Tottel's Pension Fund Trustee Handbook

Tottel's Pension Fund Trustee Handbook

Ninth Edition

Roger Self

Tottel Publishing Ltd
Maxwelton House
41-43 Boltro Road
Haywards Heath
West Sussex
RH16 1BJ

© Tottel Publishing Ltd 2005

Reprinted 2007 and 2009

A CIP Catalogue record for this book is available from the British Library.

ISBN 978 1 84592 175 0

Typeset by Columns Design Ltd, Reading, Berkshire
Printed and bound by CPI Antony Rowe, Eastbourne

Preface

The purpose of this book, now in its ninth edition and with its second publisher, is the same as at the time it was first published, namely to offer some help to the thousands of managers and employees who have taken on the role of serving as pension fund trustees.

The publication of this edition comes at a time of great difficulty for UK pension provision. A very large proportion of the country's final salary schemes have been closed to new entrants, and very many schemes are also now frozen so that no member is building up any further pensionable service. Where an alternative is being offered, this will usually take the form of a money purchase arrangement – perhaps still an occupational pension scheme run by trustees – but often a fully insured contractual arrangement not set up as a trust.

The combination of a three-year period running from 2000 to 2002 of stock markets falling in value globally, the continued prospect of low long-term inflation which means that government bonds are more expensive than in the past, and the greater longevity of pensioners have all served to put pressure on pension schemes. In a defined contribution scheme, the members have taken the hit. In the final salary scheme the hit has been taken by the employer.

To help deal with the acute distress caused to many scheme members, the Government intervened to create two new compensation schemes: in the case of the more limited initiative, the financial assistance scheme, the compensation is to be met by taxpayers, while the on-going pension protection fund will be financed by a levy on private sector defined benefit schemes.

Against this background, the independent Pension Commission is due to publish its final report in November 2005 setting out the options for the future of UK pension provision as a whole. The preliminary reports issued in October 2004 have been widely read and absorbed and the message we have received is clear: in general, we shall have to pay more in taxes and savings to build up adequate pensions, we shall have to carrying on working into later life, and we shall retire with less income than we might have expected.

It is worth remembering that this book was first published also during troubled times. The revelations in 1991 that the occupational pension schemes of the Robert Maxwell group of companies had been systematically looted dominated national television news. A spate of other stories told of how many companies, experiencing financial difficulties in a long and severe recession, had turned to their pension funds for cash advances. The result? The company failed. The pension scheme was found to be under-funded. Employees lost not only their jobs, but also their pensions.

At that time, as now, the trust of many ordinary employees that their pensions were safe was severely tested.

Then, the House of Commons Select Committee on Social Security called for action. The Government set up the Pension Law Review Committee under Professor Goode which made 218 recommendations. The Government responded with a White Paper in June 1994 which by the summer of 1995 had become the *Pensions Act 1995*. Most of the Act's measures came into force on 6 April 1997.

Under this new legislative regime, it became clear that if occupational pension schemes were to survive, then much would depend on the continuing energy and integrity of the ordinary trustee. The *Pensions Act 1995* gave them new statutory powers. It also codified their duties and imposed tough sanctions in cases of non-compliance. Yet in the end these reforms did not work. Nearly a decade later, new reforms are being put in place by the *Pensions Act 2004*.

It is not the job of this book to propose political solutions. It is, however, the job of this book to offer guidance to pension fund trustees so that they can carry out their duties.

Pension fund trustees themselves are also coming to terms with their new duties after the Government's endorsement of the recommendations issued in March 2001 by Paul Myners. The Myners principles and the 'conversance' and 'trustee knowledge and understanding' requirements introduced by the *Pensions Act 2004* do not require the 'professionalisation' of the lay trustee. Trustees are not suddenly required to become investment experts. They remain entitled to make use of the expertise of others.

Yet, Paul Myners and the Government insist that pension fund trustees should have sufficient expertise to be able to evaluate whether the advice they receive is complete, up to date and based on appropriate assumptions. Importantly, trustees are reminded that they should exercise their own judgement when considering and acting upon advice – irrespective of the source of that advice. This is a reasonable expectation of any pension fund trustee. It is the aim of this book to help pension fund trustees realise this expectation.

In this book, I have always stressed two important points:

- Occupational pensions are an employee benefit. They do not exist in a vacuum but rather form part of the overall remuneration policy of the employer.

- Trustees should not expect to be pension experts. They must rely on a host of advisers whom they appoint. What is important is that they must understand the nature of their relationship with those advisers and be prepared to question them critically. If necessary, they should seek alternative advice.

The aim of this book is simply to give all pension fund trustees the confidence to undertake their appointed task of safeguarding the pension rights of their scheme's members.

I regard this book as a bit of a workhorse and so I am grateful to Tottel Publishing for welcoming it into their stable.

Roger Self
June 2005

Contents

	Page
Preface	v
Table of Cases	xiii

	Paragraph
Chapter 1 Occupational pension schemes	
Overview	1.1
Types of occupational pension scheme	1.2
Contributory and non-contributory schemes	1.9
Pensions as an employee benefit	1.11
The law relating to occupational pension schemes	1.12
Chapter 2 Trust-based and contract-based pensions	
Two approaches	2.1
Personal pension schemes	2.2
Group personal pension arrangements	2.6
Stakeholder pension schemes	2.10–2.11
The personal pension tax regime	2.15
Financial services regulation	2.16
Chapter 3 The trustee body	
Different structures	3.1
Individual trustees	3.2
Corporate trustees	3.3
Trust corporation	3.4
Independent trustee	3.5
Management committees	3.6
Pensioneer trustee	3.7
Custodian trustee	3.8
Chapter 4 How trustees are chosen	
Appointment and removal	4.1
Those disqualified from acting as trustees	4.2
Trustees appointed by the Pensions Regulator	4.4
Member-nominated trustees	4.5
Employer-nominated trustees	4.23
Duration of appointment, removal and retirement of trustees	4.24
Practice since 1997	4.28
Reform of nomination and selection of member trustees	4.29
Chapter 5 Trustee duties, powers and discretions	
General principles	5.1
Trustee's knowledge and understanding	5.1A
Main trustee duties	5.2
Main trustee powers	5.3
Main discretionary powers	5.4
New statutory powers and duties	5.10

Chapter 6   Trust deed and rules
Overview   6.1
Announcement, undertakings and overriding legislation   6.2
Effect of conversance requirement   6.2A
Power of amendment   6.3
Protected and detrimental modifications   6.4
Statutory modifications   6.5

Chapter 7   Pensions in the context of industrial relations
View that trustees cannot negotiate   7.1
Duty to consult   7.1A
Pension negotiations   7.2
Relationship between trustees and negotiators   7.3
Pensions and contractual obligations to members   7.4
Clearance statements   7.5

Chapter 8   Trustees and the employer
The employer as settlor of the trust   8.1
Powers of the employer   8.2
Payment of pension contributions   8.3
Time off for trustees   8.8
Employment protection rights   8.9
Protection as a whistle-blower   8.10
Provision of information   8.11
Employer provides the administration services   8.12

Chapter 9   Trustees and the pension fund members
Duty to act fairly between differing groups   9.1
Trustees and active members   9.15
Trustees and early leavers   9.20
Trustees and pensioners   9.25
Trustees and surviving dependants   9.29
Trustees and divorced partners   9.30
Disclosure of information and communications   9.31
Giving advice   9.44

Chapter 10   Professional advisers
Expert advice   10.1
Advisers to employers or to the trustees?   10.2
Whistle-blowing duties   10.4
How to choose – beauty parades   10.5
Appointment and removal of professional advisers   10.6
Access to information   10.7

Chapter 11   Trustees and the pensions manager
Pensions management   11.1
Trustee panel   11.1A
Pensions administration agreement   11.2

Delegation of trustees' powers   11.3
Maladministration   11.4
Trustee relationship with pensions manager   11.5
Data Protection Act 1998   11.6

Chapter 12 Trustees and the pensions consultant
Society of Pension Consultants and Association of Consulting
    Actuaries   12.1
Services offered by pension consultants   12.2

Chapter 13 Trustees and the scheme actuary
Introduction   13.1
Institute and Faculty of Actuaries   13.2
Principles of how a pension scheme is funded   13.3
Actuarial methods and assumptions   13.4
Changes arising from the Pensions Act 2004   13.7
Trustee relationship with scheme actuary   13.13

Chapter 14 Trustees and the pensions lawyer
Association of Pension Lawyers   14.1
Services offered by pension lawyers   14.2
Trustee relationship with pension lawyers   14.3
Whistle-blowing   14.4

Chapter 15 Trustees and the fund accountant
Introduction   15.1
Eligibility to be an auditor   15.2
Pension scheme accounts   15.3
Fraud prevention   15.6
Trustee relationship with accountant   15.7

Chapter 16 Investing pension fund assets
Introduction   16.1
Trustee investment powers   16.4
Financial services legislation   16.5
Pensions Act 1995   16.6
Pensions Act 2004   16.6A
Asset management   16.9
Appointing investment managers   16.14
Performance measurement   16.21
Self-investment   16.22
Custodial and administrative arrangements   16.23
Corporate governance issues for trustees   16.25
Socially responsible investment   16.26
Additional voluntary contributions   16.27
The valuation of bonds and equities   16.28

Contents

Chapter 17 Investment issues after Myners
Introduction   17.1
Voluntary code for pension fund investment   17.2
Revised text of principles   17.3
Legislative proposals   17.6

Chapter 18 Conduct of trustee meetings
Introduction   18.1
Who chairs the trustee meeting?   18.2
Setting the agenda   18.3
Reaching decisions   18.4
Recording decisions   18.5
Frequency of meetings   18.6

Chapter 19 Special situations
Pension fund surpluses   19.1
Mergers and takeovers   19.5
Scheme reconstructions   9.6
Employer ceases to trade   19.7

Chapter 20 Resolution of individual disputes
Introduction   20.1
Internal dispute mechanisms   20.2
The Pensions Advisory Service   20.7
Pensions Ombudsman   20.8
The courts and tribunals   20.14

Chapter 21 Breaches of trust
Introduction   21.1
Unintentional and innocent   21.2
Negligent and culpable   21.3
Culpable and fraudulent   21.4
Breaches of statutory law   21.5

Chapter 22 Protection for trustees
Introduction   22.1
Trustee Act 1925   22.2
Statutory protection   22.3
Indemnity and exoneration clauses   22.4
Liability and negligence insurance   22.5
Limitations on indemnity and exoneration clauses
and liability and negligence insurance   22.6
Employer reimbursement policies   22.7
Legal costs   22.8
Liability of a corporate trustee   22.9
Protection after winding up   22.10

Chapter 23   Compensation schemes
Introduction   23.1
Financial Assistance Scheme   23.1A
Pensions Protection Fund   23.1B
Fraud Compensation Fund   23.2
Financial Services Compensation Scheme   23.3
Unpaid contributions   23.4
Contracted-out schemes   23.5
EU Insolvency Directive and the Francovich case   23.6

Chapter 24   Training opportunities for trustees
Introduction   24.1

                                                                Page
Appendix 1 The combined DB/DC scope document   351

Index   359

Table of Cases

A

Air Jamaica Ltd v Charlton [1999] OPLR 11, [1999] PLR 247   7.1
Allen, C, Determination by the Pensions Ombudsman [2002]
    PLR 333   18.5
Armitage v Nurse (CA) [1998] Ch 241, [1997] PLR 51   22.4
Associated Picture Houses v Wednesbury Corporation (CA)
    [1948] 1 KB 223, [1947] 2 All ER 680   5.4, 5.5, 9.1, 18.5

B

Barber v Guardian Royal Exchange Assurance Group (ECJ) [1990]
    PLR 95, [1990] IRLR 240   1.14, 9.3
Barclays Bank plc v Holmes [2000] PLR 339   19.6
Bartlett v Barclays Trust Co Ltd [1980] 1 All ER 139   3.4
Beckmann v Dynamco Whicheloe Macfarlane Ltd (ECJ) [2002]
    All ER (D) 05 (Jun), [2002] PLR 287, [2002] 64 PBLR   1.14, 19.5
Bradstock Group Pension Scheme Trustees Ltd v Bradstock
    Group plc [2002] PLR 327   23.1A

C

Coloroll Pension Trustees v Russell (ECJ) [1995] All ER (EC) 23,
    [1994] OPLR 179, [1994] PLR 211   9.2
Courage Group's Pension Schemes, Ryan v Imperial Brewing, Re
    [1987] 1 All ER 528, [1989A] PLR 67, [1987] WLR 495   7.1, 19.4
Cowan v Scargill [1984] 2 All ER 750, [1990] PLR 169   16.26

D

Defrenne v Sabena (No. 2) (ECJ) [1976] ICR 547, [1976] ECR 455   9.3

E

Edge v Pensions Ombudsman (HC) [1998] 2 All ER 547, [1998]
    OPLR 51, [1997] PLR 15; (CA) [1999] 4 All ER 546,
    [1999] OPLR 179, [1999] PLR 215   9.1, 18.5, 19.4, 20.13

F

Francovich v Italy (ECJ) [1992] ECR I–5357, [1992] IRLR 84   23.6

G

Glossop v Copnall [2001] All ER (D) 92 (Jul), [2001] OPLR 287   11.4

H

Harris v Lord Shuttleworth (CA) [1995] OPLR 79, [1994] PLR 47   5.8
Henderson v Stephen Harwood & ors [2005] PLR 209   20.11A
Hillsdown Holdings v Pensions Ombudsman [1997] 1 All ER 862,
    [1996] OPLR 291, [1996] PLR 427   7.1, 19.5, 19.6
HR v JAPT [1997] OPLR 123, [1997] PLR 99   22.9

I

Imperial Group Pension Trust v Imperial Tobacco Ltd [1991]
2 All ER 597, [1990] PLR 263, [1991] IRLR 66   8.2, 19.4
International Power v Healy (HL) [2001] OPLR 15, [2001] PLR 121   19.4

K

Kemble v Hicks (No. 2) [1999] Ch 53, [1999] OPLR 1   19.6

L

Londonderry's Settlement, Re [1964] 3 All ER 855, [1965] Ch 918   18.5

M

Martin & ors v South Bank University (ECJ) [2003] PLR 331   19.5
McClorry, Re (CA) (1998, unreported)   5.8
Mettoy Pension Trustees v Evans [1991] 2 All ER 513, [1990] PLR 9   19.4

N

National Grid Co plc v Mayes & others (CA) [1999] All ER (D) 126,
[1999] OPLR 95, [1999] PLR 37; (HL) [2001] UKHL 20,
[2001] 2 All ER 417, [2001] OPLR 15   19.4
Nicol & Andrew v Brinkley [1996] OPLR 361   7.5

O

Outram v Academy Plastics (CA) [2000] OPLR 321, [2000] PLR 283   8.11

P

Preston v Wolverhampton Healthcare NHS Trust (ECJ) [2000] PLR
171; (HL) [2001] UKHL/5, [2001] 3 All ER 947, [2001]
OPLR 1, [2001] PLR 39   9.3

R

R (on the application of Britannic Asset Management Ltd) v Pensions
Ombudsman [2002] EWCA Civ 1405, [2002] 4 All ER 860,
[2002] PLR 527   20.9

S

Scally v Southern Health and Social Services Board [1991] 4 All ER
563, [1991] PLR 195, [1992] 1 AC 294   8.11
Schmidt v Rosewood Trust Ltd [2003] PLR 145   18.5
South West Trains v Wightman [1997] OPLR 249, [1998] PLR 113   7.1, 7.5
Speight v Gaunt (CA) [1883] 9 App Cas 1   5.1
STC Submarine Systems v Piper [1994] OPLR 13, [1993] PLR 185   8.8

T

Thrells Ltd (1974) Pension Scheme in Liquidation v Lomas [1993]
2 All ER 546, [1992] OPLR 21, [1992] PLR 233   19.4
Trustees of the NUS Officials and Employees Superannuation Fund v
Pensions Ombudsman [2001] All ER (D) 439 (Oct)   7.5

U

UNIFI v Union Bank of Nigeria [2001] IRLR 712, [2001] PLR 239   7.1
University of Nottingham v Eyett [1999] 2 All ER 445, [1999]
     OPLR 55, [1998] PLR 27   8.11

W

Wakelin v Read [2000] PLR 319   20.11A
Westminster City Council v Haywood [1998] Ch 377 at 392,
     [1997] PLR 39   20.11A
Wilson v The Law Debenture Trust Corporation [1995] 2 All ER 337,
     [1995] OPLR 103, [1994] PLR 141   18.5

Chapter 1

Occupational pension schemes

Overview

1.1   This book is aimed at individuals who have been nominated either by their employer or by the general membership of an occupational pension scheme to serve as the scheme's trustees. The job of the trustees is to run the pension scheme.

Not all pension arrangements made by employers for the benefit of their employees are run by trustees:

*   The public service pension schemes (run by central government) and the local authority schemes are governed by special statutes and are not set up as trusts.

*   Private sector occupational pension schemes have to be set up as trusts. Until 6 April 2006 the pragmatic reason for this has been that HM Revenue & Customs (formerly the Inland Revenue) requires private sector occupational pension schemes to be set up as a trust if they are to receive the tax advantages that come with tax approval. From 6 April 2006, the tax legislation no longer makes this requirement of occupational pension schemes in order for the key tax reliefs to be applied. *Section 252* of the *Pensions Act 2004*, however, requires that a UK-based occupational pension scheme is to be set up as a trust if it is to accept any payments to fund benefits for any scheme member unless the scheme is exempted by regulations from this requirement. There are also, however, a number of private sector, unapproved and non-registered, occupational pension schemes which are not set up as trusts. These cater almost exclusively for high earners.

*   Many, mainly smaller, employers have chosen in recent years to provide pension cover for their employees by using personal pensions, which are individual contractual arrangements between each member and the pension provider – usually an insurance company. The employer may have facilitated what are known as group personal pension arrangements, a collection of what are still individual contracts between each member and the personal pension provider. Personal pensions are not generally governed by the requirements of trust law. The great majority of stakeholder pension schemes operate as a form of group personal pension arrangement and so are not run by trustees.

It is difficult to say exactly how many occupational pension schemes there are which are set up as trusts. The Pension Scheme Registry knew of 94,071 'live' private sector occupational pension schemes as at 31 March 2004. However, the great majority of these occupational pension schemes have very few members – typically just two or three directors of a small company. (The number of 'live' occupational pension schemes includes not only those which are open to new members but also closed schemes which new members cannot join, frozen schemes where members are no longer building up pension rights and frozen schemes which are also in the process of winding up.)

The Registry reports that as at 31 March 2004 there were 17,931 live occupational pension schemes with twelve or more members which are set up as trusts. These can range from a small, insured, money purchase scheme sponsored by a small company and covering a dozen or so members to the large, self-administered, final salary schemes with thousands of members sponsored by the UK's largest companies.

Below the terms just used to describe various kinds of pension scheme such as *insured, money purchase, self-administered, final salary* are explained. For all these schemes the job of the trustee is essentially the same – to run the pension scheme.

Types of occupational pension scheme

1.2   Occupational pension schemes can be divided into several different types. As a trustee, it is important to know what the differences are between various kinds of scheme, especially as it is possible for a scheme to change from one type to another and this will have important consequences for its members. Also, it is very common for an occupational pension scheme to be set up under a single trust but have two or more distinct sections which operate under different rules.

Registered pension scheme

1.3   *Approved, exempt approved* and *unapproved schemes* are terms that have been used by HMRC to define what kind of tax privileges, if any, are granted to the scheme. Yet these terms become of historical interest only on 6 April 2006 when the new pensions tax regime comes into force. Under the new pensions tax regime, registering a pension scheme brings the following substantial tax advantages that will apply without restriction to the vast majority of individuals:

- employee contributions will be granted relief from income tax either by being deducted from earnings before the deduction of income tax (relief under a net pay arrangement) or by HMRC adding a contribution equal to the tax relief at the basic rate of tax with the employee being able to reclaim any higher rate tax relief (relief at source);

- employer contributions will give rise to neither an income tax charge on the employee nor a national insurance contribution charge on either the employee or the employer;

- employer contributions will be deductible against the employer's liability to pay either corporation tax or income tax (although in some cases the relief will have to be spread over more than one tax year);

- income, once received by the scheme, is free of income tax and capital gains realised on the sale of investments is free of capital gains tax;

- lump sum payments made on the death of a member will not be subject to inheritance tax.

Employer-financed retirement benefit schemes

1.4   Before the *Finance Act 1989*, approval from the Inland Revenue (now HMRC) would have been withdrawn from any existing exempt approved scheme if the employer provided an employee with benefits from both the exempt approved scheme and an *unapproved scheme*. This ceased to be the case in 1989 and it became possible for employees to be provided with retirement benefits up to then Inland Revenue limits from an exempt approved scheme and also with further top-up benefits provided by an unfunded unapproved retirement benefit scheme (UURBS). Employers found it necessary to do this because also from 1989 new employee members of approved schemes became subject to the pensionable earnings cap which set a cash ceiling on the contributions and benefits payable in respect of high earners. In 2005/06 its last year of operation, this ceiling stood at £105,600. Unapproved schemes have simply been schemes or arrangements for paying retirement benefits to employees to which no special tax privileges are applied. Many funded unapproved retirement benefit schemes (FURBS) have been set up as trusts. Yet the system of granting tax privileges by awarding approval to pension schemes that meet certain conditions is abandoned on 6 April 2006 as explained in **1.3**. Since there are no longer to be approved schemes, there can no longer be unapproved schemes. Under the new tax regime, pension schemes which are not registered are to be known as 'employer-financed retirement benefit schemes'.

Defined benefit and defined contribution schemes

1.5   A *defined benefit scheme* usually operates by linking the employee's eventual retirement benefit to his or her pay. They are often therefore called *salary related schemes*.

In most cases, the employee's pay at or near retirement is chosen so that the benefit promise is effectively inflation-proofed over the employee's working life. They are then commonly called *final salary schemes*. However, some schemes operate by calculating the average pay earned by the employee while a member of the scheme. The pay for each year is revalued to take account of either earnings or price inflation over the time until the pension is to be calculated. These are therefore called *average salary schemes*. During the late 1990s a new kind of defined benefit scheme known as a *cash balance scheme* has been introduced into the UK. In a cash balance scheme the employee's benefits are calculated as a defined percentage of pay but expressed as a lump sum amount.

A *defined contribution scheme* simply provides the employee with the pension which can be bought with the capital sum which that employee accumulates in an individualised retirement savings account. The capital sum is built up from regular defined contributions to the scheme made by the employer and usually also by the employee, plus any money transferred by the employee into the scheme from previous pension arrangements, plus the cumulative investment return net of any charges. Such schemes are also called *money purchase schemes*.

The advantage of a defined benefit scheme is that in principle a greater degree of certainty is given to the employee's promised level of benefits. They can be used more flexibly, especially in cases of early retirement, to provide higher benefits than could be obtained by defined contribution schemes, where investment returns are very dependent on the length of time the money has been invested. With a defined benefit scheme, the investment risk is borne by the sponsoring employer who underwrites the benefit promise. The mortality risk, i.e. the risk of the pensioner living longer than expected, is also borne by the sponsoring employer in the case of a final salary or average salary scheme, but in the case of the third type of defined benefit scheme mentioned, the cash balance scheme, the mortality risk is borne by the pensioner.

We say that a greater degree of certainty is given *in principle* by defined benefit schemes but this has been true only to the extent that the employer is able to deliver the promised or expected benefits. In recent years, this has not always been the case. Employers have become insolvent at a time when the defined benefit scheme has become underfunded with the result that many members have lost a large part of their expected benefits. The considerable distress that has been caused has prompted the government to take steps to try and rectify matters. The Pensions Act 2004 has introduced the Financial Assistance Scheme to provide some limited help to members of defined benefit schemes where the sponsoring employer became insolvent during the period 1 January 1997 to 5 April 2005 where underfunding led to the loss of expected pension rights. The Pensions Act 2004 also introduces the Pension Protection Fund, financed by levies of defined benefit occupational pension schemes, to provide replacement benefits up to a specified level where the scheme winds up from 6 April 2005 onwards. For trustees of defined benefit schemes many lessons from this failure to deliver the 'pension promise' must now be learned.

The advantage of a defined contribution scheme is that it appears to be more easily understandable. If contribution levels are high enough, they can provide good benefits even if the actual level of the benefit cannot be known in advance. Each employee has an individual account so early leavers from the scheme do not subsidise those who stay to retirement as can happen in schemes which operate simply on the defined benefit basis. One problem is that the level of retirement benefit has been often extraordinarily dependent on the investment conditions prevailing at the time of the employee's retirement (although 'lifestyle' funds are designed to lock in earlier gains from riskier investments by switching the member's fund progressively into safer investments in the run up to the member's planned retirement age). Also, the regular stream of payments in retirement is often secured by purchasing an annuity. The amount of pension that can be secured by any given capital sum will vary over time because annuity rates depend on the medium-term outlook for inflation. With a defined contribution scheme both the investment risk and the mortality risk is borne by the employee.

The distinction between defined benefit and defined contribution schemes is perhaps not as great as is often claimed. Final salary schemes are funded by contributions to produce the targeted benefit. Money purchase schemes can be funded to produce the same targeted benefit. The key difference is simply that the employer is seen to underwrite the target in a final salary scheme.

Some schemes also combine the two approaches in what is known as a *money purchase underpin* or a *final salary underpin*. In a money purchase underpin employees are guaranteed that their benefits, either on transferring benefits from the scheme or at retirement, will be calculated as the greater of the amount obtained using the defined benefit and the defined contribution method. This will be so whether the employees are early leavers from the scheme who have preserved their pension rights in the scheme or have remained active members of the scheme up to the time they began to draw their pension.

In a final salary underpin an employee receives money-purchase-style benefits but these are guaranteed never to be less than a defined minimum amount, although any guarantee is only as strong as the employer's ability to ensure the guarantee is honoured.

Insured and self-administered schemes

1.6   In an *insured scheme* all the benefits are provided by an insurance company with whom the trustees have taken out a contract to pay regular premiums. The pensions administration and investment strategy are invariably the responsibility of the insurance company. Over 95% of all occupational pension schemes are insured. There are many thousands of *executive pension plans*, often with only one member, which are special insured schemes designed for senior employees.

In a *self-administered scheme*, the trustees are responsible for the overall investment strategy and can decide who will administer the scheme. Although there are far fewer self-administered schemes than insured schemes, they are on average far larger. Benefits of scale mean that once a pension fund has grown to, say, £20m, it is usually more cost effective for the fund to operate on a self-administered basis rather than to remain insured.

There are also a very large number of *small self-administered schemes*. Such schemes have fewer than 12 members and, in most cases, all the members are senior directors of the sponsoring company. Small self-administered schemes have been subject to especially strict HMRC monitoring under the pre-2006 system of tax approval because, like executive pension schemes, they can be used to provide loans to, and invest in the assets of, the sponsoring company.

Contracted-in and contracted-out schemes

1.7   Occupational pension schemes that are *contracted in* provide employees with a pension which is additional to the one they accrue at the same time in the State Earnings Related Pension Scheme (SERPS) or State Second Pension (S2P). Employees and the employer pay National Insurance contributions at the not-contracted-out rate. Technically such schemes are known as *participating schemes* or *not-contracted-out schemes*.

Occupational pension schemes that are *contracted out* provide employees with a pension that replaces either in part or in total the *additional pension* that they would otherwise have accrued in SERPS or S2P during that same period of employment. In return for the reduced amount of state retirement pension, the employee and the employer are liable to pay National Insurance contributions at a lower rate than would be the case if the employee were either a member of a contracted-in occupational pension scheme or not a member of any occupational pension scheme at all.

It is not true to say that the contracted-out pension the employees receive when they reach state pension age will always *completely* replace their additional pension from SERPS or from S2P. First of all, the state's Pension Service calculates employees' additional pension entitlement from SERPS with reference to any periods of contracted-out employment between 6 April 1978, when SERPS first began, and 5 April 1997, when the links between contracted-out employment and SERPS were broken, as if those employees had not been contracted out at all. This preliminary calculation gives the employees' *notional* additional pension entitlement from SERPS. However, this notional entitlement is then offset by an amount known as a *contracted-out deduction* (COD). The COD is equal to the value of the *guaranteed minimum pension* (GMP) that the employees are taken to have accrued during their periods of contracted-out employment at any time between April 1978 and March 1997. After the offset is applied, the resulting figure is the employees' *net* additional pension entitlement.

The net additional pension paid from SERPS after the COD offset may or may not initially be a zero amount. (Non-zero amounts may be payable because the employee ceased being an active member of the scheme and became an *early leaver*. As a result his or her GMP may have been revalued by the scheme at a different rate from that used by the state to revalue SERPS.) However, once in payment, employees' entitlement to increases on their notional additional pension payable by the state through SERPS may overtake the amount of the GMP after taking into account the more limited increases payable on GMPs by the occupational pension scheme.

The long and short of this explanation is that a pensioner who was contracted out from SERPS before 6 April 1997 will often also receive some additional pension from SERPS covering those periods of contracted-out employment.

For pension rights built up between 6 April 1997 and 6 April 2002, the date S2P began, these residual links with additional pension provided by SERPS have been broken. During this period employees were either contracted in and built up rights to SERPS or they were contracted out and built up no further rights to additional pension.

Secondly, now that S2P has come into operation, an employee who is contracted out through membership of an occupational pension scheme may also build up rights to additional pension. A top-up additional pension is provided by S2P to any employees earning above the National Insurance lower earnings limit but who earn less than £27,800 in 2005/06 during any period they are contracted out by an occupational pension scheme. The introduction of S2P restores the links between contracted-out employment and the state additional pension. Apart from pension rights built up in the last five years of SERPS, many employees in membership of contracted-out pension schemes have enjoyed, and now once again enjoy, residual rights under the state additional pension.

Contracting-out tests

1.8   Until 6 April 1997, an occupational pension scheme could be contracted out by the *guaranteed minimum pension* (GMP) test. The employee becomes entitled to the payment of a defined benefit called the GMP which is payable at state pension age. As explained above, the amount of the individual's accrued GMP is deducted at state pension age from the employee's additional pension entitlement under SERPS. Once in payment GMPs have to be increased each year in line with the rise in prices. For GMPs built up from 6 April 1988 until 5 April 1997 part of the increase is paid by their scheme (the first 3%) and the state provides any further increase necessary to match the rise in inflation. For GMPs built up before 6 April 1988, the state pays all of the annual increase.

Alternatively, an occupational pension scheme may be contracted out by the *protected rights* test. Statutory defined minimum payments have to be made each month by the employer into the member's scheme account where they are invested. This capital sum is known as the member's protected rights fund and is used at retirement from age 60 to buy a pension. The amount of pension built up from the protected rights fund before 6 April 1997 is treated by the Government to be equal in value to the notional GMP the employee would have accrued if he or she had been contracted out by the GMP test. The employee's SERPS pension is reduced by the COD offset explained above by the amount of this notional GMP even though in practice the amount of pension actually bought by the protected rights will undoubtedly be either greater or less than the notional GMP. Once in payment, any pension bought with the protected rights fund built up before 6 April 1997 must increase each year in line with inflation up to a ceiling of 3% in any one year. The state pays for any further increase necessary to match the annual rise in inflation.

Since 6 April 1997 new contracting-out tests have replaced the tests described in the previous paragraphs. From that date a member of a contracted-out scheme ceased to build up any rights to additional pension from SERPS. All pension rights built up from 6 April 1997 until 5 April 2005 provided by a defined benefit occupational pension scheme (whether contracted out or not) have to increase once in payment as a statutory minimum each year in line with prices up to a ceiling of 5% in any one year. If inflation is higher than 5%, the state is not responsible for any further increase. Pension rights built up in defined benefit schemes from 6 April 2005 must, once in payment, give rise to pensions that increase each year in line with prices up to a ceiling of $2\frac{1}{2}\%$. Pension rights built up in defined contribution schemes from 6 April 1997 to 5 April 2005 must, if they came into payment before 6 April 2005, also increase each year in line with prices up to a ceiling of 5% in any one year. But pensions secured from rights held in a defined contribution occupational pension scheme are not required to increase at all if they come into payment on or after 6 April 2005.

A scheme is able to contract out employees if it satisfies an overall quality test known as the *reference scheme* test. In return for the loss of future SERPS or S2P benefits, the employee and employer together pay National Insurance contributions at a lower contracted-out rate. Alternatively, under a revised protected rights test, a scheme may contract employees out of SERPS or S2P if the employer pays a flat-rate percentage of earnings (known as *minimum payments*) each month to the scheme to build up a protected rights fund for each contracted-out employee. The National Insurance contributions payable by the employer and employee are reduced by an amount equal to the minimum payments, but this is less than the total reduction gained from the reference scheme test. After the end of the tax year, HMRC's National Insurance Contributions Office pays over to the scheme an age-related percentage as a top-up in respect of each contracted-out employee. The percentage rises according to the age of the employee.

Since 6 April 2002 the saving to the employer is 3.5% of earnings between the National Insurance lower and upper earnings limits in the case of the reference scheme test and 1.0% in the case of the protected rights test. For both these contracting-out tests the National Insurance saving for the employee is 1.6% of earnings between the two limits.

The level of National Insurance contributions payable by employers and employees where the employees are contracted out from S2P by an occupational pension scheme reflects the fact that a top-up amount of additional pension is still payable for those earning above the National Insurance lower earnings limit but less than £27,800 (2005/06). In short, employees who earn below this limit but above the National Insurance lower earnings limit and who are members of a contracted-out occupational pension scheme will nevertheless build up some entitlement to additional pension from S2P.

Contributory and non-contributory schemes

1.9   If the employees are required as a condition of membership to make contributions to the occupational pension scheme out of their pay, the scheme is termed a contributory scheme. If no such requirement is made, it is termed a non-contributory scheme. In both cases, it has in the past been a general condition of social security law that employees have the right to make additional voluntary contributions but from 6 April 2006 it no longer will be a requirement of the social security legislation for trustees to offer AVCs.

Funded and unfunded

1.10   If the occupational pension scheme builds up assets which are invested, it is termed a *funded scheme*. If benefits are provided from income on a pay-as-you-go basis, it is termed an *unfunded scheme*. In practice all private sector, exempt approved and, from 6 April 2006, all private sector, registered occupational pension schemes are funded. On the other hand, many of the public service schemes are unfunded, but not all: for example, the local government scheme is funded.

Pensions as an employee benefit

1.11   It is very important not to lose sight of the fact that occupational pensions exist first and foremost because they have been seen by the sponsoring employers as a necessary element of the remuneration package, needed to attract, retain and motivate employees.

They have also been vital in allowing employers to react flexibly to the need to allow employees to retire but in a way which can avoid financial hardship.

Although death, and ill-health benefits can be provided by other insured benefit provisions, they form part and parcel of the benefit package of most occupational pension schemes.

In practice, and over the long term, the average defined benefit occupational pension scheme probably costs employers around 20% of pensionable payroll. The figure will obviously be a little lower in contributory schemes where there is an employee contribution than in a non-contributory scheme. However, because of the effect of higher investment returns in the late 1980s, surpluses arose which helped to lower the average employer contribution rate. During the 1990s these surpluses began to be run down, with the consequence that employer contribution rates to defined benefit schemes have begun to rise to their long-term norm. Furthermore, the early years of this century witnessed:

- a sustained fall in the world's stock markets, and the prospect of only modest long-term prospects for investment returns in general; and

- in the UK, revised demographic data which show that the average 60-year-old who had retired in 1999 could expect to live as much as one-third as long again compared to a 60-year-old who had retired in 1970.

The result is that employer contribution rates to defined benefit schemes began to climb very sharply. Many employers sought to control their pension costs, and the term 'pensions crisis' has become the phrase on everyone's lips.

Surveys show that over half of defined benefit schemes have been closed to new entrants, although in most cases existing members can continue to build up pension rights as before. Yet such a move does not reduce employer costs very quickly.

On reviewing the options, employers are seeking to change the nature of future pension provision for existing members, to look at ways of deterring early retirement and to persuade employees to bear more of the pension cost and/or risk. Pensions have begun to be the cause of industrial relations unrest as employees have become angry that the 'pension promise' which they believed had been made to them is broken.

One common approach in the recent past has been to close the defined benefit scheme to new entrants and offer instead a defined contribution arrangement. This may be in the form of a separate defined contribution, trust-based occupational pension scheme, or as a new defined contribution section within the same trust fund as the closed defined benefit scheme. Alternatively, new employees may be offered a contract-based defined contribution arrangement such as is described in **CHAPTER 2**.

In a defined contribution scheme the employer contribution will be determined either by collective or individual bargaining or by the employer's decision on what is needed and what is affordable.

Pensions are, therefore, part of the employee remuneration package. Trustees of occupational pension schemes have very particular concerns which are specified by trust law and Acts of Parliament. They do not normally negotiate on pensions, although there are exceptions. Yet, trustees should remember that occupational pensions are provided as an employee benefit and they form part of the industrial relations life of the organisation for which they work.

The law relating to occupational pension schemes

1.12   Occupational pension schemes are governed by two distinct strands of UK law: statutory law and trust law.

Statutory law

1.13   Statutory law is set by Acts of Parliament, which are the primary legislation, and associated Statutory Instruments, which are the secondary legislation.

The main statutes governing occupational pension schemes originate from the Department for Work and Pensions which frames social security law and from the Treasury/HMRC which is responsible for taxation law. The Acts of most importance to the trustees of occupational pension schemes are the *Pension Schemes Act 1993*, the *Pensions Act 1995*, the *Welfare Reform and Pensions Act 1999*, the *Child Support, Pensions and Social Security Act 2000*, the *Finance Act 2004* and the *Pensions Act 2004*.

Occupational pension schemes are also affected by other statutory law including:

- the *Equal Pay Act 1970*;

- the *Race Relations Act 1975*;

- the *Sex Discrimination Act 1976*;

- the *Disability Discrimination Act 1995*;

- the *Employment Rights Act 1996*;

- the *Industrial Tribunals Act 1996*;

- the *Data Protection Act 1998*;

- the *Financial Services and Markets Act 2000*, and

- the *Civil Partnership Act 2004*.

European law

1.14   European Community law is important in any consideration of occupational pensions. Directives issued by the EU are incorporated into new UK statutory legislation and in some cases can be relied upon by individual citizens seeking redress through the courts. The European Court of Justice (ECJ) has the final authority on the interpretation of the European Treaty and its judgments are binding.

In fact, it was precisely in the area of occupational pensions that European law first impacted significantly on the lives of ordinary UK citizens. The *Barber* judgment (see **9.3**) enforced equal treatment for men and women in the setting of normal pension ages under pension scheme rules. This was so even though there was no UK legislation in place to effect this change until the relevant sections of the *Pensions Act 1995* came into force. Similarly, pension rights for part-time employees were largely initially stimulated by case law from the ECJ. Later, anti-discrimination requirements against part-time employees were confirmed by a directive issued by the European Commission and incorporated into UK employment law. In recent years a similar process has resulted in the protection of the pension interests of disabled people and fixed-term workers and the anti-discrimination provisions protecting employees against discrimination on the grounds of religion or belief and sexual orientation.

Yet European law's impact on pensions is not just concerned with discrimination issues. It acts to protect the employment benefits of workers whose employer changes when businesses are sold and, although there was formerly an exemption for occupational pensions, the recent cases of *Beckmann v Dynamco Whicheloe Macfarlane Ltd* and *Martin and ors v South Bank University* by the ECJ shows that this exemption is quite narrowly limited to 'old-age benefits' and not necessarily, say, to enhanced early retirement pensions. The protection of employees' pension rights upon the insolvency of their employer is also an area covered by European law – see **23.6**.

It is expected that European law will increasingly be used to prevent member states from imposing unnecessary barriers to the free movement of workers by disallowing tax relief on pension contributions to schemes established in other member states, or to the freedom on pension service providers to operate across internal EU borders. The 2003 Directive on the activities and supervision of institutions for occupational retirement provision, known as the 'IORP Directive', has already greatly influenced UK pensions law having been very influential in shaping the Pensions Act 2004, especially in setting prudential standards for UK occupational pension provision.

Trust law

1.15   As explained above, most UK occupational pension schemes have been established as *irrevocable trusts* because this has been a condition for the granting of full tax relief but now the same requirement is made by the social security law in order to maintain the separation of the funds underpinning a pension scheme from those which are under the control of the sponsoring employers – and this is also a requirement made under European law through the IORP Directive (see **1.14**).

Trusts have a very long history. Essentially they have been used to protect the financial interests of persons who have been unable to look after themselves or their affairs.

A standard definition of a trust has been given in the book *Law of Trusts and Trustees* by Sir Arthur Underhill:

> 'A trust is an equitable obligation imposing upon a person (who is called a trustee) the duty of dealing with property over which he has control (which is called the trust property) for the benefit of persons (who are called beneficiaries …) of whom he may himself be one; and any one of whom may enforce the obligation. Any act or neglect on the part of a trustee which is not authorised or excused by the terms of the trust instrument, or by law, is called a "breach of trust".'

Property is not to be taken in its usual sense. It refers to any financial assets held by the trust. *Equitable* refers to the special system of law called *equity* which is founded on principles of *natural justice* and *fair conduct*. It supplements the common law (i.e. case law made by judges) and tends to be more flexible. *Trust instrument* means the trust deed and rules.

Under trust law, the assets of an occupational pension scheme are placed under the legal ownership of the scheme's trustees. Yet the beneficiaries (active members, early leavers who have preserved their pension in the scheme, pensioners, surviving dependants of former members and the employer) also own the assets according to the principles of equity.

The employer who established the irrevocable trust is known as the *settlor* of the trust.

Supporters of trust law claim that such a system has unrivalled flexibility. However, trust law has long had critics who do not see it as a suitable body of law to regulate occupational pension schemes. Following the revelations in the *Maxwell* case in the early 1990s, the House of Commons Social Security Committee wrote in its report:

> 'We are in no doubt, as a Committee, about the urgent need to reform the law as it applies to pension funds. We believe that trust law gives an inadequate legal underpinning to occupational pension schemes.'

Nevertheless, the Pension Law Review Committee (set up by the Government under Professor Goode to review the framework of law and regulation within which occupational pension schemes operate) confirmed the role of trust law to regulate occupational pension schemes. The Goode Committee reported that:

> 'Trust law in itself is broadly satisfactory and should continue to provide the foundation for interests, rights and duties arising in relation to pension schemes. But some of the principles of trust law require modification in their application to pensions.'

The Government accepted this recommendation. In fact, the *Pensions Act 1995* which came into effect on 6 April 1997 can be seen as an affirmation of the role of trust law, especially in the importance it places on the central role of pension fund trustees.

Since 1997, the Government has also affirmed the importance of the principle of occupational pension schemes being governed by trustees. However, there are still powerful counter currents. Stakeholder pension schemes which were first established in April 2001, for example, may be set up as personal pension schemes governed by individual contracts between the pension provider and each member. In the early days the emphasis was much more on stakeholder pension schemes being run by trustees. In the event, although both forms of governance are permitted, most stakeholder pension schemes are set up under the individual contract model. In part, it has been in the interests of the stakeholder pension providers that this should be so but in fact there has been no demand from employers to bring stakeholder pensions under the trust-based model.

A further counter current is represented by those who have doubts that trustees prove effective stewards of their scheme's investments. The most important voice to express such doubts has been that of Paul Myners, who was asked by the Government to carry out a review of institutional investment. The results of that review, which was published in March 2001, are likely to be profound. This matter is explored further in CHAPTER 17.

Yet perhaps the greatest criticism of trust-based occupational pension provision stems from the fact that around 400 occupational pension schemes wound up between 1 January 1997 and 5 April 2005 and left possibly 85,000 active and deferred members facing substantial pension losses. Those losses were caused by the pension fund not having enough assets needed to meet the benefits they were expected to provide. Many critics, not totally unjustifiably, believe that it was ultimately the moral responsibility of the trustees of those schemes to have ensured that such a disaster did not happen.

The Pensions Regulator

1.16   The Pensions Regulator came into being on 6 April 2005, replacing from that date its predecessor the Occupational Pensions Regulatory Authority (Opra). The Pensions Regulator has been established by the *Pensions Act 2004* and has been set the following four objectives:

- to protect the benefits of members of occupational pension schemes;

- to protect the members of all stakeholder pension schemes (see **2.10**) and those personal pension schemes where there is a *direct payment arrangement* in place (see **2.7**) so that an employer either deducts from employees' earnings contributions to pass over to the personal pension provider and/or the employer pays its own contributions directly to the employees' personal pension scheme;

- to reduce the risk of situations arising when may lead to the compensation being payable from the Pension Protection Fund (PPF);

- to promote, and to improve understand of, the good administration of *work-based pension schemes* – ie occupational pension schemes, personal pensions where there are direct payment arrangements in place and stakeholder pension schemes.

The role of the Pensions Regulator is essentially to enforce the requirements of the pensions legislation and will also intervene where necessary to uphold the principles of trust law.

The Pensions Regulator's web site is
http://www.thepensionsregulator.gov.uk/.

It is strongly recommended that all pension fund trustees should make themselves familiar with this web site and visit it routinely. Furthermore, the Pensions Regulator offers a free news alert service so that developments can be communicated by e-mail. This service can be accessed at http://www.thepensionsregulator.gov.uk/onlineServices/mailinglist/index.aspx.

Checklist 1

- As a trustee of an occupational pension scheme that is *exempt approved* or, from 6 April 2006, *registered* by HMRC you should understand the very significant tax advantages that arise from this tax status and should ensure that no action is taken which might endanger those privileges.

- It is important to know whether your occupational pension scheme provides pensions essentially on a *defined benefit* basis or a *defined contribution* basis as this determines whether the employer or the employees bear the investment risk.

- If your scheme is *self-administered*, you as trustees are responsible for the scheme's overall investment strategy.

- Whether the scheme is to be contracted in or contracted out is a decision for the employer (who must consult with employees and recognised trade unions) but the trustees will have to ensure that the scheme provides the minimum levels of benefit that are a condition of contracting out and meets the administrative standards required by the National Insurance Contributions Office.

- Whether employees make contributions to the scheme from their pay or whether all the contributions are made by the employer makes no difference to the general statutory and trust law rights of employees as members of an occupational pension scheme and which you as trustee must uphold.

- Pensions are an employee benefit and therefore form part of the employees' remuneration package. As a trustee you should be aware of this but it is not the job of trustees generally to negotiate on levels of pension provision with employee representatives or the employer. This should be left to other industrial relations forums.

- As a trustee, you must ensure that your scheme is run in accordance with UK statutory law and you may face penalties if you fail to take all reasonable steps to ensure that the law is upheld.

- As a trustee, you have a duty to all concerned to ensure that the scheme is run in accordance with the terms of its *trust deed and rules*. If you deliberately betray that duty, you could be found by the courts to have committed a breach of trust.

- The *Pensions Act 1995* confirmed the prime importance of your role as a trustee in the running of an occupational pension scheme.

- The trust-based model of pension provision is, however, now facing stiff competition from contract-based pension provision and the failure by some defined benefit schemes to be able to pay promised benefits when they were wound up has caused many to question the ability of trustees to safeguard the interests of their members.

- Pension fund trustees are advised to make themselves familiar with the web site of the Pensions Regulator and to arrange that they are alerted to new developments using the Regulator's news alert service.

Chapter 2

Trust-based and contract-based pensions

Two approaches

2.1 There are two basic approaches to the governance of private pension provision in the UK outside the public sector. The pension scheme may either be set up as a trust and be run by trustees or it may be set up on a contract basis between each individual member and the pension provider. By and large, occupational pension schemes outside the public sector are set up as trusts but most personal pensions are contract-based. Stakeholder pension schemes, which became available for the first time on 6 April 2001, may either be trust-based or contract-based although in practice most are contract-based.

There are two essential differences between trust-based and contract-based pension provision. The most obvious of these differences is that in the case of a trust-based scheme the scheme is governed by a trustee, or body of trustees, who are obliged to act in accordance with the general principles of trust law. These principles are set out in **CHAPTER 5**. These principles do not apply outside trust-based arrangements. Personal pensions, and most stakeholder pension schemes are governed in the main by the terms of the written contract made between the individual member and the pension provider.

This first difference leads directly to the second essential difference. In a trust-based scheme there is a body of people, the trustees, who can stand in between the individual members of the scheme and the pension service providers. The relationship between the individual members and the trustees is governed by an important principle, that of the trustees acting in the best interests of the members. The relationship between the trustees and the pension providers on the other hand is governed by the law of contract.

This second difference has an immediate practical effect. Subject to the contractual obligations between the trustees and the providers, the trustees can decide to replace a pension provider, say the scheme administrator if it is giving poor service, or the investment manager if its investment performance is below expectations. But if they do so, the members remain in the same pension scheme and subject to the same entitlements. This is not usually the case in a contract-based scheme. If the individual members are dissatisfied with the service given by their pension provider, their main option is to bring that contract to a close and seek to become a member of another pension scheme. This difference may not amount to much on its own if the terms of the contract between the individual member and the original service provider permit a penalty-free exit from the pension scheme – as is the case with all stakeholder pension schemes.

Yet it could be argued that a group of trustees who are committed to carrying out their duty to act in the best interests of their members can negotiate the very best terms for the management of the scheme and the investment of its assets. These advantages stemming from benefits of scale will naturally be greatest in the case of a large trust-based self-administered occupational scheme.

This book's aim is essentially to point out to pension fund trustees how they can carry out their duty to act in the best interests of their members. The only prior requirement of the trustees in order to carry out this duty is their own commitment to do so. The practical expertise needed to do so can be provided by the advisers whom the trustees have appointed, although it is clear that, especially as regards investment, trustees will need to become familiar with the issues for which they are responsible. If trustees carry out this duty, they will bring far more expertise to bear in acting in the best interests of their members than any one individual member in a contract-based scheme would be likely to be able to muster.

Personal pension schemes

2.2   Retirement annuity contracts, sometimes known as *section 226 contracts*, were the precursor of the modern personal pension. Until 30 June 1988 they were available to employees who were not members of an occupational pension scheme and to the self-employed. Although no new retirement annuity contracts have been set for individuals since 1 July 1988, anyone who already held a contract before that day is still permitted to contribute to it.

Personal pensions themselves first became available on 1 July 1988. They are all established as defined contribution arrangements (see **1.5**) and have been able to receive contributions from individual employees and their employers and from the self-employed. An employee may choose a special kind of personal pension known as an *appropriate personal pension*, to contract himself or herself out of SERPS or S2P.

A personal pension must have received approval from HMRC and/or have become a registered pension scheme on or after 6 April 2006 if the members are to benefit from the tax advantages. This entails compliance with the relevant tax legislation. The tax rules governing personal pension schemes changed on 6 April 2001 and change again on 6 April 2006 when they become the same as those applying to registered occupational pension schemes.

Because personal pension schemes are classified as *controlled investments* it has generally been the case that they must be marketed and sold only by a person authorised to do so under the requirements of the *Financial Services and Markets Act 2000*. But from 1 July 2005 employers who contribute to a personal pension or stakeholder pension scheme are exempted from the requirements of this Act which limit the promotion of these schemes to authorised persons. The exemption is also dependent on the employer not receiving any direct financial benefit from the scheme such as a commission paid to the employer by the provider of the scheme or any reduction in the amount of the premium of any insurance policy issued to the employer by the provider of the scheme. The employer is also required to make certain disclosure statements to the employees.

HMRC estimates that in the 2001/02, some 5.1 million employees and nearly 1.2 million self-employed persons were contributing to either a personal pension or a stakeholder pension scheme.

Contributions may be paid to a personal pension in two distinct ways. Under the first method, the individual (and possibly the individual's employer) may contract with the personal pension provider to pay in a specified sum on a regular basis. Individual members will normally do this by setting up a direct debit or standing order arrangement through their bank. If this regular stream of payments continues over the term of the contract, the accumulated capital sum arising from the investment roll-up on the contributions, less deductions for charges, will be available to provide the member with his or her pension benefits. If, however, the member ceases to pay contributions during the term of the contract (and the contract is not continued by the operation of some waiver of contribution insurance policy), the personal pension contract will normally become 'paid up'. Depending on the terms of the contract, some of the charges that fell due to be deducted over the intended term of the contract may be deducted immediately from the accumulated capital up until the date the contributions were suspended.

To avoid a continuing commitment to make contributions to a single personal pension, the individual may prefer to use the alternative method of paying contributions, which is solely to make a commitment to pay a single premium lump sum payment to the personal pension contract. There will then be no commitment on the individual to make any further payments although the contract will usually permit him or her to do so.

Criticisms of personal pensions

2.3   The greatest criticism of personal pensions is that the charging structure of many personal pensions has made them unsuitable saving products for those on low or even moderate earnings. This has been especially the case when the individual member has been unable to continue making contributions for the full term of the contract. There is evidence to suggest that the advent of stakeholder pension schemes, with their controlled charging structure, has had a beneficial knock-on effect in relation to personal pensions more generally. Nevertheless a combination of charges that amount to, say, 1.5% of the value of an individual's personal pension at a time when real investment returns (i.e. actual investment returns net of price inflation) may be expected to average around, say, 6% a year has the overall effect or reducing the value of the investment return by a quarter.

Mis-selling of personal pensions

2.4   Personal pensions impacted on the attention of the trustees of occupational pension schemes during the late 1980s and early 1990s because very large numbers of them were sold in contravention of the rules made under the financial services legislation.

A very large number of employees who could have joined their employers' occupational pension scheme were persuaded instead by independent financial advisers, insurance company representatives and other tied agents to buy a personal pension contract. In other cases, existing active members of an occupational pension scheme were persuaded to opt out of that scheme and take out a personal pension. Many of this group were also persuaded to transfer their accrued occupational pension scheme rights out of the scheme and over to their personal pension. Other individuals who retained deferred pension rights in an occupational pension scheme run by their former employer and who were then approaching retirement were also persuaded to transfer their accrued rights to a personal pension.

Because employers contribute to an occupational pension schemes and because occupational pension schemes nearly always provide more generous ill-health benefits and death benefits than personal pension schemes, such personal pension sales were usually non-compliant with the duty on the sales person to provide best advice. The mis-selling of personal pensions has undoubtedly been one of the biggest financial scandals of recent years and has caused a great deal of misery to the individuals affected and their families. It severely damaged the reputation of the insurance industry and also has cost billions of pounds in reinstatement or compensation costs.

The chief cause of the mis-selling scandal was ineffective regulation of a market that was and still is largely driven by commission-based sales.

Legal basis

2.5   Most personal pensions are insurance contracts made between an individual and an insurance company. They are usually established by a *deed poll*. This is a legal document that establishes the personal pension scheme and is important because it allows any dependant of the member to enforce any obligations assumed by the personal pension provider to pay benefits to that dependant. Without the deed poll mechanism, a contract can only be enforced by the parties who actually entered into that contract. However, a deed poll does not establish a trust such as described at **1.15**. The contributions paid by the member to the personal pension provider become the property of that personal pension provider. Some personal pensions adopt a limited form of trust known as a *trust of policy* which can be used to mitigate inheritance tax considerations upon the death of a member. Some, but not many, personal pensions are, however, set up as full trusts.

Group personal pension arrangements

2.6   Group personal pension (GPP) arrangements are collections of individual personal pension contracts taken out with the same personal pension provider and which are sold by independent financial advisers, insurance company representatives and other tied agents to the employees of a particular employer. The employer in effect facilitates the sale of the individual personal pensions by offering access to the personal pension provider's representative or an independent financial adviser. The employer may also offer a payroll check-off facility through which employees may pass on their personal pension contributions to the personal pension provider. The employer may, moreover, choose to make its own contributions on behalf of all or some of the employees direct to the personal pension provider. If so, it is likely that the employer's contribution will be a term of the contract of employment between the employer and the employee concerned.

In any case, the benefits of scale arising from the fact that a number of personal pension sales have been made on a collective basis often means that the contractual terms for the investment of contributions are more favourable than would be the case if the personal pension had been bought individually outside the GPP arrangement. This collective basis can mitigate the criticism mentioned above that the charging structure of personal pensions has often in the past made them unsuitable as savings vehicles, particularly for those on low or modest earnings.

GPP arrangements have become very popular especially amongst smaller employers. The GPP arrangement can often be 'badged' with the employer's name and so to all intents and purposes it takes on the outward appearance of a defined contribution occupational pension scheme.

GPPs have become popular with employers in many ways because they have not involved the establishment of a trust and they are not subject therefore to the requirements of trust law nor to the statutory requirements set out in the *Pensions Act 1995* which apply in the main only to occupational pension schemes.

Direct payment arrangements

2.7   It should be noted, however, that since 6 April 2001, certain requirements of the *Welfare Reform and Pensions Act 1999* have come into force which have helped level the playing field between defined contribution occupational pension schemes and GPP arrangements. The requirements also apply to individual personal pension contracts outside any GPP arrangements. The enforcement of these requirements is also one of the main objectives set for the Pensions Regulator by the *Pensions Act 2004*.

The requirements relate to the monitoring of employers' payments into a personal pension scheme and operate whenever a *direct payment arrangement* is found to exist between an employer and any employee and where that employee is a member of a personal pension scheme. Here a *direct payment arrangement* is defined as an arrangement where contributions fall to be paid by or on behalf of the employer to the employee's personal pension either:

- on the employer's own account but in respect of the employee; or

- on behalf of the employee out of deductions made from the employee's earnings.

In such circumstances the employer is required to prepare, maintain and from time to time revise a record of its direct payment arrangements which shows the rates and due dates of contributions payable under those arrangements. The employer is required to send to the personal pension provider a copy of this record, and of any subsequent revisions made to it. The *Personal Pension Schemes (Payments by Employers) Regulations 2000 (SI 2000/2692)* stipulate that the copy of the record must be sent so that it is likely that it becomes available to the personal pension provider no later than the date upon which the first contribution payable by reference to the record falls due for payment.

The personal pension provider must notify the Pensions Regulator if a contribution under the direct payment arrangements has not been paid by its due date, and the provider has 'reasonable cause' to believe that the failure is likely to be of 'material significance' to the Pensions Regulator in the exercise of any of its functions. The notice must be given to the Pensions Regulator and the employee within a 'reasonable period' after the due date.

A code of practice issued by the Pensions Regulator will give guidance on how term such as 'reasonable cause', 'material significance' and 'reasonable period' are to be construed.

Penalties for non-compliance

2.8   In cases of default the Pensions Regulator can impose a civil penalty in the form of a fine on the employer where the employer does not take all reasonable steps to comply with the personal pension provider's request for payment information or to pay a contribution under a direct payment arrangement by its due date.

The Pensions Regulator can also impose a fine on the personal pension provider if it fails to take all reasonable steps to comply with the requirement to give the Pensions Regulator notice of a material failure by an employer to pay over contributions in accordance with the record of contributions.

Unbundled GPP arrangements

2.9   It is possible to reproduce in a GPP arrangement some of the advantages of benefits of scale and independent advice that is available to trust-based occupational pension schemes. This works by the employer establishing a management committee which includes an external pension consultant. There is a set of overall contracts between each individual member and the personal pension provider. Yet this provider simply puts in place the overall legal documentation. The day-to-day administration of these contracts and the investment management of the underlying assets can be carried out by other organisations appointed, and possibly from time to time replaced in case of unsatisfactory performance, by the management committee. This is termed an *unbundled* arrangement because the administration and investment functions are no longer bundled together with the underlying personal pension contracts. Since no trust has been set up, the members of the management committee are not likely to be seen as trustees.

Stakeholder pension schemes

2.10–2.11 Stakeholder pension schemes first became available on 6 April 2001, having been established by the *Welfare Reform and Pensions Act 1999*. Essentially, stakeholder pensions are defined contribution schemes which are:

(a) legally established either as an occupational pension scheme or as a personal pension scheme; and

(b) legally governed either by trustees and therefore set up as a trust, or set up as an individual contract between the individual member and the stakeholder pension provider.

In practice there are three kinds of stakeholder pension schemes. These are stakeholder pension schemes which are:

● trust-based occupational pension schemes which are established by employers, or groups of employers, or by other affinity groups such as trade unions;

● trust-based personal pension schemes which operate in the form of group personal pension arrangements established by personal pension providers and governed by trustees appointed by employers, or groups of employers, or by other affinity groups such as trade unions;

● contract-based personal pension schemes governed uniquely by contracts between the individual members and the stakeholder manager employed by the personal pension provider.

The key characteristic of any stakeholder pension scheme is that it must be registered by the Pensions Regulator and, to be so registered, the scheme must comply with a set of minimum standards laid down in the legislation:

● the scheme, if in existence before 6 April 2006 had to be tax approved by the then Inland Revenue (now HMRC) and, for any period from that date to be a registered pension scheme under the provisions of the *Finance Act 2004*;

● in relation to stakeholder pension schemes where the contract began before 6 April 2005 any charges made from each member's pension account must not exceed 1/36,500 of the value of that member's pension account for each day the member remains in the scheme, although extra charges can be made if they are for additional services which are completely optional and provided under a separate contract but, in relation to new stakeholder pension contracts entered into from 6 April 2005, the maximum charge has been increased so that the maximum charge is set at 3/73,000 for each day over the first 10 years that the contract is held, and 1/36,500 for each day thereafter;

- the scheme must offer a default investment option based on what is known as the 'life-style option' available to members who do not wish to choose between a number of different investment options – the 'life-style option' involves the adoption of an investment strategy designed progressively to reduce the potential for significant variation in the value of the member's rights caused by market conditions and which must be put in place at least five years before the member's intended retirement date;

- the scheme must comply with detailed disclosure requirements;

- members must be free to make contributions of any amount, provided it is not less than £20, at any frequency they wish although when employers are deducting employee contributions from their pay the employer can impose limitations on how often the employees can vary the amount that is to be deducted for each pay period. Restrictions can be placed, however, on the payment by members of contributions by means of cash or credit card;

- the scheme must not only provide transfer values as with any occupational or personal pension scheme but must also accept any transfer payment coming from another tax-approved pension arrangement;

- if the scheme ever ceases to be registered with the Pensions Regulator , it cannot accept any further contributions and must immediately begin to wind up and complete its winding up normally within twelve months by making transfer payments to a registered stakeholder pension scheme or by complying with a request from a member for a transfer to another tax-approved pension arrangement.

The access requirement

2.12   Since 8 October 2001 all employers with more than four employees have been required to designate a stakeholder pension scheme and offer access to that scheme to any 'relevant employees'. Here 'relevant employees' means any employee who is either employed in this country or employed abroad by an employer resident or incorporated in this country and who both earns in excess of the National Insurance lower earnings limit and is not entitled to membership of an occupational pension scheme.

However, the following groups of employees will not be regarded as 'relevant employees'. They are those:

- who will become eligible for membership of an occupational pension scheme after an initial waiting period of no more than twelve months from the time they started in that employment;

- who are temporarily excluded from membership of an occupational pension scheme because they are currently aged under 18;

- who are excluded from membership of an occupational pension scheme because they started in that employment when they were aged less than five years below the scheme's normal pension age;

- who, had they wished to join an occupational pension of the employer at some time in the past, would have qualified for membership of the scheme, but who, in the event, are now excluded from the scheme because they did not join the scheme at that earlier opportunity;

- who were once members of an occupational pension scheme of the employer but chose to opt out of membership and are now as a result excluded from membership of that scheme;

- who have been employed by the employer for less than three months;

- whose earnings have not equalled or exceeded the National Insurance lower earnings limit in any week within the last three months;

- who are ineligible under UK tax law to make contributions to a stakeholder pension scheme (e.g. employees working abroad who do not satisfy the residency conditions).

There is, however, an exemption for one group of employers from the requirement to designate a stakeholder pension scheme even if some of the employees fall into the category of 'relevant employees'. An employer does not need to comply with the access requirement if it is a term of the contract of employment of every 'relevant employee', other than those who have not yet reached age 18, that the employer will make contributions to a personal pension for that employee and, if requested to do so by that employee, offer a payroll deduction service so that contributions will be deducted from the employee's pay and passed directly to the personal pension provider. The employer must pay at a rate of not less than 3% of the employee's basic pay (i e excluding overtime, bonuses and the like) but this can be made conditional on the employee making a contribution to the same scheme at a specified rate.

If the arrangement was already in place on 8 October 2001, the employer's contribution rate must equal or exceed that of the employee but if the condition that the employee must pay a contribution at a specified rate did not come into effect until on or after 8 October 2001, or if the employer's contribution rate ceases to be equal to or exceed that of the employee after that date, the employee cannot be required to make any contribution in excess of 3% of basic pay.

This exemption only applies if the personal pension does not impose any exit charges on the member, i.e. the personal pension cannot impose any penalty on members who cease contributing to the scheme or transfer their funds out of the scheme.

Where the access requirement applies, the employer must designate at least one stakeholder pension scheme which is registered by the Pensions Regulator and which offers membership to all the employer's 'relevant employees'. Before designating a stakeholder pension scheme, the employer must consult with its relevant employees or any organisations representing them.

If a stakeholder scheme designated by the employer subsequently ceases to be registered with the Pensions Regulator, that scheme must also cease to be the employer's designated stakeholder scheme.

The employer must supply all relevant employees with the name and address of the designated stakeholder scheme, or schemes, and also allow representatives of the designated scheme, or schemes, reasonable access to all the relevant employees so that they can supply them with further information. The selling and marketing of stakeholder pension schemes is regulated by the Financial Services Authority.

There had been concern that employers might be held legally responsible if they designated a stakeholder pension scheme which turned out to perform badly. However, the legislation specifies that an employer, in designating a stakeholder pension scheme, is under no duty to investigate or monitor, or make any judgment as to the past, present or future performance of the scheme.

The employer, if requested to do so by a relevant employee who has become a member of a scheme which the employer has designated, is required to:

- deduct the employee's chosen contributions to the scheme from the employee's pay; and
- pay them to the stakeholder scheme within the specified time.

Because a stakeholder pension is legally either an occupational pension scheme or a personal pension scheme, contribution schedules will have to be drawn up for stakeholder pension schemes. These schedules are subject to the same requirements as apply to occupational and personal pension schemes in general. Furthermore, similar sanctions also apply in cases of failure to comply with these requirements.

There are certain limitations on the freedom of employees to change the rate and frequency of their own contributions which they have asked the employer to deduct from their pay. First, the rules of the stakeholder pension scheme are able to stipulate that the provider can refuse to accept any contribution which is less than £20. Conversely, any contribution of £20 or more must generally therefore be accepted, whether this is a regular or a one-off payment. For these purposes any tax relief, any contracting-out minimum payments and any age-related rebate payments will not count towards the £20 minimum level.

Second, the employer may decide that an employee not be permitted to change the amount of his or her contributions deducted via the payroll more than once every six months. The employer must, however, stop making any deductions and paying them over to the stakeholder scheme as soon as practicable when requested to do so by the employee. If this happens, the employer, if asked to do so by the employee, is not obliged to restart any further payroll stakeholder deductions from that employee's pay for a further six months.

Trust-based stakeholder schemes

2.13   Where a stakeholder pension scheme is set up as a trust, whether that scheme is legally an occupational or a personal pension scheme, the trustees of that scheme will be subject broadly to the same requirements that are placed by statute and trust law on the trustees of a defined contribution occupational pension scheme. *Section 6* of the *Welfare Reform and Pensions Act 1999*, together with *Schedule 1* to that Act, achieves this effect. Unless otherwise stated, any duty described in this book as falling on the trustees of an occupational pension scheme should be taken as also falling on the trustees of any trust-based stakeholder pension scheme unless that duty relates only to a defined benefit occupational pension scheme.

In addition, the Pensions Regulator has the power to prohibit anyone from acting as a trustee of a stakeholder pension scheme and to fine the trustee if he or she fails to take reasonable steps to secure that the scheme complies with all the minimum standards set out in **2.10** above.

At least one trustee and at least one third of the total number of trustees of a trust-based stakeholder pension scheme must be independent. That is to say, this minimum number of trustees must be neither connected with, nor an associate of, any person providing services to the scheme or otherwise managing the scheme (other than as a trustee). If there is a corporate trustee (see **3.3** and **3.4**) and no individual trustees of the stakeholder pension scheme, at least one of the directors of the corporate trustee and at least one-third of the total number of directors must also be independent as defined immediately above.

The trust documentation must not require the trustees of a stakeholder pension scheme to need the consent of any other person before making any decision about investments. Nor must the trust documentation prevent the trustees, unless required to do by an Act of Parliament, from amending the trust documentation to provide for different investments to be held.

Personal pension, contract-based, stakeholder schemes

2.14   Essentially, stakeholder pension schemes that are legally established as a personal pension, and which are set up under contract, are just the same as personal pension schemes with the importance difference that the minimum standards set out in **2.1** above must apply – in particular the minimum charges that can be imposed.

The personal pension tax regime

2.15   Personal pensions and all stakeholder pension schemes are subject to a new tax regime informally known as the *personal pension tax regime* which was established by the *Finance Act 2000* and which came into force on 6 April 2001 but this tax regime, just as with the tax regimes that apply to occupational pension schemes will cease to apply on 6 April 2006.From that date, personal pensions and occupational pensions will be subject to the same tax legislation. In this edition of the *Pension Fund Trustee Handbook* we no longer summarise the personal pension tax regime.

Financial services regulation

2.16   All contract-based schemes (personal pensions, free-standing additional voluntary contribution schemes) and all stakeholder pension schemes, including those legally established as occupational pension schemes, are subject to regulation under the financial services legislation in the manner they are promoted to potential members but see **2.2** above for an explanation of the exemption for employers who contribute to their employees personal or stakeholder pension schemes which was introduced on 1 July 2005. Occupational pension schemes and additional voluntary contribution schemes taken out by the trustees of an occupational pension scheme are not, though, subject to financial services regulation in the manner that they are promoted to potential members.

The day-to-day investment management of an occupational pension scheme's assets and of the assets of an AVC scheme, however, just as with all pension assets held in contract-based schemes, must be generally carried out by those who are authorised to do so under the financial services legislation (see **16.5** below).

Reduction in yields

2.17   Where a commercial body provides any form of pension scheme it quite legitimately needs to cover its operational costs, the costs of investing contributions and managing the scheme's assets as well as generating a surplus either for further investment in operations or, in the case of a company, for distribution to its shareholders. The costs of operations will also include the costs of promoting the scheme to potential members and this may include commission payments made to third parties such as independent financial advisers.

Where there is the involvement of an employer, these costs will generally be less than in the case of individual arrangements.

The overall effect of these costs is that the commercial pension providers will either charge their client a fee or they will not pass on the full investment return earned on the scheme's assets to the client in the form of pension benefits. In the latter case, there will be a measurable annual 'reduction in yield' (RIY) that will bring down the investment return from that actually achieved.

As an example, take an individual who pays £1,000 as a single premium into a personal pension scheme and draws a pension after 25 years. If the scheme's investment return over that entire period is a 7% p a nominal return ('nominal' means without taking inflation into account) that will produce a capital sum of about £5,427. If however the scheme's charging structure has the net result of an annual RIY of 1.1%, the nominal return is reduced to 5.9% p a with the result that the end capital sum is about £4,192. In other words, in the example, the capital sum is about 77% of what it would have been without the charges.

The annual RIY will vary widely between different providers. It may also vary according to:

- the way in which the pension arrangement was sold;
- the amount of contributions paid into the scheme;
- the overall size of the fund; and
- the length of the term of the contract.

However, if these factors are held constant, a comparison of the annual RIY associated with each provider gives an objective ranking of the providers in terms of their charges.

The Financial Services Authority (FSA) maintains on its web site an interactive set of tables which show the monetary effect of the RIY resulting from the charging structures of UK personal pension schemes and stakeholder pension schemes. The FSA assumes that the contributions will attract a 7% p a nominal investment return over the entire term of the contract.

The tables may be found at http://www.fsa.gov.uk/tables and, because they are interactive, they allow the viewer to choose the appropriate contribution rate and contract term for each of the providers listed. In each case the tables for each named scheme show the monetary amount of explicit charges and deductions that will be deducted over the term of the policy to the chosen retirement date. In other words, the capital fund that would have been built up on the contributions paid at the chosen rate over the entire term of the contract up to the chosen retirement date will be reduced by the amount shown in the 'charges & deductions' column of the tables.

In addition, the tables show the 'charges deducted in the early years'. This is the monetary amount that would have been deducted if, instead of continuing with the policy for the intended term, the individual ceased making contributions after the first three years.

It is striking when looking at the results just how large the variation is between the lowest and highest charging schemes.

Checklist 2

- Pension schemes may be trust-based or contract-based.

- Personal pension schemes are generally contract-based individual arrangements between the member and the personal pension provider.

- Personal pensions can be very effective vehicles for saving for retirement but in the past many have been mis-sold. In some cases, their charging structures has made them unsuitable for low or moderate earners.

- Although 'controlled investments' within the meaning of the Financial Services and Markets Act, employers can be exempted from the rules governing the promotion of personal and stakeholder pension schemes.

- Group personal pensions can mimic the appearance of defined contribution occupational pension schemes.

- New *direct payment arrangements* have been enforced since 6 April 2001 in cases where an employer has agreed to make payments to an employee's personal pension.

- Stakeholder pension schemes became available on 6 April 2001 and can be legally established as occupational pension schemes or as personal pension schemes. Employers of 'relevant employees' have been required to offer those employees access to a stakeholder pension since 8 October 2001.

- Since 6 April 2001 a new personal pension tax regime has governed personal pension schemes and all stakeholder pension schemes (including those legally established as occupational pension schemes) but from 6 April 2006 all personal and stakeholder pension schemes become subject to the same new tax regime as also applies to registered occupational pension schemes.

- The effect of charges and deductions in reducing the overall yield obtained by investment returns on contributions still varies markedly between different personal and stakeholder pension scheme providers.

Chapter 3

The trustee body

Different structures

3.1   How a trustee body, charged with the care of an occupational pension scheme, is structured will be set out in the *trust deed and rules*, the legal document which constitutes the scheme.

From the point of view of trust law, the structure of the trustee body does not in any way change the overall legal obligations which are placed on the trustees. The trustee body will still have the same job to do.

Occupational pension schemes vary enormously. Consider some examples:

- a small scheme for three or four directors in a small family firm;

- a scheme administered by an insurance company for fifty employees working for a small service company based in one small town;

- a large scheme with three thousand employees in ten different sites throughout the UK.

Each of these very different occupational pension schemes will be under the care of a trustee body. In the first example all the members can themselves be trustees and will be intimately connected. In the second example, it is likely that all the trustees will know all the members, and probably will have met their families. Yet some will be senior managers, some will be office staff, some will be part of the sales force.

In the third example, the trustees will know only a very small proportion of the total number of members. Only personnel records will indicate whether a member is married. A member may have a financially dependent, physically handicapped child but this may not be known to the trustees. The pensions department may be located at company headquarters in London, three hundred miles from the most distant company site. The ten sites could vary enormously in size and character: for example, one site could have a thousand industrial staff in the Midlands and be highly unionised while another site might be a formerly independent, small company in Wales with fifty employees and which is fiercely proud of its own identity.

It is no wonder that different structures for trustee bodies have evolved to cope with such varied situations.

Individual trustees

3.2 The trust deed and rules may commonly provide for trustees to be appointed as individuals. In some cases a minimum number and a maximum number will also be specified. Just how individuals are appointed, how long a time they serve as trustees and how they can be replaced will also be defined in the trust deed and rules. These areas are dealt with more fully in CHAPTER 4.

Individual trustees, other than professional, independent trustees hired for their expertise, are still generally unpaid, although, of course, they may recover their expenses and those who are employees of an employer participating in the scheme continue to receive their normal wage or salary. This general practice of relying on unpaid lay trustees was challenged by Paul Myners in his review of institutional investment. For more details see *Principle 1* in **17.4** and **17.5**.

One advantage of individuals serving as trustees is that they provide the human touch in what may be a large occupational pension scheme, with its own bureaucracy and form-filling. The trustees may be well known by the members and be on hand, both formally and informally, to listen to problems and give advice, although there are certain pitfalls in this area – see CHAPTER 9.

One problem that arises is that the trust deed will need to be amended whenever a trustee resigns and a new replacement is appointed. Also, any change in who are the trustees has to be notified to the National Insurance Contributions Office and to the Pensions Regulator which maintains a register of occupational pension schemes. Because of these, and certain other reasons, many occupational pension schemes make use of a corporate trustee.

Corporate trustees

3.3 Instead of individual men and women serving as trustees, the trust deed and rules may specify that there is a single *corporate trustee*. This simply means that a company acts as the trustee body. The company will usually be a specially named and constituted subsidiary company of the main company that employs the workforce. Yet this does not necessarily mean that the trustee body becomes totally institutionalised.

What happens is that the various possible processes for the selection and appointment of individual trustees are mirrored exactly in the selection and appointment of the directors of the corporate trustee. They are usually termed *trustee directors* and they have, in general, the same role as individual trustees.

Throughout this book, whenever we use the term 'trustees', we generally mean to include 'trustee directors'.

One procedural advantage is that there is no need to change the trust deed whenever an individual trustee director resigns and a replacement is appointed.

From a legal point of view, the trustee body remains unchanged as the same corporate trustee.

A second advantage stems from possible extra legal protection for the individuals who serve as trustee directors; the theory being that the corporate trustee is sued not the individual directors. See **CHAPTER 22** for more details.

There may also be advantages concerning VAT if a corporate trustee is used because the trustee company may be included in a group VAT registration with the employer. The employer can then deduct the VAT on supplies of certain goods and services made to the trustee which would not otherwise be deductible.

It is quite useful to have a corporate trustee rather than individual trustees if the pension scheme includes land as one of its investments. This is because under the *Trustee Act 1925* no more than four individual trustees can be involved in a settlement for the sale of land. On the other hand, also under the *Trustee Act 1925*, a sole trustee (unless it is also a trust corporation – see **3.4** below) cannot give a valid receipt for the proceeds of a sale of land by the trust so there would be a need to appoint a separate trustee for this purpose. All of this may seem pretty arcane and the scheme's lawyer should be able to devise a solution in either case!

It should be remembered that, since a corporate trustee is a company, it will have to comply with all the requirements of the *Companies Acts*. This may include the need both to appoint auditors and to have the accounts of the corporate trustee audited. It also includes the requirement that the private address of each director of the corporate trustee must be held by the Registrar of Companies. It should be noted that a director of a corporate trustee should be made automatically to resign if he or she individually becomes disqualified from acting as a trustee. This would be the case, for example, if the director became personally bankrupt. If the director were not to resign, the corporate trustee itself would be disqualified from acting as a trustee.

Trust corporation

3.4   The trust deed may give the sponsoring employer power to appoint a trust corporation. A trust corporation is a company set up to provide trustee services as a commercial business. Many banks and insurance companies, for example, have established trust corporations.

A trust corporation is therefore a corporate trustee but not one that is a subsidiary of the sponsoring employer. Trust corporations are staffed by professionals who are delivering a service in return for a fee. They do not have any intimate connection with the membership.

A trust corporation has to be established under the law of one of the member states of the European Union and usually be registered under the UK

Companies Acts, or their equivalent in another member state of the European Union. Generally speaking, it must also have capital of not less than £250,000 of which not less than £100,000 has been paid up (i e the shareholders have actually paid this amount to hold the shares).

Many are in membership of The Association of Corporate Trustees (TACT):

> TACT
> 3 Brackerne Close
> Cooden
> Bexhill on Sea
> East Sussex
> TN39 3BT
> Tel: 01424 844144
> email: tact@cooden.fsbusiness.co.uk
> Web site: http://www.trustees.org.uk.

It is generally accepted that the courts will impose a higher duty of care on a trust corporation than on an individual trustee or trustee director of an 'ordinary' corporate trustee. It was held in one legal case that:

> ' ... a professional corporate trustee is liable for breach of trust if loss is caused to the trust fund because it neglects to exercise the special care and skill which it professes to have.' (*Bartlett v Barclays Trust Co Ltd* [1980] 1 All ER 139.)

This distinction has been maintained in the proposals issued by the Government in February 2002 for new legislation to require trustees who undertake investment duties to be familiar with the issues with which they are concerned. These proposals arise out of the review of institutional investment by Paul Myners. For more details see **17.7**.

Independent trustee

3.5   An *independent trustee* means a trustee who has no connection with the employer and is neither a member nor a beneficiary of the occupational pension scheme. The term is usually applied to specialist corporate trustees or trust corporations who offer professional trustee services in return for a fee but may also refer to an individual who is unconnected with the employer or membership.

A number of larger pension schemes in recent years have appointed independent trustees to be members of their trustee boards. In some cases the trust deed and rules have been amended to give the independent trustee reserve powers and so have a veto over certain kinds of changes – often with a view to safeguarding the existing members' interests in the event of a hostile takeover. A typical set of requirements embedded in the trust deed and rules might be that:

- there must always be an independent trustee so that, although the present independent trustee could be removed, this could only be done if another independent trustee were found as a replacement;

- the independent trustee has power to veto any proposal that it considers would prejudicially affect the accrued rights of beneficiaries;

- the independent trustee can close the scheme to new entrants or effect a wind up to protect accrued rights;

- if the independent trustee is removed it has the right to advise all beneficiaries in writing of the reasons for its removal.

In other cases, the independent trustee is not 'embedded' in the trust deed and rules and has exactly the same powers and duties as the other trustees. In practice the independent trustee may be seen to be more strongly placed since it can draw on its corporate and professional resources.

In October 2003 the Independent Pension Trustees Group (IPTG) was established to promote awareness of the importance of the role of the independent trustee in the operation of occupational pension schemes and to promote best practice and define the relationship between independent trustees, employers and beneficiaries. In July 2004 the IPTG released a code of guidance for use by those appointed as independent trustees to occupational pension schemes. It covers six key areas:

- appointment procedures;

- dealing with co-trustees and third parties;

- investment;

- risk management;

- compliance;

- insolvency.

Of interest to lay trustees is what the IPTG's code says about the role of an independent pension trustee appointed alongside lay trustees. It stresses that the independent trustee must be aware of where the powers set by the scheme's trust documentation reside between the various trustees and be aware that there may be powers or roles that are reserved to particular trustees. It states that independent trustees are not professional advisers and the trustees should still seek specialist advice where appropriate.

The guidance emphasises that an independent trustee should stimulate debate between the trustees and 'should not dominate proceedings'. The independent trustee should ensure that discussions of issues should be 'at the appropriate level for all trustees to understand and follow'. Independent trustees should also 'consider their position where decisions are taken in which they hold the minority view, and take appropriate action (if any) in the light of all the circumstances and any legal obligations'.

The IPTG operates under the auspices of the Pensions Management Institute (PMI).

> Gillian King
> Head of Education
> The Pensions Management Institute
> PMI House
> 4–10 Artillery Lane
> London
> E1 7LS
> Tel: 020 7392 7400
> email:gking@pensions-pmi.org.uk
> http://www.pensions-pmi.org.uk.

In certain circumstances the independent trustee is statutorily appointed. Under the provisions of *ss 22–26C* of the *Pensions Act 2004*, but as substantially amended by the *Pensions Act 1994*, an independent trustee may be appointed to the trustee body of a defined benefit scheme, if one is not already in place, if the employer becomes insolvent. The requirement does not apply to defined contribution (money purchase) schemes. Until 6 April 2005, the independent trustee in such circumstances was appointed by the insolvency practitioner put in place to wind up the company. While the integrity of the main providers of independent trustee services is not doubted, the statutory legislation itself in the past has not prohibited independent trustees from exercising trustee powers for their own benefit. For example, in a case where an independent trustee has been appointed to an occupational pension scheme of a company which has gone into receivership, it was possible that a company associated with the independent trustee could place the scheme's assets with an insurance company in return for a substantial commission payment. It would seem that such an action would nevertheless have been a breach of trust. The legislation was changed to prohibit the appointment of any independent trustee upon an employer's insolvency if that independent trustee was connected or associated with anyone who has an interest in the assets either of the scheme, or of the employer, other than as a trustee of the scheme.

An important disadvantage of having an independent trustee, especially for smaller schemes, is the cost of the fees, while others judge that the membership ought to be able to rely on a combination of member-nominated and employer-nominated trustees, supported by their external professional advisers, without drawing on outsiders to act as trustees.

The issue of fees that may be charged by independent trustees who are appointed to wind up a defined benefit scheme of an insolvent employer has proved to be highly controversial. TPAS, the Pensions Advisory Service, drew attention to the lack of control over the activities of such independent trustees and the sometimes 'extortionate' charges that they could then levy. TPAS called for greater accountability for the costs in winding up a pension scheme and believed that independent trustees, who had sole control over the whole wind-up process, had such an important role they should be licensed. TPAS stated:

'At present, anyone or any organisation can set themselves up in business as an independent trustee without needing any authorisation. No standards of knowledge, ability or resources are required. Regulation of this sector of the market would be in the interests of the many trustees who are competent and responsible.'

There was a considerable amount of sympathy with the stance being taken by TPAS. In the event the *Pensions Act 2004* has now changed the legislation so that the Pensions Regulator itself has been given power to appoint an independent trustee rather than the insolvency practitioner and where the independent trustee to be appointed is registered on a list maintained by the Pensions Regulator.

In order to qualify for appointment as an independent trustee in these circumstances the person:

● must have no interest in the assets of the employer or of the scheme otherwise than as a trustee of the scheme, and

● must have no connection with, nor be an associate of, either the employer, any person acting as the insolvency practitioner or the official receiver acting in relation to the employer's insolvency.

Management committees

3.6   The term *committee of management* or *management committee* tends to be used in a variety of senses.

A management committee may provide a local forum for active members, especially in a large occupational pension scheme where the active members are spread over many sites. As such it serves as a *pensions consultative committee*.

Similarly, some employers negotiate with trade unions and employee representatives on pensions. This may be through the standard negotiation machinery or through special pension negotiating committees, and the term *management committee* might be used in this context.

However, if either of these kinds of bodies under the terms of the trust deed and rules have any trustee duties, powers and discretions delegated to them, the members of such management committees are trustees. Their actions will be governed by trust law.

It is common to find in a large multi-site company that the trust deed and rules specify that certain discretionary powers are not exercised by the main trustee body. Rather they are delegated to local management committees. These may be discretionary powers such as deciding who should receive a dependant's pension after a member has died and to whom any lump sum should be paid. The argument is that it is better that such decisions are taken at local level. For a fuller discussion see **5.4**.

Sometimes the term *management committee* is reserved for another central body operating alongside the main trustee body – the trustee board itself. A standard division of labour might give the trustee board responsibility for investment matters, for holding the scheme assets, strategic issues such as powers of amendment to the trust deed and powers exercisable when the occupational pension scheme is wound up, while the management committee oversees day-to-day administration.

Pensioneer trustee

3.7   *Pensioneer trustee* is a term uniquely associated with *small self-administered schemes*. These are occupational pension schemes which have less than twelve members. They usually provide benefits to directors of small companies. Pensioneer trustee services are provided on a fee-payment basis usually by insurance companies and specialist consultancies.

Many, but far from all, pensioneer trustees are in membership of the Association of Pensioneer Trustees (APT):

> APT
> c/o Mr Trevor Harvey
> Pensioneer Trustees (London) Ltd
> Chalfont Court
> Hill Avenue
> Amersham
> Buckinghamshire
> HP6 5BB
> Tel: 01494 788117
> Web site: http://www.pensioneers.org.

HMRC has maintained a list for inspection of all approved pensioneer trustees. This may be viewed on the following web address: http://www.hmrc.gov.uk/pensionschemes/apt-list.htm.

Custodian trustee

3.8   The term *custodian trustee* is sometimes used. Quite simply, the custodian trustee's job is to hold financial assets. In the strict sense, a custodian trustee has to be a trust corporation and can only be removed by a court order. Such a custodian trustee in fact is hardly ever used by occupational pension schemes. The term is sometimes applied to what is properly known as a *holding trustee* who is appointed and removed under the terms of the trust deed and rules. However, most usually the term refers to a nominee custodian. A nominee custodian is usually engaged by the investment manager and is not actually a trustee of the scheme at all. Their role is discussed at **16.23**.

Checklist 3

- The structure of the trustee body will in part reflect the size of the sponsoring employer and whether or not employment sites are geographically widespread, but this does not change the nature of the trustees' duties.

- The trustee body may be made up of *individuals acting as trustees* or there may be a *corporate trustee* with individual *trustee directors*. There are technical differences between the two sorts of trustee boards but trustees and trustee directors have essentially the same duties.

- Professional trustees, often constituted as trust corporations, can serve as *independent trustees* alongside individual trustees or a corporate trustee with trustee directors. They charge a fee for their services.

- An *independent trustee* must be appointed in specific circumstances (e g in the case of most defined benefit schemes, when the employer becomes insolvent).

- If members of a *management committee* are charged with carrying out any trustee duty, they are acting as trustees and are subject to trust law.

- Special trustee arrangements apply to *small self-administered schemes*.

- It is not usual for the *custodian* of an occupational pension scheme's assets to be a trustee.

Chapter 4

How trustees are chosen

Appointment and removal

4.1   Until the coming into force on 6 April 1997 of certain sections of the *Pensions Act 1995*, the appointment and removal of trustees had been governed solely by the trust deed and rules, and also, in the case of a corporate trustee, the articles of association of that company. If the trust deed and rules do not say how the trustees should be appointed or removed, then *ss 36–39* of the *Trustee Act 1925* provide a set of default rules. In cases of dispute or difficulty, the courts can interpret the trust deed and rules in the light of general principles of trust law. In the case of a corporate trustee, how the trustee directors are appointed and removed will also be subject to company law. Until the coming into force of the relevant measures in the *Pensions Act 1995*, the power to appoint and to remove trustees in most cases lay exclusively with the employer.

Those disqualified from acting as trustees

4.2   Again, until the coming into force of certain sections of the *Pensions Act 1995*, anyone was eligible to act as a trustee with the exceptions of minors, those certified as insane and those declared bankrupt. However, since 6 April 1997, the following are specifically excluded from acting as a trustee of an occupational pension scheme:

(a)   the scheme's actuary;

(b)   the scheme's auditor;

(c)   anyone who has been prohibited by an order made by the Pensions Regulator;

(d)   anyone disqualified by the Pensions Regulator for being a trustee of any scheme following that person's removal as a trustee of another scheme by the courts on the grounds of misconduct or mismanagement;

(e)   anyone who has been temporarily suspended from acting as a trustee by an order made by the Pensions Regulator;

(f)   anyone who has been convicted of an offence involving dishonesty or deception (unless the conviction has become spent under the Rehabilitation of Offenders Act 1974);

(g)   anyone who is an undischarged bankrupt;

(h)   anyone who has made an undischarged arrangement with his or her creditors;

(i)   anyone who has failed to make a payment as required under the terms of a county court administration order;

(j)   anyone disqualified by the Pensions Regulator on the grounds of mental disorder;

(k)   any director of a company which itself has been disqualified from acting as a trustee (also applies to a partner in a Scottish partnership);

(l)   anyone who has been disqualified from acting as a company director; and

(m)   a company disqualified by the Pensions Regulator because it has gone into liquidation.

If any of the above ignores the ban from acting as a scheme trustee, they are guilty of an offence and liable, if convicted, to a fine and imprisonment.

However, anything done as a trustee by someone who was in fact disqualified will not automatically become invalid.

Except in the case of the scheme actuary and auditor, the Pensions Regulator has the power to waive the disqualification or to revoke its own disqualifying order.

These exclusions also apply in the case of trustees of a stakeholder pension scheme.

The Pensions Regulator has the power to issue an order suspending a trustee in a number of situations generally for a period of up to 12 months, but this can be extended by a period of a further 12 months. Such situations include when proceedings either are pending or have been instituted against the trustee for an offence involving dishonesty or deception but have not been concluded, or where a petition for an individual's bankruptcy or, in the case of a corporate trustee, a petition for the winding up of the company has been presented to the court.

Register of prohibited persons

4.3   The Pensions Regulator maintains a register of those who have been prohibited from acting as a trustee under *s 3* of the *Pensions Act 1995*.

Under measures contained in the *Pensions Act 2004* the Pensions Regulator is required to make the prohibition register available for inspection by the public. The Regulator is also permitted to publish, in a medium of its choosing and so including therefore on its web site, a list of those whose names appear on the register. The full name, including initials and titles, and date of birth must be listed if the Pensions Regulator has a record of these details, even if these details are not recorded on the register itself. The pension schemes themselves are, however, not named.

The Pensions Regulator's register of disqualified trustees may be viewed at the following web address:
http://www.thepensionsregulator.gov.uk/regulatoryActivity/prohibitedTrustees/
prohibited-12.aspx.

The legislation requires the Pensions Regulator to show this summary in three lists:

(a)   those trustees who are prohibited in respect of all trust schemes;

(b)   those trustees who are prohibited in respect of only one scheme; and

(c)   those trustees who are prohibited in respect of one or more particular descriptions of trust schemes, but not in respect of all trust schemes.

The legislation does not allow the Pensions Regulator to give any other information than is shown in this summary.

The Pensions Regulator has pointed out that individuals may be automatically disqualified from acting as a trustee for other reasons, such as bankruptcy or conviction of an offence involving dishonesty or deception, but that its register of prohibited trustees does not include the names of such trustees. The only way one can find out whether a person has a conviction is to ask that person, but one can find out whether someone is an undischarged bankrupt by contacting the Individual Insolvency Register:

> Bankruptcy Public Search Room
> 4th Floor, East Wing
> 45/46 Stephenson Street
> Birmingham
> B2 4UZ
> Tel: 0121 698 4000
> Web site: http://www.insolvency.gov.uk/eiir/IIRFAQ.asp.

The hope has been that the legislation, by providing easier access to the register for those responsible for appointing trustees, has reduced the risk of prohibited persons being appointed as trustees. To prevent inequity, the Pensions Regulator will not publish a person's name until either the time limits for appeals and for applications to review the disqualification decision are passed, or when it is unlikely that there will be an appeal or application for review, or when an appeal or review is pending.

Trustees appointed by the Pensions Regulator

4.4   Once it has removed an existing trustee the Pensions Regulator has the power to appoint a replacement trustee who will act in the same way as an independent trustee appointed by the Pensions Regulator (see **19.7**).

In fact the Pensions Regulator has a general power to appoint a trustee to an occupational pension scheme if it is satisfied that it is necessary to do so in order to make sure that:

- the trustees as a whole have, or exercise, the necessary knowledge and skill for the proper administration of the scheme;

- there are enough trustees for the proper administration of the scheme; or

- the scheme's assets are administered properly.

The Pensions Act 2004 extended this provision so that trustees of an occupational pension scheme, or the sponsoring employer, or any member of the scheme are free to make a request to the Pensions Regulator for the appointment of such an independent trustee from its panel so that the trustee body as a whole have, or exercise, the necessary knowledge and skill for the proper administration of the scheme or to look after the scheme's assets properly.

Any such trustee would in practice be an independent trustee whose fees and expenses would have to be paid by the employer or out of the scheme's resources or partly by the employer and partly out of those resources. The Pensions Regulator has the power to specify how the cost should be met among these parties and also to provide that any amount paid out of the resources of the scheme should be treated as a debit due from the employer.

The appointment could be on a temporary basis. The Pensions Regulator 's predecessor Opra published guidance for the use of the independent, professional trustees it appoints in such circumstances. The aim of the guidance is to ensure that professional trustees do not spend money or time unnecessarily and so deplete the scheme's funds beyond the amount needed to carry out the action required.

Member-nominated trustees

4.5   A trust law purist may say that it does not matter how trustees are chosen since in all circumstances they must conscientiously carry out their various trustee duties impartially and not represent sectional interests.

Following the *Maxwell* imbroglio which broke in 1991, and other revelations, considerable doubts were expressed by some commentators about the wisdom of exclusively relying on trustees drawn from the senior management of the sponsoring employer, or even, in some rare instances, relying on the sponsoring company itself serving as the sole trustee. It was felt that the scope for a breach of trust in such circumstances was too great, especially in circumstances where the company was experiencing financial difficulty. While some commentators went so far as to say that directors of the company should be debarred from being trustees, others countered by arguing that employers would withdraw their support from occupational pension funds if they did not have a direct input in their trustee bodies.

In the event the Pension Law Review Committee which had been established by the Government recommended that:

(*a*)   employers should not have the sole power to appoint trustees, and should not be able to veto a trustee selected by the scheme members;

(*b*)   schemes should be able to retain their then present arrangements for the appointment of trustees, unless the members exercised their right to make appointments.

Following extensive consultation, the Government introduced measures in the *Pensions Act 1995* and the *Occupational Pension Schemes (Member-nominated Trustees and Directors) Regulations 1996 (SI 1996/1216)* which offered employers, trustees and scheme members the following choices with effect from 6 October 1996:

- The employer was permitted to propose *alternative arrangements* that did not give the members the right to nominate and select at least a third of their scheme's trustees, or which curtailed the powers of any member-nominated trustees, or which gave the employer a right to remove member-nominated trustees; and provided that it was not rejected by the membership under the *statutory consultation procedure* this alternative arrangement was originally to stand for a period of up to six years.

- If the employer did not propose an alternative arrangement, or the employer's alternative arrangement was rejected by the members, the existing trustees had to implement the general requirement of the *Pensions Act 1995* and implement arrangements which meet the general requirements set out in the Act (e g to give the members the right to nominate and select one-third of their scheme's trustees, with a minimum of two trustees or a minimum of one trustee if the scheme has less than 100 members). These general requirements are set out in full below. The existing trustees implemented these arrangements by proposing *appropriate rules*. These appropriate rules were originally to stand for a period of up to six years provided they were not rejected by the membership under the statutory consultation procedure.

- In the case of an impasse, the trustees could implement a set of *pre-scribed rules* for the nomination and selection of member-nominated trustees. Alternatively this set of default rules could be adopted from the outset.

We set out below the relatively complex requirements in force at the time of writing relating to the general requirements for member-nominated trustees, the right of employers to propose alternative arrangements, the requirements relating to appropriate rules proposed by the scheme trustees, the statutory consultation procedure for testing the acceptability of the proposed arrangements for appointing trustees, and the fall-back set of prescribed rules set out in the regulations.

In its December 1998 Green Paper *A New Contract for Welfare: Partnership in Pensions* and in a separate consultation paper issued at the same time, the Government announced that it intended to reform the legislation governing the nomination and selection of member trustees. These reforms were contained in the *Child Support, Pensions and Social Security Act 2000* but were never brought into force and are now repealed by the *Pensions Act 2004*. Those reforms were to have applied to an occupational pension scheme when its current arrangements expired at the six-year time limit. However, in February 2002, the Government, having announced that it would be delaying the implementation of the new legislation, introduced amending regulations on 6 October 2002 which automatically extended the duration of existing alternative arrangements and appropriate rules for the nomination and selection of member-nominated trustees or trustee directors for a further four years. The amending regulations in question are the *Occupational Pension Schemes (Member-nominated Trustees and Directors) Amendment Regulations 2002 (SI 2002/2327)*. As a result, alternative arrangements and appropriate rules that were endorsed via the statutory consultation procedure before 6 October 2002 automatically continue for a total period of ten years. No action is required by either the employer or the trustees to begin another statutory consultation procedure. Revised rules apply, however, in the case of new arrangements or appropriate rules made on or after 6 October 2002, and these are explained at **4.14** and **4.15** respectively.

The *Pensions Act 2004* introduces new requirements for member-nominated trustees which will be bought into force to dove-tail with the expiry of the validity of the existing procedures put in place by the *Pensions Act 1995*. These are explained at **4.29** below.

The member-nominated trustee requirements do not apply to trust-based stakeholder pension schemes. However, at least one trustee and at least one-third of the total number of trustees of a trust-based stakeholder pension scheme must be independent as explained at **2.13** above.

General requirements before proposed changes

4.6   The *Pensions Act 1995* makes the following general requirements of any arrangements for the nomination and selection of trustees. These requirements, however, do not apply to any *alternative arrangement* proposed by the employer.

As explained above, these general requirements will be replaced from 2006 onwards by the new requirements made by the Pensions Act 2004, which are explained at **4.29** below.

Right to be nominated

4.7   Any person who has been nominated and selected in accordance with the *appropriate rules* proposed by the existing trustees and approved under the *statutory consultation procedure* automatically becomes a trustee. However, if the employer so wishes, the appropriate rules must give the sponsoring employer the right to veto any person who is not a scheme member (ie the person is neither an active member, nor a deferred pensioner nor a pensioner). For example, a trade union official who is not a scheme member can be nominated and selected as a member-nominated trustee provided the employer does not object.

Removal of member-nominated trustees

4.8 A member-nominated trustee can only be removed with the agreement of all the other trustees. Member-nominated trustees who were employees but cease to be employees will not lose their right to continue as trustees provided they have become either deferred pensioners or pensioners. Any member-nominated trustee who was a scheme member when appointed (ie was either an active member, deferred pensioner or pensioner) must, however, cease to be a trustee if he or she ceases to be a scheme member.

Treatment of vacancies

4.9 Where a vacancy for a member-nominated trustee is not filled because insufficient nominations are received, the arrangements must provide for the filling of the vacancy, or for the vacancy to remain, until the end of the next period in which persons may be nominated and selected. This period must be defined in the appropriate rules but must end at the time the trustees' period of office ends.

Period of office

4.10 The arrangements must provide for the period of office of any member-nominated trustees to be for a minimum of three years and a maximum of six years.

Minimum number of member-nominated trustees

4.11 The arrangements must ensure that the members nominate and select at least one-third of the total number of trustees, with a minimum of at least two such member-nominated trustees (unless the scheme has in total less than 100 members in which case the minimum is one member-nominated trustee). The selection arrangements may provide that more than the statutory minimum number of trustees can be nominated by the members, provided that the sponsoring employer has consented.

Status of member-nominated trustees

4.12 The arrangements must not allow the functions of member-nominated individual trustees to differ from those of any other trustees. Therefore, member-nominated individual trustees could not systematically be excluded from sitting on any investment sub-committee. However, this rule does not apply to trustee directors in the case of a corporate trustee although the requirements of the *Companies Act* are relevant. (Exceptions are also made in the case of the special statutory powers that can be given to a trustee appointed by the Pensions Regulator.)

Schemes excepted from the general requirements

4.13 The general requirements outlined above apply both to defined benefit and defined contribution schemes. There are, however, specific kinds of scheme which are excepted from the general member-nominated trustee requirements. They include:

- small self-administered schemes;

- schemes which have in place an independent trustee appointed by the insolvency practitioner to the sponsoring employer (see **19.7**);

- schemes which have less than two members;

- unapproved schemes (employer-financed retirement benefit schemes from 6 April 2006);

- schemes providing only death benefits;

- industry-wide schemes where the sponsoring employers are unassociated and where one-third of the trustees can be classed as independent;

- schemes where the employer is the sole corporate trustee and all the members are either current or former directors of the company provided that at least one-third of the members are current directors;

- insured schemes where no further contributions are payable;

- schemes which have been modified under the *Coal Industry Act 1994* and certain other statutory schemes; and

- wholly insured schemes where the insurance company and the sole corporate trustee are connected, provided the insurance company is neither the employer nor connected to the employer.

Employer's alternative arrangements

4.14 Initially, in the case of existing schemes, the employer had the right to propose *alternative arrangements* at any time during the period from 6 October 1996 to 5 May 1997, except that if the employer gave the existing trustees a written notice stating that it would not be proposing any alternative arrangement at any time during this period, that decision could not then be revoked during the same period. If the employer did tell the existing trustees that it did not wish to propose alternative arrangements, the trustees could then go ahead and propose their own *appropriate rules*. If the employer had not announced that it would be proposing alternative arrangements by 5 May 1997, the employer normally became prevented from doing so during the following six years, ie to 6 April 2003. In the case of a new scheme, an employer has one month in which to propose alternative arrangements. If it does not, it is normally precluded from doing so for the next six years.

(However, note the effect of the four-year extension mentioned at **4.5** above and further discussed below.)

In any case where the employer does decide to propose alternative arrangements, the employer, rather than the existing trustees, becomes responsible for carrying out the *statutory consultation procedure* which is explained at **4.17** below. If, before 6 May 1997, the employer did propose alternative arrangements, the employer had six months, or by 5 October 1997 if earlier, in which to gain acceptance from the membership. If under the statutory consultation procedure approval was gained, the existing trustees then were obliged to implement the alternative arrangements. If approval was for the existing arrangements to continue, they were immediately in place, otherwise the existing trustees had six months in which to implement the alternative arrangements. Once in place, an alternative arrangement was to operate for a maximum of six years. After this time the mandate given by the members via the statutory consultation procedure was to lapse and a new statutory consultation procedure had to be undertaken. However, as explained at **4.5**, alternative arrangements that had received approval via the statutory consultation procedure by 6 October 2002 were able to continue for a further four years.

If an employer wishes to propose a new alternative arrangement on or after 6 October 2002, and this proposal is accepted under the statutory consultation procedure, approval is given for a maximum period of four years. Provided that the trustees give their consent, the employer may propose a new alternative arrangement at any time.

If the trustees do not give their consent, the employer may still propose a new alternative arrangement at any time on or after 6 October 2002 provided that it is to replace an existing alternative arrangement already in place. On the other hand, if there is no alternative arrangement in place in relation to the scheme, and the employer last proposed an alternative arrangement before 6 October 2002, the employer is prevented from proposing a new alternative arrangement until the end of a period of ten years from the date of its last proposal for putting in place a new alternative arrangement. Similarly, if there is no alternative arrangement in place but the employer, without the trustees' consent, wishes to propose an alternative arrangement on or after 6 October 2002, it can do so, but if the proposal fails to be accepted under the statutory consultation procedure the employer is prevented from making a further such proposal for a further four years.

Note that all the above time limits relate to the period of validity of the alternative arrangement itself, not to the maximum term of office of member-nominated trustees or trustee directors themselves. The term of office of member-nominated trustees or trustee directors continues to be defined by the rules made by the alternative arrangement.

Employers have only proposed alternative arrangements if they wished to have in place nomination and selection procedures for the trustees that, in one or more ways, did not fulfil all the general requirements set out from **4.6** to

4.12 above. Examples might include alternative arrangements in which there are either no 'member' (i e non-management) trustees or fewer than a third; where the status of member trustees differs from that of management trustees; where the power of selection and removal of all trustees is exercised by the employer; and where member trustees can remain in office for more than six years. In many cases there were existing arrangements that had been negotiated between the employer and recognised trade unions that did not meet the general requirements set out above. If such an arrangement were to continue to operate, the employer had to propose them as an alternative arrangement and gain approval for it via the statutory consultation procedure.

Appropriate rules

4.15   Once the existing trustees knew that the employer would not be proposing *alternative arrangements*, which for existing schemes in the first instance was 6 October 1996 at the earliest and 5 May 1997 at the latest, they had six months in which to propose *appropriate rules* and have put in place the eventual arrangements for the nomination and selection of member-nominated trustees. If the employer announced that it would be proposing alternative arrangements but in the event those proposals were rejected under the *statutory consultation procedure* explained below, the trustees always had six months from the date of the opt-out failure to implement the requirements for member-nominated trustees. Since the latest date for an opt-out failure during the introduction of the new procedures was 5 October 1997, the latest date for implementation of appropriate rules was 6 April 1998.

All appropriate rules must meet the general requirements for member-nominated trustees set out above. In addition the appropriate rules:

● must determine the procedure for the nomination and selection of a person to fill a vacancy as a member-nominated trustee;

● may determine, or provide for the determination of, the conditions required of a person for filling such a vacancy;

● must provide for a member-nominated trustee to be eligible for re-selection at the end of his or her period of office;

● must specify, in the case where a vacancy for a member-nominated trustee is not filled because insufficient nominations have been received, the start date of the next period in which persons may be nominated and selected (the end of this period must coincide with the end of the trustees' period of office); and

● must provide that, where the employer so requires, a person who is not a member of the scheme must have the employer's approval to qualify for selection as a member-nominated trustee.

There was considerable scope for the trustees to propose appropriate rules which were designed to meet the circumstances of their scheme. For example, if there were, say, four sites in which the sponsoring company operates in the

UK, the trustees may have decided that active members at each site should nominate and select one trustee and that the pensioners should nominate and select a fifth trustee. There would then be five constituencies each selecting one member-nominated trustee. In such circumstances, five separate ballots could have taken place and the candidate in each ballot with the highest number of votes would have been selected. The trustees may also have proposed that in order to be put forward as a candidate, any person should have received, say, ten nominations from other members of that constituency.

As another example, a company may employ a large number of distinct employee groups and have only recently established an occupational pension scheme. The trustees may have wished to keep the trustee board to a maximum of five, of whom two will be nominated by the active members. The trustees may also have decided that pensioners should not be involved in the nomination and selection process. Because they expected a large number of nominations, the trustees may then have proposed that selection should be by ballot of the active members using the single transferable vote system, which would favour the selection of a universal second choice compromise candidate who was broadly acceptable to all active members.

Once in place, the *appropriate rules* were to have operated for a maximum of six years. After this time the mandate given by the members via the statutory consultation procedure was to have lapsed and a new statutory consultation procedure would have had to be undertaken, but as explained at **4.5** appropriate rules which had received approval via the statutory consultation procedure by 6 October 2002 can now continue for a further four years.

In the case where trustees propose new appropriate rules on or after 6 October 2002 and this proposal is accepted under the statutory consultation procedure, approval is given for a maximum period of ten years. Note that this differs from the case of new alternative arrangements proposed on or after 6 October 2002 which, if approved under the statutory consultation procedure, only have four years' validity. The reason for the difference is that any appropriate rules automatically will comply with the proposed new requirements for all schemes to have a minimum number of member-nominated trustees or trustee directors as described at **4.29** below.

Relevant events

4.16   As explained above, once, via the *statutory consultation procedure*, an *alternative arrangement* proposed by the employer, or an arrangement governed by *appropriate rules* proposed by the previous trustee body, is in place, the authority for that arrangement was to have lapsed after a maximum of six years, although as already noted this period has now been extended by a further four years as set out at **4.5** above.

However, the regulations stipulate that in certain situations the trustees must consider whether it would be detrimental for the approval of the appropriate rules or of the alternative arrangement to continue to have effect before this time limit is reached. The situations envisaged in the regulations are the occurrence of a *relevant event*, that is:

- a bulk transfer of members into or out of the scheme where the individual consent of each member has not been obtained;
- a new employer becoming a participating employer;
- an existing employer ceasing to be a participating employer; or
- an employer becoming a wholly owned subsidiary of another employer and that other employer not employing members of the scheme.

In the wake of any of the above relevant events, if the trustees consider that the continuation of the existing arrangement would be detrimental to the interests of the members, they may give notice to the employer that the existing alternative arrangement or appropriate rules will cease to have effect. In this case, the employer has one month in which to give the trustees notice that it intends to propose an alternative arrangement under the statutory consultation procedure. The employer then has six months in which to gain acceptance for the alternative arrangement. If the employer does not propose an alternative arrangement, or if the employer's alternative arrangement is rejected, then the trustees must propose appropriate rules under the statutory consultation procedure. The trustees have six months in which to gain acceptance for the proposed *appropriate rules*.

In the case of a new scheme, the requirement to implement the member-nominated trustee requirements (ending the statutory consultation procedure) must currently come into play within six months of the date the scheme received HMRC approval. In the event, it is likely that new schemes will adopt a procedure for member-nominated schemes that complies with the requirements of the Pensions Act 2004, as set out at **4.29** below.

Statutory consultation procedure

4.17   The *statutory consultation procedure* is the detailed set of pro-cedures for obtaining the views of members of occupational pension schemes as set out in *Schedule 1* to the *Occupational Pension Schemes (Member-nominated Trustees and Directors) Regulations 1996 (SI 1996/1216)*. Some details of the statutory consultation procedure differ according to whether it is the employer who has proposed *alternative arrangements* or the existing trustees who have proposed *appropriate rules*. Other details are common to both situations. The statutory consultation procedure does not form part of the new procedures for deciding on the nomination and selection of member nominated trustees introduced by the *Pensions Act 2004*.

The employer proposes alternative rules

4.18   The employer must send a notice to each active member, each pensioner (ie each retired active member; not widows, widowers or dependants), and any deferred pensioners whom the existing trustees have decided should also be consulted. This notice must contain a general statement which explains that if the *alternative arrangements* proposed by the employer are not approved, the trustees will put in place arrangements for the nomination and selection of member-nominated trustees that comply with the general requirements which we have outlined above (see **4.6** to **4.13**).

The employer's notice must contain details of the alternative arrangements proposed which must include:

(a)   the proposed total number of trustees for the scheme;

(b)   the procedure proposed to be adopted for the selection of trustees;

(c)   the period proposed as their period of office;

(d)   if it is proposed that the functions of any trustees should differ from those of other trustees, the differences in those functions (and in the case of trustee directors, whether any special rules for decisions to be made by particular directors are proposed and, if so, what they are); and

(e)   whether it is proposed that, if at the time the arrangements come into force the trustees already include member-nominated trustees, they should continue or cease to be trustees and, if they are to cease, the time when they are to do so.

The existing trustees propose appropriate rules

4.19   The existing trustees must send a notice to each active member, each pensioner (ie each retired active member; not widows, widowers or dependants) and any deferred pensioner whom they have decided to consult. This notice must contain a general statement that the existing trustees are required to put in place arrangements for the selection of member-nominated trustees and to implement *appropriate rules* to regulate those arrangements.

The trustees' notice must contain details of the appropriate rules proposed. Those details must include the following particulars:

(a)   the total number of trustees for the scheme;

(b)   the number of trustees to be selected by the members;

(c)   the number of trustees to be selected by the employer;

(d)   whether, if a vacancy for a member-nominated trustee is not filled because insufficient nominations are received, the vacancy is to be filled or to remain and, if it is to be filled, the procedure proposed to be followed;

(e)   the period for which selection as a member-nominated trustee is to have effect (not being less than three but not more than six years).

Common procedures

4.20   Any notice sent out by either an employer proposing alternative arrangements or by the trustees proposing appropriate rules must also include details of:

4.20   *How trustees are chosen*

(a)   whether any, and if so what conditions are proposed for persons to be considered as eligible for nomination;

(b)   the number of members of the scheme proposed to be required to make a nomination;

(c)   in cases where a vacancy is not filled because insufficient nominations are received, the period proposed as the next period in which persons may be nominated and selected; and

(d)   the procedure proposed for selection where the number of persons nominated to fill vacancies exceeds the number of vacancies.

In addition, the notice must explain that all the active members, all the pensioners (ie each retired active member; not widows, widowers or dependants) and, if the trustees have so decided, any deferred pensioners that the trustees have included in those to be consulted, either:

●   are being given a period within which they may object to the proposals and may be balloted if at least 10% of the total number of members consulted (or 10,000 members if less) have objected within the period; or

●   are being balloted directly.

In either case, if the trustees have decided that some deferred pensioners should be consulted, the notice must explain the 'effect of that determination'.

In the case where the members must register objections, the notice must explain that if the required number of objections are not received within the stated period the proposals will be treated as approved, but that if at least the required number of objections are received within the notice period then a ballot will be held of all the members to be consulted. The notice must also explain:

●   the manner in which objections may be made;

●   the length of the objection period which must last at least one month beginning from the date the notice is given to the members; and

●   the number of members who can vote (provided that the objection period ends before the beginning of the first scheme year).

Whenever the members are being balloted, the notice must explain that the proposals must be approved by a ballot of all the members to be consulted.

The notice must also:

●   explain the procedure to be used for the ballot, including whether it is to be conducted so that those voting can do so in secret; and

●   give the last date on which votes may be cast which must be at least one month after the date on which the notice is given.

Where a ballot is to be held, the following rules apply:

- the result must be obtained by a simple majority of those voting;

- if the employer undertook the statutory consultation procedure, the employer must inform the trustees of the result as soon as it is known;

- if the existing trustees undertook the statutory consultation procedure, the existing trustees must inform the employer of the result as soon as it is known;

- if approval is given by the ballot, the proposals shall be treated as approved from the date the result of the ballot is known.

The statutory consultation procedure will not be invalidated if it is subsequently discovered that the procedures followed meant that members did not have the opportunity to make objections to the proposals, provided that the number of potential objections would not have made a material difference to the result.

Prescribed rules

4.21   The prescribed rules may be seen to have been as a default set of rules for the appointment of member-nominated trustees, to be used when all proposals put to the members under the statutory consultation procedure have been rejected. Alternatively, they may have been seen by existing trustees and employer alike as an attractive option in their own right, in which case they could be adopted at the outset without the need for any statutory consultation procedure. It should be noted, however, that any ballot held under the prescribed rules for the selection of member-nominated trustees will involve only the active members. They are not suitable, therefore, for adoption if the trustees wish, or feel they have a duty to involve pensioners, or even deferred pensioners, in the selection process.

The existing trustees must invite nominations for the filling of vacancies by giving notice in writing to the active members specifying the last date on which nominations may be made, which must not be earlier than one month after the date on which the notice is given. The notice must set out the terms for the arrangements that the trustees are making to comply with the general requirements that would apply under the *Pensions Act 1995* to any set of appropriate rules, e.g. to have in place at least one-third of the trustees as member-nominated trustees (see **4.6** to **4.13**).

The notice must also give the following details:

(a)   the total number of trustees for the scheme;

(b)   the number of trustees to be selected by the members;

(c)   the number of trustees to be selected by the employer;

(d)   whether, if a vacancy for a member-nominated trustee is not filled because insufficient nominations are received, the vacancy is to be filled or to remain and, if it is to be filled, the procedure proposed to be followed; and

(e)   the period for which selection as a member-nominated trustee is to have effect (not being less than three but not more than six years).

Any person may be nominated to be a member-nominated trustee (including any of the existing trustees) subject to the sponsoring employer being able to veto the nomination of any person who is not an active member, deferred pensioner or pensioner of the scheme. Any nomination must be made in writing by an active member of the scheme and be supported by at least one other member. Nominees must give their written consent to the nomination.

If the number of valid nominations does not exceed the number of vacancies, those persons become member-nominated trustees. If the number of valid nominations exceeds the number of vacancies, those vacancies must be filled by those nominees elected by a ballot of the active members.

No later than 14 days after the last date on which nominations can be made, the existing trustees must give notice in writing to all the active members specifying:

- the procedure to be used for the ballot (including whether it is to be conducted so that those voting can do so in secret);

- the last date on which votes may be cast (being a date not less than 14 days nor more than one month after the date on which the notice is given); and

- the arrangements to be made for overseeing the conduct of the ballot, and for the counting of the votes and the declaration of the result.

In the ballot itself each active member may vote only for one nominee in respect of each vacancy. The vacancy or vacancies will be filled by the nominee or nominees for whom the most votes are cast. Any tie must be resolved by drawing lots.

The existing trustees may decide that in the event of insufficient nominations any remaining vacancy will be filled by the first valid nomination received during the period for which selection as a member-nominated trustee is to have effect. Alternatively, if the existing trustees have decided that in the event of insufficient nominations any vacancy will remain and further nominations will be sought, the next period in which persons may be nominated and selected to fill that vacancy is the period beginning either:

- if the new trustees consent, the day after the last day specified in the notice inviting nominations; or

- the day when nominations could be made to select a new member-nominated trustee if the vacancy had been filled and the member-nominated trustee had completed the period of office.

4.22   Any employer who proposes an alternative arrangement but fails to give effect to the statutory consultation procedure would be liable to be fined by Opra/the Pensions Regulator. Trustees also face possible prohibition orders and fines if they fail to take all reasonable steps to secure compliance with the requirements to make arrangements for persons selected by members of the scheme to be trustees and to implement those arrangements and the appropriate rules or prescribed rules.

Employer-nominated trustees

4.23   The sponsoring employer will usually appoint some senior company managers as trustees. It is likely that certain company executives or managers (including one or more of the following positions: company secretary, managing director, finance director, human resources director or personnel manager) would be appointed trustees *ex officio*. Of the company officers, the role of the finance director might seem to be especially critical and a useful presence on the trustee board. Certain members of the employing company's board, such as the chairman, might serve as employer-nominated trustees.

Trust law requires that, when acting as trustees, senior managers must, in the case of any conflict of interest, carry out their duties as trustees in preference to the interests of the company. It is wrong, however, to suppose that all matters will give rise to a conflict of interest. After all, it is generally in the interests of the scheme members that the sponsoring employer flourishes and that the pension scheme serves to attract, retain and motivate the employees without imposing unmanageable costs on the employer. Nevertheless, conflicts can and do arise and employer-nominated trustees will be aware that, just as with member-nominated trustees, they owe a duty to put the interests of the pension scheme members above all other considerations.

Prior to the introduction of the mandatory requirement for member-nominated trustees being introduced by the Pensions Act 2004 (see **4.29**), it has been possible for the employer alone to select all the trustees, or for member-nominated trustees drawn from the membership to be appointed subject to the employer's approval. However, such an arrangement would mean that the members of the scheme would have foregone their right to nominate at least one-third of the trustees through the statutory consultation procedure.

Duration of appointment, removal and retirement of trustees

4.24   In the case of individual trustees, the appointment of a new trustee is normally made by the execution of a deed amending the trust deed and rules. The formal power of appointment is specified in the trust deed and is usually given to the employer. In the case of a corporate trustee, the trustee directors will normally be appointed under the articles of association of the corporate trustee company.

Member-nominated trustees

4.25   Prior to the introduction of the new measures contained in the *Pensions Act 2004*, special conditions set down in the *Pensions Act 1995* have governed the duration of appointment, removal and retirement of member-nominated trustees (unless such member-nominated trustees have been nominated and selected by the members under the rules governing an *alternative arrangement* proposed by the employer). As explained above:

- selection as a member-nominated trustee must be for a period of at least three years but not more than six years;

- the appropriate rules adopted by a scheme to govern the arrangements for nominating and selecting member-nominated trustees must provide for a member-nominated trustee to be eligible for reselection at the end of his or her period of service;

- a member-nominated trustee cannot normally be removed from the trustee board without the agreement of all the other trustees;

- if a person was a member-nominated trustee when appointed but subsequently ceases to be either an active member, a deferred pensioner or a pensioner of the scheme, he or she automatically ceases to be a trustee. (Note that member-nominated trustees who lose their jobs with the sponsoring employer can currently continue to act as trustees provided they do not decide to transfer their pension rights out of the scheme, and it is this provision which persuaded many employers to choose to propose an *alternative arrangement*.);

- if a member-nominated trustee resigns, a replacement member-nominated trustee should be selected, probably within six months.

Employer-nominated trustees

4.26   The trust deed and rules, or articles of association in the case of a corporate trustee, will normally specify how long trustees serve on the trustee body, how they may be removed or simply retire.

Individuals who have been nominated by the employer will normally stop being trustees if they leave their employment. In the case of management trustees appointed *ex officio* they may cease to be trustees if they no longer hold that specific post.

It should be noted, however, that the appointment of an individual trustee does not automatically end if the trustee leaves the employment or ceases to be a member of the scheme. The procedure laid down in the trust deed and rules must be followed (but if the trust deed and rules are defective, trust law lays down a procedure of last resort). In the case of individual trustees, a trustee can normally only retire if an appropriate deed is executed by a solicitor. In the case of a trustee director, the corporate trustee as such does not change in such circumstances, but a new trustee director has to be appointed none the less.

Removal because of disagreement

4.27   The *Pensions Act 1995* permits the decisions of the trustees to be taken by agreement of a majority unless the trust deed and rules specify otherwise. In practice, at most trustee meetings a consensus approach is sought. Yet a serious disagreement may arise and this might involve an attempt by the employer to remove 'troublesome' trustees (provided that the trust deed and rules stipulate that the power of removal is held by the employer). In the case of an attempt to remove any member-nominated trustee (unless nominated and selected under an *alternative arrangement* proposed by the employer), since 6 April 1997 the agreement of **all** the other trustees is required. The vacancy would then have to be filled in accordance with the *appropriate rules* which had been approved by the *statutory consultation procedure*.

It should be remembered that the power granted to an employer to remove trustees is generally thought to be exercisable only on a *fiduciary* basis. That is to say, the employer must use it as would a trustee acting in the best interests of the beneficiaries as a whole. Some pension lawyers disagree and argue that the removal of a trustee by the employer is not necessarily bound by any *fiduciary* duty and that at least in some cases the employer may look to its own interests when exercising any power it has to remove a trustee. However, in any case, if the threatened trustees believe that the employer's attempt to remove them is improper, they should report the matter to the Pensions Regulator. They may also resist through the courts or through the Pensions Ombudsman (see **20.7**).

If a trustee or a small group of trustees disagrees with the decision that the majority of the trustees propose to take, but a breach of trust is not involved (see **21.4**), the conflict may in the end result in that trustee or small group of trustees resigning. It would then be obvious to the members that any consensus had broken down. In the case of member-nominated trustees, this would give rise to a vacancy or vacancies that would then have to be filled in accordance with the appropriate rules.

Practice since 1997

4.28   Survey evidence overwhelmingly shows that, since the requirements of the *Pensions Act 1995* came into force, the great majority of employers who sponsor self-administered occupational pension schemes have exercised their right to propose *alternative arrangements*. That is to say these employers have opted out of the statutory, member-nominated trustee requirements. Furthermore, the great majority of statutory consultation exercises resulted in only a handful of members in each scheme raising objections. The objection route, with its hurdle of needing 10% of those consulted to object (or 10,000 if lower), has been a stiff target in the absence of any widespread, organised opposition to an employer's proposal.

The 1997 annual survey carried out by the National Association of Pension Funds (NAPF) at the time the member-nominated trustee measures were first being implemented found that among 531 private sector pension schemes:

- 83% had adopted an *alternative arrangement* proposed by the employer;

- 11% had adopted *appropriate rules* proposed by the trustees; and

- 5% had adopted the *prescribed rules* set out in the legislation.

In the main, the few serious challenges made to proposals for alternative arrangements took place when the employer's proposal made no specific provision to ensure that there was a scheme pensioner among the trustees and there happened to be a powerful and organised pensioners' action group that could mobilise opposition. In some cases, an employer's proposal met organised opposition from trade union members in the scheme but this seemed to be relatively rare. In many cases, the employer's proposal was for the maintenance of the pre-existing arrangements for the nomination and selection of trustees. If there was a recognised trade union already involved in the nomination and/or selection of some trustees, this would mean that the trade union would tend to support the employer's opt-out proposal.

There are a number of important points to be made about current practice. Although employers' proposals for schemes to opt out of the statutory member-nominated trustee requirements have usually succeeded, it is still very common:

(a)   for there to be trustees drawn from the general membership; and

(b)   for the general membership to be involved in the formal process of appointing these member trustees.

The NAPF found that, among private sector final salary schemes, the appointment of member trustees:

- in 75% of schemes involved the active scheme members; and

- in 43% of schemes involved pensioners.

In some 16% of schemes trade unions were formally involved in some way in appointing member trustees.

Therefore it has not been uncommon to find that in a scheme where an employer's alternative arrangement is in place (and so the formal general requirements set out at **4.6** to **4.12** above do not have to apply), up to one half of the trustees will have been appointed following a ballot of the active members and pensioners. This fact begs the question therefore why an alternative arrangement was proposed. In some cases the answer lies in the employer anticipating problems in not being able to remove member-nominated trustees appointed according to appropriate rules. Also an employer may prefer not to have deferred pensioners, now working for another employer, acting as trustees of the pension scheme.

Research carried out by Incomes Data Services and published in April 1998 indicated that where member trustees are in post, their term of office is very often three years. Towards the end of the trustee's term, a fresh nomination and selection procedure is carried out so that a new member trustee is ready to take the place of the resigning member trustee. In some schemes the existing member is immediately able to seek re-nomination. In others this is forbidden and the trustee must always stand down, although he or she could seek a further nomination at the end of the next term. Vacancies are often filled from a reserve list of shortlisted nominees from the last nomination and selection process or by the person who received the next highest number of votes in a ballot. A replacement member trustee will usually serve the rest of the former trustee's term of office and will then usually be eligible for re-nomination and re-selection.

Reform of nomination and selection of member trustees

4.29   As signalled at **4.5** above, the Government indicated in its 1998 Green Paper *A New Contract for Welfare: Partnership in Pensions* and in a separate consultation paper issued at the same time, that it intended to reform the legislation governing the nomination and selection of member trustees. The Government stated:

> 'We believe that all funded schemes set up under trust should have member-nominated trustees. That is the way to give members a proper feeling of ownership of and commitment to their scheme. We also believe that schemes with significant numbers of pensioners must be given the chance to elect a pensioner trustee. The present provisions do not always achieve either. They are also very complicated both to understand and to operate. We therefore propose changes which will not only provide considerable simplification, but will also ensure that the member-nominated trustee provisions actually deliver member-nominated trustees. They will mean that schemes must have trustees who are nominated and elected by members and that there should be provision for a pensioner trustee in large mature schemes.'

In October 1999 the then DSS issued a further consultation document setting out the Government's current proposals on changes to the member-nominated trustee requirements following responses to the December 1998 Green Paper. The proposals were in fact devised by a working group made of DSS officials, representatives of various pensions organisations, the TUC and Opra (the Pension Regulator's predecessor). Under these revised proposals all trust-based occupational pension schemes (save for the existing exceptions) would be required to have at least one-third member-nominated trustees but the requirement that mature schemes should always have a pensioner among the trustees was dropped.

Under these measures, there would be two different ways to nominate and select member-nominated trustees:

- a statutory route – where the trustees will be responsible for implementing nomination and selection procedures as set out in legislation; and

- a scheme-specific route – where the employer will be able to propose nomination and selection procedures to suit the scheme. At least one-third of the trustees must be nominated by members, but the nomination and selection procedure can be whatever the employer chooses. The arrangements will have to be approved by scheme members under a *statutory consultation procedure*.

The proposals were enacted in the *Child Support, Pensions and Social Security Act 2000* but, as signalled at **4.5** above, in February 2002 the Government announced that the implementation of these new measures contained in the *Child Support, Pensions and Social Security Act 2000* would be delayed until the results of the simplification review being carried out had been studied. In the event, the Government decided a new approach was needed given its decision to replace Opra with a new kind of pensions regulator which could supervise occupational pension provision using a less prescriptive approach by, for example, issuing codes of practice rather than relying on more inflexible rules set out in regulations made by Parliament. The measures in the *Child Support, Pensions and Social Security Act 2000* were not brought into force and have now been repealed by the *Pensions Act 2004*.

Nomination process

4.30   The new measures in the *Pensions Act 2004* requires trustees of an occupational trust scheme generally to make arrangements for at least one-third of the total number of trustees to be member-nominated trustees. There is therefore no bar on member-nominated trustees representing more than one third of the trustee body. Also the Act gives the Secretary of State the power to raise this minimum threshold from one-third to one-half and in accordance with future regulations to modify how this is achieved in relation to particular cases. Prior to the Secretary of State exercising such a power, however, the employer has to give its approval if more than one-third of the trustees are to be member-nominated. In June 2005, the Pensions Minister explained that the Government would shortly be consulting on regulations governing member-nominated trustees and that, as part of that consultation the Government would be asking for views on whether the move to 50% member-nominated trustees could be achieved by 2009. At the time of writing the Pensions Regulator was on the point of issuing a draft Code of Practice on the simplified member-nominated trustee requirements which are due to come into force in April 2006.

The arrangements must be put in place *within a reasonable period* of the date when the measure first applies to the scheme, and what constitutes a *reasonable period* is to be covered by a code of practice issued by the Pensions Regulator.

The duty to ensure that the arrangements are put in place falls squarely on the existing trustees. The Pensions Regulator has the power to impose a fine on any trustee who has failed to take all reasonable steps to secure compliance if the arrangements securing at least one-third member-nominated trustees are not in place or are not being implemented.

The *Pensions Act 2004* defines *member-nominated trustees* as trustees of an occupational pension scheme set up under trust and who are nominated by a process in which at least the following are eligible to participate:

- all the active members or, an organisation which *adequately represents* the active members, and

- all the pensioner members or, an organisation which *adequately represents* the pensioner members.

There will be no prohibition on the trustees deciding on the nomination process involving both individual scheme members and organisations which adequately represent either active members or pensioners. There is no prohibition either on the involvement of deferred pensioners in the nomination process although it is expected that most existing trustee bodies will choose not to do so.

The meaning of the phrase *adequately represents* with reference to the participation of an organisation in the nomination process will also be covered in the code of practice to be issued by the Pensions Regulator. At the time of writing, the Pensions Regulator has indicated that this code of practice is expected to be issued for consultation during the early summer of 2005, and to be formally issued in the autumn of 2005 so as to be ready for implementation of the new member-nominated requirements from April 2006.

Selection process

4.31 The *Pensions Act 2004* stipulates that selection process must involve some or all of the members of the scheme.

If the employer so requires, the nomination and selection process must provide that a person who is not a member of the scheme must have the employer's approval in order to qualify for selection as a member-nominated trustee.

If the number of nominations is equal to or less than the number of vacancies, the nominees can be deemed to be selected (subject to the qualification that the employer may have taken the right to make it a condition that anyone who is not a scheme member can only be selected with the employer's approval).

The Act also makes provision to ensure that the arrangements will not leave vacancies unfilled for an unreasonable length of time. These provisions are as follows:

4.31   *How trustees are chosen*

- the nomination and selection process must take place *within a reasonable period* of any requirement to fill a vacancy;

- where a vacancy remains unfilled because either no or too few nominations have been received, the nomination and selection process must be repeated at *reasonable intervals* until the vacancy is filled.

Again what constitutes a *reasonable period* or a *reasonable interval* will be covered by the code of practice issued by the Pensions Regulator.

Treatment of member-nominated trustees

4.32   The *Pensions Act 2004* requires that the member-nominated trustee arrangements put in place for any scheme must stipulate that a member-nominated trustee can only be removed with the agreement of all the other trustees.

The Act also prevents the member-nominated trustee arrangements from excluding member-nominated trustees from exercising functions which other trustees can exercise simply on account of their being member-nominated trustees.

Exceptions from the requirement

4.33   The *Pensions Act 2004* provides for certain occupational pension schemes set up under trust to be excepted from the requirement to have in place arrangements for member-nominated trustees. The exceptions are where this does not apply in the case of an occupational trust scheme if:

- every member of the scheme is a trustee of the scheme and no other person is such a trustee;

- every trustee of the scheme is a company (in which case *s 242* applies).

Other kinds of exceptions from the member-nominated trustee requirement will be made in regulations not yet issued at the time of writing but these are likely to follow closely the exceptions that have applied under the *Pensions Act 2005* as set out at **4.13** above.

Member-nominated directors

4.34   For the avoidance of doubt, the requirements set out above in relation to the trustees also apply broadly to the directors of a corporate trustee so that, for example, where a trust-based scheme is governed by a single corporate trustee company, one-third of the directors of that company have to be member-nominated directors.

Where every trustee of a trust-based occupational pension scheme is a company, the requirement of the *Pensions Act 2004* is for at least one-third of the directors of each company to be member-nominated directors.

The Act also allows a company that is trustee in relation to more than one scheme to treat the schemes as if they were a single scheme for the purposes of meeting the member-nominated directors' requirement. The company can however elect not to do so.

Checklist 4

- The Pensions Regulator has the power to prohibit or suspend a person from acting as a trustee of a particular scheme and the legislation disqualifies certain categories of persons from being trustees.

- The Pensions Regulator has the power to install a replacement trustee or an additional trustee if it judges it to be necessary.

- The *Pensions Act 1995* introduced statutory rules for the nomination and selection of member-nominated trustees although the employer has had the right to propose alternative arrangements which will stand provided they are not rejected by the membership under a statutory consultation procedure. If they have not been rejected, the existing trustees had to implement the employer's proposals. This alternative arrangement was then to stand for a maximum of six years when it automatically would have lapsed, but in 2002 a four-year extension was granted for alternative arrangements in place before 6 October 2002.

- If the employer has not proposed an alternative arrangement, the existing trustees had to either propose appropriate rules for an arrangement for the nomination and selection of member-nominated trustees in accordance with the general requirements of the *Pensions Act 1995* or to adopt a default set of prescribed rules. If the existing trustees proposed appropriate rules, these rules would stand provided they were not rejected by the membership under a statutory consultation procedure. If they were not rejected, the existing trustees had to implement their proposals. The appropriate rules were then to stand for a maximum of six years when they automatically would have lapsed, but again a four-year extension has been granted for appropriate rules put in place before 6 October 2002.

- On or after 6 October 2002, the same arrangements apply to new schemes, but an alternative arrangement will be valid for only four years while a scheme adopting the appropriate rules would be valid for ten years.

- In case of an impasse, the prescribed rules governing the nomination and selection of member-nominated trustees could be adopted without going through a statutory consultation procedure.

- In proposing appropriate rules, the existing trustees had to follow the general requirements of the *Pensions Act 1995,* but also, as trustees, be guided by their fiduciary duty to all classes of the membership.

- In the statutory consultation process, the existing trustees have had to decide whether some of the deferred pensioners (e g those for whom they hold a current address) should be included with the active members and pensioners among those to be consulted.

- Under the rules, those pensioners to be consulted under the statutory consultation procedure have not included widows, widowers and dependants.

- If a *relevant event* occurs (e.g. a bulk transfer, or a new participating employer), the trustees have a statutory duty to consider whether they should give notice that either the current alternative arrangement or the appropriate rules should cease to have effect and be replaced.

- A member-nominated trustee, selected under either the appropriate or prescribed rules, who is still an active member, a deferred pensioner or a pensioner cannot be removed by the employer and can only be removed during his or her period of office with the agreement of all the other trustees, or by the Pensions Regulator.

- Any trustee who is removed and has reasonable grounds for fearing that his or her removal is to facilitate a breach of trust should report the matter to the Pensions Regulator.

- The *Child Support, Pensions and Social Security Act 2000* contained revised requirements for the nomination and selection of trustees by the members but these measures were never brought into effect and have been repealed by the Pensions Act 2004.

- The *Pensions Act 2004* is introducing new requirements for member-nominated trustees which, subject to those kind of schemes which are excepted from the requirements, requires trust-based occupational pension schemes to have at present at least one-third of the trustees nominated by all the active members or an organisation adequately representing them and by all the pensioner members or an organisation adequately representing them and where the selection process involves some or all of the members. The Government has taken powers to raise the minimum proportion of the trustees that must be nominated by the members from one-third to one-half, perhaps by 2009.

- Other than in the case of member-nominated trustees, the appointment of trustees is determined by each scheme's trust documentation and the power of appointment of trustees will normally lie with the employer.

Chapter 5

Trustee duties, powers and discretions

General principles

5.1   As explained in **CHAPTER 1**, trustees must carry out all their responsibilities mindful of both the statutory law and trust law under which they operate. A certain number of general principles derive from trust law.

The Occupational Pensions Board, the governmental body responsible for supervising occupational pension schemes until 6 April 1997, issued a booklet entitled *Pension Trust Principles* for all trustees. *Pension Trust Principles* summarises the general duties of all trustees of occupational pension schemes in five points:

(a)   to act in accordance with the trust deed and rules of the scheme, within the framework of the law;

(b)   to act prudently, conscientiously and honestly and with the utmost good faith;

(c)   to act in the best interests of the beneficiaries and strike a fair balance between the interests of different classes of beneficiary;

(d)   to take advice on technical matters and any other matters which they do not understand; and

(e)   to invest the funds.

Traditionally, the responsibilities of trustees are divided into three categories: duties, powers and discretionary powers. *Duties* are usually very specific tasks which the trustee must ensure are carried out. *Powers* are rights which the trust deed and rules give to trustees. *Discretionary powers* are those powers given to trustees by the trust deed and rules which permit a choice to be made. Note that the trust deed and rules are likely to give duties, powers and discretionary powers to the employer as well as to the trustees.

The duties placed on the trustees by the trust deed and rules are not the only duties that trustees must carry out. Statutory duties are also placed on the trustees by the legislation, notably by the *Pensions Act 1995* and the *Pensions Act 2004*.

The Pensions Regulator produces guidance for pension fund trustees which is made freely available. Rather than summarise it here, we urge trustees to become familiar with this guidance directly by visiting the relevant pages on its web site at http://www.thepensionsregulator.gov.uk/trustees/guidance/index.aspx.

It is accepted that trustees, in carrying out their duties, must exercise a proper care when investing trust funds and that the standard of care required of trustees in general has been that as first set out back in 1883 in the case of *Speight v Gaunt*. The judge held that:

> '[A] trustee sufficiently discharges his duty if he takes in managing trust affairs all those precautions which an ordinary prudent man of business would take in managing similar affairs of his own.'

As noted at **3.4** a higher standard of care is expected from professional, paid trustees, but as a government consultation paper issued in February 2002 stated in quoting the well-known legal maxim:

> 'In contrast, unpaid, non-professional trustees are required to take such care as an ordinary prudent man would take, if he were minded to make an investment for the benefit of other people, for whom he felt morally bound to provide.'

Despite the use of terms such as 'man', 'he' and 'his', it is not the case that this standard is nowadays only expected of men and not of women.

Trustee's knowledge and understanding

5.1A   Following the review of institutional investment carried out in 2001 by Paul Myners, the sufficiency of this general standard of care described above has been challenged, at least in relation to the exercise by pension fund trustees of their duty to invest the fund. Following further discussions the government has reinforced the general duty of care placed on trustees by trust law by including in the *Pensions Act 2004* a new requirement for pension fund trustees to have a certain degree of relevant 'knowledge and understanding' of the issues with which they are concerned.

In particular the *Act* requires a pension fund trustee must, in relation to an occupational pension scheme of which he or she is a trustee, be conversant with:

- its trust deed and rules (see **CHAPTER 6**);

- any statement of investment principles that they are required to maintain (see **16.8**);

- the statement of funding principles which must in future be maintained by the trustees of defined benefit occupational pension schemes (see **13.11**);

- any other document recording policy for the time being adopted by the trustees relating to the administration of the scheme generally.

The Pensions Regulator makes it clear that 'being conversant with' should be taken to mean to be familiar with these documents and able to make use of them to carry out trustee functions.

The *Pensions Act 2004* also requires a pension fund trustee to have knowledge and understanding of the law relating to pensions and trusts, the principles relating to the funding of occupational pension schemes and the investment of the scheme's assets and other matters that may be set out in regulations.

The *Occupational Pension Schemes (Trustees' Knowledge and Understanding) Regulations 2005*, however, disapply these requirements for individual trustees for six months from the date on which they are appointed as a trustee (except, of course, in relation to independent trustees, professional trustees or trustees who hold themselves out as experts).

Scope documents

5.1B   Prior to the establishment of the Pensions Regulator in April 2005, its predecessor, Opra, worked with various pension professionals to establish and develop a checklist of the areas of knowledge that trustees are required to have. This checklist has two versions: one for defined contribution schemes and one for both defined contribution and defined benefit schemes. These checklists have become known as the *scope documents* and were published in revised form in February 2005. The combined defined contribution/defined benefit scope document is reproduced in **APPENDIX 1**.

The scope documents will form the basis for a draft syllabus and qualification for trustee training to be developed by the Financial Services Skills Council and the Qualifications and Curriculum Authority, although it will not be mandatory for trustees to take the qualification – see **CHAPTER 24**.

Code of Practice

5.1C   In March 2005, the Pensions Regulator issued a consultation document containing in draft its *Code of Practice no. 3: Trustee knowledge and understanding (TKU)*. This Code of Practice sets out how pension fund trustees can comply with the legislation. The scope documents mentioned above complement the Code of Practice, and are to be published alongside it.

This Code of Practice is a key document for any pension fund trustee and all readers of this handbook are urged to become familiar with it. The draft Code is described below and the final version of the Code will be available on the Pension Regulator's web site, http://www.thepensionsregulator.gov.uk/codesAndGuidance/codes/index.aspx.

The Pensions Regulator has been at pains to reassure trustees that their first task is to work out what they need to learn and to concentrate only on what is appropriate for their needs and circumstances. It points out that if their schemes are small, fully insured or defined contribution only, they may have fewer learning needs than other trustees. The Pensions Regulator also states that the learning which is required of trustees should be measured in days, not weeks, although as mentioned in **5.1A** above, the legislation allows new pension fund trustees to take up to six months to complete it if they wish.

Moreover, the Pensions Regulator reassures pension fund trustees that they are to continue to take advice as they always have done and there is no requirement for trustees to become experts themselves. And while the role of the Pensions Regulator is to check on progress, it is also to advise and assist trustees, their advisers and training providers in every way that it can.

The main points made in the March 2005 draft of the Code are set out below. Please not that this is not a comprehensive summary and is also based on the draft Code circulated for consultation. Readers should therefore ensure that they read the final version of the Code.

Application and readership

5.1D   The *Code of Practice no. 3: Trustee knowledge and understanding (TKU)* applies to all trustees, individual and corporate, of all occupational pension schemes including any stakeholder pension scheme set up under trust, irrespective of the size of the scheme.

Scope of the body of knowledge

5.1E   The scope of knowledge that is required is set out under nine high-level principles:

1   The law relating to trusts – this includes an understanding of the special nature of a pension trust and the duties, obligations and powers of trustees to operate pension schemes in accordance with the law and the trust deed and documents.

2   The law relating to pensions – this includes occupational pensions legislation in outline and the key provisions of related legislation that affects pension schemes and impacts on the role and activities of trustees.

3   Investment: defined benefit and defined contribution occupational pension scheme arrangements (including AVCs) – this includes the different types of assets available for investment and their characteristics.

4   Funding: defined benefit occupational pension scheme arrangements – this includes the principles relating to the funding of defined benefit occupational pension schemes and the way in which funding is dependent upon the financial circumstances of the sponsoring employer and the value of the liabilities of the scheme.

5   Contributions: defined benefit occupational pension scheme arrangements – this includes the principles relating to the funding of defined benefit occupational pension schemes and the way in which contribution levels are dependent upon the funding of the scheme.

6   Strategic asset allocation: defined benefit occupational pension scheme arrangements – this includes the principles relating to the suitability of different asset classes to meet the liabilities of the scheme.

7   Funding: defined contribution occupational pension scheme arrangements (including AVCs) – this includes the principles relating to the
funding of defined contribution arrangements and the risks borne by the
scheme members.

8   Investment choices: defined contribution occupational arrangements
(including AVCs) – this includes the principles relating to the choice of
investments.

9   Fund management: defined benefit occupational pension and defined
contribution occupational pension arrangements (including AVCs) –
this includes the principles of fund management and how performance
can be measured.

How much knowledge is the trustee expected to have?

5.1F   The draft Code does not prescribe the exact body of knowledge
which applies equally to all trustees in all circumstances. Instead the scope
outlined above represents a framework of matters which trustees need to
know and understand.

The breadth of knowledge that each individual trustee has to have is that
appropriate for their role. This role will vary according to the scheme
but trustees should know and understand sufficient for their role and
be knowledgeable enough to ask challenging questions of the scheme
advisers.

The trustee of a defined contribution occupational pension scheme, with no
link to a defined benefit occupational pension scheme, is unlikely to need to
know and understand items 4, 5 and 6 above in relation to the funding,
contributions and strategic asset allocation for a defined benefit scheme.

Trustees are expect to use a training needs analysis so that any gaps in their
knowledge and understanding can be identified and a learning plan devised to
close those gaps.

The Pensions Regulator recognises that trustees may elect to take training
courses and/or obtain accredited qualifications if they wish but there is no
mandatory qualification.

What level of knowledge is the trustee expected to have?

5.1G   The degree of knowledge and understanding required is that which is
appropriate for the purposes of enabling individuals properly to exercise the
function of trustee of their own schemes.

At the most basic level, all trustees will need some investment knowledge,
even if the decision-making power on investments is delegated or if the
scheme assets are invested exclusively in the life insurance contracts.

At a more advanced level where the trustee takes on a specialist role such as the chair of an investment sub-committee, there is an expectation that the investment knowledge and understanding for that role is deeper, broader and more technical than that of the trustee which invests exclusively in insurance policies.

In all instances the trustee needs to know enough and understand enough to be able to ask challenging questions of their advisers.

Newly appointed trustees

5.1H   The six-month initial period where newly appointed lay trustees are not required by the legislation to have knowledge and understanding nor to be conversant with their scheme's documentation is designed to enable them to acquire the necessary knowledge and understanding.

The draft Code advises newly appointed trustees to familiarise themselves with the scheme's trust deed, rules and relevant documents. It also notes that pre-appointment training is good practice and should be encouraged.

The draft Code reminds newly-appointed trustees that they remain responsible in law, and are therefore accountable, for any decisions that they take during the initial six month period and advises that, were the Pensions Regulator to have cause or concern about a scheme, it would take into account the length of time that newly appointed trustees have had to acquire the appropriate knowledge and understanding.

Updating trustee knowledge and understanding

5.1I   The Pensions Regulator strongly recommends that the process of reviewing the body of knowledge and checking a trustee's understanding against that body of knowledge is undertaken on at least an annual basis.

In addition to an annual review, trustees may find that they need to acquire new areas of knowledge in the event of both internal and external scheme changes, or if the trustee takes on a new function.

The draft Code notes that internal scheme changes that may prompt a revisiting of knowledge and or an acquisition of new knowledge may, for example, relate to an unexpected deficit in a defined benefit scheme or the proposed closure of the scheme to new entrants. External changes which may prompt trustees to look again at their knowledge base are, for example, relevant changes in the investment markets or in the law or regulations.

Demonstrating knowledge and understanding

5.1J   The Pensions Regulator will ask trustees how they have met the legislative requirements on trustee knowledge and understanding in the scheme return and so pension fund trustees will need to consider how they can respond to this request. Also, in line with the Pensions Regulator's remit to concentrate its resources on those schemes where there is the greatest risk, there will be an additional focus on trustee knowledge and understanding where schemes come to the Regulator's attention because of other perceived failings. In such cases the trustees concerned may expect that their learning activities will be looked at on a regular basis, and may be a matter for further enquiry in the light of actual or potential scheme difficulties.

Pension fund trustees will need to demonstrate what active steps they have taken to fill the gaps in their knowledge and understanding as revealed by the review of their training needs.

The draft Code suggests that trustees may consider recording what learning activities they have undertaken and what knowledge and understanding they have acquired during each year, and then reporting this record to scheme members.

It lists some examples of good practice in relation to the record keeping of learning activities: training needs analyses, training plans, training logs, minuted training events at the start of trustee meetings, and regular individual performance appraisals where appropriate.

The Pensions Regulator takes the view that the best demonstration of trustee knowledge and understanding is a well-run scheme, particularly where trustees can respond effectively in adverse situations. It states that a well run scheme is likely to have documentary evidence of its trustee decision-making processes so that it is clear how and why trustees have arrived at their decisions.

The requirement to be conversant with scheme documents

5.1K   As explained at **5.1A** above, it is a statutory requirement that trustees must be conversant with particular scheme documents. The draft Code gives further details suggesting that the pension fund trustees should know the essentials of how their scheme works, what their powers are, and what policies they or their predecessors have agreed which are currently applicable.

The draft Code states that trustees should have sufficient knowledge of their technical documentation to enable them to ask relevant questions of their advisers.

Trustees should have access to the scheme documents at any time.

The document types with which the trustees must be conversant

5.1L   The legislation requires pension fund trustees to be familiar with the scheme's trust deed and rules, any current statement of investment principles

(SIP) and any current statement of funding principles (SFP) and other documents recording the trustees' policy for the administration of the scheme generally. The draft Code points out that of the documents stated, the SFP is only a requirement of schemes which provide defined benefits.

An individual director of a corporate trustee must be familiar with the corporate trustee's company documents so far as is necessary to exercise the function of a trustee properly.

Other documents with which pension fund trustees need to be conversant will include those that record current policy for the administration of the scheme, the scheme booklet, announcements and member communications, minutes of trustee meetings and the annual report.

Yet the draft Code suggests also that must determine whether there are other documents containing current policy which are not listed in the Code but with which nevertheless they must be familiar.

Review of the Code

5.1M   The Pensions Regulator explains that it wishes to consider the effectiveness of the Code to trustees and other users and will therefore start the review process of the Code within a two-year period from the date after which it comes into force.

Main trustee duties

5.2   The five general duties identified in **5.1** form the core of any trustee's duties. One further general duty often quoted is that a trustee should not profit from the assets of the fund. This does not mean of course that a trustee cannot also be a scheme member who will eventually draw a pension in the usual way. Indeed the *Pensions Act 1995* also clarified trust law by specifically authorising member trustees to exercise discretionary powers even if they may benefit as members of the scheme. Rather, the general duty not to profit from the assets of the fund means that it is absolutely forbidden for a trustee to deal in investments with the pension fund.

Other specific duties will be specified in any trust deed and rules and will usually be distinguished by the phrase 'The trustees shall ... '.

In practice, trustees can delegate many of these duties to the professional administrators employed in the pensions department, whether the administration is provided by an insurance company, or contracted out to a third party administrator, or whether it is an in-house administration team employed either by the pension fund or the company. Such duties are often simply part of the day-to-day administration and management of the occupational pension scheme. See **CHAPTER 11** for a general discussion of this topic.

The ultimate responsibility for ensuring that these duties are carried out, nevertheless, remains with the trustees.

Main trustee powers

5.3   One of the main powers given in the trust deed and rules is the power to delegate. This is vital since it is impossible for part-time lay trustees to carry out all the duties of a large, modern occupational pension scheme. A related power is the ability to employ agents to carry out these duties (e g the appointment of an investment manager to look after the funds). Other powers that may be included in the trust deed and rules include the power to open bank accounts, to borrow money, to order accounts and audits and to buy annuity contracts (contracts with insurance companies to provide members with regular pensions). This list is far from exhaustive.

Main discretionary powers

5.4   One of the advantages that supporters of trust law argue in its favour is its flexibility. A prime example is the use of discretionary powers by trustees. Certain benefits can be awarded if circumstances permit even if all those circumstances are not codified in the trust deed and rules. The exercise by trustees of their discretionary powers must be reasonable. The trustees' exercise of a discretionary power would probably be challenged if it seemed to be capricious or irrational. In short, the trustees must consider the circumstances carefully before exercising any discretionary power and in so doing bear in mind the five general principles outlined in **5.1** above.

In exercising any discretionary power, it is unlikely that the decision of the trustees would be overturned by the courts or by the Pensions Ombudsman if the trustees follow the rules (first applied in a context outside trust law) which are known as the *Wednesbury Principles*:

- The trustees must ask themselves the correct questions.

- They must direct themselves correctly in law; in particular they must adopt a correct construction of the trust deed and rules.

- They must not arrive at a perverse decision, i.e. a decision to which no reasonable body of trustees could arrive, and they must take into account all relevant, but no irrelevant, factors.

Powers which are discretionary in one scheme may not be so in another. Nevertheless, there are some which are almost always discretionary, such as who should receive any death-in-service lump sum that becomes payable under the scheme's rules.

Discretionary powers that affect all benefits rather than those of one individual will almost certainly only be exercisable with the consent of the employer – an example is the level of any discretionary pension increase.

In a very large organisation, the pension manager is likely to present the bulk of individual discretionary decisions to the trustees for their consideration with a bare minimum of detail – unless there are particular complications. In some instances, where undue delay would be caused by waiting until the next trustee meeting (such as in the payment of a death-in-service lump sum) it is the practice in many schemes for the pensions administrator to contact just two or three trustees for a decision. It is important that the trustee body as a whole has properly delegated the discretionary power to the sub-committee of trustees in such circumstances.

The major discretionary powers that trustees usually exercise without needing the specific consent of the employer are considered below.

Death-in-service lump sum

5.5   If a member dies while still in employment as an active member of the scheme most occupational pension schemes pay out a lump sum. Prior to 6 April 2006, the maximum that is allowed by HMRC for an approved scheme is four times salary (the salary is limited in some cases to the current level of the pensionable earnings cap) plus a refund of the employee's own contributions with reasonable interest but this limit ceases to apply from that date.

From 6 April 2006, no liability to income tax arises on a lump sum death benefit which is either a *defined benefits lump sum death benefit*, an *uncrystallised funds lump sum death benefit* or a *transfer lump sum death benefit*. Provided the lump sum death benefit is not paid into the deceased employee's estate, it is also free of inheritance tax.

The lump sum amount that the trustees can pay is not discretionary since it is specified in the trust deed and rules. Rather, the discretionary power lies in deciding who receives the money.

In relation to exempt-approved schemes operating under one of the tax regimes before 6 April 2006, HMRC says:

> 'The lump sum may be paid to the employee's legal personal representatives or a nominated beneficiary, or distributed at the discretion of the trustees/administrator: it is not necessary to limit nomination or distribution to dependants. The money may continue to be held under the rules of the pension scheme for a period not exceeding 2 years if this is necessary for the trustees/administrator to determine who is to benefit … '.

In relation to registered schemes operating under the new pensions tax regime from 6 April 2006, the above guidance in practice will still apply to defined benefits lump sum death benefit payable by defined benefit schemes and uncrystallised funds lump sum death benefit payable by defined contribution schemes.

Standard practice is to encourage all employees on joining the pension scheme to complete an expression of wish declaration whereon the employee states who should receive any such lump sum. This declaration may be placed in a sealed envelope or, alternatively, confidentially recorded so that the details appear on that individual's benefit statement each year. This way the employee will be prompted to revise the declaration if circumstances have changed.

Trustees should take account of this expression of wish but are not bound by it.

The following factors may come into play:

- The trust deed and rules may define the category of potential beneficiary more narrowly than HMRC or than is permitted by the *Finance Act 2004*.

- The member may inadvertently not have completed an expression of wish form, or it may be very out of date, being written, for example, before he or she was married.

- The nominee may have pre-deceased the member.

- The trustees may find it *unreasonable*. For instance, the member may have recently nominated as the beneficiary a brain-washing religious cult who advised extreme fasting and the member's spouse, having the care of their three young children, may be left in straightened circumstances, about to lose the family home.

- The member may have left the money to a proscribed military or political group.

- The member may have recently split with his partner without being divorced and moved in with a new partner. The member may have recently changed the nomination or not. Of the ex-partner and new partner, one may be rich, the other poor; one or the other or both may have care of the employee's children.

The trust deed and rules will typically allow the trustees to split any lump sum between different beneficiaries and this gives more scope in dealing with difficult decisions. It might be, for example, in the case of a split marriage, that the trustees would ensure that any children would directly benefit from the lump sum by setting up a suitable trust.

However, the trustees may find that they are bound by a court order that requires them to pay the death-in-service lump sum payment to a divorced member's former spouse – see **9.24**.

There are two further possible complications. First, the member may have copied the expression of wish declaration to the beneficiary. Secondly, the *Occupational Pension Schemes (Disclosure of Information) Regulations 1996 (SI 1996/1655)* specify that where a member or a beneficiary of a scheme has died and rights or options are available to a person in consequence, the information on any survivor's rights or options must be provided automatically to that person within two months after the trustees have been notified of the death and, on request, to any personal representative of the deceased person or anyone authorised to act on behalf of the survivor within two months of the request. (Note, however, that any person may be limited to making one request only during a three-year period.)

There are those who argue that not to act according to the member's wishes because the trustees think it unreasonable smacks of paternalism. Others see a way out if inheritance tax were ever to cease to be relevant to most estates and in such conditions, as a change in practice, they urge that the sum should be paid to the member's estate so that it is disposed of in accordance with the member's will – if there is a will!

In many large schemes, the exercise of this particular power of discretion may be taken by trustees in local management committees. Some feel this is better because they are closer to the people concerned. Others might feel this is precisely the wrong approach and members would be happier if they knew the decision would be taken by those who were more remote and so less likely to be prejudiced.

When trustees have taken a decision, the facts and the decision itself should be clearly minuted. It should be clear that the trustees considered their decision properly but the reasoning that led to the decision should not be recorded in the minutes. The theory is that the Pensions Ombudsman or the courts will not reverse an exercise of discretion unless it can be shown that it was taken in error or through prejudice. In other words, the trustees' decision should abide by the *Wednesbury Principles* set out at **5.4** above. The issue of how the trustees' decision should be recorded in the minutes of the trustees' meeting, and in what situations the minutes of this meeting should be disclosed to interested parties, the court or to the Pensions Ombudsman, are both examined at **18.5**.

Other lump sum payments

5.6   In many schemes, lump sum payments are also made in the case of early leavers who die before drawing their deferred pension and in the case of pensioners who die within the first five years of retirement. Many of the remarks made above for death-in-service pensions will apply in these cases.

Survivors' pensions

5.7   The trust deed and rules may give the trustees some discretionary powers in respect of pensions to widows, widowers and dependants. Some scheme rules have stipulated that only widows' and widowers' pensions are provided although when the *Civil Partnership Act 2004* comes into effect the statutory rights of a surviving civil partner must be respected .

Statutory law imposes certain markers:

(a)   if the member had entitlement under the scheme to a guaranteed minimum pension (GMP), the scheme must pay a widow's or widower's GMP (WGMP) to the widow or widower for any period during which a category B retirement pension, or a widowed mother's allowance, widowed parent's allowance, widow's pension or bereavement allowance is payable to the member by the state. If the widow or widower stopped being entitled to widowed parent's allowance or bereavement allowance from the state when aged over 45, the occupational pension scheme must nevertheless continue to pay a WGMP. However, WGMPs do not have to be paid under the legislation if the recipient is under state pension age and cohabiting with a person of the opposite sex (in which case the WGMP could be suspended) or has remarried (in which case it could be ended altogether). The scheme rules may, however, be more generous. Note that in the case of a widower a WGMP is payable only in relation to pensionable service since April 1988. The term legal widow or widower means the person to whom the member was married at the time of death, but this includes partners in a marriage by habit and repute in Scotland. Similar requirements apply under the contracting-out legislation to protected rights pensions and the rights payable to a widow or widower under a scheme contracted out by the reference scheme test after 5 April 1997. Note that a divorced person under the law does not become a widow or widower of their former spouse upon that person's death. Note also that under the *Civil Partnership Act 2004* a surviving civil partner is to be entitled to receive the equivalent amount that a widower is entitled to receive in relation to contracted-out rights accrued by the deceased member in relation to pensionable service since April 1988 and in respect of all pensionable service by the member from the date the Act comes into force, and a surviving civil partner is entitled to the same benefits as would be paid to a surviving spouse.

(b)   The total amount of all survivors' pensions is limited by HMRC rules prior to 6 April 2006.

(c)   A survivor's pension may be paid to a dependant and this term may be defined in the scheme's trust deed and rules but, if the scheme is exempt approved, it cannot be used in a wider sense than as defined by HMRC or, as from 6 April 2006, the meaning of 'dependant' as defined in *para 15* of *Sch 28* to the *Finance Act 2004*. This latter definition is as follows:

> (1) a person who was married to the member at the date of the member's death
>
> (2) a child of the member if the child has not reached the age of 23 or has reached that age and, in the opinion of the scheme administrator, was at the date of the member's death dependent on the member because of physical or mental impairment.
>
> (3) a person who was not married to the member at the date of the member's death and is not a child of the member if, in the

opinion of the scheme administrator, at the date of the member's death:

-     the person was financially dependent on the member, or

-     the person's financial relationship with the member was one of mutual dependence, or

-     the person was dependant on the member because of physical or mental impairment.

(4) the rules of the pension scheme can also include as a dependant, a person who was married to a scheme member when that member first became entitled to a pension under the scheme but who was no longer married to that member at the time that member died.

(d)   the *Employment Equality (Sexual Orientation) Regulations 2003 (SI 2003/1661)*, as amended by the *Employment Equality (Sexual Orientation) (Amendment) Regulations 2003 (SI 2003/2827)* make it unlawful, except in relation to rights accrued or benefits payable in respect of periods of service prior to 1 December 2003, for the trustees or managers of an occupational pension scheme to discriminate on the ground of sexual orientation against a member or prospective member of the scheme in carrying out any of their functions in relation to it (including in particular their functions relating to the admission of members to the scheme and the treatment of members of it) but note the separate provisions made by the *Civil Partnership Act 2004* in relation to surviving civil partners in relation to the deceased partner's pensionable service since April 1988. .

Within these constraints, and acting in accordance with the trust deed and rules, trustees might therefore use their discretion to:

- pay part of the survivor's pension to a former spouse and part to the spouse at the date of the member's death. However, the need for the use of trustee discretion in the matter of pensions and divorce may be circumscribed by mandatory court orders earmarking pension rights and, from 1 December 2000, by the sharing out of pension rights between the divorcing parties by the courts at the time of divorce itself – see **9.24**. However, the use of trustee discretion in cases where there has been no marriage or civil partnership, and so no divorce or ending of a civil partnership, may remain. For example, the trustees may discover that an unmarried member had a relationship with two partners and had recently parented a child in each family unit. The trustees might decide, if permitted by their trust deed and rules, to split the survivor's pension equally between the two partners.

- pay a dependant's pension to a gay or lesbian partner, elderly parent or disabled friend provided that prior to 6 April 2006 HMRC would accept that the person and the member have been financially interdependent or that from that date the person falls within the definition of a dependant given at (c) above.

Trustees who have such discretionary powers will need a substantial amount of detailed information on the circumstances of both the deceased scheme member and the survivor.

Ill-health pensions

5.8   Perhaps one of the most tricky decisions for trustees in the use of their discretionary powers can be whether or not to award a member an enhanced early retirement pension on the grounds of ill-health. The decision may be at the discretion of the trustees but inevitably takes place within an employment context. It may be that the employer wishes to secure the early departure of an employee and has 'promised' an ill-health early retirement pension as a way of avoiding an unfair dismissal claim. However, such considerations cannot be allowed to bind the trustees in how they decide to use their discretion since they have a responsibility to safeguard the fund from improper use in the wider interest of all the members. On the other hand, the employee may have been dismissed and awarded only a deferred pension and it is not apparent that the trustees ought to have considered an enhanced early retirement pension on the grounds of ill-health. This is especially the case where it only becomes apparent later that the employee had been suffering from an undiagnosed illness which had in fact been the cause of the employee being unable to carry out his or her job. In such cases, the trustees may well consider they can revisit their earlier decision.

This last point does not conflict with the principle that has been reasonably clear since the Court of Appeal judgment in the case of *Re McClorry*. This is that the date at which an employee ceases to be employed is the date at which the test of incapacity set by the scheme's trust documentation must be applied.

There are important guidelines for trustees in considering whether or not to grant ill-health pensions:

- the trustees should obtain medical information from the employee and the employer, and where they consider it necessary, from an independent source;

- the trustees should consider and follow the requirements of the trust deed and rules – in many cases the rules will specify that members may receive a higher benefit if they are totally unable to perform any work and a lower benefit if they are prevented by illness from performing their own job but capable of working in another job;

- the trustees should try to set consistent standards and treat the claim fairly;

- the trustees should ignore the industrial relations context;

- if the trustees decide that an enhanced early retirement pension on the grounds of ill-health should be payable, the trustees should consider whether they ought to obtain periodic medical reports on the member's

81

health (at least until the member reaches the normal pension age for the scheme) to ensure that pension funds are not being misappropriated – the scheme auditors may be consulted on the best method. The trustees would not want to be heavy-handed in carrying out this duty and so cause a genuinely sick member any anxiety. It may be that a pensioner welfare service is available to assist.

One particular case decided by the Court of Appeal that may be of use to trustees who are having to decide whether an ill-health early retirement pension may be payable is that of *Harris v Lord Shuttleworth*. Here the Court of Appeal decided that the phrase 'retirement from the service by reason of incapacity' meant that the member had left the employer's service at some date before reaching normal pension age by reason of some physical or mental disability or ill-health so serious that, at the time of leaving service, it was probable that the member would be unable by reason of disability to follow his or her present or similar employment with the employer or any other employer during any part of the period before reaching normal pension age.

It should, however, always be remembered that any court decision will normally depend on the specific circumstances of that case and in particular what the scheme's own trust deed and rules require.

Late joiners

5.9   If an employee declines to join the pension scheme on first becoming eligible to do so, or if an existing member decides to opt out, the trustees will often have discretion over whether that employee, having changed his or her mind, may later join the scheme. The trust deed and rules may lay down certain conditions that have to be met, such as a satisfactory medical examination, but in many cases the final decision will rest with the trustees. This issue in the recent past took on importance in view of guidance from the former Securities and Investments Board (now the Financial Services Authority). This guidance recommended that those who had been mis-sold personal pensions rather than joining or maintaining their membership of occupational pension schemes should ideally, at least if they were still employees of an employer who participated in the scheme, be allowed to join or rejoin the pension scheme both for future and past service upon payment of a suitable transfer value.

New statutory powers and duties

5.10   The *Pensions Act 1995* and the *Pensions Act 2004* set out a large number of new statutory powers and duties that complement pre-existing powers and duties made under earlier legislation or other quasi-statutory powers and duties imposed by authorities such as HMRC. These powers and duties are explained at the appropriate point in this handbook. Penalties can be imposed on trustees who fail to take all reasonable steps to secure compliance with these duties and in so doing act to prevent a breach of the statutory law.

Checklist 5

- Traditionally, trustees have five main duties:

    - to act in accordance with the trust deed and rules, within the framework of the law;

    - to act prudently, conscientiously and honestly and with the utmost good faith;

    - to act in the interests of the beneficiaries and strike a fair balance between the interests of different classes of beneficiary;

    - to take advice; and

    - to invest the funds.

- The standard of care required by a lay trustee has been that of the 'ordinary prudent man or woman of business'.

- The *Pensions Act 2004* has introduced the new requirement that pension fund trustees should be *conversant* with their schemes trust deed and rules, its statement of investment principles, its statement of funding principles (where applicable) and certain other documents recording trustee policy.

- The *Pensions Act 2004* also requires pension fund trustees, after an initial six-month period, to have *knowledge and understanding* of the law relating to pensions, the principles relating to the funding of occupational pension schemes and the investment of their assets to the degree appropriate for the purposes of enabling the individuals concerned properly to exercise their functions as trustees.

- The Pensions Regulator has published the *scope documents* as a checklist of the areas of knowledge that trustees are required to have.

- The Pensions Regulator must issue a Code of Practice on the requirement for trustees to be *conversant* with their key documentation and to have *knowledge and understanding*.

- Trustees have various powers given to them by the trust deed and rules, including the power to delegate.

- Trustees have discretionary powers given them by the trust deed and rules, some of which must be exercised only with the agreement of the employer and some of which should be exercised by the trustees acting on their own.

- The use of the trustees of their discretionary powers will not normally be questioned by the courts or by the Pensions Ombudsman provided the trustees have:

  - asked themselves the correct questions;

  - directed themselves correctly in law, in particular by adopting a correct construction of the trust deed and rules; and

  - not arrived at a perverse decision (i e one at which no reasonable body of trustees could arrive) and have taken into account all relevant, but no irrelevant, factors.

Chapter 6

Trust deed and rules

Overview

6.1 For all practical purposes, an occupational pension scheme set up under a trust arrangement must operate under a signed and delivered document called the *trust deed*. The actual rules of the scheme are usually set out in a schedule or in an attached document.

Often in the past, in order to set up an occupational pension scheme quickly, a short *interim deed* usually established the scheme. An interim deed contains the basic material needed to operate the scheme as a trust and so could act as a sufficient legal basis for HMRC to grant tax relief on a temporary basis. Confirmation of the tax relief then had to wait until the definitive trust deed and rules were signed and delivered. It is important to note that a definitive deed cannot make fundamental changes to the interim deed.

If after a period of two years the interim deed had not been replaced by a definitive trust deed, HMRC could demand that all the tax reliefs granted on a provisional basis should be repaid.

However, this interim authorisation procedure was withdrawn on 6 April 2002 except for new schemes set up as a result of a *corporate reorganisation* – i.e. where:

- the new scheme is set up to receive a bulk transfer from another pension schemes of funds and/or employees; and

- the bulk transfer has been brought about by a change, or intended change of:

  - ownership of an employer; or

  - ownership of all or part of an employer's trade or business.

Unless these conditions are met, applications for the tax approval of an occupational pension scheme from 6 April 2002 but before 6 April 2006 can no longer be made if that scheme's definitive documentation is not yet operative.

Yet, from 6 April 2006, the status of an exempt-approved pension scheme where tax approval depends on the scheme being set up under irrevocable trust ceases to exist and it is irrelevant for the purpose of benefiting from the tax reliefs granted by the *Finance Act 2004* to any registered pension scheme whether the scheme is established as a trust or not.

Yet if the scheme is an occupational pension scheme that has its main administration in the United Kingdom, then under *s 252* of the *Pensions Act 2004* if the scheme is not established under irrevocable trust, the trustees must ensure that no funding payment is accepted. The establishment of occupational pension schemes under trust ensures the legal separation of the assets of the occupational pension scheme from those of the sponsoring employers and *s 252* achieves this requirement of the European Directive 2003/41/EC on the activities and supervision of institutions for occupational retirement provision (the IORP Directive).

Trust deeds vary enormously from one scheme to another and some prove defective when it comes to important changes, such as on a takeover of the sponsoring company. In recent times there were calls for legislation that would impose a basic standard trust deed and rules with optional variations. Others (especially solicitors) argued that the necessary degree of flexibility required to suit the needs of different companies and different workforces could only be delivered by a tailor-made trust deed and rules.

Announcement, undertakings and overriding legislation

6.2   The trustees or the employer may have made formal announcements to the members which describe changes to contribution levels and benefits. However, the formal trust deed and rules may not have been amended to reflect these changes. Such formal announcements remain valid and are binding on the trustees so new trustees reading the trust deed and rules should ensure that any formal announcements to members have also been appended.

When Parliament creates pensions law, the new measures may need to be incorporated into each trust deed and rules before they become operative or they may be *overriding*. The operation of overriding legislation means that the new measures must be applied even if the existing trust deed and rules make no equivalent measure or even contradict it. Most new legislation is not incorporated into the trust deed and rules and so a reading of the latter will not give a complete picture.

The Pension Law Review Committee set up under Professor Goode recognised that this was a problem. However complicated the definitive trust deed and rules are to read, they at least ought to be the final word. The Committee urged that scheme authorities should be encouraged to consolidate their trust deeds and rules at least every five years. The Government accepted the recommendation but said that this was a measure to be dealt with by best practice and not by legislation.

An example of the effect of new legislation on the trust deed and rules is given by the pension sharing on divorce requirements brought in by the *Finance Act 1999*. In this example, if a new scheme had not gained HMRC approval by 10 May 2000, the new pension sharing provisions had to be included in trust deed and rules. Even if an application for approval had been made before that date, the trust deed and rules would have had to be resubmitted with the new pension sharing provisions included. On the other hand for all schemes already approved before 10 May 2000, and which continued to be approved on and after 1 December 2000, when the pension sharing provisions actually came into force, these provisions were applied by statutory override. Yet HMRC made it clear that pension schemes were not expected to rely on overriding provisions indefinitely. In this case, the trustees should ensure that the pension sharing provisions are incorporated into the trust deed and rules at the earliest 'convenient opportunity' – this was defined as the next occasion on or after 1 December 2000 when the trust deed and rules were being amended other than in a trivial way. From 6 April 2006, the new tax regime applies to registered pension schemes and the old approval system ceases to exist.

Yet the social security legislation continues to make new requirements on occupational pension schemes and achieve this effect by use of a statutory override. The overriding requirements made by the *Pensions Act 2004* are listed in *s 306* of that *Act*.

A list of 'relevant legislative provisions' (i.e. statutory provisions which have overridden the trust deeds and rules of occupational pension schemes but which may not be reflected in the scheme's documentation) can be found in *s 67A(9)* of the *Pensions Act 1995* – this section being inserted into the *1995 Act* by *s 262* of the *Pensions Act 2004*.

Effect of conversance requirement

6.2A   As explained at **5.2**, the *Pensions Act 2004* requires a pension fund trustee, in relation to an occupational pension scheme of which he or she is a trustee, to be *conversant* with its trust deed and rules and the draft code of practice issued for consultation purposes, as explained at **5.12**, suggests that trustees should have access to the scheme documents *at any time*.

In practice, this may present trustees with difficulties if their trust deed and rules has not been consolidated to take in all the amendments made both locally and by the overriding legislation. The cost and time of consolidating trust deeds and rules is not inconsequential, and pension law firms might be hard-pressed to consolidate the trust deeds and rules of all their clients over a short period. This may now prove to be even more the case in the light of the redrafting of the benefit and contribution rules following from the persistent deficits arising in defined benefit occupational pension schemes and the desire to abandon old HMRC contribution and benefit limits from 6 April 2006 to free up their scheme design.

The patchwork amendment of trust deeds and rules over the years has also produced another problem – that of internally self-contradictory trust deeds and rules leading to unresolvable ambiguities and in some cases outright nonsense.

Yet these practical difficulties in fact make it even more important that the aim of the *Pensions Act 2004* legislation is realised. Every pension fund trustee must have an up-to-date copy of the scheme's trust deed and rules. The trustees and the settler of the trust, i.e. the principal employer, should then agree to address any deficiencies that are found.

Power of amendment

6.3   The clause usually seen as the most important clause in the trust deed and rules is the *power of amendment clause*. It is usually very widely drawn because it is virtually impossible to amend an amending clause. Indeed, the amending clause in the definitive deed must be the same as in any interim deed. It is usually possible to use the power of amendment to amend a trust deed and rules retrospectively. Nevertheless, any amendment will ordinarily require the consent of the trustees who cannot abandon their fiduciary duty to protect the interests of the beneficiaries.

Protected and detrimental modifications

6.4   *Section 67* of the *Pensions Act 1995* introduced new overriding legislation from 6 April 1997. This stated that any power to modify a pension scheme cannot be exercised in a manner which would reduce for any member any existing entitlements (i.e. pensions already in payment) or accrued rights to pension (i.e. rights already built up in the scheme through the member's past pensionable service) unless the trustees themselves have approved of the modification and the consent of each individual member has been obtained for the reduction in his or her accrued rights. Indeed, no modification of the pension scheme is allowed at all until the trustees are satisfied, after taking professional actuarial advice, that the modification would not reduce any existing entitlement or accrued rights or, if it would do so, that the members have given their consent.

The *Pensions Act 2004* replaces these provisions of the *Pensions Act 1995* with new provisions in relation to existing entitlements and accrued rights which it calls '*subsisting rights*'. In relation to any scheme amendment that would modify any member's subsisting rights, the test which the trustees must apply depend on whether or not the proposed amendments amount to a '*protected modification*'. A protected modification is an amendment which, on taking effect, would or might result in:

- any of the subsisting rights of a member, or of a member's survivor, which are defined benefit rights becoming or being replaced by defined contribution rights; or

- the reduction in the amount of any pension currently in payment, or

- any other modification which is added to the list of protected modifications by future regulations.

Where the amendment proposes to make a protected modification to the trust deed and rules, the *informed consent* of each affected member must be obtained. This involves the trustees in giving each affected member written information which adequately explained the nature of the modification and its effect on that person, giving the member written notification that he or she can make representations to the trustees about the proposed modification and in practice affording the member a reasonable opportunity to make any representations and giving the member written notification that his or her consent is required. The modification can then be made if each member affected has given his or her consent and provided that modification is then put into effect within a reasonable period after the member has given that consent to the retrospective change.

If the amendment to the trust deed and rule which is to change any member's subsisting rights is not a protected modification but nevertheless falls into the category of a '*detrimental modification*', the trustees have a choice of how to proceed. A detrimental modification is an amendment which on taking effect would or might adversely affect any subsisting right of any member or the scheme or of any survivor of a member of the scheme. The choice open to the trustees is either to obtain the informed consent of each affected member just as if it were a protected modification or instead to ensure that the actuarial equivalence requirements are met.

The actuarial equivalence requirements consists of three elements:

- The *information requirement*: requires the trustees to take all reasonable steps to give each affected member written information explaining the nature of the modification and its effect in his or her particular case; to give that member written notification that he or she may make representations to the trustees about the proposed modification and in practice affording the member a reasonable opportunity to do so; and to give that member written notification that the actuarial equivalence test will apply.

- The *actuarial value requirement*: the trustees must make adequate arrangements to secure that the actuarial value of each affected member's subsisting rights will be maintained after the scheme amendment is made.

- The *actuarial equivalence statement*: the trustees must within a reasonable period beginning with the date on which the amendment is made, obtain an actuarial equivalence statement from the scheme actuary which certifies that the actuarial value in relation to an affected member immediately after the time the modification takes effect is equal to or greater than the actuarial value of the member's subsisting rights immediately before that time.

Any protected modification or detrimental modification can only be made if the trustees have given their approval for the scheme amendment to be made. Trustee approval is given if the trustees themselves have exercised a power given to them by the trust deed and rules to make the modification. If the trust deed and rules, however, have given the power to make such a scheme amendment to the employer, the *Pensions Act 2004* still requires the trustees to give their approval to the employer exercising this power. The trustees can only give their consent to a protected modification if the informed consent of each affected member has been obtained and can only given their consent to a detrimental modification being made if either the informed consent of each member has been obtained or the actuarial equivalence requirements are met.

In the case where each member's informed consent is required, the trustees must notify each affected member. In the case where the actuarial equivalence requirements are to be applied, the trustees must take all reasonable steps to notify each affected member.

The *2004 Act* gives the Pensions Regulator the power to declare any scheme amendment void unless the above requirements are met.

These provisions did not affect the ability of trustees and employers to modify the trust deed and rules to change the benefits that active members can build up in relation to future pensionable service. Note, however, that the Pensions Act 2004 has introduced new provisions which requires employers to consult scheme members where they propose (or the trustees propose) to make significant changes to the pension arrangements to apply to future pensionable service. These consultation requirements are discussed at **7.5**.

Statutory modifications

6.5   The *Pension Schemes Act 1993* and the *Pensions Act 1995* have given trustees the power to modify the trust deed and rules to achieve any of a specified list of purposes. Most of the purposes are to allow the trustees to modify their schemes so that they comply with various legislative requirements.

The Pensions Regulator has direct power to modify the trust deed and rules of an occupational pension scheme for specific purposes set out in the legislation. In some cases, the trustees could approach the court to see if they can be granted authority to amend the trust deed and rules, and in some cases the court itself can directly amend the trust deed and rules.

Checklist 6

- As a trustee of an occupational pension scheme that is *exempt approved* by HMRC or that from 6 April 2006 is a registered pension scheme under the *Finance Act 2004* you should understand the very significant tax advantages that arise from this tax status and should ensure that no action is taken which might endanger those privileges.

- The trustees must observe the trust deed and rules.

- A trust deed and rules can be overridden by Acts of Parliament, and sometimes by announcements that have been made in the name of the trustees to the members – all of which the trustees must take into account when reading their trust deed and rules.

- The trustees should periodically ensure that their trust deed and rules are consolidated and brought up to date.

- It is virtually impossible to amend the power of amendment clause but, provided the terms of the power of amendment clause are respected, the trust deed and rules can be amended.

- *Section 67* of the *Pensions Act 1995* has prevented scheme amendments that result in the retrospective worsening of an individual's already accrued pension rights, and a similar provision is often made by the trust documentation of individual schemes.

- *Section 67* of the *Pensions Act 1995* is being substituted by new provisions made by the *Pensions Act 2004* which introduce an actuarial equivalence test.

- The Pensions Regulator, the courts and the *Pensions Acts* can help trustees to amend their trust deed and rules for specified purposes if the power of amendment clause does not give them the ability to do so. The courts can give the trustees authority to make an amendment if the trustees have any doubts about whether they have a right to do so.

Chapter 7

Pensions in the context of industrial relations

View that trustees cannot negotiate

7.1   The following advice is crystal clear:

'As a trustee you are not a representative of the group or interest from which you are drawn: your duty is to serve all the different classes of beneficiary impartially. Nor, by the same token, are you a negotiator. There may well be negotiations on pension benefits between representatives of the employer and the workforce, but the trustees' meeting is not the arena for these.'

Source: former Occupational Pensions Board publication *Pension Trust Principles*.

For those who are trustees, their only responsibility, at least while they are wearing their trustee hats in a trustee meeting, is to ensure that the obligations imposed by the trust deed and rules and any overriding legislation are met.

Member trustees nominated through a process involving a recognised trade union sometimes feel frustrated by the fact that they should not normally seek improvements in benefit provision in trustee meetings.

Member trustees might try to table an agenda item asking, for example, that pensionable pay be based on all earnings rather than just earnings above the current National Insurance lower earnings limit. The trustee chairing the meeting may refuse the item properly pointing out that the trustee meeting is not a negotiating forum. Subsequently, the company may inform the trustees that, owing to a favourable actuarial report and valuation (nowadays a much rarer occurrence than in the past), it wants to bring in this particular improvement, especially as the improvement disproportionately benefits lower paid members. The trustees would almost certainly agree to the proposed rule change provided they felt that other classes of beneficiaries would not be disadvantaged, for example if the current pensioners were granted a reasonable annual increase. However, to the member trustees it would appear that the issue does not appear on the agenda if they propose it, but does appear if the company proposes it.

Nevertheless, the trust deed and rules may give trustees some discretionary powers which they can exercise with the consent of the employer. An example might be the level of increase granted to pensions in payment. Clearly, in such circumstances the trustees will be operating within the terms of the trust deed and rules if they approach the employer to suggest a figure.

It is recognised that pensions are subject to negotiations in an industrial relations context. And, indeed, advice from the former Occupational Pensions Board on the ways it would assist a scheme to modify its trust deed and rules so that a payment of a pension fund surplus may be taken by the employer (see **CHAPTER 19**) implied that pension negotiations would have taken place beforehand.

It is also clear from recent court cases that in certain circumstances it is correct for the trustees to negotiate with the sponsoring employer. For example, Justice Knox in the case of *Hillsdown Holdings v Pensions Ombudsman* reports the opinion of another judge, Justice Millet who:

' … contemplates as perfectly proper a process of bargaining between trustees of a pension fund and the employer in the context of a desire by an employer to obtain payment of at least part of a surplus and a desire by the trustees to secure increased benefits for their members.'

The reference to Justice Millet in fact comes from the well-known case of *Re Courage's Group Pension Schemes* in which he said that:

'Where the employer seeks repayment, the trustees … can be expected to press for generous treatment of employees and pensioners and the employer to be influenced by the desire to maintain good industrial relations with its workforce.'

In these kinds of cases, it is perfectly proper for the trustees to negotiate with the employer but the acid test, as Justice Knox points out in the *Hillsdown* case, is that both the trustees and the employer should both have a legitimate interest to preserve, and here 'legitimate interest' means acting in accordance with the trust deed and rules. The trustees should not through negotiation consent to any course of action which is specifically forbidden by the trust deed and rules.

The kind of negotiation between trustees and the employer which the courts have noted with approval is a bargaining situation where each side has something to give or withhold by way of necessary consent and there is no absolute bar on what is sought to be achieved, e g a change in the trust deed and rules that can be made using the power of amendment clause.

The trustees must always act in the best interests of the members but it is acknowledged that those best interests are likely to be well served by consultation with the employer, with a view to ensuring that pension fund trustees take a decision which fits in, so far as practicable and permissible, with an employer's business strategy.

Although the use of surpluses has in the past usually been at the centre of such trustee/employer consultation, it may be that investment strategies will also become an important item on the agenda in discussions between the employer and the trustees. As explained at **16.6** and **16.8**, since the coming into force of the *Pensions Act 1995*, the trustees have absolute responsibility for the investment strategy, as set out in the scheme's Statement of Investment Principles. The employer is not allowed to have any reserve powers to veto the trustees' approach but the trustees must consult the employer. Clearly this makes sense for the trustees of a defined benefit scheme where the employer bears the investment risk. It would be counter-productive for the trustees to set out on an investment strategy that implied a rate of funding which the employer was either unwilling or unable to support. From April 2006 when the risk-based levy relating to the new Pension Protection Fund (PPF) begins to be collected, this area becomes even more complex for the trustees of a defined benefit scheme. Riskier funding policies might imply lower employer contributions but they also imply a higher risk-based levy.

The point also to bear in mind is that in these situations the trustees, as a whole, are negotiating with the employer: the bargaining forum is not a trustee meeting but a meeting between the trustees and the employer. At a trustee meeting, there can be no bargaining because, quite simply, the employer is not present.

The case of *South West Trains v Wightman* heard by Justice Neuberger in December 1997 is of particular interest because it looks at whether a collective agreement negotiated between an employer and a trade union can affect the terms of a pension scheme's trust deed and rules. Justice Neuberger held that all the aspects of a restructuring proposal that had been satisfactorily negotiated in an industrial relations joint working group and had been agreed by the employer and the trade union, including some re-negotiated pension rights, acted to bind the employer and the employees concerned contractually on an individual basis.

One group of employees had argued that the provisions of the scheme's trust deed and rules would provide them with more favourable benefits and objected to a proposed amendment to the scheme which would take in the changes that had been negotiated. However, because of the contractual agreement, Justice Neuberger held that it was arguable that the trustee of the pension scheme concerned could in any case refuse to pay the employees concerned a pension at a higher rate than that agreed with the employer. However, the correctness of the arguments put forward did not have to be decided in this case because Justice Neuberger had already held that the employer could enforce the binding pensions agreement by restraining any employee claiming a pension on a more generous basis than that agreed under the binding agreement.

In general, however, it would seem a good idea to make sure that the trust deed and rules are properly amended before a change is implemented. Furthermore, it should be noted that *s 67* of the *Pensions Act 1995* prevents changes that reduce a member's already accrued rights unless either each member potentially affected consents to the change or the change is actuarially equivalent (see **6.3** above).

Many pension lawyers share the opinion that there is in fact a contractual relationship between the employer and the trustees which the trustees can, and probably should, enforce if the employer fails to comply with the terms of the trust. Speaking at the 2001 conference of the Association of Pension Lawyers, Duncan Buchanan pointed out that deeds of adherence admitting new employers as participating employers in an occupational pension scheme often contain an express covenant that the employer will comply with the terms and conditions of the scheme. He said:

> 'Of course, in practice it is rare that the trustees need to enforce these contractual provisions because the employer complies with the terms and conditions of the scheme. That said, I believe that there is a clear contractual relationship between the employer and trustees.'

In June 2001, the Central Arbitration Committee (CAC) delivered its decision in the case of *UNIFI v Union Bank of Nigeria*. The issue to be decided was whether negotiation on matters relating to pensions came under the ambit of 'pay' in the sense in which that word is used in the Schedule and Model Method set out in the *Trade Union Recognition (Method of Collective Bargaining) Order 2000 (SI 2000/1300)*. The decision of the CAC also contains a very useful summary of the wider issue of whether pension rights are generally included as part of an employee's 'pay' outside the area of equal treatment, where it is already clearly established that pensions represent 'deferred pay'.

The CAC's deliberations acknowledged that, after the judgment of the Privy Council in the case of *Air Jamaica Ltd v Charlton*, it is now generally accepted that the rights of employees in relation to their membership of an occupational pension scheme derive from their contracts of employment and 'are not inappropriately described as "deferred pay"'. The particular details of this case concerned the employer's contributions to a money purchase arrangement and the CAC concluded on the facts that the obligation on the Bank of Nigeria to negotiate with UNIFI on 'pay' included all matters relating to the levels or amount of employer's pension contributions.

The CAC also distinguished the issues of whether employer contributions to a defined contribution arrangement and to a defined benefit scheme are both 'pay'. The implication of the CAC's decision is that in general employer contributions to a defined contribution arrangement are 'pay', but in the case of a defined benefit scheme it is the benefit payable, rather than the employer's contributions, which can be considered 'pay'. The CAC stated:

> 'Having considered the relevant authorities and sought to establish whether guidance can be obtained from the Parliamentary debate, we next consider what assistance can be gained by bringing to bear our industrial relations experience on whether pay includes any, and if so which aspects, of the term 'pensions' in the collective bargaining context and any relevant case law. Our conclusion is that employer pension contributions (in a defined contribution scheme) and the benefits payable (in a defined benefit scheme) are now seen as an integral and important part of a worker's pay

and the two aspects of a worker's financial reward for his or her services are intertwined.'

Yet so much of the above discussion on the trustees' role in negotiating with employers has arisen in earlier years where the underlying problem to be negotiated was the happy problem of how to deal with a pension fund surplus in a defined benefit scheme. Today, the problem is the decidedly less happy problem of negotiating how to deal with a pension deficit. The role of trustees here is discussed further at **7.5** below.

Duty to consult

7.1A   Measures in the *Employment Relations Act 2004* have put into effect the *EC Directive on Informing and Consulting Employees (Directive 2002/14/EC)* which give employees the right to be consulted and informed about matters that affect them at work. The *Information and Consultation of Employees Regulations 2004 (SI 2004/3426)* made under that Act came into force on 6 April 2005.The legislation is being phased in over three years to give smaller firms longer to prepare. The legislation will apply to firms with:

- 150 or more employees from 6 April 2005;

- 100 or more employees from 6 April 2007; and

- 50 or more employees from 6 April 2008.

The onus is on employees to ask for information and consultation arrangements to be agreed, but employers are obliged to set up arrangements where 10% of the workforce ask for this. If employers do not abide by such arrangements, employees or their representatives can complain to the Central Arbitration Committee, and a penalty of up to £75,000 can be imposed.

The Department of Trade & Industry also published guidance on the require-ments made under the Act. This explains that 'changes in contractual relations' would fall under the scope of this new legislative duty on em-ployers to consult and that in the Department's view 'changes in contractual relations' would include the introduction of, or a change to, compulsory retirement age and also changes to an occupational pension scheme but in this latter case only where there was a contractual right to participate in the scheme as that right would form part of the contract.

7.1B   Yet whether or not employee membership of an occupational pension scheme was a contractual right, *Sections 259–261* of the *Pensions Act 2004* is introducing a separate requirement that employers must consult on future changes they or the trustees of the scheme wish to make in relation to an occupational pension scheme.

Section 259 of the *2004 Act* does no more than provide the government with a power to introduce regulations which will set out the circumstances in which an employer will have to consult. These regulations, which were issued in draft in June 2005, will also set out the types of decisions leading to major or significant changes to occupational pension schemes that will trigger the requirement to consult. The draft sets out the following list of proposals affecting rights deriving from future pensionable service in an occupational pension scheme and which must be the subject of prior consultation:

- to increase the age at which benefits under the scheme become payable to active or prospective members;

- to stop admitting new members, or certain categories of new members, to the scheme;

- to stop active or prospective members from accruing further benefits under the scheme;

- to free the employer from its liability to contribute to the scheme;

- to introduce a requirement for employees to contribute when the scheme was previously non-contributory;

- in respect of defined contribution occupational pension schemes, to effect any reduction in the employer's contribution rate so that, when expressed as a percentage of pensionable earnings, the reduction is by a margin of two percentage points or more, or so that the effect of the reduction is that the employer's contribution is reduced below three per cent of pensionable pay;

- to increase member contributions by two percentage points of pensionable earnings or more;

- in respect of defined benefit occupational pension schemes, to change any of the benefits that may be provided under the scheme to defined contribution, or to reduce the rate of future accrual of benefits under the scheme, or to reduce the rate of future accruals of benefit, or to increase member contributions by two percentage points of pensionable earnings or more.

The draft regulations also require employers with contract-based pensions involving a direct payment arrangements (see **2.7**) to consult before making any of the same changes in employer or employee contributions described above for defined contribution occupational pension schemes.It is noteworthy also that the regulations will prevent the trustees of an occupational pension scheme from making certain kinds of decisions about the scheme unless they have first notified the employer of the proposed decision and they are satisfied that the employer has undertaken any consultation required by the regulations.

Yet in order to give certainty s 259 also provides that that the validity of any decision which will become subject to prior consultation with the scheme members before it is implemented will not itself be affected by any failure to comply with these regulations.

Section 261 of the *2004 Act* deals with how the regulations are to prescribe how the consultation process will have to be carried out including making provision for the time periods for consultation, the information that must be provided to those consulted, and who is to be consulted, including any discretion the employer may have as to the persons to be consulted. The draft regulations propose that the employer must conduct the consultation over a period of at least two months.

The requirements to be made under the regulations will also contain provision about representatives that employees may have and the method of selecting those employees. This section of the *2004 Act* also makes provision for the regulations to be made to protect employee representatives involved in the pensions consultation process from suffering any detriment or unfair dismissal by reason of carrying out their consultation duties, and to ensure they are given adequate time and remuneration to carry out their consultation duties. This mirrors existing protection provided to employee representatives under the *Employment Rights Act 1996* and the protection given by the *Information and Consultation of Employees Regulations 2004* mentioned in **7.2** to '*I&C*' representatives.

Employers and trustees will be required to demonstrate to the Pensions Regulator that they have complied with the requirement to consult the members when they have been obliged by the regulations to have done so. The regulations will also give the Pensions Regulator the power to waive or relax the duty on the employer to consult in appropriate circumstances.

The draft regulations also require the employer to communicate to the scheme's trustees any representations received by the employer as part of the consultation process which relate to proposals made by the trustees.

The requirements will be introduced in the following stages depending on the number of employees employed by the employer:

- 150 or more employees from 6 April 2006;

- 100 or more employees from 6 April 2007; and

- 50 or more employees from 6 April 2008.

Employers with 50 or fewer employees are not required to comply with this statutory duty to consult employees on future pension changes.

Pension negotiations

7.2   Although the ownership of the pension fund and, at least theoretically and now historically, of surpluses that arise in the fund, can be a matter of dispute, it is much more generally accepted that the eventual pension itself can be seen as a form of *deferred pay* for the employee. Such conclusions can be drawn from judgments of the European Court of Justice.

If pensions are part of the overall remuneration package offered by an employer to employees, then it is clear that individual employees, staff associations and trade unions will seek to negotiate with the employer over pensions.

Pensions can have effects on pay negotiations. In the mid-1980s one company found it had a surplus in the pension fund and a temporary cut in the employee pension contribution level was negotiated. After the ending of the employee contribution holiday, it proved very difficult to restore employee contributions to their original level. Especially resistant were young employees who had joined the company during the contribution holiday. The matter was resolved by restoring the contribution levels at the same time as granting a slightly higher than expected pay increase.

Similarly, a company, finding that the pension fund was enjoying a surplus, while it, itself, needed to control costs, succeeded in negotiating a lower pay-round increase with its employees by simultaneously agreeing that the pension scheme would become non-contributory.

The greater general awareness of pensions issues among employees and the general public in recent years encouraged many trade unions during the 1980s until the late 1990s to seek benefit improvements in their members' pension schemes. The process had also been helped by the codification by the former Inland Revenue (now HMRC) of how pension fund surpluses should be reduced – see **19.1**. In many ways, the Chancellor of the Exchequer in the *Finance Act 1986* placed pension fund surpluses on negotiating tables across the land.

Similarly, the ending of the ability of employers to make membership of the pension scheme a condition of employment, the measures introduced during the 1980s on disclosure of information and the encouragement of member-ship of personal pensions – all measures introduced by the Government of the day as part of its pension reform programme – led to greater emphasis on improved pension communications.

Employers and trade unions were drawn into alliances to protect occupational pension schemes. One result was that pensions moved up the negotiating agenda.

By 2003, pension negotiations once again have risen to near the top of the negotiating agenda between employers and organised labour, with the trustees often sitting uncomfortably in the middle. By then, however, the cause was not how to divide up a surplus, but how to proceed when falling stock markets, greater pensioner longevity and the prospect of only moderate, single-digit investment returns in future had together revealed a large deficit in many formerly well-funded schemes.

Since then many final salary schemes have been closed to new entrants. In many cases trade unions and other forms of staff representative bodies have been unable to prevent this from happening, mainly because employees who were existing members of the scheme were not threatened.

In other cases, employers have approached the membership, via their representatives, to seek ways of reducing pension costs relating to existing members. Such proposals have included moving for future service from a 1/60th to a 1/80th accrual rate, removing enhanced early retirement provisions and often also increasing the employee contribution rate. It must be said that any plan to resist such proposals by the trade unions is likely to be hindered if in early years the final salary scheme has been closed to new entrants, who have themselves been offered cheaper alternative provision. The new entrants would wonder why they are being asked to contemplate industrial action to support their fellow workers in the more generous scheme when they themselves have already been denied that provision with the passive acceptance of the trade unions.

Some of those in the personnel and human resources field are also becoming concerned about the longer-term implications of different pension arrangements depending on the date an employee joins the company. One can have two colleagues with the same experience and responsibilities who joined the employer within a week of each other. Yet one will be building up a defined benefit in a 1/60th final salary scheme; the other may be in a defined contribution scheme receiving a 5% employer contribution. After a few years, the cost of the two remuneration packages, all else being equal, will differ markedly and this can cause resentment.

It should be noted, however, that by the summer of 2002, some employers had proposed closing final salary schemes for all further accrual. In some cases, this provoked industrial action and the withdrawal of that proposal but in many cases active members are not in membership of defined contribution schemes while a few years ago they were accruing benefits linked to their final salary. Such moves are now in many cases subject to the duty on the employer to consult with the employees affected in advance of making the changes – see **7.1A–7.1B** above.

Relationship between trustees and negotiators

7.3   Although the trustees will not negotiate on pensions in meetings of the trustee body, it is quite likely that as individuals they will be involved in any such negotiations either directly or indirectly.

When the negotiations are concluded, the employer will invite the trustees to agree any necessary changes to the trust deed and rules. Normally, this should not present any problems since it is unlikely that the package negotiated will involve any diminution in the accrued benefits for any scheme members.

However, the trustees might want to consider that they are still acting in the interests of *all* beneficiaries. For example, and now perhaps a rather hypothetical example at that, if a pension fund surplus has been completely used to grant the employer a contribution holiday and to improve the accrual rate for all current members, the trustees might have a problem since existing and deferred pensioners would have been excluded from the benefit improvements.

In February 1999, the Pensions Ombudsman criticised the corporate trustee of one scheme for leaving benefit improvements to negotiations between the employer and the trade unions. The Pensions Ombudsman held that the trustee had failed in its fiduciary duty to the beneficiaries by not considering making recommendations in respect of the disposal of a surplus – particularly in respect of those members whose interests may not be properly considered in the collective bargaining process. The language was precise. The trustee did *not* have a duty to make recommendations: rather it had a duty to *consider* making recommendations for benefit improvements.

Pensions and contractual obligations to members

7.4   The case of *South West Trains v Wightman* (discussed at **7.1**) shows that there can be a complex interaction between, on the one hand, the employment rights of an employee as set out in the employee's contract of employment, and, on the other hand, the provisions of the pension scheme's trust deed and rules. The case of *Trustees of the NUS Officials and Employees Superannuation Fund v Pensions Ombudsman* concerned the treatment of an element of the remuneration of one employee. The employee had been offered an increase in salary by his employer, but on condition that the increase would not count as pensionable earnings. The rules of the member's pension scheme, however, in effect provided that salary increases were pensionable. The employee had raised an objection to this condition at the time the offer was made, although he had accepted the increased salary.

In the High Court, Justice Lightman held that the employer had offered a non-pensionable increase and that, in accepting the increase, the employee had also accepted that the increase was non-pensionable. It was, said the judge, not open to the employee to accept one element of the employer's offer but not the other. Although not stated explicitly, the result of the judgment seems to confirm the judgment in *South West Trains v Wightman* that the terms of the employee's contract, provided it is clear that they have been accepted by both parties, can override the provisions of the trust deed and rules.

More generally, consideration in recent times has turned to the question of whether employees may, in particular circumstances, have a contractual right to continue to accrue pension rights while employed under the terms of their employment contract. Would it breach the terms of employees' contracts of employment if, say, the employer closed an occupational pension scheme so that existing employees ceased to build up pensionable service under the scheme from a specified date?

Alternatively, could there be circumstances where, say, the employer closes a defined benefit scheme for future service for all employees but offers them instead membership of a defined contribution scheme, with the result that the employees could successfully claim a breach of their employment contract because they were being offered inferior benefits?

The decisions are much discussed at the time of writing. In any particular case, of course, the outcome will depend not only on the actual terms of the employment contract itself but also on the terms of any other statements that have been made by the employer to the employees concerned. The outcome will also depend on whether the employees concerned can be seen to have accepted or rejected the variation in the terms of their employment contract.

However, this is a question of employment law that centres on the employer and the employees as the two parties involved. It might be thought that the trustees themselves might not be directly involved although, of course, the resolution of any such employment law question would be of significant importance to the trustees concerned.

It may also be the case, as pointed out by Duncan Buchanan at the Association of Pension Lawyers 2001 annual conference, that contractual rights may exist between the scheme members and the trustees. Such contractual rights are distinct from the fiduciary rights that members can enforce against the trustees and which arise from the terms of the trust deed and rules.

An example is contained in the case of *Nicol & Andrew v Brinkley* where, following the sale of a business between two employers, an employee was offered, in return for transferring his accrued pensionable service to a new scheme established by his new employer, a transfer credit of seven years' pensionable service. However, various errors meant that the transfer credit had been too low and the trustees of the scheme tried to rectify matters by reducing the service credits. In giving judgment, Sir John Vinelott held that the offer of the service credit of seven years, which had been accepted by the member, had clearly given rise to a contract and that it was absurd to suppose that the terms of that contract could now be altered.

Clearance statements

7.5   In April 2005 the Pensions Regulator issued guidance setting out the principles under which it will act to carry out its statutory duty under the *Pensions Act 2004* to prevent claims arising on the Pension Protection Fund (see **23.1B**) from underfunded defined benefit schemes following the insolvency of the sponsoring employer (see **19.7**). The *Pensions Act 2004* gives the Pensions Regulator powers to issue in particular:

- *contribution notices* where there is an action, or failure to act, by an employer to avoid pension liabilities – see also **23.1A**, or

- *financial support orders* in circumstances when the employer in relation to the scheme is a service company or insufficiently resourced.

In order that employers who are involved in corporate restructuring some certainty that their proposed actions will not result in the imposition of such a notice or order by the Pensions Regulator, the *Pensions Act 2004* has also established the mechanism whereby the Pensions Regulator can issue a clearance statement. The intention is that those concerned could gain assurance via the clearance statement that the action they intended would not be found later to fall foul of the legislation. Clearance was therefore introduced with the underlying aim of protecting jobs, particularly where clearance is needed to prevent the employer becoming insolvent and the continuation of appropriate deal activity involving employers with defined benefit schemes.

Among such deals are the arrival at potential compromise arrangements between the trustees of an underfunded defined benefit occupational pension scheme and the employer sponsoring that scheme who wants to be relieved of a debt obligation to the trustees clearance procedure – see again **23.1A**. Since 6 April 2005 it is very important for the trustees of defined benefit schemes to be aware that any decision by the trustees to take action which will, or is intended to, result in any debt which is or may become due to the scheme not being paid in full must be notified to the Pensions Regulator unless certain conditions are met. These conditions and further details of the notifiable events requirements introduced by the Pensions Act 2004 are described at **23.1C**.

The Pension Regulator's guidance *Clearance statements*, is very important reading for any trustees who are, or may be placed in such a negotiating position. The document is available at http://www.thepensionsregulator.gov.uk/pdf/clearanceGuidance.pdf.

A key section of the guidance is reproduced below.

CLEARANCE STATEMENTS – ROLE OF THE TRUSTEES INVOLVED IN COMPROMISE NEGOTIATIONS WITH THE SPONSORING EMPLOYER OF AN UNDERFUNDED DEFINED BENEFIT OCCUPATIONAL PENSION SCHEME

81. The pension scheme, if in deficit, is an unsecured creditor of the employer. Usually, because of the size of the deficit, it is a material unsecured creditor and although not identical to a large unsecured bank loan, it does have many similarities in the form of:

•   its size relative to other unsecured creditors;

•   its importance – particularly in cases where there is a large number of active members; and

•   its ability to exert leverage over the company, particularly because of trustees' ability to whistleblow to the regulator, with the regulator's powers to issue contribution notices or financial support directions.

---

82. The trustees should therefore learn from the way a bank with a large unsecured loan would look to negotiate with a company.

83. In order to negotiate, and to protect scheme members' interests, trustees need to understand the sponsoring employer's financial position and the strength of its commitment to the funding of the scheme. They should monitor corporate activity and seek the employer's agreement to be given information at an early stage subject to the usual restrictions such as those on handling price-sensitive information.

84. If the trustees are concerned, they should raise their concerns with the sponsoring employer and, where appropriate, other companies in the group.

85. Trustees can also contact the Pensions Regulator who will be able to help and advise them.

Confidentiality

86. Trustees must understand that information they receive in their position as trustees is confidential. This is particularly important when it comes to sensitive information – involving either scheme members or the employer. Trustees cannot expect to be given 'inside information' from the employer if they pass it on.

87. One way of ensuring that all parties understand the importance of confidentiality is to enter into a confidentiality agreement. This should ideally be done every time a new trustee joins the board, rather than waiting until there is an important issue which the employer is reluctant to discuss because of confidentiality issues.

Conflicts of interest

88. Many trustee boards have members who may have a conflict of interest – for example, trustees who are directors of the employer or union representatives. Trustees must remember that at all times they must act in the interests of scheme members and other beneficiaries not just the active members.

89. Trustees and employers should plan in advance their approach for when a conflict of interest arises. They may for example set triggers which would result in an independent trustee being appointed.

90. The issue of conflict becomes more important when the trustees are negotiating with the employer when a type A event* is likely. The regulator expects a trustee who could be involved in both sides of the negotiation (for example a finance director or chief executive) to ensure that the trustees have the appropriate information on a timely basis and to draw his fellow trustees' attention to the potential conflict and to absent himself from trustee meetings when the issue is discussed and to play no part in decision making.

91. Trustees may need to commission an investigating accountant or insolvency specialist with industry knowledge to assess the financial circumstances of the employer or group of companies before negotiating, particularly if the conflicted trustee is the trustee board's main source of financial knowledge.

Negotiations

92. As noted above, in order to negotiate properly, trustees must understand the employer's financial situation and its commitment to the pension scheme. They must also understand the position of the scheme and its funding.

93. Most importantly, they need to understand the impact of the type A event on the scheme and what they can demand in negotiations.

94. We have identified some areas which can mitigate the effect of a type A event on the pension creditor and which should be carefully considered during negotiations.

* Type A events

Type A events generally have one or more of the following three effects on the pension creditor:

- Change in priority: a change in the level of security given to creditors, with the consequence that the pension creditor might receive a reduced dividend in the event of insolvency. For example: the granting or extending of a fixed charge or floating charge

- Return of capital: a reduction in the overall assets of the company which could be used to fund a pension deficit. For example: dividends, share buy backs, dividend strips, distribution in species, demergers

- Change in control structure: a change or partial change in the group structure of an employer, which reduces the overall employer covenant, and could affect the ability of an employer to meet a potential debt under section 75 of the Pensions Act 1995 and lead to the regulator imposing a financial support direction. For example: change of employer or participating employer change of parties connected or associated with the employer.

Source: Paragraphs 81 to 94 of the guidance Clearance Statements issued by the Pensions Regulator.

Checklist 7

- It is accepted that those serving as a scheme's trustees, while acting in the capacity of trustees, do not generally seek to negotiate on pension provision with the employer.

- Regulations made under the *Pensions Act 2004* will introduce a new requirement on employers to consult with employees where the employer or trustees propose to make future certain changes to occupational pension schemes or to a personal or stakeholder pension direct payment arrangement. The *Information and Consultation of Employees Regulations 2004 (SI 2004/3426)* may also be relevant where employees have a contractual right to membership of a pension scheme.

- A trustee meeting, where only the trustees, their secretary and advisers are present, is not a negotiating forum between the employer and trade unions.

- In the exercise of those discretionary powers where the trustees must seek the agreement of the employer, the trustees would not normally be seen as negotiating with the employer.

- There are, however, circumstances where the trustees would be expected by the courts to negotiate with the employer, such as when the employer seeks to persuade the trustees to take a course of action which is not forbidden by the trust deed and rules.

- In many organisations, trade unions or staff representatives negotiate on pension provision with the employer and it has now long been recognised that pensions are a form of deferred pay.

- The decision of the Central Arbitration Committee in the case of *UNIFI v Union Bank of Nigeria* has clarified the question of whether negotiation between an employer and employee representatives on matters relating to pensions come under the ambit of 'pay' in the sense in which that word is used in the Schedule and Model Method set out in the *Trade Union Recognition (Method of Collective Bargaining) Order 2000*.

- If the employer and trade unions have negotiated changes to the pension scheme rules, the trustees will normally accept the changes to the trust deed and rules provided no class of beneficiary has been disadvantaged by the changes.

- It might be the case that employees already in membership of an occupational pension scheme could have a contractual right to accrue future pensionable service under the terms of the contract of employment.

- Contractual obligations can arise between the trustees and the employer, and between the trustees and the members, that are distinct from the fiduciary relationship that arises under trust law.

- Trustees of defined benefit schemes should negotiate with the sponsoring employer in accordance with the guidance issued by the Pensions Regulator in its guidance on clearance statements when any Type A event is at issue.

Chapter 8

Trustees and the employer

The employer as settlor of the trust

8.1 The person who creates the trust is known as the *settlor* of the trust and in the case of most occupational pension schemes this will be the employer.

In the report issued by the Occupational Pensions Board way back in 1982, the view of the Board members was that:

> 'The concepts developed in trust law become rather strained when applied to a modern pension scheme. Under trust law the employer is considered to be the "settlor" who endows the trust from which the members or "beneficiaries" draw their pensions, overlooking the fact that the members as well as the employer often contribute to the scheme and the employer's contributions can scarcely be considered as an act of unilateral benevolence.
>
> Trust laws seem to pre-suppose that the two interests (of the settlor and the beneficiaries) will be co-incident but in pension schemes there is a potential source of conflict between the interests of employer and the interests of members.'

The law of trusts has in the past developed in the context of ordinary family trusts where the settlor does not have a continuing financial interest in the trust: this is not the situation with an employer and an occupational pension scheme.

The employer is not only the settlor of the trust, but also a potential beneficiary under the trust deed and rules. For example, surpluses in a defined benefit scheme can be reduced by making a payment to the employer (see **19.1**) and the trust deed and rules may specify that any surplus remaining after the winding up of the scheme may be given to the employer, although the making of such payments is now subject to rigorous conditions and surpluses themselves have very largely disappeared.

The employer, therefore, as settlor of the trust, decides what the provisions of the trust deed and rules will be. The trustees are then under a duty to carry out the provisions of that trust documentation. As mentioned in **7.1** the trustees and the employer probably have a contractual relationship so that the trustees could enforce the terms of the trust against the employer. If on the other hand the trustees failed to carry out their duties under the trust, then the employer probably would seek to remove those trustees under the powers granted to it by the trust deed and rules.

Among the reasons commonly cited by employers for the inclusion of occupational pensions as an element of the overall employee remuneration package are that:

- they offer a means of effecting a smooth transition for older employees from employment to retirement;

- they can be designed to offer the employer a degree of control over when employees retire, which in particular can reflect changing demands on the job market;

- they can be the vehicle for provision of life insurance benefits allowing the employer to assume a degree of social responsibility by being able to protect the employee's family more economically than the employee could do so on an individual basis;

- they are seen as an essential element in a competitive remuneration policy necessary for attracting, motivating and retaining skilled employees; and (somewhat less positively)

- they have simply been inherited by the current management.

Since 1988 there has been a trend among employers away from occupational pension schemes and over to contract-based personal or stakeholder pension schemes. Funding difficulties with defined benefit schemes have prompted many employers to close these schemes to new entrants, or in some cases to freeze the scheme so no member accrues further pensionable service. Many employers have also decided that they need to focus on the core business rather divert their energy in providing services to an occupational pension scheme and so find it more productive to transfer the responsibility to a personal pension provider, which is in practice an insurance company. Other employers, however, take the view that the value of the occupational pension funds which they sponsor is so great that it is more cost effective for them to work with trustees appointed to a trust they have created. The pension fund can then be run on a self-administered basis so that the mutual interest of the employer and members can remain the primary aim and the trustees retain control.

Powers of the employer

8.2   The employer as settlor of the trust has very substantial powers.

Many of the discretionary powers under the terms of the trust deed and rules can be exercised by the trustees only with the consent of the employer.

The power of amendment contained in the trust deed and rules will allow the employer to make extensive changes to how the scheme operates and the benefits it offers. The trustees will, however, usually have to agree to these changes. The power is also circumscribed by the *Pensions Act 1995* (as amended by the *Pensions Act 2004*) as explained at **6.3** above to avoid reducing the already accrued rights of scheme members.

The employer will normally be able to wind up the scheme at any time. Prior to the coming into force of the requirements governing member-nominated trustees the employer also usually had the sole power to appoint and remove the trustees. Although an employer can, if approval is gained through the statutory consultation procedure explained at **4.17**, at the time of writing retain the unique power to appoint all the trustees, the *Pensions Act 2004* will ensure that occupational pension schemes will generally in future always have among their trustees a proportion who have been nominated directly or indirectly by the scheme members – see **4.29**. The employer naturally will retain the unique power to appoint and remove employer-nominated trustees.

The trust deed and rules will normally assign certain powers to be exercised only by the employer. It may be that some of those powers can be seen as *fiduciary powers* which simply means that the employer must act in a trustee-like way when exercising those powers. If the power in question is a fiduciary power, the employer would need to exercise that power by taking into account only the interests of the members and to disregard its own interest. Many of the powers given to the employer, however, will not be fiduciary powers. Such powers are given absolutely to the employer and so when exercising those powers the employer may first and foremost have regard to its own interest.

Trust law also defines the principle of a *fraud on a power*, meaning simply that a person who has a limited power must exercise that power in good faith for the end designed, otherwise the exercise will be void.

In an important development in 1990, in the case of *Imperial Group Pension Trust Ltd v Imperial Tobacco Ltd*, the then Vice Chancellor (the senior judge in the Chancery Division which hears pension law cases) Sir Nicolas Browne-Wilkinson, held that an employer must exercise any powers given to it by the trust deed and rules subject to an *implied duty of good faith*.

The phrase 'implied duty of good faith' is a kind of legal shorthand used to refer to the employment law concept that in contracts of employment there is an implied obligation that:

> ' ... the employers will not, without reasonable and proper cause, conduct themselves in a manner calculated or likely to destroy or seriously damage the relationship of confidence and trust between employer and employee'.

In other words, since the *Imperial* case it has been accepted that this general obligation of an employer applies as much to the exercise of its rights and powers under a pension scheme as it does to the other rights and powers that exist under employment law.

Payment of pension contributions

8.3   It is a general condition of tax approval that the employer contributes to the occupational pension scheme. However, employer contributions can currently be suspended under the *Finance Act 1986* as one of the authorised methods of reducing a pension fund surplus – see **19.2**.

It had always been the duty of the trustees to check that any contributions due from the employer were properly paid over to the scheme. The auditor's report which must appear in the trustees' annual report previously had to contain a statement of whether or not contributions payable to the scheme during the scheme year had been paid in accordance with the rules and, in the case of defined benefit schemes, with the recommendation of the actuary. Now, where the scheme is required to have in place a *schedule of contributions* (see **8.5** below) or a *payment schedule* (see **8.6** below), the auditor's statement must state whether, in the auditor's opinion, contributions have been paid in accordance with that schedule.

Schemes that are contracted out have always had to satisfy further requirements: in particular, employers with contracted-out money purchase schemes have always had to forward the minimum payments within 14 days of the end of each tax month to the scheme's trustees.

Where employee and employer contributions have not been paid when due, there have been instances where the contributions have been made good by the National Insurance fund – see **23.5**.

The law governing the payment of pension contributions was radically altered by the *Pensions Act 1995* and the main requirements made by that Act, and the associated regulations, regarding employee contributions in general, the schedule of contributions applying to schemes subject to the minimum funding requirement and the payment schedule applying to money purchase schemes are still in place today. Subsequently the *Welfare Reform and Pensions Act 1999* modified the legislation made in the *Pensions Act 1995* on the payment of contributions, as well as introducing a new requirement on employers in respect of any contributions that they have agreed to pass on or make directly to a personal pension or stakeholder pension scheme held by an employee – see **2.7**. Recently, the Pensions Act 2004 has further modified these requirements.

Employee contributions

8.4   The legislation applies special requirements to contributions which are deducted from an employee's earnings by the employer's payroll and then passed over to the trustees of the occupational pension scheme. These requirements relate to:

● the maximum time that the contributions can be held by the employer before they are passed over to the trustees; and

● to the circumstances in which late payment of these contributions should be reported to the Pensions Regulator.

Section 49(8) of the Pensions Act 1995 and reg 16 of the Occupational Pension Schemes (Scheme Administration) Regulations 1996 (SI 1996/1715)

stipulate that contributions deducted from employees' pay must be passed by the employer to the trustees within 19 days, beginning at the end of the calendar month in which the contributions were deductions were made.

Section 49(9)(a) of the *Pensions Act 1995* stipulates that if the employer fails to comply with the requirement to pass over the employees' contributions within 19 days from the end of the calendar month in which they were deducted from their pay, the Pensions Regulator has the power to levy a fine on the employee. This fine can be up to £5,000 if the employer is an individual person and up to £50,000 in other cases (e.g. where the employer is a company).

The reporting requirement is dealt with in *s 49(9)(b)* of the *Pensions Act 1995*, but this has been rewritten by the *Pensions Act 2004*. The amended reporting requirement still falls on the trustees and they have a duty to report to the Pensions Regulator a failure by the employer to pay over contributions deducted from employees' earnings within the 19-day period ending with the calendar month in which the contributions were deducted. But the amended reporting requirement makes the duty to report conditional. If the trustees have 'reasonable cause' to believe that the failure is *likely to be of material significance* in the exercise by the Pensions Regulator of any of its functions, they must, except in circumstances set out in regulations, give notice of the failure to the Pensions Regulator and to the members within a 'reasonable period'.

Under *s 49(10)* of the *Pensions Act 1995*, again as amended by the *Pensions Act 2004*, the Pensions Regulator has the power to fine the trustees if they fail to comply with the revised reporting duty – the fine can be up to £5,000 in the case of an individual trustee and up to £50,000 in the case of a corporate trustee.

The *Pensions Act 2004* requires the Pensions Regulator to issues various codes of practice which will give guidance on the meaning of such phrases as 'reasonable cause', 'likely to be of material significance' and 'reasonable period'.

In practice, since January 2004 when the Pension Regulator's predecessor, Opra, issued its *Update 5*, the reporting requirements placed on the trustees have been eased so that not every infraction of the employer's duty to pay over the contributions in line with the statutory requirements needs to be reported. These reporting requirements as they are to apply under the Pensions Act 2004 are explained at **8.7** below. It is important, however, to bear in mind that these changes in the duty of trustees to report late payments has not changed the existing statutory duty on the employer to pay over contributions by the required date. This not only applies to the duty to pay over contributions deducted from employees' pay within 19 days of the end of the calendar month in which they were deducted. The employer is required also to pay over all contributions which are due to the trustees of an occupational pension by the due date set out in the scheme's schedule of contributions (see **8.5**) or payment schedule (see **8.6**).

Schedule of contributions for defined benefit schemes

8.5   Since 6 April 1997, trustees of schemes that are subject to the minimum funding requirement or MFR (i.e. most defined benefit schemes) have had a duty to prepare and maintain a *schedule of contributions* following the scheme's first MFR valuation. The schedule of contributions is the central mechanism for delivering the MFR and enables trustees to check that contributions are paid into the scheme promptly and at an appropriate rate. It also ensures that non-payment of contributions is quickly identified so that action to enforce payment can be initiated promptly. In September 2005, the MFR is to be replaced by the new scheme funding rules for defined benefit schemes but, although this differs substantially from the MFR, it also requires the adoption of a schedule of contributions. For a discussion of the new scheme funding rules, see **13.9–13.12**.

Under the existing MFR, the schedule should separately identify employer and employee contributions and the due dates for payment. (Employees' AVC payments also have to be shown separately.) Any schedule of contributions that is certified by the scheme actuary on or after 19 March 2002 must also show separately any extra contributions that the employer must pay in order to bring the scheme's funding up to the 90% level. The trustees and the employer should agree the rates of contributions to be entered on the schedule, subject to the requirement that they can be certified by the scheme's actuary to be adequate to meet the MFR. There is some flexibility to revise the schedule during inter-valuation periods provided the revised rates can be certified by the actuary as still satisfying the MFR. In the event of the employer and trustees being unable to agree what the long-term funding rate for the scheme should be, the trustees must set the contributions at a rate adequate to secure that the scheme complies with the MFR.

The first schedule of contributions had to be drawn up following the first MFR actuarial valuation after 5 April 1997. From that point on, the schedule has had to be revised after every subsequent actuarial valuation in order to take into account any change in the funding position of the scheme. The schedule has to be in place within twelve weeks after the actuary has signed the valuation report. Under the transitional arrangements to be put in place for the new scheme funding rules, trustees will have to obtain their first valuation based on a reference date which is not later than the third anniversary of the last effective date of the valuation under the MFR before 23 September 2005. The latest date therefore for a valuation under the new scheme funding rules is 22 September 2008 and the trustees would need to obtain the valuation report and put in place the schedule of contributions within 15 months of this effective date (12 months for EU cross-border schemes).

Under *s 227* of the *Pensions Act 2004* and the *Occupational Pension Schemes (Scheme Funding) Regulations 2005* issued in draft in March 2005, the schedule of contributions prepared under the new rules must show the rates and due dates of all contributions (other than voluntary contributions) payable towards the scheme by or on behalf of the employer and the active members during the period of five years after the date on which the schedule is certified (two years in the case of an EU cross-border scheme). It must show separately:

- the rates and due dates of contributions payable by or on behalf of active members of the scheme;

- the rates and due dates of the contributions payable by or on behalf of the employer; and

- If separate contributions to cover expenses which are likely to fall due for payment by the trustees or managers in the schedule period are made to the scheme, the rates and due dates of those contributions.

Where additional contributions are required in order to give effect to a recovery plan, the rates and dates of those contributions must be shown separately from the rates and dates of contributions otherwise payable. The schedule must be signed by the trustees or manager of the scheme, and make provision for signature by the employer in order to signify his agreement to the matters included in it. The scheme actuary must also certify the schedule.

The draft code of practice on the new scheme funding measures, which was also issued by the Pensions Regulator in March 2005, states that:

- trustees should ensure that the schedule is sufficiently clear to enable them to monitor payment of amounts and their due dates. Where the schedule refers to payments expressed as percentages of pay, it will normally be necessary for the employer and the trustees to have access to the pensionable payroll relevant to each payment in order to determine the monetary amount due. As a result the schedule will not always be the only document needed for monitoring purposes;

- trustees should however seek to avoid the need to refer to other documents when interpreting a schedule. For example, where there are many different rates in force, rather than refer to 'contributions in accordance with the rules', the schedule should provide a reasonable explanation of those rates;

- a schedule should not show any due date for member contributions later than the 19th day of the month following deduction from pay;

- trustees do not need to refer to contributions covering individual augmentations or general benefit improvements in the schedule unless these were planned and due to be paid when the schedule was certified but the trustees' policy on augmentations and the exercise of discretions should be included within the statement of funding principles.

In practice, it often makes sense for the 'due dates' that are to be specified in the schedule of contributions to be set at the 19th day of each month in view of the separate requirements applying to the payment of contributions that have been deducted from employees' pay. At the same time, since this date is the statutory long-stop, it also makes sense for the trustees and employer to agree in practice to process the payments much earlier. For example the due date may be set as the 19th day of the month but a written statement is made to the effect that the employer has agreed to aim to pay the contributions by the seventh day of each month.

Under the requirements relating to schedules of contributions relating to the new scheme funding rules, any outstanding unpaid contributions due according to the schedule are a debt on the employer which has also been the case in relation to schedules of contributions under the MFR But under a new development introduced under *s 228* of the *Pensions Act 2004* the Pensions Regulator has the power to fine the employer if, without reasonable excuse, it fails to make a payment required by the schedule of contributions or to pay a debt of unpaid contributions to the trustees.

The Pensions Regulator under the MFR and the new scheme funding rules has the power to fine any trustee up to £5,000 in the case of an individual or £50,000 in case of a corporate trustee for:

- failing to prepare or revise a schedule of contributions within the specified time; or

- failing to report to the Pensions Regulator and to the membership any non-payment of contributions by the employer in the circumstances set out in the legislation.

Under *s 231* of the *Pensions Act 2004*, the Pensions Regulator, where the trustees fail in their duties to enforce the schedule of contributions, has the power to impose a schedule of contributions on the scheme setting out the contributions to be paid and the dates by which they are to be paid.Some defined benefit schemes are not subject to the MFR or the new scheme funding rules and so their trustees do not have to put in place a schedule of contributions. For example, small schemes with less than 12 members and where all the members are trustees and decisions require either unanimity or the consent of an independent trustee are exempted from the new scheme funding rules and so also from the need to prepare a schedule of contributions.

The new funding rules for defined benefit schemes introduced by the *Pensions Act 2004* involve the trustees of the scheme seeking the agreement of the employer on a number of key matters. These are discussed at **13.11B**.

Payment schedules for defined contribution schemes

8.6   Late arrival of the contributions, whether employee or employer contributions, is especially important with defined contribution (money purchase) occupational schemes since the delay translates directly into lost investment opportunities. Since 6 April 1997, *ss 87–89* of the *Pensions Act 1995* have required the trustees of most defined contribution occupational pension schemes to prepare, maintain and revise a *payment schedule* showing:

- the rates of contributions payable to the scheme by the employer and separately by the active members;

- any amounts payable to the scheme by the employer to cover expenses that are likely to be incurred during the scheme year; and

- the due dates on or before which the contributions and other payments must be made.

The payment schedule must contain separate entries for the rates and the due dates of contributions payable to the scheme by the employer (and if there is more than one employer, rates and due dates for each employer's contributions must be shown) and by the active members of the scheme. (Note that AVCs do not have to be listed.)

However, where an insurance premium is payable, the payment schedule does not have to contain separate entries for identifying the contributions making up that premium that are payable by the employer and the active members. The detailed requirements have been set out in Part IV of the *Occupational Pension Schemes (Scheme Administration) Regulations 1996 (SI 1996/1715)* mentioned at **8.4** above.

If the trustees fail to take all reasonable steps to put in place, maintain and revise a payment schedule, or to carry out these reporting requirements, the Pensions Regulator has the power to impose a fine not exceeding £50,000 on a corporate trustee, and not exceeding £5,000 on an individual trustee.

Any amounts shown on the payment schedule that remain unpaid after the due date, whether payable by the employer or not, will automatically be treated as a debt from the employer to the trustees. The Pensions Regulator has the power under the *Pensions Act 1995* to fine any employer if any amount payable on the employer's own account in accordance with the payment schedule has not been paid by the due date. The fine on the employer is one of up to £50,000 in the case of a corporate employer, and up to £5,000 in the case of an individual.

A number of kinds of defined contribution schemes are exempt from the requirement to operate a payment schedule. They include small self-administered schemes and certain kinds of executive pension plans, provided that in both kinds of scheme all the members are trustees and every member has to agree each decision.

Just as in the case of schedules of contributions, trustees and employers usually agree that the 19th day of each month is the most practicable choice of due date because of the separate requirements applying to the payment of contributions that have been deducted from employees' pay. Because this is the statutory long-stop with no room for error, the trustees and employers will usually arrange to aim to pay the contributions by, say, the 7th day of each month but keep the 19th day of the month as the official due date.

Trustees' duty to report late payment of contributions

8.6A   Trustees of occupational pension schemes are required to report, in certain circumstances, the late payment by the employer of:

- contributions which the employer has deducted from employees earnings (see **8.4**);

- contributions which are payable under the schedule of contributions of a defined benefit occupational pension scheme subject either to the MFR or the new rules on scheme funding (see **8.5**);

- contributions which are payable under the payment schedule of a defined contribution occupational pension scheme (see **8.6**).

In order to carry out these duties, trustees will need to ensure that they have a robust procedure in place for monitoring receipt of contributions. Those carrying out monitoring will usually need access to details of the the relevant pensionable payrolls of all employers participating in the occupational pension scheme.

The trustees need to investigate any apparent employer failure to adhere to legislative requirements to pay contributions deducted from the employee's earnings within 19 days of the calendar month in which the contributions were deducted and any contributions which are not paid in accordance with the schedule of contributions or the payment schedule and this will be so whether or not there is a requirement to report the failure to the Pensions Regulator.

Trustees must report to the Pensions Regulator any late payment of contributions by the employer if they have *reasonable cause* to believe that late or non-payment is likely to be *materially significant* to the Pensions Regulator in the exercise of its functions.

Trustees must have *reasonable cause* to believe that a contribution failure has actually taken place. So, for example, they should satisfy themselves that before making a report they have taken into account any legitimate agreed payments made directly by the employer for scheme purposes, such as to pay pensions; contributions paid directly to a scheme insurer or investment manager and any additional voluntary contributions which have been included with the employer's overall payment.

The Pensions Regulator advises that where the trustees have identified a contribution payment failure, they should normally discuss it with the employer as soon as practicable, with a view to finding out the cause of the failure, taking steps to avoid a recurrence in the future and rectifying any underpayment.

Trustees are likely to need to report contribution failure to the Pensions Regulator where one or more of the following situations apply:

- the employer appears to be involved in the fraudulent evasion of the obligation to pay contributions deducted from employees' earnings;

- contributions remain unpaid 90 calendar days after the due date (unless it is a one-off or infrequent administration error, which is discovered after the 90 days, and which is already corrected when found);

- the trustees become aware that the employer does not have adequate procedures or systems in place to ensure the normal correct and timely payment of contributions and appears not to be taking adequate steps to remedy the situation;

- discussions with the employer reveal there is no early prospect of contribution underpayments being corrected, for example because of the financial circumstances of the employer or for any other reason.

On the other hand, trustees are unlikely to need to report late or non-payment where if the contribution failures stem from administrative lapses which are corrected within reasonable timescales and where reasonable steps are being taken to avoid recurrence;

If the trustees decide that they have *reasonable cause* to believe that a contribution failure has occurred and that it is of *material significance* to the Pensions Regulator, they must report it within a *reasonable period* and the Pensions Regulator advises that a *reasonable period* means no later than five working days from the date they concluded that a report is needed.

Reporting late payment to members

8.6B   The trustees are also required to notify members in certain circumstances where there has been late payment by the employer of contributions. The draft code of practice issued by the Pensions Regulator in March 2005 states that the trustees are to report to members failure to pay over contributions no later than the date when a report is made to the Pensions Regulator.

When Opra, the Pension Regulator's predecessor, issued *Update 5* in January 2004 setting out its relaxation on when it needed to receive failure reports from trustees relating to isolated late payments of contributions where the problem had since been rectified and other 'innocent' failures to comply with the deadline for payment by the employer of contributions, it nevertheless emphasised that the relaxation did not apply to the reporting requirements on trustees in certain circumstances to report late payments to the members. These member reporting requirements have been set by:

- *reg 16A* of the *Occupational Pension Schemes (Scheme Administration) Regulations 1996 (SI 1996/1715)* in relation to contributions deducted from an employee's earnings;

- *reg 23* of the *Occupational Pension Schemes (Minimum Funding Requirement and Actuarial Valuations) Regulations 1996 (SI 1996/1536)* in the case of late payment of contributions listed on a schedule of contributions of a defined benefit scheme subject to the MFR; and

- *regs 20 and 21* of the *Occupational Pension Schemes (Scheme Administration) Regulations 1996 (SI 1996/1715)* in the case of late payment of contributions listed on a payment schedule of a defined contribution scheme.

The common rule for all three kinds of late payment has been that if the contributions have still not been paid 60 days from the date on which they became due, the trustees are required to notify the scheme members about the late payment and to do so within 90 days of that due date.

Update 5 stated:

'From the date of this Update, Opra only expects trustees to report when contributions remain outstanding 90 days or more after their due date.

However, we do expect trustees to comply with the legal requirement to notify scheme members when contributions are paid 60 days, or more, late. They must do this within 90 days of the due date. We regard this disclosure to be important in keeping members informed about the way their scheme is run, and to provide any members who have significant concerns with the opportunity to tell Opra about those concerns.

In practical terms, this means:

- any contributions paid late but received within the 90-day period do not normally have to be reported to Opra;

- trustees must report all contributions still outstanding at the end of the 90-day period to Opra immediately;

- when reporting to Opra

    - trustees should confirm that they have notified members of the late payment of the contributions; and

    - if they receive any contributions after the 90-day period but before they make their report to Opra, this should be noted in the report.'

Draft guidance issued by the Pensions Regulator in June 2005 in relation to reporting late payments due under a defined contribution scheme's payment schedule does not differ fundamentally from the earlier guidance. It states:

'Trustees must report material late payments to the Pensions Regulator and scheme members. Circumstances which are likely to be material and in which trustees should report include:

i.   where there is a late payment involving possible dishonesty or a misuse of assets or contributions. For example, trustees may have concerns that the employer is using the contributions to alleviate cashflow difficulties;

ii.   where there is a failure to pay contributions which carries a criminal penalty. For example, where the employer is knowingly concerned in the fraudulent evasion of the obligation to pay member contributions;

iii.   where contributions remain unpaid 90 after the due date (unless it is a one-off or infrequent administration error, which is discovered after the 90 days, and is corrected when found);

iv.   where the trustees become aware that the employer does not have adequate procedures or systems in place to ensure the normal correct and timely payment of contributions due;

v.   where there is no early prospect of outstanding contributions being paid, for example because of the financial circumstances of the employer or for any other reason.'

Payments to personal pension schemes

8.7   The *Welfare Reform and Pensions Act 1999* introduced a new requirement for the monitoring of employers' payments to personal pension schemes. The requirement came into force on 6 April 2001.

The aim of the new legislation was in part to redress an imbalance in the then regulatory safeguards dealing with the payment of pension contributions that have emerged between:

- those employees who are members of an occupational pension scheme; and

- those employees who are members of a personal pension into which their employer has agreed to make a direct contribution or simply to offer a payroll deduction facility to pass on employee contributions to the personal pension provider on a net-of-tax basis.

The many regulatory requirements to pay contributions on time placed on employers who sponsor occupational pension schemes, whether of the defined benefit or the defined contribution variety, had persuaded many employers who wished to make pension provision for their employees to prefer the use of personal pensions, which were then subject to a much lighter regulatory touch. The imbalance in the regulatory requirements had therefore created a distorting effect which has fed through to employers' choice of pension provision.

Also, from 6 April 2001 stakeholder pension schemes became available. As explained in **2.11** above, stakeholder pensions may be legally established as occupational pension schemes, in which case the rules relating to employee contributions described at **8.4** above and the rules relating to payment schedules used in money purchase occupational pension schemes described at **8.6** above both apply.

However, stakeholder pension schemes may also be legally established as personal pensions. In order for there to be a level playing field between these two types of stakeholder pension schemes, similar legislation to protect the members of personal pension-based stakeholder pension schemes against non-payment, incorrect payment and delayed payment of contributions was needed. The decision was taken to extend the scope of this legislation to all personal pensions.

If the personal pension-based stakeholder pension scheme is set under trust, the trustees will be responsible for implementing the new requirements.

The detail of these requirements relating to a *direct payment arrangement* between an employer and a personal pension scheme provider are set out in **2.7** above.

Time off for trustees

8.8   Since 6 April 1997, the *Employment Rights Act 1996* requires an employer who sponsors an occupational pension scheme to give any employee who serves as a trustee to that scheme paid time off during working hours to perform trustee duties and to undergo relevant training. There has been, however, no mandatory requirement on the employer to provide training although the trustee knowledge and understanding requirements described at **5.2** imply that trustees will need training opportunities. (This requirement for paid time off during working hours was originally contained in the *Pensions Act 1995*.)

There was an error in the original legislation with the result that this right to paid time off work applied to employees who were 'trustees' but not employees who were 'trustee directors'. It is notable that there were reports of this drafting error being exploited. Amendments made by the *Welfare Reform and Pensions Act 1999* ensure that the requirement applies to employees who are directors of a trust company in the same way as they do to employees who are individual trustees.

The amount of time that an employee is permitted to take to perform trustee duties or undergo relevant training, the timing of this paid time off, and any conditions subject to which the time off may be taken will be those which are:

'reasonable in all the circumstances having regard in particular to:

(a)   how much time off is required for the performance of the duties of a trustee of the scheme and the undergoing of relevant training, and how much time off is required for performing the particular duty, or, as the case may be, for undergoing the particular training; and

(b)   the circumstances of the employer's business and the effect of the employee's absence on the running of that business'.

The employee trustees should receive the pay they would normally have received if they were working normally for the time they were engaged in performing trustee duties or relevant training. If payment varies with the amount of work done, the amount payable should be calculated by reference to the average hourly earnings for that work for the employee trustee concerned. The right to be paid an amount under these rules does not affect any right of employees to pay under their contract of employment, but the amount of pay due and the amount of contractual pay due can be mutually offset.

Where a dispute arises, the trustee can present a complaint to an employment tribunal if he or she feels that the employer has refused paid time off unreasonably. The trustee should present the complaint within three months of the refusal.

Before the introduction of this legislation in 1997, the issue of paid time off to carry out trustee duties had been the subject of some tribunal cases, notably the case of *STC Submarine Systems v Piper* where the Employment Appeal Tribunal ruled that the trustee, who was also a trade union branch secretary, had been entitled to paid time off work to attend training on developments in equal treatment in relation to pensions.

Employment protection rights

8.9   The *Pensions Act 1995* introduced some new measures of employment protection for all employee trustees irrespective of how long they have served as employees. These new measures are now contained in the *Employment Rights Act 1996*. The Act provides that:

' … an employee has the right not to be subjected to any detriment by any act, or any deliberate failure to act, by his employer done on the ground that, being a trustee of a trust scheme which relates to his employment, the employee performed (or proposed to perform) any functions as such a trustee.'

The dismissal of an employee will be treated as an unfair dismissal under the *Employment Rights Act 1996* if the reason, or the principal reason, for the employee's dismissal or redundancy is connected to the employee's activities as a trustee.

The employee trustee must normally present a complaint of detriment in employment or unfair dismissal to an employment tribunal within three months of the event.

It should be remembered that it will not automatically follow in all cases that, if an individual is dismissed as an employee, he or she will also cease to be a trustee of the scheme, although in practice this is usually the result. The *Welfare Reform and Pensions Act 1999* ensures that these employee protection measures apply in the same way to employees who are directors of a trust company as they do to employees who are individual trustees.

Protection as a whistle-blower

8.10   *Section 70* of the *Pensions Act 2004* introduces new 'whistle-blowing' duties which will fall on a wider range of people than were affected by the similar measures contained in the *Pensions Act 1995*. The duty imposed by *s 70* falls on:

- a trustee or manager of an occupational or personal pension scheme;

- a person who is *'otherwise involved in the administration of such a scheme'*;

- the employer in relation to an occupational pension scheme;

- a professional adviser in relation to such a scheme;

- a person who is otherwise involved in advising the trustees or managers of an occupational or personal pension scheme in relation to the scheme.

The nature of the whistle-blowing duty is described at **10.4** but here we touch on the position of an employee who blows the whistle to the Pensions Regulator.

The *Pensions Act 2004* gives a certain measure of protection to whistle-blowers who have other duties which may be contravened by reporting breaches of the law. The code of practice acknowledges the potential impact of a report on the relationship between those making the report and either their client, or, in the case of employees, their employer. The code nevertheless states:

'The Employment Rights Act 1996 (ERA) provides protection for employees making a whistleblowing disclosure to the Pensions Regulator. Consequently, where individuals employed by firms having a duty to report disagree with a decision not to report to the Pensions Regulator, they may have protection under the ERA if they make an individual report in good faith. The Pensions Regulator expects such individual reports to be rare and confined to the most serious cases.

The Pensions Regulator will, if requested, seek to protect the identity of reporters. However, this cannot be guaranteed. Even if the Pensions Regulator does not explicitly reveal the name of the reporter, their identity may become apparent in the course of an investigation.

In all cases, the Pensions Regulator expects reporters to act conscientiously and honestly, and to take account of expert or professional advice where appropriate.'

Any failure to report without 'reasonable excuse' is a civil offence. In this respect, the Pensions Regulator considers that a reporter has a reasonable excuse if:

- based on the information that the person could reasonably be expected to have had at the time, he or she could not have identified the breach; or

- a breach was identified but not reported, because at that time the reporter could reasonably have regarded it as not materially significant to the Pensions Regulator.

In judging what was reasonable, the Pensions Regulator will take the circumstances of the breach and the position of the reporter into account. It will consider if the appropriate procedures were in place to allow the report to be made. Failure to put procedures in place to allow reporting as soon as reasonably practicable will not be a reasonable excuse for a late or absent report.

Provision of information

8.11   Regulations made under the *Pensions Act 1995* require the employer to provide trustees with information relevant to a defined benefit scheme's funding position (which in turn the trustees must provide to the scheme actuary whom they have appointed). The *Occupational Pension Schemes (Scheme Administration) Regulations 1996 (SI 1996/1715)* require the employer (and any actuary or auditor acting for the employer) to disclose within one month of its occurrence any event which there is reasonable cause to believe will be of material significance in the exercise by the trustees or professional advisers of any of their functions.

In addition, these Regulations require the employer to disclose on request to the trustees such information as is reasonably required for the performance of their duties or those of the professional advisers. In this way, the onus is placed on the trustees to establish a suitable arrangement with the employer that will ensure that they have access to relevant information and are kept informed as changes take place and events occur.

Under employment law, the House of Lords has ruled in the case of *Scally v Southern Health and Social Services Board* that the implied duty of mutual trust and confidence in the employment relationship means that an employer must take reasonable steps to bring the existence of a valuable right (such as that relating to an occupational pension scheme) to the attention of the employee. However, in giving this judgment Lord Bridge set conditions limiting the extent of this duty on the employer. The following conditions must apply:

- the terms of the contract of employment have not been negotiated with the individual employee but result from negotiation with a representative body or are otherwise incorporated by reference;

- a particular term of the contract makes available to the employee a valuable right contingent upon action being taken by the employee;

- the employee cannot, in all the circumstances, reasonably be expected to be aware of the term unless it is drawn to his or her attention.

This means that the employer's duty to provide information does not abrogate pension scheme members of all responsibility for any decision they may take regarding options they are free to take under the scheme. If the employee has access to accurate and complete information describing the scheme, the employer is entitled to assume that the employee will exercise any option granted under the scheme knowing the implications of doing so. This point has been made by Mr Justice Hart in the case of *University of Nottingham v Eyett* where he held that the employer had not breached the implied duty of mutual trust and confidence. In that case, the employer had simply not taken action positively to alert the employee that by delaying his voluntary early retirement by one month, his pension would be a greater amount because of the way final pensionable earnings were calculated under the scheme rules.

The same general issue came before the Court of Appeal in April 2000 in the case of *Outram v Academy Plastics*. It was suggested in this case that an appellant alleging that an employer had failed to carry out any duty to give advice on pensions would generally often need to show that such a duty to do so arose out of the contract of employment, rather than more generally looking for a test for liability for causing economic loss to another person. Lord Justice Chadwick, one of the appeal judges hearing this case, gave credence to the view that:

> 'the duties owed by an employer, or former employer, in relation to its employees were in a state of development, particularly in the field of economic loss suffered by an employee as a result of action or omission by the employer ancillary to the performance of the contract of employment itself.'

However, this aspect of the case could not be tried by the Court of Appeal because the appellant's barrister had expressly rejected the suggestion that the claim could be put on a contractual basis.

Employer provides the administration services

8.12   The trustees are responsible and will be held accountable for the proper running of their occupational pension scheme but generally the task of the day-to-day administration of the scheme is delegated by the trustees to a pensions administration department – see **CHAPTER 11**. However, in the *Occupational Pension Schemes (Scheme Administration) Regulations 1996 (SI 1996/1715)*, it is recognised that if the trustees are to be held responsible for ensuring proper administration, then the trustees must be perfectly clear about the terms on which administrative services are provided. Accordingly, the Regulations include a requirement that where it is the employer who makes provision for the administration of the scheme, it must disclose to the trustees the terms on which these services are provided. In particular, this should mean that the trustees will be clear about whether the administrators owe a duty of confidentiality primarily to the employer or to them as trustees.

Checklist 8

- The employer is the settlor of the trust and so can devise a trust deed and rules which will serve its purpose of providing pensions that fit in with its overall remuneration policy.

- The trust deed and rules will give the employer specific powers to amend the scheme, but usually the trustees will have to agree to the changes and no retrospective worsening of members' accrued rights is permitted under the *Pensions Act 1995* as substituted by the *Pensions Act 2004* – unless either all members give their consent or the benefits before and after the change are actuarially equivalent.

- In certain cases the employer must exercise powers given to it by the trust deed and rules in line with fiduciary principles.

- Under employment law, the employer must exercise powers subject to an implied duty of good faith.

- If an employer, without reasonable excuse, fails to pay over contributions that had been deducted from employees' earnings within the prescribed time limit, the employer may be liable to a fine imposed by the Pensions Regulator.

- The trustees are responsible for enforcing a schedule of contributions (schemes subject to the minimum funding requirement or the new scheme funding rules) or payment schedule (defined contribution schemes) and for ensuring that the employer makes the correct contributions or payments to the scheme within the specified time limits. Similar duties now apply when an employer makes payments to a personal or stakeholder pension scheme.

- Any employee trustee must be given paid time off work to attend to trustee duties.

- An employee trustee is given special employment rights protection against unjust treatment and unfair dismissal by the employer.

- An employee trustee or employee involved in administration of the pensions scheme who blows the whistle on the employer cannot be sued by the employer for breach of confidence.

- The employer must inform the trustees whenever material events take place and must disclose on request to the trustees information that they reasonably require.

- If the employer provides the pension administration services, the employer must disclose to the trustees the terms on which the services are provided.

Chapter 9

Trustees and the pension fund members

Duty to act fairly between differing groups

9.1   Under trust law, it has always been held that trustees should act in the best interest of all the scheme's beneficiaries and strike a fair balance between the different classes of beneficiary. This is also embodied in social security law where, for example, early leavers who preserve their pensions in the scheme are protected against unfair curtailment of benefit. Naturally, trustees must observe the general law, such as the *Race Relations Act 1975* and the *Disability Discrimination Act 1995*.

The Pensions Regulator's predecessor, Opra, in its *Guide for Pension Scheme Trustees* listed the various classes of beneficiary of an occupational pension scheme as possibly including all the following:

- active members (current employees);

- pensioner members;

- deferred pensioners;

- prospective members;

- widows and widowers of members;

- dependants and future dependants of members; and

- the employer.

Opra commented that the trustees must consider the interests of all these classes of beneficiary, striking a balance so that an appropriate weight is given to the interests of each class, depending on the issue being considered. Opra then made an important point – giving due consideration to each class 'does not necessarily mean treating all classes equally'.

The Vice Chancellor, Sir Richard Scott, senior judge in the Chancery Division, the division of the High Court that hears pensions law, discussed the issue of whether trustees could favour one class of beneficiaries over another in a judgment where he overturned an earlier Determination of the Pensions Ombudsman. The Pensions Ombudsman had found that the trustees of a pension scheme had committed maladministration because they breached their duty to act impartially between the different classes of beneficiaries when considering how to use a pension fund surplus.

In particular, in his Determination, the Pensions Ombudsman had said:

'The trustees' duty to act impartially between the different beneficiaries does not equate with a duty to exercise their discretion on all occasions in such a way to produce equal benefits of equal value to all beneficiaries. Nor does it even require that all beneficiaries receive some benefit from an exercise of a discretion. It is permissible to exercise a discretion in such a manner as to omit particular beneficiaries, or a class thereof. But the discretion to exclude those beneficiaries must not be the result of undue partiality towards the interests of the preferred beneficiaries.'

In the appeal in the case of *Edge v Pensions Ombudsman* heard in December 1997, the Vice Chancellor said that he agreed with all of the above bar the final sentence and in particular the phrase 'undue partiality'. The Vice Chancellor said:

'The trustees are entitled to be partial. They are entitled to exclude some beneficiaries from particular benefits and to prefer others. If what is meant by 'undue partiality' is that trustees have taken into account irrelevant or improper or irrational factors, their exercise of discretion may be flawed. But it is not flawed simply because someone else, whether or not a judge, regards their partiality as 'undue'. It is the trustees' discretion that is to be exercised. Except in a case in which the discretion has been surrendered to the court, it is not for a judge to exercise the discretion. The judge may disagree with the manner in which the trustees have exercised their discretion but, unless they can be seen to have taken into account irrelevant, improper or irrational factors, or unless their decision can be said to be one that no reasonable body of trustees properly directing themselves could have reached, the judge cannot interfere. In particular he cannot interfere simply on the ground that the partiality shown to the preferred beneficiaries was in his opinion undue.'

This is a very robust defence of the right of trustees to exercise the discretionary powers given to them by the trust deed and rules as they see fit. There is the exception that the trustees must not take into account 'irrelevant, improper or irrational factors' etc – the *Wednesbury principles* discussed at **5.4** above – but otherwise the Vice Chancellor has upheld the principle that the courts should not reverse the decision of properly appointed trustees who are carrying out their duties and exercising their powers in accordance with their trust deed and rules. There is, however, a clear tension between the view of the Pensions Ombudsman and the Vice Chancellor over exactly what 'striking a fair balance between the various classes of beneficiaries' actually means.

In July 1999, the Court of Appeal heard the Pensions Ombudsman's appeal against the Vice Chancellor's High Court judgment in *Edge v Pensions Ombudsman*. The Pensions Ombudsman argued that the Vice Chancellor was wrong to hold that, in the exercise of their discretionary power to amend the rules, the trustees were not subject to a duty to act impartially as between individual classes of beneficiaries. He also argued that it was wrong to hold that the trustees were themselves the judges of whether their exercise of the power was fair between included and excluded beneficiaries.

The Court of Appeal held that the beneficiaries concerned had no right to insist on an increase in benefits as a means of reducing the scheme surplus but in the words of Lord Justice Chadwick: 'Their right was to have the matter properly considered'. He added that: 'the trustees must, in deciding whether or not to increase benefits (and, if so, which benefits), act in a way which appears to them fair and equitable in all the circumstances.'

In coming to such a fair and equitable decision the trustees would need to consider the circumstances in which the surplus had arisen, but that did not mean that they would be bound to take any particular course as a result of that consideration. The main purpose of the scheme was to provide retirement and other benefits for employees of the participating employers, and the trustees 'must consider the effect that any course which they are minded to take will have on the financial ability of the employers to make the contributions which that course will entail'.

In the end the Court of Appeal affirmed the *Wednesbury Principles* explained at **5.4** above as being appropriate guidance for trustees in exercising discretionary powers. Lord Justice Chadwick held that if the trustees follow those principles 'they cannot be criticised if they reach a decision which appears to prefer the claims of one interest – whether that of the employers, current employees or pensioners – over others. The preference will be the result of a proper exercise of the discretionary power.'

The *Wednesbury Principles* emphasise that the trustees' decision must not be perverse. It must be a decision at which a reasonable body of trustees could arrive. As an absurd example, suppose the trustees decided under a discretionary power that no pension increases would be payable to pensioners with red hair. This would be unreasonable. It could also be attacked because the trustees were taking into account irrelevant matters. It is so unreasonable that it might be described as being done in bad faith. Other examples might occur to readers. Suppose that the trust deed and rules gave the trustees the discretionary power to award a dependant's pension to any financial dependant of an employee and member of the scheme who had died. What if the trustees were prepared to do so for an opposite-sex partner but not for a same-sex partner where in both cases there was incontrovertible evidence of financial dependency? The same arguments apply as in the case with denying pension increases to those with red hair. (In the latter case, in addition to being open to challenge under the *Wednesbury Principles*, the discrimination could well be challenged in the courts under the separate head of failing to comply with *reg 9A* of the *Employment Equality (Sexual Orientation) (Amendment) Regulations 2003 (SI 2003/2827)* – see **9.5** below. Here statutory law has moved, as a result of European law, to reinforce a set of principles adopted in the interpretation of trust law.)

Equal treatment

9.2   European law has been the driving force in achieving equal treatment for men and women in the matter of:

- access to occupational pension schemes; and
- the contributions and benefit provisions of occupational pension schemes.

It should be remembered that judgments of the European Court of Justice (ECJ) in its interpretation of the European Treaty are the supreme authority under UK law. The key to equal treatment and pensions questions lies in a series of judgments of the ECJ made over the years in connection with its interpretation of what was formerly Article 119 of the EEC Treaty, the Equal Pay Article. (Articles 117 to 120 of the EEC Treaty have now been replaced by Articles 136 EC to 143 EC and Article 119 has now become Article 141 EC). The ECJ has ruled that pension benefits count as pay for all purposes of Article 141 EC. If pensions are pay, then pension rights have to respect the principle of equal treatment for men and women. In one of the judgments (*Coloroll Pension Trustees v Russell*) given in 1994, the ECJ made two important rulings of importance to trustees.

> 'The direct effect of Article 119 of the EEC Treaty may be relied on by both employees and their dependants against the trustees of an occupational pension scheme who are bound, in the exercise of their powers and performance of their obligations as laid down in the trust deed, to observe the principle of equal treatment.'

> 'In so far as national law prohibits employers and trustees from acting beyond the scope of their respective powers or in disregard of the provisions of the trust deed, they are bound to use all the means available under domestic law, such as recourse to the national courts, in order to eliminate all discrimination in the matter of pay.'

It is quite clear therefore that trustees have a direct responsibility under the law to ensure that their pension scheme observes the principle of equal treatment. The *Pensions Act 1995* sets out an equal treatment rule that states in effect that where a member is employed to perform work of equal value to that performed by a member of the other sex, any terms treating the member less favourably will be treated as modified to remove the inequality. In a legal defence it will be for the trustees (rather than the employer) to prove to the court that any difference in treatment of men and women is due to a material factor which is not sex-related.

Trustees might not have been able to make alterations to the trust deed and rules because they did not have the power to do so, or if the procedure was unduly complex, protracted or involved gaining consents which could not be obtained or could only be obtained with great difficulty. In this case they have been helped by the equal treatment provisions contained in the *Pensions Act 1995* that give trustees the ability to modify the trust deed and rules by simple resolution to ensure that the scheme conforms with the equal treatment rule set out in the Act.

Interpretation and exceptions

9.3   The ECJ has given certain derogations to trustees regarding equal treatment. The law can become complex but the following summary will serve as a basic pointer:

- Periods of pensionable service before 17 May 1990 (i.e. the date of the *Barber* judgment by the ECJ) do not have to give rise to equal benefits and any attempt to equalise benefits retrospectively that involves a worsening of benefits could conflict with UK trust law.

- Periods of pensionable service on or after 17 May 1990 but before the scheme rules were changed to eliminate discrimination between men and women must give rise to equal benefits by granting to the dis-advantaged sex the same advantages as those enjoyed by the advantaged sex.

- Equal treatment for periods of pensionable service after the date the scheme rules were changed can generally be achieved by reducing the advantages which the advantaged sex used to enjoy.

- In defined benefit schemes there is no requirement that unisex actuarial factors must be used, so that commutation rates for retirement lump sums, for example, do not have to be equal.

- In all schemes, the amount of any employee contributions must be on a sex-equal basis. In defined benefit schemes, it is the pension that has to be on a sex-equal basis and so any difference in the employer's funding level due to different actuarial factors for men and women is permitted. It is not entirely clear what the requirement is for defined contribution (money purchase) schemes but some lawyers hold that, provided both employee and employer contributions are calculated on a sex-equal basis, it does not matter that non-unisex annuity rates will produce unequal pension amounts. (Note that the UK contracting-out legislation insists that any protected rights fund (see **1.8**) when used to secure an annuity must be used to do so using unisex annuity rates.)

- Bridging pensions payable to pensioners to compensate for the current inequality in state pension ages may be payable to men and not women between the ages of 60 and 65. But as the state pension age for women begins to rise in 2010, bridging pensions, if paid to men over 60, will also have to be paid to women over 60 until they reach state pension age.

- The Pensions Ombudsman in January 2000 issued a decision in which he held that guaranteed minimum pensions (GMPs) built up from 17 May 1990 until 5 April 1997 under the contracting-out legislation had to be equalised as a separate element of a member's pension. However, the High Court quashed his direction but only on the argument that the Ombudsman did not have jurisdiction to determine the question. The judge did not refer the question to the ECJ for a preliminary ruling.

- Where a transfer value has been based on unequal benefits for pensionable service on or after 17 May 1990 and is lower than if it had been based on equal benefits, the receiving scheme must increase the benefits to the level that could have been bought by the higher transfer value.

- The exclusion from the pension scheme of part-time employees, or any other category of employees, has constituted indirect discrimination if there is no objective justification for the exclusion unrelated to the sex of the members and if the exclusion affects a far greater number of one sex than the other. However, since 1 July 2000, the *Part-time Workers (Prevention of Less Favourable Treatment) Regulations 2000 (SI 2000/1551)* ensures that, unless there is an objective justification, it has become unlawful in any case to discriminate in pension terms and conditions against part-time employees irrespective of sex discrimination issues.

- National rules relating to time limits for bringing actions under national law may be relied on against employees who assert their right to join an occupational pension scheme, provided that they are not less favourable for that type of legal action than for similar actions of a domestic nature, and that they do not render the exercise of rights conferred by Community law impossible in practice. In May 2000, the ECJ in the case of *Preston v Wolverhampton Healthcare* upheld the UK time limit that prevented a claim being valid if it was made more than six months after the employee had left the employment concerned. However, it rejected the UK legislation that limited to no more than two years any backdating of scheme membership in restitution for unlawful denial of scheme access. The House of Lords later decided that in such cases membership could be backdated to the date the employee was first unlawfully excluded from membership – although this could not be earlier than 8 April 1976, the date of the judgment in *Defrenne v Sabena* when the ECJ first demonstrated that Article 119 EEC (now Article 141 EC) could be relied upon in legal claims.

Women on maternity leave

9.4   The legislation provides for special treatment of women members who are taking maternity leave. *Schedule 5* to the *Social Security Act 1989* provides that any period of *paid* maternity leave must be pensionable. Paid maternity leave will involve receipt of either statutory maternity pay or contractual maternity pay. During periods of *paid* maternity leave the member:

- must continue to accrue pensionable service;

- must still be covered by death-in-service benefits;

- need only pay any employee contributions calculated on the actual maternity pay she is receiving; and

- must have any benefits that fall to be calculated based on the pensionable earnings she would have received if she had been working normally.

In the case of a member of a defined contribution (money purchase) scheme during any period of *paid* maternity leave, any contribution the employee is required to make is calculated on the actual maternity pay she is receiving, while the employer makes its contributions based on the pay she would have received if she had been working normally. But this will result in a shortfall and so the employee will not receive the same pension benefits as if she had been working normally. Some lawyers believe that the employer should also pay during any period of *paid* maternity leave a top-up payment equal to the difference between the employee's actual contributions and the contributions she would have paid if she had been working normally.

Any member taking her minimum 26 weeks' 'ordinary maternity leave' must continue to accrue pension rights even if, unusually, her period of employment has been so short that she does not qualify for statutory maternity pay. Note that the *Employment Act 2002*, in extending the statutory maternity pay period from 18 to 26 weeks, also equalised the duration of the statutory maternity pay period and the ordinary maternity leave period.

A period of *unpaid* maternity leave that falls after the period of ordinary maternity leave or any period of paid maternity leave does not have to be pensionable, but the period of pensionable service before and after this period of unpaid maternity leave must be treated as continuous. The rules of the scheme may specify that the period is pensionable or that the employee is able to make additional contributions to make this period pensionable. In some schemes, periods of unpaid maternity leave will become pensionable automatically, provided the member returns to work for a minimum period.

Extension to paternity and adoption leave

9.5   It should be noted that *Sch 5* to the *Social Security Act 1989* introduced legislation not only to prevent 'unfair maternity provisions' but also 'unfair family leave provisions', and that these existing provisions have force in conjunction with the paternity, adoption and maternity leave provisions introduced by the *Employment Act 2002* and the secondary legislation introduced under that Act. *Section 265* of the *Pensions Act 2004* amends *Sch 5* to the *1989 Act* to provide that employer pension contributions during periods of paid paternity leave and paid adoption leave should be made as if the scheme member was working normally. Statutory paternity pay is payable for two weeks and statutory adoption pay is payable for 26 weeks.

Other forms of discrimination

9.6   Under the provision of *Race Relations Act 1975* it would clearly be unlawful to deny access to pension schemes or provide inferior pension benefits on the ground of race or ethnicity. The pensions aspects of discrimination on other grounds are not always so clear. There are at present a number of developments at a European and UK level to prevent unlawful discrimination against particular groups of people in society, other than in the areas of sex discrimination and discrimination against part-time employees which have been discussed immediately above.

Disability discrimination

9.7 The *Disability Discrimination Act 1995 (Pensions) Regulations 2003 (SI 2003/2770)* came into effect on 1 October 2004 and were drawn up by the Government to implement in UK domestic law the provisions prohibiting indirect or direct discrimination against disabled employees without objective justification as set out in the European Council Directive 2000/78/EC. They have amended the *Disability Discrimination Act 1995* by repealing *s 17* of that Act which had inserted a non-discrimination rule into every occupational pension scheme. Instead these 2003 Regulations have deemed that a new non-discrimination rule is included in the governing documentation of every occupational pension scheme. This new non-discrimination rule makes the following requirements:

(a)   The trustees of the scheme must refrain from discriminating against a relevant disabled person in carrying out any of their functions in relation to the scheme and this includes in particular their functions relating to the admission of members to the scheme and the treatment of members of the scheme.

(b)   The trustees must not subject a relevant disabled person to harassment in relation to the scheme and ensure that the other provisions of the scheme are to have effect subject to the non-discrimination rule.

It is unlawful for the trustees of an occupational pension scheme to discriminate against a relevant disabled person contrary to requirement (a) of the non-discrimination rule or to subject a relevant disabled person to harassment contrary to requirement (b) of the non-discrimination rule.

The non-discrimination rule, however, does not apply in relation to pension rights accrued, or benefits payable, in respect of periods of service prior to 1 October 2004 but it does apply to communications with members or prospective members of the scheme in relation to such rights or benefits.

The legislation gives trustees of an occupational pension scheme the power to make the necessary alterations to their scheme's trust deed and rules so that it conforms with the non-discrimination rule by resolution if they do not otherwise have power to do so, or if the procedure for doing so is liable to be unduly complex or protracted, or involves the obtaining of consents which cannot be obtained, or can only be obtained with undue delay or difficulty.

It also places a duty on the trustees to make reasonable adjustments in relation to provisions, criteria or practices (including scheme rules) applied by them where these place a relevant disabled person at a substantial disadvantage in comparison with persons who are not disabled.

Age discrimination

9.8   European Council Directive 2000/78/EC states as general policy that any direct or indirect discrimination in employment based on age should be prohibited throughout the Community and sets 2 December 2006 as the latest date for implementation. Nevertheless, it allows occupational pension schemes to fix ages for admission or entitlement to retirement or invalidity benefits (including the fixing under those schemes of different ages for employees or groups or categories of employees, and the use of age criteria in actuarial calculations) without that amounting to discrimination on the grounds of age, provided this does not result in discrimination on the grounds of sex.

Questions that may be relevant to many schemes, however, include for example whether a defined contribution scheme that has a contribution structure that means that higher employer contributions are paid to older employees than to younger employees would fall foul of the age discrimination provisions, or whether it would come under the exceptions noted above.

The key issue has been whether the future legislation would remove the existing ability of an employer to dismiss an employee who has reached normal retiring age without that employee having recourse to making a claim for unfair dismissal to an employment tribunal. Some commentators argued that the current situation where employees lose the right to take a complaint for unfair dismissal to an employment tribunal once they have reached their normal retiring age is incompatible with the requirements of the Directive. In December 2004 the Government announced that legislation, which will come into force in the autumn of 2006, will provide for a national default retirement age of 65 and a right for employees to request working beyond the set retirement age. The decision to have a national default retirement age will be reviewed after five years.

In coming to this decision, the Minister noted that the earlier consultation process had indicated that any legislation limiting the options open to employers to individually justified retirement ages only could risk adverse consequences for occupational pension schemes at the time the legislation was introduced. She feared that in such circumstances some employers would instead reduce or remove benefits that they offered to employees to offset the increase in costs.

Currently employers can set the age at which their employees retire without any need to justify their choice. In come cases, employees may have to retire at age 60 or even younger, whether or not they wish to continue working. From the autumn 2006 implementation date, employers will only be able to set their own retirement age for all or some of their workforce below age 65 where they can objectively justify this. Such a decision by the employer will be subject to challenge and to succeed in implementing a retirement age below 65 the employer will have to show that it was appropriate and necessary to do so.

This default retirement age at 65 is not to be taken as a compulsory retirement age. The default age will be accompanied by a right for employees who want to continue to work beyond the default age or their employer's own justified retirement age to have their request considered seriously by their employer. This right will follow the model of the right to request flexible working for parents with young children. The Minister said:

> 'This policy will ensure that employers listen to employees who want to keep working and think about whether they can agree. In doing so, it will help promote a culture change including on workforce planning and the design of employee benefits, and move towards a position where fixed retirement ages are relied on only where they can be objectively justified by the employer.'

This decision on retirement age has no direct implications for occupational or state pension arrangements. The Government has emphasised that it has no plans to change the state pension age once it has been equalised for men and women at 65, and occupational pension schemes will still be able to set normal retirement ages when this is needed.

In 2011 the Government will review whether a policy of retaining a default retirement remains appropriate. The review will take into account the relevant data on trends in life expectancy, the number of individuals working beyond 65 and the impact of the regulations on business, including the evolution of business practice with respect to the degree of reliance on retirement ages for workforce planning. If at the point of the review the evidence suggested that the UK no longer needed the default retirement age at 65, it would be abolished.

Fixed-term workers

9.9   European Council Directive 1999/70/EC applies the principle of non-discrimination to those in fixed-term employment through the European Union. The UK Government introduced measures in the *Employment Act 2000* and the *Fixed-term Employees (Prevention of Less Favourable Treatment) Regulations 2002 (SI 2002/2034)* to prevent discrimination against such employees. The regulations require employers to offer fixed-term employees access to occupational pension schemes on the same basis as offered to permanent employees unless different treatment can be objectively justified. However, the regulations also make it clear that a difference in the pension provision offered to fixed-term employees and to permanent employees can be objectively justified if the terms of a fixed-term employee's contract of employment, taken as a whole, are at least as favourable as the terms of the comparable permanent employee's contract.

Guidance issued by the Department of Trade and Industry at the time the regulations were laid before Parliament explained that where a fixed-term contract was for a period less than the vesting period applied by the rules of an occupational pension schemes, any move to allow the fixed-term employee access to the scheme might lead to a disproportionate cost with no benefit to the employee. Nevertheless, it should be noted in this context that the December 2002 Green Paper and accompanying technical paper explored proposals for the immediate vesting of occupational pension scheme rights. The implications of such a change would be the same for those employees on short fixed-term contracts as for employees on permanent contracts who nevertheless leave their employer after a short period.

Sexual orientation

9.10   European Council Directive 2000/78/EC states as general policy in relation to employment that any direct or indirect discrimination based on sexual orientation should be prohibited throughout the Community and set 2 December 2003 as the latest date for implementation. The Directive permits the scheme rules to restrict survivors' benefits to the legal widows and widowers because the Directive is expressed to be 'without prejudice to national laws on marital status and the benefits dependent thereon'. In the UK, however, from 5 December 2005 the *Civil Partnership Act 2004* will permit same-sex couples to register their partnership and as a result be treated under the law in the same way as a married opposite sex couple. Scheme rules which currently restrict survivor's benefits to the surviving widow or widower of a marriage will also then need to provide the survivor's benefit to the surviving partner of a civil partnership. *Section 55* of the *Civil Partnership Act 2004* confers a power on the Government to amend various kinds of legislation relating to pensions for the purpose of providing pensions for surviving civil partners or dependants of deceased civil partners. The power will be used to require contracted-out defined benefit pension schemes to take account of periods of pensionable service from April 1988. Contracted-out defined contribution schemes would be required to provide survivor benefits from the protected rights accrued from April 1988, if the member is in a civil partnership at the point of retirement.

On 1 December 2003 the *Employment Equality (Sexual Orientation) (Amendment) Regulations 2003 (SI 2003/2827)* came into force. These insert a new *reg 9A* into the *Employment Equality (Sexual Orientation) Regulations 2003 (SI 2003/1661)* which makes it unlawful, except in relation to rights accrued or benefits payable in respect of periods of service prior to 1 December 2003, for the trustees of an occupational pension scheme to discriminate on the ground of sexual orientation against a member or prospective member of the scheme. It is unlawful therefore for trustees to discriminate on the grounds of sexual orientation in any matter relating to the admission of members to the scheme and to the treatment of members of the scheme. *Regulation 9A* also makes it unlawful for the trustees to subject to harassment a member or prospective member of the occupational pension scheme.

A non-discrimination rule is deemed to be included in the governing documentation of every occupational pension scheme so that every occupational pension scheme is treated as including the requirement that the trustees or managers of the scheme refrain from doing any act which is unlawful by virtue of *reg 9A*.

As with the legislation governing disability discrimination, this legislation gives trustees of an occupational pension scheme the power to make the necessary alterations to their scheme's trust deed and rules so that it conforms with the non-discrimination rule by resolution if they do not otherwise have power to do so, or if the procedure for doing so is liable to be unduly complex or protracted, or involves the obtaining of consents which cannot be obtained, or can only be obtained with undue delay or difficulty.

Religion or belief

9.11   Also as a result of the European Council Directive 2000/78/EC, the *Employment Equality (Religion or Belief) (Amendment) Regulations 2003 (SI 2003/828)* came into force on 2 December 2003. These make changes to the *Employment Equality (Religion or Belief) Regulations 2003 (SI 2003/1660)* that are comparable to the changes made in respect of the anti-discrimination measures on the ground of sexual orientation described immediately above.

Early retirement programmes

9.12   As a result of a downsizing operation, the employer may propose that especially attractive early retirement terms are offered to older employees. Trustees should seek actuarial costings of the operation and ask whether a cash injection from the employer is necessary to finance the extra cost – which can be quite considerable. It may be that the early retirement programme is offered to all employees over a certain age. Or it may be that the employer's consent will also be needed and certain employees with vital skills will not be offered the favourable early retirement option. Trustees should ensure that they are being fair among members.

It is not to say that the occupational pension scheme should not be involved in financing an early retirement programme. Perhaps a surplus is available and the trustees reason that favourable early retirement terms on a temporary basis are as reasonable as an employer contribution holiday, although such surplus and contribution holidays are rarer now than in earlier times. If the early retirement programme *and* an employer contribution holiday is proposed, trustees should consider whether the interests of other classes of beneficiaries (younger members, early leavers and pensioners) are being sacrificed. In cases of redundancies, the trust deed and rules may often specify that the employer must bear the cost of providing unreduced or enhanced early retirement pensions. As ever, the key in deciding what policy the trustees should adopt is to see what the trust deed and rules say.

Augmentation of benefits to senior executives

9.13   It is boardroom practice very often to offer an *augmented* (i e increased) pension to a senior director who joined the company and contributed greatly to steering it through difficult times. The employer may offer the maximum approvable pension to this executive. The trust deed and rules should be checked to see if there is a power to augment benefits, and, if so, whether the extra cost, as determined by the scheme actuary, of providing the enhanced benefits should be met by the employer making a special contribution. At the end of the day, the trustees should not seek to define the employer's remuneration policy. Conversely, the trustees do owe a duty to strike a balance between the interests of the different classes of beneficiary.

Treatment on bulk transfers

9.14   Trustees of the main occupational pension scheme must be alert to the situation of the employer who wishes to transfer members of, for example, a separate senior executive scheme into the main scheme. Such schemes will have few members and are therefore subject to wild fluctuations in their funding level. The executive scheme could be underfunded, and a top-up payment may be due from the employer. If, as part of some harmonisation exercise, these members are to be transferred into the main pension scheme but in a separate section which provides superior benefits, trustees must take independent actuarial advice to ensure that a fair bulk transfer payment is made to cover the new liability.

Not to do so could unfairly damage the interests of existing beneficiaries and be a breach of trust. The employer might point to a current scheme surplus and argue that it should be used to cover the new liability. Again, the trustees must question whether this strikes a fair balance between the different groups of beneficiaries. It may be that the trustees feel the balance is fair and that no other group will suffer as a result: for example, the surplus is also sufficient to pay the usual discretionary increases on pensions-in-payment over the foreseeable future (although this is much less likely to be the case now than in the closing decades of the last century). In any case, it would still be expected that the bulk transfer payment would be sufficient to cover the past service liabilities of the transferring employees.

Similar situations can arise as a result of a merger or takeover – see **19.5**.

Trustees and active members

New employees

9.15   Trustees should be concerned that newly recruited employees who are eligible to join the occupational pension scheme are encouraged to do so.

To this end, effective communications have been important and are considered below. Many schemes have also decided to abandon lengthy waiting periods or minimum age requirements in their eligibility criteria to encourage membership.

Many schemes also have adopted the process of *automatic membership*: new employees are automatically entered into the scheme unless they positively decide to opt out.

On the other hand, the widespread perception of a 'pensions crisis' that became apparent during 2002 may mean that there is less need to sell the idea of membership of a good scheme. Ironically, the same pension crisis has caused many defined benefit occupational pension schemes to close to new entrants. In this situation new employees may be offered membership of a defined contribution occupational scheme or contract- based pension scheme such as group personal pension arrangement. Where contract-based provision is offered the developments regarding promotional material given at **2.2** are relevant.

Pensionable earnings cap

9.16   Since 1989 trustees have been advised to ensure that the employer and personnel staff involved in recruiting senior staff are aware that all new employees are caught by the pensionable earnings cap. The problem has been the employer's, not the trustees', since an approved scheme is prevented from providing benefits on earnings over the cash ceiling set by the cap. (Nevertheless, trustees will not want new senior executives who became members of the scheme to be unaware of the limitation. The pensionable earnings cap, however, will cease to be part of the new pensions tax regime beginning on 6 April 2006 although trustees may have incorporated the cap into their own scheme's rules. If so, and also if the trustees are content that the pensionable earnings of members who are subject to the cap on 5 April 2006 should continue to be capped in this way, there is nothing to prevent the cap remaining in place during a transitional period ending in April 2009. HMRC will publish each year a notional pensionable earnings cap figure so that an uprated figure can continue to be used. The legislation to achieve this effect is contained in the *Pension Schemes (Modification of Rules of Existing Schemes) Regulations 2004* which were issued in draft in June 2004.

Benefit redesign

9.17   Benefit redesign may offer a way of making the occupational pension scheme more attractive to employees. For example, the introduction of a *money purchase underpin* will mean that early leavers are not going to lose out. Younger employees might prefer a *starter defined benefit scheme* with low employee contribution rates and a slower accrual rate or one that is money purchase based, although to achieve the same effect it would now be much more common to offer a stakeholder pension scheme with a matched employer contribution up to a defined limit. Some schemes have successfully brought in *age-related employee contributions*. For instance, younger employees may need to maximise take-home pay but will be willing to contribute 2.5% of salary; older employees will be motivated to pay 6.0%. Benefit redesign is, however, the responsibility of the employer, although trustees will need to be consulted and involved. It must also be admitted that benefit redesign issues relating to final salary schemes since 2002 in the vast majority of cases have become centred on the employer's perceived need to control costs rather than attract new entrants. Indeed, the commonest benefit redesign has precisely been to close the scheme to new entrants, offering them instead access to some other form of pension provision. Some employers have sought to control costs but remain with a defined benefit approach by switching for future service to a cash balance or average salary scheme design. Other common ways that costs can be controlled include an increase in the employees' contribution rates (or allowing employees to continue to pay at their current rate but in return of a lower rate of benefit accrual) and less generous early retirement terms.

Opting out

9.18   Trustees should also consider what their attitude is towards those who remain in employment but opt out of the pension scheme. Much, as always, may depend on the trust deed and rules but in many cases trustees may have discretion to decide their policy. Will the employer continue to cover these employees for death-in-service lump sums? And if so, will it do so at the same or a lower level than for pension scheme members? Will those who request a transfer have their transfer value restricted to benefits that were accrued since 6 April 1988, as is allowed by the legislation, or will all their pensionable service count?

If an employee opts out, or refuses to join when first eligible, but then seeks to join or rejoin the scheme, will the trustees impose a medical examination to avoid selection against the pension scheme? (A medical examination may well be required by any insurer who has been engaged to provide death-in-service lump sum benefits.) Will a maximum re-entry age be set in such a case?

Similar issues have arisen in the past as a result of the mis-selling of personal pensions during the late 1980s and early 1990s. Employers and trustees had to decide whether those who had been mis-sold personal pensions were to be allowed to restore the missed past service upon receipt by the scheme of an adequate transfer value, and whether there would be a different policy on re-entry for those who were no longer employees, i.e. would they be reinstated as deferred pensioners.

Personal pensions

9.19   Whatever policy is adopted towards employees who have personal pensions, it would be wise to ensure that it is consistent. It should be remembered that many new employees may already have personal pensions set up several years ago and face severe upfront paid-up charges under these older contracts if they stop their contributions in order to join the occupational pension scheme. However, it is no longer always the case that an employee needs to stop contributing to a personal pension scheme in order to become a member of an occupational pension scheme. Concurrency is currently an option for those whose earnings have not exceeded £30,000 in any of the previous five tax years (but not counting any year before 2000/01). From 6 April 2006 there is full concurrency so that an employee may be an active member of her employer's occupational pension scheme and at the same time and in respect of the same earnings she may contribute to one or more personal or stakeholder pension schemes.

Trustees should be aware of whether the employer is willing to contribute directly to an employee's personal pension.

Trustees and early leavers

9.20   The rights of the early leaver may not always be uppermost in the trustees' considerations. Trustees may think that those who have left the company should take a back seat. Even if understandable, such an approach is not honourable. In a contributory scheme, the early leavers will have paid contributions to the scheme during their time as employees and, if they have chosen to defer a preserved pension with the scheme, thereby becoming deferred pensioners, they will have shown good faith and confidence in the scheme. The great majority of the UK working population are early leavers after all.

The *Social Security Act 1973* introduced the preservation requirements for early leavers. Before that time, an employee could lose all pension rights if he or she left employment before normal pension age, even after 39 years' service! The *Social Security Act 1985* introduced the revaluation and transfer legislation which is now to be found in the *Pension Schemes Act 1993*. Before that time, an early leaver's pension could be compulsorily frozen in the scheme without any increases except those applying to any guaranteed minimum pension. It is now generally acknowledged that the pension industry's hostility to the situation of the early leaver caused much resentment and lost occupational pension schemes much support.

General principle

9.21   In the legislation, the pension entitlement of the early leaver is known as *Short Service Benefit (SSB)* as opposed to the *Long Service Benefit (LSB)* of those who stay until retirement. The *Pension Schemes Act 1993* states:

> 'A scheme must not contain any rule which results, or can result, in a member being treated less favourably for any purpose relating to short service benefit than he is, or entitled to be, treated for the corresponding purpose relating to long service benefit.'

The above rule, however, does not apply to benefit improvements made after the member has left employment.

A scheme's normal pension age is defined in the *Pension Schemes Act 1993* as the earliest age at which the member is entitled to receive benefits (other than any GMP under the contracting-out legislation) on retirement from that employment other than in circumstances where special provision for early retirement on grounds of ill-health or otherwise is being made. Active members who qualify to become deferred pensioners in the scheme have a right to draw their pension when they reach the normal pension applying at the date they left pensionable service. This has been subject to the qualification that if the scheme's normal pension age was less than age 60, deferred pensioners would not have a right to draw pension until age 60. This rule is changed by *s 263* of the *Pensions Act 2004* so that short service benefit must be payable from no later than age 65 except where normal pension age is over 65, in which case short service benefit must be paid from normal pension age.

Section 72 of the *Pensions Act 1993* is also modified so that payment of short service benefit from an age other than normal pension age under the amended legislation just described does not conflict with the basic principle that short service beneficiaries are not treated less favourably than long service beneficiaries.It is not uncommon to find that the payment of an unreduced early retirement pension is subject under the scheme rules to the exercise of a discretionary power in any particular case. The power may be exercisable by the trustees or the employer. In such a situation it is quite possible that an active member is offered an unreduced early retirement pension at say, age 55, while a deferred pensioner of the same age who contacts the scheme to ask if he or she can be paid an immediate pension is offered an early retirement pension with the normal actuarial reduction applied.

Trustees must also decide whether deferred pensioners should be consulted about the nomination and selection rules for member-nominated trustees (see **4.18**).

Trustees should not forget deferred pensioners when considering the use of any discretionary powers that they are free to exercise under the provisions of the trust deed and rules.

Revaluation of deferred pensions

9.22   For defined benefit schemes, there are a number of points in relation to the revaluation of the deferred pensions (in excess of any GMP which is in effect revalued in line with national average earnings):

- For those employees who left before 1 January 1986 there does not have to be any revaluation at all.

- Deferred pension rights that were accrued on or after 1 January 1985 for those who left on or after 1 January 1986 but before 1 January 1991 have to be revalued at a minimum over the period of deferment in line with the rise in prices or at 5% compound per annum if this is less.

- For those who have left on or after 1 January 1991 all deferred pensions rights have to be revalued at a minimum over the period of deferment in line with the rise in prices or at 5% compound per annum if this is less.

Around one quarter of the larger private sector final salary schemes give trustees discretionary power to revalue deferred pensions by more than the statutory amount. In many cases, the rise-in-prices-or-5%-compound formula (known as Limited Price Indexation or LPI) is used irrespective of the date the member actually left the scheme.

Average salary schemes must revalue the deferred pensioners against the same index as is used to calculate the pensions of those retiring from active service.

GMPs have been abolished for pensionable service after 5 April 1997. All the pension rights of early leavers from defined benefit schemes which have accrued from that date are revalued using the LPI formula.

Deferred pensions preserved in defined contribution (money purchase) schemes will simply continue to participate in the fund's investment growth less, where applicable, any administrative charge levied by an insurance company.

Transfer payments

9.23   An actuary will calculate transfer values for early leavers who wish to take their pension out of the scheme in accordance with the legislation, in particular the *Occupational Pension Schemes (Transfer Values) Regulations 1996 (SI 1996/1847)*. The legislation requires that transfer values should normally reflect any customary discretionary benefits that are paid.

A discretionary increase on pensions-in-payment is the main example and, of course, the transfer value will be larger if it reflects these increases. The legislation does, though, permit trustees specifically to forbid the actuary to take account of such discretionary increases so that the transfer value is kept low. However, under the *Occupational Pension Schemes (Transfer Values) Regulations 1996* the trustees must not instruct the actuary to ignore discretionary increases unless they have consulted him or her, and have obtained a written report on the implications for the state of the scheme funding if they go ahead and indeed instruct him or her to ignore dis-cretionary increases. The report must include the actuary's opinion as to whether or not there would be any adverse implications for the funding of the scheme if the trustees did not instruct the actuary to ignore discretionary increases. Members requesting transfer values have a right to see this report. In other words, it is now theoretically harder for trustees to justify not allowing the actuary to take into account discretionary benefits when calculating transfer values if the actuary's report makes it clear that it would not have difficult funding implications for the scheme.

Under the requirements of the *Occupational Pension Schemes (Disclosure of Information) Regulations 1996 (SI 1996/1655)* members must be told as part of the information given on the basic benefits provided by the scheme whether discretionary increases are taken into account in calculating transfer values.

In the case of defined benefit schemes, a member's right to a quoted transfer value must, since 6 April 1997, normally be guaranteed for a minimum period of three months. Furthermore, since that date such schemes gradually became subject to the *minimum funding requirement* (MFR) (see **13.7**) and the Transfer Values Regulations require in such cases that the transfer value is calculated on a basis which is no less favourable to the early leaver than that used in assessing the actuarial valuation of the liabilities under the MFR.

If the trustees fail without reasonable excuse to pay the member's transfer value within six months, the transfer value must be increased with interest in accordance with the requirements of the Transfer Values Regulations. It might also be the case that the Pensions Ombudsman, if involved, would find that the trustees were guilty of maladministration.

In August 2003 the *Occupational Pension Schemes (Transfer Values) Regulations 1996* were amended so that transfer values can be reduced in circumstances where the defined benefit scheme making the transfer is underfunded. Such a reduction cannot normally be applied once the member has been quoted the value of the transfer which is to be guaranteed for a three month period. If the scheme is at least 100% funded against the MFR, the transfer value cannot be reduced below the MFR minimum. If the scheme is less than 100% funded against the MFR, the transfer value can be reduced but by no more than in due proportion the amount of the shortfall against 100% funding against the MFR.

Where members of a defined benefit schemes have requested a transfer value quotation and the amount to be quoted is reduced because of underfunding it may be the case that the member's best interests will be better served by deferring taking any transfer value out of the scheme until a later date. The trustees should ensure that the situation is fully explained to the member requesting the transfer.

It is possible that a transfer value from a defined benefit scheme can be reduced even during the currency of the three months guarantee period if the transferring scheme goes into wind-up. In such cases the member must be informed of any reduction and a new three-month guarantee period begun.

Death before retirement

9.24   Many schemes will provide an immediate widow's, widower's or dependant's pension to the survivor of a deferred pensioner in the event of his or her death before pension age. Some schemes will also pay a discretionary lump sum to a nominated survivor. The trust deed and rules will determine what pension, if any, is paid and trustees may have discretionary powers to determine who should receive it – see **5.4**. Problems may arise if the survivors of a deferred pensioner are unaware of their rights although, in the case of contracted-out schemes, the scheme administrator will be informed by the National Insurance Contributions Office if a widow's or widower's contracted-out pension is payable.

Trustees and pensioners

9.25   During the early 1990s, there were a number of groups of pensioners exercising pressure on their occupational pension schemes and persuading the trustees to pay them due regard. It seemed likely that such examples would be part of a continuing trend and indeed pensioner groups have continued to be active in lobbying trustees to pay due attention to the interests of pensioner members, not only in regard to the issue of pension increases but in other more general areas such as arguing against payments from surplus to be paid to the sponsoring employer. It must be said, however, that in recent years the closure of underfunded defined benefit schemes has often left pensioners in a relatively privileged position compared to active members since pensions in payment are awarded a higher priority than other benefits when a scheme is wound up – see **19.11**.

There are repeated calls from pensioner action groups to be represented on the trustee body and pensioners have to be involved in the nomination and selection rules for member-nominated trustees. Following strong opposition, however, the Government in 1999 backed away from a proposal it had made that large mature schemes should have a reserved place on the trustee board for a pensioner member. Whether pensioners are able to nominate candidates for selection as member-nominated trustees, and whether active members, in cases where they can nominate member trustees, could nominate pensioners have been questions that are determined by the scheme rules governing trustee selection although pensioners or an organisation adequately representing their interests must be involved in the nomination process under the new member-nominated trustee requirements introduced by the *Pensions Act 2004* (see **CHAPTER 4**). Where pensioner trustees are in place, their input has generally been very highly regarded. It is often suggested that pensioner trustees can be more single-minded in carrying out their trustee duties because they have no conflicts arising from any employment contract with the sponsoring employer.

Pension increases

9.26   A key concern of pensioners, if not of all scheme members, is the ability of the occupational pension scheme to grant annual increases to pensions-in-payment so that their value is preserved in real terms.

The trust deed and rules will specify how pensions-in-payment will be increased. On 6 April 1997, legislation contained in the *Pensions Act 1995* introduced Limited Price Indexation (LPI). The legislation was then modified on 6 April 2005 by the *Pensions Act 2004*. The effect is that pension rights accrued in pensionable service from 6 April 1997 to 5 April 2005 have had to give rise to pensions which, once in payment, as a minimum, have to rise each year in line with the rise in prices up to a ceiling of 5%. For pension rights which have come into payment before 6 April 2005, the LPI formula capped at 5% a year has applied to pension rights build up since 6 April 1997 either in defined benefit or in defined contribution schemes.

Yet for pensions coming into payment on or after 6 April 2005 to a member of a defined contribution scheme, there is no requirement for the member concerned to choose to use the available fund to secure a pension or annuity that increases in payment at all. From that date the trustees of defined contribution occupational pension schemes have been required to advise members who are about to liquidate their fund to secure a pension about the different types of annuities available. The trustees can obtain booklets from the Pensions Regulator for distribution to members who are about to use their defined contribution fund to secure retirement benefits, and this will satisfy the statutory requirement to give the required advice.

For members of defined benefit schemes, pensionable service from 6 April 1997 to 5 April 2005 must at a minimum continue to give rise to a pension that increases once in payment in line with prices capped at 5%. But pensionable service on or after 6 April 2005 needs only give rise to a pension payable from the scheme that increases in line with prices capped at 2.5%.

The introduction of compulsory LPI on pension rights built up from 6 April 1997 to some measure compensated members of schemes contracted out by the GMP test for the loss of future GMP rights from the same date. GMPs, once in payment, are in effect increased in line with the full rise in prices.

This LPI formula does not necessarily apply to pensioners who have retired, other than on the grounds of ill-health, before age 55. Once a pensioner, who retired before age 55, reaches age 55 the whole amount of the missed pension increases then become payable and the pension must be uprated normally thereafter.

Any discretionary increases above the LPI formula can be offset against the following year's LPI increase.

AVC contributions do not have to give rise to increasing pensions.

9.27   Most of the larger occupational pension schemes in the private sector have granted increases which have restored, or nearly restored, the original purchasing power of pensions-in-payment.

Full annual increases in line with the retail prices index (RPI) are hardly ever given as a right under the rules of private sector schemes. In recent years the norm among the larger schemes is to have a rule that will raise each year all pensions-in-payment in line with the RPI up to the LPI limit of 5% and then give the trustees discretionary powers to grant an additional increase. Note that this goes beyond the statutory requirement which requires LPI increases only on pension rights earned after 5 April 1997. If employers and trustees wish to reduce the increases which the rules of an occupational pension scheme grant on pensionable service from 6 April 2005 to reflect the change in the LPI formula introduced by the *Pensions Act 2004* those rules will need to be changed by making an appropriate amendment to the trust documentation.

Very often, during a period of high inflation, the pension increase is lower than the RPI. Then, a few years later, special targeted increases are made to groups of pensioners over a specified age in a series of 'catching-up' exercises.

Trustees who have discretionary powers to award pension increases, which will almost always involve the need to obtain the consent of the employer, may feel in a very exposed position. Yet the decision of the employer, the advice of the scheme actuary and the history of custom and practice may mean that in the event there is very little scope for discretion and a figure will emerge.

When general benefit improvements are being considered, perhaps as a result of the distribution of a surplus, pensioners would undoubtedly challenge a decision not to award a reasonable increase, with perhaps special weighting for those who have been retired the longest.

Some smaller schemes simply grant a fixed increase of 3% a year (although they are obliged to offer the LPI formula on post-5 April 1997 service as explained above). When inflation was high members' pensions provided by these schemes would have declined in *real* value.

Example

An employee has a pension of £100 p m. If inflation is, say, 7%, the pension will need to be increased by 7% to retain its *real* value, i e increased to £107 pm. The 7% increase is said to be a *nominal* increase as it just preserves the *real* value of the pension. If the scheme actually grants 3% fixed pension increases only, the pension is increased to £103 p m. Because $103/107 \times 100$ comes out at 96.26%, we can say that the pension has declined in *real* value by 3.74%.

Some other schemes did not grant any increase at all prior to the new legislation coming into force, other than the statutory increase on any GMP if the scheme had been contracted out. Therefore a scheme offering a fixed increase was seen as generous in comparison.

Ironically, at a time of low inflation those schemes which promise 3% fixed increases are often providing a more generous increase than those which promise full price inflation.

Example

An employee has a pension of £100 pm. If inflation is, say, 1%, the pension would need to be increased by 1% to retain its *real* value, i.e. increased to £101 pm. As before, this increase is said to be a *nominal* increase as it just preserves the *real* value of the pension. If the scheme actually grants 3% fixed increases only, the pension is increased to £103 pm. Because 103/101 × 100 comes out at 101.98%, we can say that the pension has increased in *real* value by 1.98%.

Under such conditions, a 3% fixed increase can become a very costly benefit provision. Removal of a right to a fixed 3% increase, however, except in relation to pension rights built up after the date of any rule change, is very likely to be challenged for falling foul of *s 67* of the *Pensions Act 1995*, as amended. This is the measure that prevents the worsening of any accrued rights without the consent of all the members affected or the benefits before and after than change having to be actuarially equivalent (see 6.3).

Even schemes which do not promise a fixed increase could find that that they are meeting the cost of granting *real* increases if there were ever to be a period of deflation – that is when the retail prices index becomes negative. This is because the trust deed and rules of pension schemes allow for pensions to be *increased* to take account of inflation, but do not permit them to be *reduced* in *nominal* terms during a period of deflation.

Example

An employee has a pension of £100 pm. If inflation was, say, −1% (i.e. deflation of 1%), the pension would need to be reduced by 1% to retain its *real* value, i.e. reduced to £99 pm. As before, this reduction is said to be a *nominal* reduction as it just preserves the *real* value of the pension. However, the trust deed and rules of the scheme are likely to preclude such a reduction and in practice the pension would remain at £100 pm. Because 100/99 × 100 comes out at 101.01%, we can say that the pension has increased in *real* value by 1.01%.

Other aspects

9.28   Trustees may also be involved in pensioner welfare activities, or the pensions administration may employ an officer with special responsibilities for pensioner welfare. Visits to the homes of pensioners may be made by volunteers and annual events organised, especially if the employer is established in a particular part of the country. As a matter of good practice, pensioners should be circulated with any pension newsletter that is produced.

Trustees and surviving dependants

9.29   Trustees may be called on to exercise discretionary powers under the trust deed and rules in deciding whether a person qualifies as a dependant of the bereaved pensioner, current active member or deferred pensioner. For more details see **5.4**.

It is quite common in the rules governing private sector schemes to find a provision stating that a spouse's pension will be reduced if he or she is more than a certain number of years younger (often ten) than the deceased. This is in part an attempt to safeguard against the so-called 'death-bed marriages' in which an elderly pensioner marries a young man or woman solely so that the latter can be provided with a pension for life. Many of the stories are probably apocryphal.

It is now rare for scheme rules to withdraw a survivor's pension in cases of the survivor later remarrying, although the practice is widespread in the public sector. Even rarer would be any private sector scheme which would suspend a survivor's pension during any period when the recipient was cohabiting. In both cases, there could be great difficulties in ensuring compliance with such a rule.

Trustees and divorced partners

9.30   The *Pensions Act 1995* gave the courts the power to make orders that will direct the trustees to pay part of a divorced member's pension rights, once they have come into payment, direct to that member's former spouse. This process is known as *earmarking* the benefit. Once the trustees receive the order they will have to inform the parties concerned of the changed circumstances and give information about the value of the pension benefits. Trustees are able to recover administrative expenses for the scheme.

The court may order the member to commute the whole or part of his or her benefit and the order will extend to the lump sum payment. As explained at **5.5**, all or part of any death-in-service lump sum may have to be paid to the ex-spouse. Earmarking orders, however, cannot be used to earmark survivors' pensions payable on the member's death. Once an earmarked pension has come into payment it will cease on the member's death. If the ex-spouse dies first, the earmarked pension may cease, be paid to the ex-spouse's estate, or revert to the member.

Once a court order is in force, it will transfer automatically if the member subsequently transfers all his or her pension rights out of the scheme to another pension arrangement.

These provisions only apply where the petition for divorce was presented to the court on or after 1 July 1996.

The Welfare Reform and Pensions Act 1999 and the *Finance Act 1999* introduced *pensions sharing* on divorce provisions available to divorces granted on or after 1 December 2000. Pensions sharing on divorce operates as an alternative to earmarking orders, and indeed also as an alternative to the long-established practice of the courts in devising financial settlements that offset pension rights against other assets. Pension sharing has the important advantage over earmarking in that it works on the 'clean break' principle and the divorced spouse does not have to wait until the ex-partner decides to draw the pension rights before being able to receive any pension benefit.

Broadly, pension sharing works as follows. Spouses A and B were a married couple until their divorce. Spouse A is a member of either an occupational or a personal pension scheme. If there is a pensions share, there is a reduction in spouse A's pension rights known as the 'pension debit' and a corresponding allocation of rights to spouse B known as the 'pension credit'. Spouse A's SERPS/S2P entitlement can also be debited and a corresponding credit granted to Spouse B. In the case of an occupational pension scheme spouse B becomes a special kind of scheme member with the right (except in an unfunded scheme) to transfer that pension credit to another pension arrangement. The rules of a scheme can insist that a person awarded a pension credit but who was not otherwise a member of the scheme must transfer that pension credit to another pension arrangement. The costs of the pension sharing to the scheme is recoverable from the divorcing couple.

Disclosure of information and communications

Disclosure of Information Regulations

9.31 Trustees should familiarise themselves with the latest amended version of the *Occupational Pension Schemes (Disclosure of Information) Regulations 1996 (SI 1996/1655)*. Most pension consultants will also have published effective guidance on the Disclosure of Information Regulations. The *Social Security Act 1985* (now revoked) introduced new requirements on trustees to provide members with certain basic information about their schemes automatically, and also rights to receive further information on request. Recognised trade unions also have rights to receive scheme information. Since 6 April 1997, the various disclosure requirements have been extended by regulations made under the *Pensions Act 1995* and cover the requirements relating to the disclosure of the scheme's audited accounts, the information to be given when a member requests to transfer pension rights out of the scheme, and what information must be given to early leavers.

Failure to comply

9.32   Before the coming into force of the *Pensions Act 1995*, if trustees failed to provide the information required by the earlier version of the Disclosure of Information Regulations, aggrieved individuals or a trade union could issue a notice requiring them to do so within 14 days. Alternatively, they could ask the former Occupational Pensions Board (OPB) to act on their behalf. Once the OPB was satisfied that there was evidence of default, it could similarly issue a notice requiring the trustees to comply within 14 days. If the trustees continued to fail to meet the requirements, the aggrieved individuals, the trade union or the OPB on their behalf could apply to the appropriate court for an order. These enforcement procedures were widely criticised as being inadequate, and since 6 April 1997 the *Pensions Act 1995* has made any breach of the new requirements a matter for Opra and now the Pensions Regulator with explicit penalties on trustees for non-compliance.

Communications

9.33   The principle of voluntary membership was introduced by the *Social Security Act 1986* (by rendering void any clause in an employment contract that has compulsory membership as a condition of employment). Although the December 1998 Green Paper *A New Contract for Welfare: Partnership in Pensions* proposed measures to encourage take-up of scheme membership, including making scheme membership once again a general condition of employment, it explained that it would still be necessary to allow certain employees the ability to opt out of scheme membership provided they could show they met certain conditions. Because of the statutory need to disclose information, the fact of voluntary membership and the rise of personal pensions, it was seen as important for trustees to mount a continuing and effective communication campaign that actively tries to sell membership of the occupational pension scheme to employees.

However, in recent years communication campaigns have tended to be directed at explaining the pension provision, and in particular, at explaining any change in the nature of that provision. For example, a defined benefit final salary scheme may have been closed to new entrants, who are instead offered membership of a defined contribution arrangement, such as a stakeholder pension scheme.

There seems also to be less emphasis on trying to persuade employees to take up membership. In certain quarters, the 'paternalist' approach to the employer/employee relationship seems currently to be out of fashion.

In large organisations, the trustees and the pensions department will need assistance in communicating any pensions message. This may be through local *pension consultative committees*, or though the local personnel function.

Below we list the basic and the optional elements of the trustees' communications package. They constitute good practice but are not themselves a summary of the requirements of the Disclosure of Information Regulations. In many cases, good practice goes beyond these statutory requirements.

All communication materials should use plain English but not patronise members. Complex subjects should not be avoided on the grounds that they are 'too difficult' for members.

The two most important points about any communication material is that:

(a)　it should aim to give as comprehensive an explanation as possible; and

(b)　it must be completely accurate.

Any misleading or inaccurate information given in a scheme handbook or benefit statement could constitute scheme maladministration (see **11.4**). If a scheme member relied on such information to his or her financial disadvantage, the Pensions Ombudsman or the courts could direct the trustees to set the matter right – see **CHAPTER 20**.

It is noteworthy that Alan Pickering, in his July 2002 report *A Simpler Way to Better Pensions*, stated that his starting point on communicating pensions was that the rules should be based on the following clear principles:

● Communications should be aimed primarily at influencing behaviour. The information should give individuals the facts that they need to decide whether to join, stay in or leave a scheme.

● Communication should provide members with basic information about their likely pension – including setting out, in broad terms, the risks: for example, in a defined contribution scheme members should receive a reminder that the final pension will depend on investment performance net of fees and annuity rates.

● Individuals should be properly informed of major events that might affect members (for example, relevant changes to scheme design or large numbers of members taking early retirement), and their options on leaving or retiring or what will happen to their pension if they die.

● It is also necessary to provide information to protect members: for example, those in a defined benefit scheme should have access to information about the funding position.

● All communications with members should be tested to see whether they are understandable and will work.

Alan Pickering was sceptical that the current disclosure requirements met these principles and proposed radical simplification to these requirements. In the technical paper accompanying the December 2002 Green Paper, the Government said it would welcome views on:

- what information items that are currently supplied automatically could instead be made available on request;

- what particular pieces of information should continue to have specific time limits attached to them; and

- what other areas of legislative prescription could be removed without having an adverse effect on members and their understanding of their pension arrangements.

There is a danger inherent in Alan Pickering's call for pensions communication to be used first and foremost to influence members' behaviour. Although clearly not his intention, it should be remembered that 'communication designed to influence behaviour' is often also, more simply, known as 'propaganda'. Information regarding one's occupational pension scheme should not be presented on the public relations principle of 'accentuate the positive and omit the negative'!

Also, the emphasis on the 'keep it simple' approach in order that all members should be able to understand inevitably means that important but difficult information – such as the detailed analysis of the pension scheme's accounts – would either be omitted or simplified and so not be available, or not easily available, neither to those members who were willing to put in the effort to come to grips with it, nor to external commentators such as trade unions and journalists.

Basic elements

9.34   Trustees may wish to consider posting some of the following material to the employee's home rather than handing it out at work. There are certain advantages: the material is less likely to be mislaid or lost and the member's family is also more likely to see it. If this option is chosen, it should be designed so that it can be easily pushed through the average-size letter box.

Handbook

9.35   A scheme handbook ought to be given to all potential new members. Amendments should be given to all members when they are made. New editions should be produced and given to all members rather than allowing amendment sheets to accumulate. The handbook should describe all the contribution conditions and the benefits offered.

Benefit statements for active members

9.36   Each member should receive an annual benefit statement which is easily understandable. Supporting material such as a newsletter can be included with the benefit statement. The annual benefit statement is the piece of scheme information that is most likely to be read in full by the recipient. The arrival of statutory money purchase illustrations (SMPI) should help members of defined contribution schemes better understand the expected value of the pension income, in today's money. Joint benefit statements incorporating the individuals' entitlement from the state as well as from their current scheme give a broader understanding of the totality of future income, even if they fail to be able to incorporate future income from deferred pension rights in a single statement.

Benefit statements for pensioners

9.37   All pensioners should be sent annual benefit statements and told of the amount of any pension increase. Again, a newsletter could be included in the mailing.

Annual report

9.38   The trustees are required to produce an annual report containing the audited accounts, the actuarial valuation and statement and other information required by the legislation. Some large occupational pension schemes have decided that a popular annual report should be given automatically to all active members and pensioners. Copies of the full annual report are, of course, still provided on request.

However, any popular annual report should not be designed so as to evade the proper provision of information about the scheme. Trustees might like to encourage their communication advisers to try to make the full annual report and accounts more 'popular' instead. The annual report can be used to give the history of the scheme over the previous year and items can be reported which are of interest to the membership at large. Trustees should, nevertheless, be reconciled to the fact that many members will not read the annual report and accounts, whether it is the popular or the formal version.

Trustees are required to prepare, revise and maintain a statement of investment principles (see **16.8**). This can be a separate document available to members on request. However, because of its importance, the trustees often choose to place it within the annual report and accounts. This seems to be a very good idea.

Optional elements

Newsletters

9.39   If the employer issues a company newsletter, it might be useful for trustees to negotiate a regular column on pension scheme news (there is rarely any shortage!). Some very large schemes may issue their own occasional newsletter.

Promotional leaflets and brochures

9.40   Attractive promotional leaflets and brochures can be designed and produced to be given to new employees to point out the advantages of belonging to the company scheme. The Maxwell affair was over 14 years ago, but as a cause of distrust among the members it has been replaced by a plethora of reports concerning the closure of underfunded final salary schemes. Such material will need to address issues of security head on. Yet, it must be acknowledged that in recent years some supplies of attractive promotional leaflets were probably junked when the scheme was closed to new entrants.

Videos/DVDs

9.41   Videos explaining the pension scheme and taking members through any major scheme redesign have been very effective. They were expensive and needed to be used very carefully in conjunction with employee meetings and supporting written material. It was often useful to lend the video out for members to take home; this involved the member's family who also had an interest in the message being relayed. It should, nevertheless, be remembered that Robert Maxwell made effective use of video presentations to members of his companies' schemes. The onward march of technology means that we are currently well advanced in a transition from videos to DVDs and if this route were to be adopted now both media would probably need to be used.

Intranet and internet sites

9.42   Electronic communication and in particular interactive media are being rapidly adopted as an extra means of communication by many pension schemes. Some schemes have set up web sites that are open to all and contain much information about the scheme – for example the contents of the latest annual report. Others put this information on a CD-ROM which is given to any member with a multi-media PC at home. A company-wide intranet is a particularly useful means of communication since it can be designed to allow members to ask 'what if' type questions based on their own personal circumstances. Ensuring the security of personal information is important in such systems.

Professional help

9.43   Most pension consultants offer extensive communication services – see **CHAPTER 12**. Help in preparing the material can also be obtained from the company's public relations department. Effective communication does not need to be expensive, but it does need to be thoughtful.

Giving advice

9.44   Trustees should be aware of the restrictions placed by the *Financial Services and Markets Act 2000* on the giving of financial advice. Only those who are directly authorised or exempted under that Act are permitted to give detailed financial advice on investments to others. Most trustees are not authorised to give financial advice.

There is no problem in trustees giving advice to members:

- about the occupational pension scheme since it is not classed as an investment;

- about general principles of why an occupational pension scheme may provide better benefits than a personal pension; and

- about the general advantages of making additional voluntary contributions.

Trustees should be wary of giving specific advice on the merits of the XYZ personal pension scheme or free-standing AVC scheme since both of these products are classed as controlled investments. However, there is a feeling that trustees and pension administrators have been too cautious in giving advice and that in practice they would not be prosecuted under the earlier *Financial Services Act 1986* if it was clearly seen that they were not in the business of giving investment advice and received no commercial benefit from so doing. Guidance from the Securities and Investments Board (now the Financial Services Authority (FSA)) in any case should have made it clear that it is not normally best advice to sell a personal pension to an active member, or potential member of an occupational pension scheme. The arrival of the concurrency option introduced in April 2001 (see **2.15**) also greatly reduced the danger of the mis-selling of personal pensions and the new tax regime will eliminate the need for anyone to have to make a choice between the two types of scheme.

The problem may commonly arise where an early leaver approaches the trustees (or a member of the pensions or the personnel department) and asks whether he/she should go for a buy-out policy with the ABC insurance company or a personal pension with the XYZ insurance company. The trustee could point out the general options of preservation in the scheme, transfer to a buy-out policy, a personal pension or to the next employer's scheme and express a general opinion. The trustee should avoid specific advice in this instance. Those selling any transfer plan will have to carry out a detailed transfer value analysis in any case.

The selling of stakeholder pension schemes from April 2001 is also a regulated activity, even if the stakeholder pension is legally established as an occupational pension scheme. The FSA regulates the conduct of stakeholder pensions business which includes the use of a set of draft 'decision trees' – a graphical critical path of decision boxes to guide the individual in deciding whether or not to contribute to a stakeholder pension scheme.

Many in the financial services industry are concerned that the limit on charges placed on all stakeholder pension schemes left very little scope for the giving of advice to potential stakeholder customers and this pressure succeeded in persuading the Treasury to raise the maximum charge on stakeholder pensions by 50% on new stakeholder pension contracts sold from 6 April 2005 for the first 10 years of the contract. However, many on the consumer side point to the distinct lack of quality in the advice given in earlier times in relation to the selling of personal pensions. There is an argument that if the quality of the product meets minimum standards, then the need for costly advice is less. This has been reflected in the FSA's approach.

Where a stakeholder is governed by trustees, they will be responsible for ensuring that those advising potential and actual members of their stakeholder pension scheme comply with the FSA's requirements. Most new stakeholder pension business is likely to be 'non-advised'. The importance of the decision trees devised by the FSA, and which are incorporated into the regulatory process, is that they should enable individuals to make a choice, where they reasonably can, without having to pay for advice, and to help identify instances in which advice or further information is necessary.

Note also that the above discussion does not concern the particular case of an employer who contributes to an employee's personal or stakeholder pension scheme because the employer has in such circumstances an exemption from the restrictions on promoting such schemes – see **2.2** for further details.

Checklist 9

- Trustees have a duty to act fairly between the different classes of members.

- Trustees are directly responsible for ensuring that their scheme's rules and actual practice respect the principle of equal treatment between men and women in matters of access, contributions and benefits.

- Scheme rules and practice must also respect other statutory requirements which prevent discrimination against scheme members or prospective scheme members on the grounds of disability, sexual orientation, or religion/belief.

- Trustees must ensure that members on maternity leave, on paternity leave, on adoption leave, employees who work part-time and workers on fixed-term contracts are treated at least in accordance with the relevant statutory requirements.

- Age discrimination will be introduced in the autumn of 2006 which is likely to have at least indirect effects on occupational pension schemes.

- Trustees must pay rigorous attention whenever there are scheme reconstructions involving mergers, demergers and bulk transfers to

---

ensure that the accrued and future pension rights of their own members are not disadvantaged nor diminished.

● If benefit improvements are to be made using a scheme fund surplus, trustees should consider the needs of all groups, although this does not mean that benefit improvements cannot be made which only favour one group of members. Such partial improvements can be made provided the use of the surplus funds in this way does not jeopardise the accrued rights and legitimate future expectations of other groups.

● Trustees should recognise the distinct interests of active members, early leavers including deferred pensioners, pensioners, widows, widowers and other dependants including divorced spouses.

● Trustees must observe the disclosure of information requirements but ought to go further and strive to enthuse members about their scheme by the use of good communications. Communication materials which are thoughtfully put together may be more effective than materials that have simply cost a good deal of money. Giving full explanations in plain English about complicated subjects is preferable to glossy materials written in a 'popular' style that leave out anything that is felt 'too difficult' for the members.

● Trustees of trust-based stakeholder pension schemes will need to ensure that those promoting the stakeholder pension scheme comply with the requirements of the FSA.

Chapter 10

Professional advisers

Expert advice

10.1   Whether individual trustees are drawn from senior management or the employees generally, it is not expected that they will bring with them an expert knowledge of trust law, pensions administration, actuarial matters, pensions accountancy and institutional investment. All trustees will need to take expert advice. Even professional trustees will need to take advice from other professionals working in a different field. Nevertheless, as explained at **5.2**, after an initial period of six months in the post, trustees should comply with the requirements introduced by the *Pensions Act 2004* to possess a certain degree of relevant *'knowledge and understanding'* of the issues with which they are concerned.

When Paul Myners published his report *Institutional Investment in the UK: A Review* in March 2001, there was a widespread view that he was proposing the 'professionalisation' of pension fund trusteeship. During the ensuing debate it has become clearer that this is not his intention nor do the measures introduced by the *Pensions Act 2004* indicate the government policy is that pension funds ought in general to be governed by professional trustees. As the Pensions Regulator states in the introduction to the consultation paper on its draft *code of guidance on trustees' knowledge and understanding* there has been:

'...no expectation that trustees should take on the mantle of an expert. The intention was always to enable trustees to understand the advice they are given by experts so that they can enter into a discussion on that advice and so that they can genuinely reach their own decisions'.

It is accepted that there are benefits in having trustees drawn from a great variety of backgrounds and with different areas of expertise. It is also accepted that pension fund trustees will need access to good quality advice from paid professional advisers.

What Paul Myners advocated, and the Government endorsed, is that, especially in the area of pension fund investment, the trustees should be *familiar with the issues concerned* so that they can effectively question and challenge the advice they are given. It must be said that it is difficult to quarrel with this view. If the trustees are in reality bamboozled by the complexity of the issues involved in running a pension scheme, they cannot be acting in the best interests of their members. In such a situation the professional advisers will in reality be those making the key decisions. The

Government states that it is seeking to ensure that *those responsible for decisions in law are those taking them in fact* – and that surely ought to be the trustees. The issues raised by Paul Myners' review are further explored in **CHAPTER 17**.

It is in fact a trustee's duty to take advice, and trustees who act in important matters without taking expert, independent advice could certainly betray the interest of the beneficiaries. They are also likely to fail to meet the many statutory requirements of the *Pensions Act 1995* and *Pensions Act 2004* and as a result possibly suffer a penalty imposed by the Pensions Regulator. Trustees who fail to take advice could in addition leave themselves open to action for a breach of trust.

Indeed, in many situations statutory law will require that the trustees obtain the expert services of an outside professional. For example, in a defined benefit scheme, an actuary must carry out the required periodic valuations of the scheme's assets and liabilities.

However, just because professional advice has been obtained, it does not follow that trustees have no choice but to follow it. If there is a difficulty, perhaps a second opinion should be sought. Ultimately, the responsibility for a decision will rest with the trustees.

The trust deed and rules will almost certainly give trustees the power to appoint professional advisers and pay them from the fund's resources.

Some advisers, in particular accountants, actuaries and solicitors, will be covered by a professional indemnity insurance. This ought to help trustees recover any losses which the fund sustains as a direct consequence of poor professional advice.

Advisers to employers or to the trustees?

10.2   The *Pensions Act 1995* made important changes on 6 April 1997 as to how professional advisers are appointed, the nature of their role and the nature of their responsibilities. In summary, trustees can be fined if, with certain limited exceptions:

- they rely on auditors, actuaries, lawyers, custodians or fund managers whom they have not appointed (e.g. the employer has appointed them instead);

- they do not appoint a scheme auditor and, except in the case of money purchase schemes where the pension is secured by annuities rather than being paid from the fund, a scheme actuary.

But in the case of the investment manager or managers, the appointment may be made either by the trustees or by someone authorised to do so on their behalf.

The overall intention of the Government was that scheme advisers should be appointed by, take their instructions from, and report to the trustees, rather than the employer.

It has always been important to understand to whom the advisers owe their primary loyalty: the trustees or the employer. Professional advisers will naturally need to ensure they comply with statutory law and the standards and codes set by their own professional associations. They will, however, owe a duty of confidence to their client. And prior to 6 April 1997 their client may have been the trustees or it may have been the employer. That dilemma has been removed.

The adviser may, however, also separately be an adviser to the employer; for example, the same accountancy firm may audit the company accounts and the pension fund accounts.

Few commentators say that trustees should not accept advice from an adviser in a firm that has also been engaged to provide services to the employer. In many circumstances, this may be appropriate. For example, the same actuary could advise both the sponsoring employer and the trustees and in most cases this will be a sensible use of resources. However, there are areas where there are genuine conflicts of interest, and the duty of trustees will be more than just to take professional advice; it will be to take *independent*, expert advice. Professional advisers should inform the trustees if they think there is a conflict of interest.

The actuary or auditor, with certain narrow exceptions, should not be connected to any of the trustees.

Advisers and beneficiaries

10.3   Professional advisers will not be directly accountable to the beneficiaries of the pension fund. If the fund has paid for the advice, though, under trust law it could be argued that beneficiaries have a right to have sight of that advice. Such a right would go beyond the specific requirements of the Disclosure of Information Regulations.

This is not the case in other jurisdictions – for example in the US, federal legislation insists that professional advisers have fiduciary duties to the members. There have been signs that this approach might one day be adopted in the UK. In its proposals for a replacement for the minimum funding requirement (MFR), the Government at one point suggested that the scheme actuary should have a statutory duty of care to the members. Also, in an early consultation paper setting out legislative proposals for an enhanced standard of care by trustees when making investment decisions the government asked:

'The ERISA provisions in the US legislation on which the current proposals are based extend to fiduciaries other than pension scheme trustees. This means that fund managers and, for example, custodians also have a fiduciary responsibility to pension scheme beneficiaries. Should a provision similar to this be introduced in the UK?'

Whistle-blowing duties

10.4   One of the criticisms of the system of regulating and supervising occupational pension schemes at the time of the Maxwell scandal in the early 1990s was that there was no specific duty on the various scheme advisers to share any misgivings they had about how a pension scheme was being run with a supervisory body. They did of course often have to give certified statements to the various supervisory bodies about the scheme, but the Report of the House of Commons Social Security Committee investigating the Maxwell case levelled some general criticism at professional advisers who adopted a rather 'letter of the law' approach.

The criticism was developed in the Report of the Pensions Law Review Committee under the chairmanship of Professor Goode. Three weaknesses in particular were identified:

- advisers reported any irregularities to those who had appointed them and on whose behalf they acted, i.e. the employer or trustees;

- there was no regulatory body with general supervisory powers over pension schemes to which such reports could be made;

- reports to a third party such as a regulator were inhibited in any case by the confidentiality that the advisers owed to their clients.

The government agreed with this analysis and the policy to rectify these shortcomings lay at the heart of the *Pensions Act 1995*.

A new powerful regulator, the Occupational Pensions Regulatory Authority (Opra), with a more wide-ranging remit than its predecessor, the Occupational Pensions Board (OPB), was created which has now been transformed by the *Pensions Act 2004* into the Pensions Regulator.

Two key advisers, the auditor and the actuary, were given under *s 48* of the *Pensions Act 1995* a statutory duty to 'blow the whistle'. They were required, when they had reasonable cause to believe that irregularities have occurred in a scheme, to make an immediate written report of the matter to Opra.

Section 48 of the *1995 Act* has now been repealed and replaced by *s 70* of the *Pensions Act 2004* which introduces new 'whistle-blowing' duties which will fall on a wider range of people. The duty to blow the whistle, however, still falls on the scheme actuary and the scheme auditor but also now falls on any professional adviser to the scheme, the trustees, any person who is 'otherwise involved in the administration of such a scheme', the employer and a person who is otherwise involved in advising the trustees of an occupational scheme in relation to the scheme.

The whistle-blowing duty which falls on any person within these groups is to report breaches of the law. More specifically, the duty to make a report will arise whenever a person who falls into one of these groups has 'reasonable cause' to believe that a duty which is relevant to the administration of the scheme in question, and which is imposed under statute or the rule of law, including the common law and trust law, is not being complied with.

It will, however, only be a duty for the person to make a report of the non-compliance if the person also believes that the non-compliance is 'likely to be of material significance' to the Pensions Regulator in the exercise of any of its functions.

When these two key conditions are met, the reporter must report the matter to the Pensions Regulator 'as soon as reasonably practicable'.

The Pensions Regulator issued a code of practice entitled *Reporting breaches of the law* on 6 April 2005 which gives guidance on how these reporting requirements should be interpreted. Trustees are advised to make themselves familiar with this code, which is available at http://www.thepensionsregulator.gov.uk/pdf/CodeRepBreaches.pdf.

It should be noted that the duty to blow the whistle will also apply to staff provided by the employer to carry out administration tasks in-house and that this will include staff performing pension payroll and similar functions as well as staff administering the pension scheme.

The duty to report applies to employers sponsoring or participating in an occupational pension scheme. In the case of a multi-employer scheme this includes any participating employer who becomes aware of a breach regardless of whether the breach relates to, or affects, members who are its employees or those of other employers.

A brief description of the protection offered to a whistleblower under *s 70* of the *Pensions Act 2004* is given at **8.10**.

How to choose – beauty parades

10.5　Current practice in how professional advisers are appointed varies from scheme to scheme. More significantly, it depends on the kind of adviser concerned. If external investment managers are engaged, it will usually be a well-thought-out process involving site visits, and the so-called *beauty parade* whereby a selected shortlist of investment managers make presentations to the trustees. Yet the shortlist may be put together with guidance from a pension consultant. So the question then becomes: 'How is the pension consultant appointed?'

The appointment of each of the individual advisers is considered in the following chapters. However, there are several general principles:

- A relationship that has grown up over the years will have the important advantage of familiarity and continuity and should not be disturbed simply for the sake of change but trustees should ensure that the services provided are still meeting the required standards.

- New appointments should involve some element of competitive tendering (although fee scales are far from being the only important criterion) and the putting together of a shortlist of likely candidates.

- Trustees should consider whether the status of golfing partner to the company chairman is an objective and satisfactory test in itself for any appointment!

Appointment and removal of professional advisers

10.6 The *Occupational Pension Schemes (Scheme Administration) Regulations 1996 (SI 1996/1715)* made under the *Pensions Act 1995* set out certain conditions for the appointment of professional advisers, and in particular for the appointment of the scheme auditor and scheme actuary. These include the requirement that appointments and terminations of these professional advisers should be given by the trustees in writing and should be acknowledged in writing by the adviser.

The scheme auditor and the scheme actuary may resign at any time by serving the trustees a notice in writing. However, the resignation will not be effective unless the notice contains either:

- a statement specifying any circumstances connected with the proposed resignation which, in the opinion of the auditor or actuary, significantly affect the interests of the members or prospective members or beneficiaries of the scheme; or

- a statement that the auditor or actuary knows of no such circumstances.

If the trustees remove either the scheme auditor or scheme actuary, he or she must, within 14 days, serve on the trustees either:

- a statement specifying any circumstances connected with the removal which, in the opinion of the auditor or actuary, significantly affect the interests of the members or prospective members or beneficiaries of the scheme; or

- a statement that he or she knows of no such circumstances.

If the removed advisor was the scheme actuary, the trustees must then give a copy of this statement to the remaining scheme auditor within 14 days of having received it. Similarly, if the removed advisor was the scheme auditor, the trustees must give a copy of this statement within the same time limit to the remaining scheme actuary (assuming the scheme is not exempt from the requirement to appoint a scheme actuary).

When the scheme auditor or scheme actuary is removed by the trustees, or resigns or dies, the trustees must make a new appointment within three months. The new auditor or actuary must be given a copy of any statement made by the former adviser on or before the day he or she is appointed, or, if later, within 14 days after the trustees receive the statement.

If the trustees fail to comply with these requirements they risk being fined by the Pensions Regulator.

In practice the Auditing Practices Board and the Institute and Faculty of Actuaries, the professional bodies regulating auditors and actuaries respectively, have published approved examples of appointment and engagement letters for the use of auditors and actuaries who are appointed by pension fund trustees.

Access to information

10.7   The Scheme Administration Regulations also set out certain requirements regarding the provision of information to advisers that are binding on trustees and on the sponsoring employer and any professional advisers employed by the employer:

- the employer, an auditor retained by the employer, or an actuary retained by the employer must furnish the trustees, the scheme auditor and the scheme actuary with any such information and explanation as may reasonably be required for the performance of the duties of scheme auditor or scheme actuary;

- the trustees must allow the scheme auditor and scheme actuary access at all reasonable times to the scheme's books, accounts and vouchers and furnish the scheme auditor and scheme actuary with such information and explanation as may reasonably be required for the performance of their duties;

- where scheme auditors or scheme actuaries consider that they have failed to obtain all the information and explanation which, to the best of their knowledge and belief, are necessary for the purposes of their audit or actuarial valuations or statements, they must make a statement to that effect and should, so far as they know, give reasons for the failure. The statement must be given to the trustees and the Pensions Regulator must be advised of the failure.

Checklist 10

- The trustees have a duty to take advice.

- Trustees should not abandon decision-making to the advisers by merely rubber-stamping what their advisers say since the trustees remain responsible for the stewardship of the scheme. They should be familiar with the issues with which they are concerned.

- The trustees should appoint all the scheme advisers (although in the case of the fund manager the appointment may be made by someone authorised to do so on their behalf).

- With certain narrow exceptions, the actuary and auditor should not be connected to any of the trustees.

- In some cases the scheme adviser (or another adviser from the same firm) may also be retained by the employer and this may be a sensible use of resources, but all should be aware of the possibility of conflicts of interest.

- Among others, any professional adviser to the trustees has a statutory duty to blow the whistle to the Pensions Regulator if he or she has reasonable suspicions that there are material irregularities.

- Trustees should appoint advisers in a professional manner by research and preparation of a shortlist.

- The appointment and removal of advisers, and of the scheme actuary and auditor in particular, are governed by statutory requirements.

- Employers and trustees must supply their advisers with the information that they require to carry out their duties.

Chapter 11

Trustees and the pensions manager

Pensions management

11.1   The pensions manager is usually a paid employee of the sponsoring employer (or, in some cases, of the corporate trustee) who has the day-to-day responsibility for the proper running of a self-administered occupational pension scheme.

The Government had originally stated that it did not intend to require the trustees to appoint the person or persons who carry out the day-to-day administration of the scheme. None the less it did wish to encourage the trustees to follow the guidance given in September 1993 by the Pension Law Review Committee that:

> 'As a matter of good practice, trustees who use the administrative services provided by the sponsoring employer in running the scheme should ensure that the services to be provided are clearly defined in the document formalising such an arrangement.'

However, the overwhelming response to the Government consultation paper that had explained that it was not the Government's intention to require trustees to appoint formally the scheme administrator was that this was a matter too important to be left to best practice. Responses highlighted the critical role played by the administrator on behalf of the trustees and pointed out that if trustees were to be held accountable for the proper running of the scheme, then they must be perfectly clear about the terms on which administrative services were provided.

As explained at **8.12**, the *Occupational Pension (Scheme Administration) Regulations 1996 (SI 1996/1715)* require that where it is the employer who makes provision for the administration of the scheme, the employer must disclose to the trustees the terms on which these services are provided.

It should therefore be clear to the employer, to the trustees and to the scheme administrators to whom the scheme administrators owe their contractual duty of confidence.

A significant proportion of the larger occupational pension schemes are served by an in-house pensions department which carries out all the day-to-day administration needed to run the scheme. The cost of maintaining the pension administration department may either be borne by the employer or by the pension scheme itself or shared between them.

Yet many of the larger schemes contract out day-to-day general administration to a third-party, external agency, perhaps a pensions consultancy, an actuarial firm or even another occupational pension scheme: but they will usually still be served by an in-house pensions manager to look after policy areas.

In smaller occupational pension schemes, which tend to be fully insured, the day-to-day administrative tasks are carried out by the insurance company. The company does not employ a pensions manager but rather the company secretary or another senior staff member will liaise on pension matters with the insurance company.

Pension managers often hold a professional qualification from the Pensions Management Institute. The Institute holds examinations each year for those who are employed in the pensions industry and who are following a study programme.

If successful in the ten-part examinations, they qualify to become Associate Members of the Institute (APMI). After further practical qualifying experience, pension managers may become Fellows of the Institute (FPMI). The PMI also has developed an examination leading to the Qualification in Pensions Administration (QPA) designed for general administrative staff working in a pensions department as well as the Qualification in Public Sector Pensions Administration (QPSPA). In addition, the Institute has introduced the Retirement Provision Diploma (RPD), which is a foundation-level qualification aimed at people whose work requires them to deal with pensions some of the time and at those who are starting out on a career in pensions. Members who have gained the RPD, QPA or QPSPA become Ordinary Members of the Institute (MPMI).

> Pensions Management Institute
> PMI House
> 4/10 Artillery Lane
> London
> E1 7LS
> Tel: 020 7247 1452
> Fax: 020 7375 0603
> email: enquiries@pensions-pmi.org.uk
> Web site: http://www.pensions-pmi.org.uk.

The PMI operates a formal system of Continuing Professional Development for those who already hold the APMI and FPMI which stresses the importance of members maintaining high standards and keeping themselves up-to-date with current developments in pensions.

Trustee panel

11.1A   The PMI also provides the Secretariat for a user group specifically for trustees and those involved with or interested in trusteeship issues. The group is known as the *PMI Trustee Group*. Details are available from the above address. In March 2005, the government announced that the PMI had agreed to coordinate the setting up of a trustees' panel to advise the government on a number of issues that currently affect trustees including their views on investment decisions and the difficulties that they face in managing conflicts of interest within the trustee body. Speaking at the PMI 2005 Spring conference, the Pensions Minister said:

> 'The government is keen to take into account trustees' thinking on occupational pension issues, as well as giving them the support and acknowledgement that is their due...The strength of this panel will lie in the fact that it will be completely independent of government, but will have access to me on a regular basis and as such give a voice to trustees of all sorts at the highest level.'

The Trades Union Congress, the National Association of Pension Funds and the Occupational Pension Defence Union have indicated their willingness to collaborate with the PMI in setting up the panel.

Pensions administration agreement

11.2   It is the responsibility of the pension fund trustees to ensure that their schemes are efficiently run. Before the 1990s, it was probably true to say that pension scheme administration was very much a backroom activity. Yet in the 1990s the office of the Pensions Ombudsman was created and more employers decided to outsource their pensions administration. Service standards and cost effectiveness were put on the trustees' agenda and then steadily proceeded to move up that agenda.

To address the issues that began to emerge from this increasing attention on the quality of pensions administration, in July 2002 various representative organisations published a Model Administration Agreement to offer trustees some help. The organisations involved were:

* the Association of British Insurers (ABI);

* the Association of Pension Lawyers (APL);

* the Law Debenture Trust Corporation;

* the National Association of Pension Funds (NAPF);

* the Pensions Management Institute (PMI); and

* the Pensions Research Accountants Group (PRAG).

In June 2005 the Model Administration Agreement's Steering Group put in place revisions to reflect recent changes in legislation and feedback from current users of the Agreement.

The aim in developing the Model Administration Agreement was that it should act as the basis for new agreements between trustees and an administrator, whether that administrator is a third party administrator or is provided by the sponsoring employer. One objective was: 'to give trustees the ability to design their own pre-delivery check, to specify performance levels and to agree the terms of maintenance'.

Yet it was also made clear that it was intended that the Model Administration Agreement could be used to serve as a comprehensive checklist for trustees who already have administration agreements in place and so therefore would, or ought to include all trustee bodies except a small number of corporate trustees who themselves directly employ the administrators running their scheme.

The question raised by this initiative is, therefore, whether trustees should seek to renegotiate their existing agreements along the lines of the model administration agreement. The accompanying press release made it clear that the authors of the agreement hoped that over time it would become the industry standard. The Executive Committee of Pensions Research Account-ants Group (PRAG), for example, issued a statement stating that it believes that:

'the model agreement will provide a useful benchmark against which agreements can be considered as they are negotiated and hopes that in due course, the model can be developed to become a standard agreement for pension administration arrangements'.

Much of the impetus for developing the Model Administration Agreement came from a speech made at the Autumn 2000 conference held by the National Association of Pension Funds by Brian Fyfe of the Engineers' and Managers' Association. He set out the experiences of smaller pension schemes by describing how he and his fellow trustees had been 'taken to the cleaners' by their administrators. Clearly, the development of the Model Administration Agreement has been felt by many to have become a pressing need. The Association of Pension Lawyers put the point for strengthening the trustees' hand quite forcefully when it stated:

'it is now more important than ever to be clear on what is required from service providers, be they employers or third party administrators. The model agreement ... will also function as a useful checklist for any trustee faced with an external provider's standard form contract'.

The message, therefore, seems clearly to be that trustees would be well advised to ensure that their own agreement follows the Model Administration Agreement and to seek to re-negotiate that agreement if it fails to do so.

The Model Administration Agreement is published with accompanying explanatory notes. This is a helpful format since it provides trustees with an agreement that is appropriately legally drafted, ready to be adapted by the parties' own legal advisers for use in any specific contract between trustees and an administrator (whether provided by the employer or an external provider). But the document also provides trustees with an explanation of why it is worded as it is.

Flexibility is provided by the use of a series of schedules which can be completed or altered by the parties to any particular agreement:

- Schedule 1 sets out general matters, such as contact emails and telephone numbers, those designated by the trustees to give the administrator instructions etc.

- Schedule 2 is a comprehensive list in detail of the services that a pension scheme administrator could provide and, where relevant, leaves space for a time limit to be specified within which the administrator is to complete each task.

- Schedule 3 is blank and is available for the parties to list any variations of the standard terms and conditions set out in the body of the agreement.

- Schedule 4 is blank and is available to list the discretions, if any, that the trustees wish to delegate to the administrator.

- Schedule 5 deals with the payment of services and is blank because the model's standard terms and conditions do not stipulate any particular fee basis. However, Appendix B to the explanatory notes provides a sample of various fee bases so that trustees can see the options and negotiate with the administrator just how the services are to be paid.

We draw attention below to certain key clauses of the Model Administration Agreement.

Clause 13 of the agreement stipulates that the administrator is to submit periodically to the trustees 'a completed and true certificate which is substantially in the form set out in Schedule 6'. Such a certificate is intended to concentrate the administrator's mind on the some of the most important issues for the trustees.

Importantly, clause 2.5 of this compliance certificate asks the administrator to aver that neither it, nor any connected party, has 'become entitled to receive any commission, fee or other similar consideration as a result of our position in relation to the scheme'. This ties in with clause 20 of the model agreement which binds the administrator to account to the trustees for any commission, fee or other consideration that it receives by virtue of acting for the scheme. It is also a welcome sign that the visibility of the costs incurred by the trustees can be an issue in relation to administration as well as investment services.

In practice, an occupational pension scheme can be administered on a day-to-day basis in accordance with established administrative procedures but the administrators may not always have in mind the actual provisions of the scheme's trust deed and rules. A claim for maladministration can easily arise if the administrative procedures fail to implement the provisions of the trust deed and rules. Clause 6.6 of the model agreement specifies that the administrator must provide services in accordance with the trust deed and rules, subject, of course, to the trustees having supplied the administrator with an up-to-date copy of the trust documentation and also ensuring that all properly made amendments are notified to the administrator.

In terms of 'blowing the whistle' (see **10.4**), the Model Administration Agreement, in respect of both in-house and third party administrators, stipulates at clause 11 that if the administrator becomes aware of any matter affecting the scheme that could be expected to lead to a report to the Pensions Regulator, the administrator must inform the trustees promptly of that matter. Originally it was the case under the Model Administration Agreement that the administrator might not have any duty under the *Pensions Act 1995* to make such a report but the Model Administration Agreement made it in any case a contractual requirement for the administrator to do so. Since 6 April 2005 an administrator is subject to the statutory duty under *s 70* of the *Pensions Act 2004* to report to the Pensions Regulator where it has cause to believe that there has been non-compliance with a duty relevant to the administration of the scheme and that failure to comply is likely to be of material significance to the Pensions Regulator in the exercise of any of its functions. Furthermore, if the administrator reasonably believes that a criminal offence may have been committed in relation to the scheme, the Model Administration Agreement makes it clear that the administrator may make a report to the Pensions Regulator without telling the trustees about it first.

One of the difficulties in practice that can arise when the trustees have engaged the services of a third party administrator is to manage properly the transition from that administrator to any eventual successor. The hand-over may be fraught because the dismissed administrator may feel little incentive to put resources into ensuring a smooth hand-over. Clause 23 of the Model Administration Agreement sets out the actions to be undertaken following the termination of an administration agreement. Specifically, it deals with the question of the hand-over of computerised records. It makes it clear that the administrator must make available to the trustees or the new administrator all the scheme's records without charge, other than the reasonable costs incurred in arranging delivery to the new location. It is also clear, however, that the basis of the provision of the data is to be the standard facility available under the software system in use by the administrator. In the event that an alternative or additional basis is requested by the trustees, the administrator is entitled to make a reasonable charge for any assistance rendered or cost incurred in producing the data in that form.

The full text of the Model Administration Agreement and explanatory notes can be downloaded from the PMI web site (http://www.pensions-pmi.org.uk/publications/administration/agreement0105.pdf).

Delegation of trustees' powers

11.3   The trust deed and rules must contain a clause which effectively allows the trustees to delegate all or any of their various duties and powers to the pensions manager. In particular, this should cover authorisation to draw cheques on a banking account and to receive money into the pension scheme account. It is sometimes mistakenly thought that trustees cannot delegate their duties and powers. In a modern pension scheme they in practice have to delegate those powers extensively. Two principles remain:

● Trustees can only delegate in accordance with the trust deed and rules.

● Trustees do not abandon their responsibilities by delegating and they should ensure that the tasks are properly carried out.

Trustees cannot delegate their discretionary powers to those who are not trustees but in practice in a large scheme they will usually be advised by their pensions manager as to which is the most suitable action in the majority of straightforward cases. Nevertheless, the formal decision must be made by the trustees.

Maladministration

11.4   Although the trustees delegate the day-to-day administration of the pension scheme to a pensions manager and a pensions administration team, the trustees remain responsible for the proper running of the scheme. Members who feel they have suffered because of maladministration of the pension scheme can raise the issue through the internal disputes resolution procedure, go to the Pensions Advisory Service (TPAS), go to the Pensions Ombudsman, or even go to the court if the maladministration amounts to a breach of trust. See **CHAPTER 20** for more details.

Trustees might well wonder exactly what constitutes 'maladministration'. Failure to apply the trust deed and rules or respect a statutory requirement seem likely candidates but these can give rise to an action in law whereas simple mal-administration may not. There is no statutory definition of maladministration but reference is often made to the so-called *Crossman Catalogue*. When the Parliamentary Commissioner Bill was being taken through Parliament, Mr Crossman, as leader of the House of Commons, gave examples of malad-ministration (see Hansard HC 18 October 1966, column 51). He mentioned bias, neglect, inattention, delay, incompetence, turpitude, arbitrariness, and so on. More recently the Parliamentary Commissioner suggested other examples, such as rudeness, refusing to answer reasonable questions, knowingly giving advice which is misleading or inadequate and faulty procedures.

However, in the case of *Glossop v Copnall*, the Vice Chancellor Sir Andrew Morritt upheld an appeal against the Pensions Ombudsman who had held that: 'Mrs Copnall's exclusion from the scheme amounted to indirect discrimination under Article 119. Failure to comply with Article 119 amounts to maladministration as a consequence of which Mrs Copnall suffered injustice ...'. The Vice Chancellor said that this conclusion was wrong because 'there are three decisions of High Court judges which show that *a mere error of law* cannot amount to maladministration' (*our emphasis*). One must bow to the authority of the Vice Chancellor and three High Court judges, indeed the Pensions Ombudsman himself was obliged to do so on this occasion, but perhaps there are others who might wonder that if a 'mere error of law' does not amount to maladministration, what will?

The debate has now been taken further. In his determination on 25 April 2002 of a complaint brought by Mr Allen (see **18.5** for a discussion of the background), the Pensions Ombudsman stated that:

> 'It would be wrong however to conclude that the absence of a breach of the law means that there is no act of maladministration. Maladministration is in some ways a wider concept than a breach of the law and respondents to complaints may sometimes find themselves judged to have acted with maladministration in circumstances where they would not be regarded as acting unlawfully.'

In order to avoid such failings, trustees might discuss with the pensions manager whether quality certification under the *BS EN ISO 9000* series might be appropriate for the pension scheme. In addition, proper training and motivation for the administrative team undoubtedly has positive effects in terms of service levels and trustees might discuss whether the *Investors In People* programme was also appropriate for the pensions department.

The question of the prevention of maladministration in the running of a pension scheme has, however, been discussed in terms of a more systemic failure in the management of UK pension schemes.

In April 2001, the firm Dunnet Shaw published *Raising the Standard of Pension Scheme Administration* as part of a pensions industry initiative to raise the general standard of pensions administration. It commented that certain commonly encountered attitudes acted to undermine good administration standards. They were:

- a systems view that only the highest volume processes justify computerised automation;

- a payroll view that pensions are non-critical and a refusal to take responsibility for the accuracy of data provided to the administrator;

- a management view that outsourced contracts allow the abdication of all responsibility for the administration function to the provider;

- the use of multiple spreadsheets and other applications instead of central and robust administration systems;

- the belief on both sides of an outsourced relationship that the service can be managed on the basis of retrospective quarterly statistics;

- the view of pensions as a low priority when it comes to investment in training and infrastructure; and

- the belief that DC administration is simpler than DB administration.

Following the publication of the April 2001 paper, a steering group was established and held its first meeting in January 2002. The steering group decided that in order to cover all the issues that had been identified, the lifecycle of a pension scheme would be reviewed and a set of high-level guidance notes should be prepared detailing what was expected of a pension administration service. Four working groups were established:

- Group A – Set up of a new scheme.

- Group B – Ongoing administration.

- Group C – Take on/transfer of administration.

- Group D – Wind up of an existing scheme.

The *Raising Standards of Administration Group* involves pension managers working for both in-house occupational pension scheme administration departments and third party administrators, as well as trustee, consultant and insurance company representatives. Details of its work, including the April 2001 paper and the subsequent deliberations, can be found at http://www.raisingadminstandards.com.

In a further initiative, the Society of Pension Consultants (SPC) (see **12.1**) has established a working party comprising SPC members and pensions software designers to look at ways to improve pensions data standards following concerns over the high rates of inaccuracy in much of the data. The SPC has stated that 20% of the UK's largest occupational pension schemes could have 'serious data problems'.

The working party is also looking at ways to improve the manner in which data is passed from one user to another by devising a common standard file format – much as in the banking industry BACS has long served as a single standard for the transmission and receipt of data. One particular aspect of the SPC's work in this area is to devise a common standard for the transmission and receipt of data between the payroll, personnel and pension administrators – irrespective of whether in any particular case any or all of these administrators are in-house or provided by a third party. Apart from the technical standard itself, which will be written in extensible mark-up language (XML), the working party is examining the possibility of a common set of data validation and reconciliation control totals which will form part of the file format.

Trustee relationship with pensions manager

11.5   The pensions manager relationship with the trustees is a key issue.

He or she will:

- provide the secretariat to support the trustees and organise the taking of minutes for trustee meetings;

- report to the trustees on what is happening in the scheme; and

- carry out the trustees' instructions.

The trustees under the trust deed and rules have overall responsibility for the scheme and they bear a fiduciary duty to the beneficiaries. Unless the pensions manager is also a trustee (which would be very rare), he or she will have no such fiduciary duty but only a contractual duty to his or her employer and a duty to follow any codes of professional conduct.

In most cases, the pensions manager will be a senior officer in the company hierarchy and in certain circumstances could be privy to confidential company information that is not known to the trustees. Therefore, he or she could be placed in a conflict of loyalty. It is for this reason that the *Occupational Pension Schemes (Scheme Administration) Regulations 1996 (SI 1996/1715)* stipulate that, in these circumstances, the employer must specify the terms on which the administration services are provided.

It is recommended that trustees seek a close and professional relationship with the pensions manager and make full use of all his or her acquired skills. However, trustees should never abdicate their responsibility for the stewardship of the pension funds and should ensure that their instructions are carried out.

Data Protection Act 1998

11.6   The trustees are also likely to rely on their pensions manager to ensure that they comply with the requirements of the *Data Protection Act 1998*. The data covered by *1998 Act* are any 'personal data' which relate to a living individual who can be identified from the data or from that and other data in the possession of the 'data controller'. In the case of a trust-based occupational pension scheme it is clear that the trustees are the data controller for the purposes of the *1998 Act* (although the employer may also be a data controller in respect of the same data).

Unlike the old *Data Protection Act 1984*, the data concerned are not restricted to those held on an electronic computer system. The *Data Protection Act 1998* applies to any 'relevant filing system'. This is defined as:

> 'Any set of information relating to individuals to the extent that, although the information is not processed by means of equipment operating automatically in response to instructions for that purpose, the set is structured, either by reference to individuals or by reference to criteria relating to individuals, in such a way that specific information relating to a particular individual is readily accessible.'

Any data controller wishing to process personal data must notify the Data Protection Commissioner and respect the eight data protection principles:

1.   Personal data shall be processed fairly and lawfully and, in particular, shall not be processed unless:

(a)   at least one of the conditions in *Sch 2* is met;* and

(b)   in the case of sensitive personal data, at least one of the conditions in *Sch 3* is also met.†

2.   Personal data shall be obtained only for one or more specified and lawful purposes, and shall not be further processed in any manner incompatible with that purpose or those purposes.

3.   Personal data shall be adequate, relevant and not excessive in relation to the purpose or purposes for which they are processed.

4.   Personal data shall be accurate and, where necessary, kept up to date.

5.   Personal data processed for any purpose or purposes shall not be kept for longer than is necessary for that purpose or those purposes.

6.   Personal data shall be processed in accordance with the rights of data subjects under this Act.

7.   Appropriate technical and organisational measures shall be taken against unauthorised or unlawful processing of personal data and against accidental loss or destruction of, or damage to, personal data.

8.   Personal data shall not be transferred to a country or territory outside the European Economic Area unless that country or territory ensures an adequate level of protection for the rights and freedoms of data subjects in relation to the processing of personal data.

* *Schedule 2* provides that processing of data can only be carried out if one of the following conditions is satisfied:

● the individual has given his or her consent to the processing;

● the processing is necessary for the performance of a contract with the individual;

● the processing is required under a legal obligation;

● the processing is necessary to protect the vital interests of the individual;

● the processing is necessary in order to pursue the legitimate interests of the data controller or certain third parties (unless prejudicial to the interests of the individual).

† *Schedule 3* provides stricter conditions for the processing of sensitive data, and this will include any information relating to a scheme member's health. At least one of the conditions set in *Schedule 3* will have to be met and in the case of occupational pension schemes the condition that is likely to have to be satisfied if sensitive information is to be held is that the member has given his or her *explicit* consent to the processing of the personal data.

Individual members have a right to ask for copies of their data. On payment of a fee (£10), the member must be provided with a description of the data, the purposes for which it is held and the recipients or classes of persons to whom it may be disclosed. The data controller is given 40 days to respond to a request but does not need to respond to repeat requests from the same individual if they are not separated by a reasonable interval.

Checklist 11

- The pensions manager heads up the pensions administration team that carries out the day-to-day running of the pensions scheme.

- The trustees are ultimately responsible for the proper running of the scheme but delegate the day-to-day running of the scheme to the pensions manager and the administration team.

- The introduction of the Model Administration Agreement by representative pension organisations in July 2002 was a significant step towards an industry standard for pensions administration.

- If the pensions manager and the administration team are employed by the sponsoring employer, the employer must make clear to the trustees the terms on which the administration services are provided.

- Administration services can be provided by external third party providers or in some cases can be provided by an administration team directly employed by the trustees.

- The administration costs can be met by the pension fund or by the sponsoring employer or be shared between the two parties.

- The trustees will be answerable if there is maladministration by the administrators to whom they have delegated responsibility for the day-to-day running of the scheme. Recent initiatives are trying to address some systemic problems in pensions administration that can lead to maladministration. There is a distinction between breaches of the law and acts of maladministration.

- As the data controller, the trustees must ensure compliance with the *Data Protection Act 1998*.

Chapter 12

Trustees and the pensions consultant

Society of Pension Consultants and Association of Consulting Actuaries

12.1　Most large occupational pension schemes engage the services of professional advisers to act as consultants. Firms which offer pension consultancy services are likely to be members of the Society of Pension Consultants or the Association of Consulting Actuaries. Many firms are members of both bodies.

> Society of Pension Consultants
> St Bartholomew House
> 92 Fleet Street
> London
> EC4Y 1DG
> Tel: 020 7353 1688
> Fax: 020 7353 9296
> email: john.mortimer@spc.uk.com
> Web site: http://www.spc.uk.com

> Association of Consulting Actuaries
> Warnford Court
> 29 Throgmorton Street
> London
> EC2N 2AT
> Tel: 020 7382 4594
> Fax: 020 7374 6220
> email: acahelp@aca.org.uk
> Web site: http://www.aca.org.uk

Most of the larger pension consultancies will charge on a time basis, with the amount depending on the seniority of the individual consultant. Administration services will more likely be charged on a fixed-fee basis. Some of the smaller consultancies earn most of their money through commission arrangements.

It is generally agreed that the pensions consultancy industry is becoming more competitive; there were a number of mergers of actuarial consultancies during the 1990s.

Services offered by pension consultants

12.2 Most of the larger firms of pension consultants will offer all of the following services to clients. This list is not exhaustive.

Actuarial services

12.3 The role of the actuary is discussed separately in CHAPTER 13.

Administration services

12.4 Pension consultants can advise on how to run an efficient and cost-effective pensions administration system, especially regarding how computer systems and software packages could be used. Some of the larger firms market their own pension administration software.

Alternatively, the larger firms will either provide an external pensions administration service themselves or advise on hiring the services of a third party pension administration provider.

See also **11.2** for a discussion of pensions administration and in particular of the new Model Administration Agreement.

Benefit design

12.5 Consultants can also advise on what benefit package the occupational pension scheme should offer to its members, bearing in mind company philosophy, competitive practice, relative cost and employee attitudes.

Communications

12.6 Firms of pension consultancies often provide through a subsidiary company the full range of member communication services.

They can design, write and produce benefit statements, scheme booklets, trustee annual reports, pension newsletters and special packages to explain pension changes, such as on the merger of a new scheme.

International benefits

12.7 Most of the larger consultancies are tied into international networks and so can advise companies which operate outside the UK.

Investment of funds

12.8 Pension consultancies will help trustees discuss their overall investment strategy and then draw up a shortlist of external fund managers to form a 'beauty parade' from which the trustees will select those who will manage the pension scheme's assets. This particular aspect of a consultant's work has become a matter of keen debate and is further discussed below.

Legal and documentation services

12.9   Some of the firms provide pension lawyer services themselves or sub-contract the work to a law firm.

National Insurance Contributions Office and HMRC negotiations

12.10   Pension consultants can liaise between the scheme and the National Insurance Contributions Office and IR SPSS, the business stream of HMRC that until April 2006 deals with the approval and monitoring of pension schemes.

Placing of insurance

12.11   The pension consultant can help either the employer or the trustees to obtain competitive rates for any insured benefits, such as permanent health insurance cover or death-in-service cover.

Retirement counselling

12.12   Seminars and weekends away can be organised by the pension consultant to counsel members on how to prepare for retirement and manage the transition from the world of full-time work.

Trusteeship

12.13   Trustee training services can be provided by the consultant as well as advice to the trustees on any matter. A consultant could advise on the appointment of an independent trustee if this was required.

Trustee relationship with pension consultant

12.14   Pension consultants will maintain a relationship of confidentiality with their client. If the client is the employer, then the consultant may not be in a position to disclose the employer's latest thinking on possible future changes in the benefit structure to employee trustees. Note, however, that as explained in **10.2**, the trustees must be responsible for appointing the scheme actuary.

In cases of a conflict between the trustees and the employer, the pensions consultant, who historically advised both parties without distinguishing between them, might advise that he or she is unable to act for both on this occasion. If so, an independent consultant from another firm might be brought in.

Whereas some schemes have a long-standing relationship with one pension consultancy, others schemes will prefer to use a variety of pension consultancies for different tasks. An experienced in-house pensions management team may also mean that some of the services offered by the pensions consultancies can more effectively be provided in-house.

Myners and investment consultants

12.15   In his review *Institutional investment in the UK*, Paul Myners discussed at length the role of investment consultants. He concluded that the investment consulting industry was highly concentrated in a small number of consulting firms – the four largest firms were found to hold at least 70% of the market share by value of funds in 1999. At the same time, he found that the level of profitability derived from doing this work for the firms involved appeared to be low. He therefore did not have any fears about conventional competition concerns, but thought that the market structure of the pension fund consulting business in the UK was:

'... likely to lead to the provision of advice that is relatively uniform, insufficiently specialised and in particular, poorly equipped currently to deal with alternative asset classes. There appears to be little assessment of the [investment] manager research activities of consultants'.

The reference to 'alternative asset classes' picks up on one of the main themes discussed in **CHAPTER 16**, which discusses the trustees' role in choosing the investment strategy that is appropriate for their scheme – see **16.9**.

Paul Myners went on to recommend that:

- contracts for actuarial services and investment advice should be opened to competition separately. Pension funds should be prepared to pay sufficient fees for each service to attract a broad range of kinds of potential provider;

- trustees should arrange for formal assessment of their adviser's performance and of any decision-making delegated to them;

- trustees should not take investment advice on an asset class from an investment consultant who lacks expertise in that asset class; and

- fees devoted to asset allocation should properly reflect the contribution it can make to the fund's investment performance.

The issue of the appointment of external investment managers, and the role of the consultant, is further discussed at **16.16** below.

Partly in response to these developments, the National Association of Pension Funds (NAPF) issued in 2001 *The Trustee/Asset Consultant Relationship – A*

Guide to Good Practice. The framework for good practice between the trustees and their investment consultant, as seen by the NAPF, involves the trustees having to define their expectations of their consultant in relation to the advice and services taken, and then recording these in a contract with the consultant. The trustees would then need to make a regular assessment of whether the consultant had delivered what was expected. This is not always a straightforward process. In considering the evaluation of the advice and service provided by an investment consultant, the NAPF warns that account needs to be taken of the extent to which trustees make final decisions or delegate them to the consultant and the extent, therefore, that the consultant should be held accountable for his or her advice.

In December 2004 the Treasury published the conclusions of its review into how effective the Myners principles have been in improving the investment decision-making taken by trustees and their investment managers. This subject is dealt with more fully in **CHAPTER 17** but at this point it should be noted that the government announced among its conclusions that as well as contracting separately for investment and actuarial advice (as the Myners principles already require), in relation to investment advice, pension fund trustees should also contract separately for advice on their scheme's strategic asset allocation and advice on fund manager selection.

Checklist 12

- Trustees or employers may engage the services of a pensions consultant.

- In many cases the consultancy involved will also be the firm that supplies the scheme actuary in which case special considerations apply (see **CHAPTER 13**).

- Pension consultancies can supply a number of useful services on a one-off basis.

- Trustees may feel that the advice and services provided by their own pensions manager and administration team are sufficient in many circumstances.

- Paul Myners raised some concerns about the role of investment consultants in his March 2001 review of UK institutional investment.

Chapter 13

Trustees and the scheme actuary

Introduction

13.1   In the case of any occupational pension scheme which is run on a
defined benefit basis, the actuary is the key scheme adviser. The advice of the
scheme's actuary has in practice determined what level of contributions had
to be paid into the scheme for it to meet its future liabilities. The *Pensions Act
1995* has if anything increased the importance of the actuary because of the
introduction from 6 April 1997 of the Minimum Funding Requirement
(MFR). The importance of the scheme actuary as the key adviser to the
trustees of a defined benefit scheme has not changed since the introduction of
the *Pensions Act 2004* but the new scheme specific funding rules introduced
by the *2004 Act* place the key responsibility for choosing the method and
assumptions that will determine the contribution rate on the trustees
themselves.

Institute and Faculty of Actuaries

13.2   Actuaries usually have a background in mathematics and are
individually members of one of two professional institutions. In Scotland,
actuaries are members of the Faculty of Actuaries. Elsewhere in the UK, they
are members of the Institute of Actuaries.

Faculty of Actuaries
Maclaurin House
18 Dublin Street
Edinburgh
EH1 3PP
Tel: 0131 240 1300
Fax: 0131 240 1313
email: faculty@actuaries.org.uk

Institute of Actuaries
Staple Inn Hall
High Holborn
London
WC1V 7QJ
Tel: 020 7632 2100
Fax: 020 7632 2111
email: institute@actuaries.org.uk
Joint Faculty and Institute web site: http://www.actuaries.org.uk.

Qualified actuaries from elsewhere in the European Union may act as scheme actuaries.

Actuaries are employed directly by insurance companies to advise on the funding level required for insured occupational pension schemes. Actuaries who are engaged to provide advice to self-administered schemes are in practice usually employed by a firm of pension consultants or consulting actuaries – see **12.1**.

A trustee of the scheme must not be appointed as the scheme actuary. The scheme actuary must not be connected with, or an associate of any of the trustees but it is permissible for the same firm to provide the actuary and an independent trustee to the same scheme providing they are different individuals. Special rules concern the appointment and removal of the scheme actuary and the exchange of information between actuary, employer and trustees – see CHAPTER 10.

Principles of how a pension scheme is funded

13.3   Defined contribution (money purchase) schemes are relatively simple and at present require little input from an actuary. If it is thought desirable, though, to fund them to produce targeted benefits for each individual member, this will require at least some actuarial input. Larger money purchase schemes which do not buy out pension liabilities by purchasing annuities from insurance companies, but rather pay pensions directly to pensioners, have to employ the services of an actuary.

Defined benefit (such as final salary, average salary and cash balance) schemes have to be funded on an actuarial basis. An actuarial valuation must be carried out to assess the ability of a pension scheme to meet its liabilities. The object of the exercise is to assess the funding level and derive a recommended contribution rate.

Actuarial methods and assumptions

13.4   In order to carry out actuarial valuations, actuaries make use of various assumptions which are employed in one of various methods.

Assumptions

13.5   The main assumptions that currently enter into an actuary's calculations are:

- the expected return (including capital growth) on investments;
- the expected increase in the income from investments;
- the expected increase in members' earnings;
- the expected increases to pensions-in-payment;

- the expected rate of revaluation of deferred pensions;

- the mortality rate among members and beneficiaries;

- the expected age at which members will retire;

- the balance between pensions and commuted lump sum payments; and

- the ages of members' husbands, wives, partners and dependants.

Often, it has been said that the assumptions themselves are not critical and what counts is the relationship between them; for example, assumptions about an investment return of 10% and earnings growth of 8% might be thought to come to much the same as assumptions about an investment return of 7% and earnings growth of 5%. In choosing which assumptions to adopt, the aim was said not necessarily to adopt the most accurate forecast. Rather, the intention was to achieve a result that observed two golden rules:

1. The contribution rate should be relatively constant over time.

2. The scheme should always have enough assets to cover the reasonable expectations members have of their benefits earned up to the date of the valuation.

A new statutory funding objective has been introduced by the *Pensions Act 2004* which involves the calculation of an actuary of a defined benefit scheme's 'technical provisions' (see **13.8** below). The *Occupational Pension Schemes (Scheme Funding) Regulations 2005* (issued in draft at the time of writing) specify that the assumptions to be used in calculating a scheme's technical provisions must be determined by the scheme's trustees after obtaining the advice of the actuary. Actuarial valuations from 23 September 2005 must therefore be based on the use of assumptions upon which the trustees have received advice from the actuary but which the trustees themselves have chosen.

Methods

13.6   However, if two actuaries used identical assumptions in an actuarial valuation, they will produce very different results if they have adopted different valuation methods.

The choice of the valuation method essentially determines when the cost of paying benefits is actually met. Some methods meet the cost as early as possible, some as late as possible. The choice of one method over another will affect the contribution rate and whether the scheme runs a larger or a smaller fund.

There are two broad groups of actuarial valuation methods: the *accrued benefits* valuation methods and the *prospective benefits* valuation methods.

Accrued benefits valuation methods

This is any valuation method in which the actuarial liability at the valuation date relates to:

- the benefits for pensioners and deferred pensioners and their dependants, allowing for future increases; and

- the accrued benefits for members in service on the valuation date.

There are four main methods that fall into this group:

- the projected unit method;

- the current unit method;

- the defined accrued benefit method; and

- the projected accrued benefits method.

Prospective benefits valuation methods

This is any valuation method in which the actuarial liability at the valuation date is the present value of:

- the benefits for pensioners and deferred pensioners and their dependants, allowing for future increases; and

- the benefits which active members will receive in respect of both past and future service, allowing for projected earnings up to their assumed exit date, and for increases thereafter;

less the present value of future contributions payable in respect of current members at the standard contribution rate.

There are three main methods that fall into this group:

- the entry age method;

- the attained age method; and

- the aggregate method.

Each of these methods has different characteristics and the *Pensions Act 2004* requires the trustees of defined benefit schemes to obtain the advice of their actuary before making any decision on the method and the accompanying assumptions that is to be used for calculating their scheme's technical provisions. Yet the decision on which actuarial method advice to adopt must be taken by the scheme's trustees – not the scheme actuary. In relation to the calculation of the scheme's technical provisions – see **13.8** below the *Occupational Pension Schemes (Scheme Funding) Regulations 2005* specify that the method to be used must be one of the accrued benefits funding methods. Which accrued benefits funding method is to be used is, as with the assumptions, to be determined by the trustees after obtaining the advice of the actuary.

In practice, in most on-going schemes used in the UK the scheme actuary in practice has adopted the *projected unit method* for normal valuation purposes. This is the accrued benefits valuation method in which the actuarial liability makes allowance for projected earnings. The *standard contribution rate* is that rate necessary to cover the cost of all benefits that will accrue in the *control period* following the valuation date by reference to earnings projected to the dates on which the benefits become payable.

Here, *standard contribution rate* is the overall contribution rate (employer's plus employees' contributions) required before taking into account any differences between the actuarial liability and the actuarial value of the assets, i e before taking account of any surplus or deficiency in the fund. *Control period* refers to the period in any accrued benefits valuation method over which the standard contribution rate is calculated to remain constant assuming that at the beginning and end of the period the funding ratio (i.e. the ratio of the actuarial value of the assets to the actuarial liability) is 100%.

Any actuarial valuation using whichever method listed above will need to calculate the value of the scheme's assets less the value of its liabilities. If this is a positive number, the scheme is in surplus, if it is a negative number the scheme is in deficit. When valuing the scheme's assets and liabilities, the actuary can value the assets at either their current *market value* or at a *discounted value*. The discounted value option in the past has been the traditional approach used by UK actuaries. It involves valuing the assets by calculating the present value of the fund's expected future income stream. However, in recent years, there has been a marked trend away from discounted valuations and over to the market value approach.

However, as we have just stated the actuarial value of the fund is the value of the scheme's assets less the value of its liabilities. When a discounted value is placed on the scheme assets, a consistent discounted value must also be placed on the scheme liabilities. By the same reasoning, if a market value is placed on the scheme's assets, a market value must also be placed on the scheme's liabilities. It is easy to understand what the market value of the scheme's assets means. After all, there is a real market out there for stocks and shares and property etc. But just what is the market for the scheme's liabilities? Trustees whose actuaries use market values should ask their actuary just how he or she has calculated the scheme's liabilities

The *Scheme Funding Regulations 2005* do not set out the type of actuarial method that is to be used for the calculations relating to the future accrual of benefits.

Guidance issued by the Pensions Regulator in March 2005 explains that the choice of actuarial method essentially determines the pace at which the emerging liabilities of the scheme are recognised in the technical provisions. So, for example, the greater the advance funding made in the technical provisions for future increases in pay, the less likely that the contribution rate required from the employer will rise in the future.

13.6   *Trustees and the scheme actuary*

The guidance from the Pensions Regulator lists a number of factors that are likely to influence the trustees' decision over which actuarial method to adopt:

- the ability, or willingness, of the employer to make advance provision for future events; so the greater the allowance made today for future pay growth in the technical provisions, the greater the financial strength of the scheme (and this will have the effect of reducing the risk-based levy that will become payable to the Pension Protection Fund (PPF) from April 2006 – see 23.1B;

- the covenant of the employer (i.e. the degree to which the employer is willing to back the scheme) relative to the size of the scheme; for example the stronger the covenant, the more able the employer is to bear changes in the required contributions arising from the effect of unbudgeted-for pay growth on the technical provisions; and

- if the scheme is closed to new entrants the cost of accrual of future benefits will rise over time when expressed as a percentage of the total pensionable paybill as the number of active members dwindles – so the trustees and employer of such a scheme may wish, therefore, to calculate the technical provisions on the projected unit method but budget for future contributions on a method that recognises today the average cost of accrual of benefits over the period until all the active members have retired (such a method could be the attained age method. However, the Pensions Regulator also points out that the smaller the proportion of active members in the scheme, the less significant the differences in the methods will be to the overall valuation result.

The Pensions Regulator in its March 2005 guidance also makes the observation that because the choice of funding method is essentially about the level of benefits that the employer is prepared to fund in advance, the decision of which actuarial method to adopt will usually be made independently of any decisions on the choice of assumptions that will be used. Yet it also states that it can be argued that decisions about the funding method adopted for the calculation of technical provisions cannot be divorced entirely from decisions on valuation assumptions. The Regulator's guidance cites an example of trustees who adopt the projected unit method using *weak assumptions* (i.e. those assumptions tending to assume, for example, higher investment returns and lower earnings growth) could give rise to lower technical provisions than adopting the defined accrued benefit method using *strong assumptions* (i.e. assumptions tending to assume, for example lower investment returns and higher earnings growth). Weak assumptions make for a lower value on liabilities (i.e. lower technical provisions) than strong assumptions when using the same method.

See **13.8** for a discussion of the requirements placed on trustees in deciding which assumptions and which actuarial method to adopt for the calculation of their scheme's technical provisions.

Changes arising from the Pensions Act 2004

13.7   The former minimum funding requirement (MFR) was introduced by the *Pensions Act 1995* but failed to deliver what its name suggested it ought to have achieved. The Pensions Act 2004 has introduced a scheme-specific funding approach for defined benefit schemes after a long period of intense consultation between government and pension professionals.

The following details relating to the transitional arrangements for the switch from the MFR to the new scheme funding rules are subject to confirmation from the DWP and are based on consultation documents issued in March 2005.

A valuation of a defined benefit scheme for the purposes of the former MFR can be made with an effective date before 23 September 2005 but no MFR valuation can be made with an effective date on or after that date. Such a valuation made under the MFR would stand for a period of up to the third anniversary of its effective date.

From 23 September 2005 actuarial valuations of defined benefit schemes must be carried out under the scheme funding requirements set by *Part 3* of the *Pensions Act 2004*. The responsibility for seeing that a proper actuarial valuation of the scheme is carried out falls on the trustees although the valuation must be carried out by a properly qualified actuary whom they have appointed and from whom they take advice.

The trustees have a maximum period of 15 months from the effective date of the valuation to obtain the valuation from the actuary and put in place the scheme's schedule of contributions.

Trustees must thereafter obtain actuarial valuations at intervals not exceeding three years provided that they obtain actuarial reports for the intervening years. If they prefer to do so, rather than obtain actuarial reports in the intervening years, the trustees may obtain full actuarial valuations at intervals of not more than one year (but this is not an option for schemes which accept contributions from employers based in other EU member states).

This requirement to obtain annual actuarial reports during the intervening years only applies to trustees after they have obtained their first actuarial valuation under the new scheme funding provisions. It does not apply to trustees who have obtained their last MFR valuation undertaken with an effective date before 23 September 2005 if fewer than three years have passed from that date. The latest effective date for the first actuarial valuation under the new rules is 22 September 2008 and the trustees would then have to obtain the valuation and put in place the schedule of contributions within the following 15 months.

Statutory funding objective

13.8   Unless the scheme is exempt, a defined benefit scheme is subject to the requirement known as the statutory funding objective. The statutory funding objective is that the scheme must have 'sufficient and appropriate assets' to cover its 'technical liabilities'.

'Technical liabilities' is a term used in the European Directive of 3 June 2003 on the activities and supervision of institutions for occupational retirement provision, generally known as 'the IORP Directive' and which is implemented in UK domestic legislation with effect from 23 September 2005. The *Pensions Act 2004* defines 'technical provisions' as the amount required, on an actuarial calculation, to make provision for the scheme's liabilities.

The *Occupational Pension Schemes (Scheme Funding) Regulations 2005* (issued in draft at the time of writing) set out how the scheme's assets and liabilities are to be determined. In short the amount of the assets is the amount shown in the scheme's accounts (less uncollectible debts and any employer-related investments held in contravention of statutory requirements. The liabilities are essentially the value of the accrued rights of members and survivors to future benefits and the value of any existing pensions in payment or lump sum which has fallen to be paid.

The *Scheme Funding Regulations 2005* provide for trustees to choose the method and assumptions appropriate for the calculation of their scheme's technical provisions and the Pensions Regulator is required under the *Pensions Act 2004* to issue a code of practice giving practical guidance to trustees on their duties in determining the basis for calculating their scheme's technical provisions.

As noted above, the *Scheme Funding Regulations 2005* state that it falls to the trustees to determine the actuarial assumptions and which accrued benefits actuarial method that their actuary is to use in carrying out the calculation of the scheme's technical provisions. The *Regulations* also stipulate that the trustees must take into account the actuary's estimate of the solvency of the scheme (as calculated on a full insured buy-out basis – see **13.10** for more details) and also act in accordance with the following principles:

- the assumptions must be chosen prudently taking account where applicable of an appropriate margin for adverse deviation

- the rates of interest used to discount future payments of benefits must be chosen prudently, taking into account *either or both* (i) the yield on assets held by the scheme to fund future benefits and the anticipated return on those assets, and (ii) the market redemption yields on government or other high-quality bonds

- the mortality tables used and the demographic assumptions made must be based on prudent principles, having regard to the main characteristics of the members as a group and expected changes in risks to the scheme, and

- any change from the method or assumptions used on the last occasion on which the scheme's technical provisions were calculated must be justified by a change of legal, demographic or economic circumstances.

Note that the *Pensions Act 2004* prevents any trust deed or rules effectively limiting the amount of a defined benefit scheme's liabilities by reference to the value of its assets. Under the statute any such provision in the trust documentation would simply be disregarded.

Statement of funding principles

13.9   The trustees must prepare, periodically review and when needed revise a *statement of funding principles*. This is a written statement of the trustees' policy for ensuring that the statutory funding objective explained above is met.

The statement of funding principles must include the following matters:

- the methods and assumptions to be used in calculating the scheme's technical provisions

- the period over which a failure to meet the statutory funding objective would be rectified and the manner in which it will be rectified

- any funding objectives set out in the trust deed and rules, or which the trustees have adopted, in addition to the statutory funding objective

- any direction issued by the Pensions Regulator under *s 231* of the *Pensions Act 2004* (see **13.11C**) following a failure:

  - by the trustees to prepare a statement of funding principles,

  - by the trustees to obtain an actuarial valuation,

  - by the actuary to be able to certify the calculation of the scheme's technical provisions,

  - by the trustees to prepare or revise a recovery plan (see **13.11**)

  - by the trustees to prepare or revise a schedule of contributions (see **13.11A**)

  - by the actuary to be able to certify the schedule of contributions

  - by the employer to make payments in accordance with the schedule of contributions and where this failure is of material significance

  - by the trustees to reach agreement with the employer within the prescribed time in any of the matters where such agreement is required (see **13.11B**).

- whether there are arrangements for a person other than the employer or a member of the scheme to contribute to the scheme and, if so, the circumstances in which they apply

- whether there is a power in the trust deed and rules to make payments to the employer out of the pension fund and, if so, the circumstances in which such a power would be exercised

- whether there is a discretionary power to provide benefits and, if so, the policy for exercising it

- the manner in which cash equivalent (minimum transfer values) are to be calculated and whether a cash equivalent may be reduced on account of the state of the funding of the scheme, and if so, the way in which it will be reduced;

- the frequency at which the trustees will obtain actuarial valuations and the circumstances in which and the occasion on which they will obtain, or will consider obtaining, additional actuarial valuations.

Trustees must prepare their first statement of funding principles within 15 months (12 months for EU cross-border schemes) of the effective date of their first actuarial valuation under the Pensions Act 2004 and then review that statement. The statement must then be reviewed, and if necessary revised, within 15 months after the effective date of each subsequent actuarial valuation.

The Pensions Regulator has the power to fine trustees who do not take reasonable steps to comply with these requirements.

Under the Disclosure of Information Regulations (see **9.25**) the statement of funding principles is a document that must be supplied to scheme members and beneficiaries within two months of a request.

The statement of funding principles is connected with the separate statement of investment principles that trustees must also prepare – see **16.8**. Clearly the two policies are deeply intertwined. In its draft code of practice issued in March 2005, the Pensions Regulator stated that trustees may combine their statement of funding principles with their statement of investment principles. Whether or not they do so, the Pensions Regulator advises that trustees should ensure that their investment policy and the agreed funding policy are compatible. The Pensions Regulator also notes that unless it is someone other than the employer who sets the contribution rate, trustees must obtain the employer's agreement to the content of the statement of funding principles. In contrast, although the trustees must consult the employer on the content of their statement of investment principles, the trustees are not required to obtain the employer's agreement to the statement of investment principles. Consequently, in practice trustees can prepare a combined statement of funding principles/statement of investment principles only where the employer agrees to it in its entirety.

Actuarial valuations and reports

13.10   The trustees must arrange for a written valuation of the assets and technical provisions of the scheme from the scheme actuary. As mentioned at

13.7 valuations are most commonly carried out every three years with the trustees arranging for actuarial reports for the intervening years. Full valuations must not be carried out less frequently than once over three years. In the case, however, of schemes which undertake cross-border activities and so accept contributions from employers in other EU member states, actuarial valuations must be carried out annually.

All actuarial valuation must be carried out by actuaries in conformity with the professional guidance issued by the actuarial profession. The effective date of an actuarial valuation is the date by reference to which the assets are valued and the technical provisions are calculated and so the actual valuation will not be available to the trustees until some time after that date. The *Scheme Funding Regulations 2005* in what all may hope to be a long-stop requirement state that the trustees must ensure that they receive the valuation from the actuary within 15 months of its effective date, and an actuarial report commissioned by the trustees for the intervening years in between a full valuation must be received within 12 months of its effective date.

The valuation must contain the actuary's certification of the calculation of the scheme's technical provisions (see **13.8**) and also the actuary's estimate of the solvency of the scheme. More precisely this is an estimate by the actuary of whether, on the effective date of the valuation, the value of the scheme's assets exceeded or fell short of the cost of purchasing annuities (as described in *s 74(3)* of the *Pensions Act 1995*) which would be sufficient to satisfy the liabilities used to calculate the scheme's technical liabilities and the amount of the excess or shortfall.

If the actuary is not able to give the required certificate, the actuary must report the matter to the Pensions Regulator within five days after the end of the period within which the actuarial valuation had to be received by the trustees (i.e. within five days of the end of the 15-month period following the valuation's effective date).

Any actuarial report received in the intervening years between full actuarial valuations must reflect the adjusted development of the scheme's technical provisions and any changes in the risks being covered.

The trustees must provide the employer with any actuarial valuation or report within seven days of the date they received it from the actuary.

The Pensions Regulator can fine trustees who have not taken reasonable steps to comply with these requirements and to fine an actuary who does not report a failure to be able to certify a calculation of the scheme's technical provisions within the permitted period.

Recovery plans

13.11 If, once the trustees have received an actuarial valuation, they can see that the statutory funding objective is not met (i.e. their scheme does not have 'sufficient and appropriate assets' to cover its 'technical liabilities'), they must within 15 months after the effective date of the valuation either prepare a recovery plan or review, and if necessary, revise an existing recovery plan.

The deadline in the case of schemes accepting contributions from employers in other EU member states is 12 months rather than 15 months and the following requirements will not apply to such cross-border schemes.

A recovery plan must be reviewed, and if necessary also be revised, where the Pensions Regulator has issued a direction under *s 231* of the *Pensions Act 2004* – see **13.11C** below.

Any recovery plan must set out the steps to be taken so that the scheme will meet the statutory funding objective, and the time it will take for this to be achieved. It must also be appropriate to the nature and circumstances of the scheme. In preparing or revising a recovery plan, the trustees must, under the *Scheme Funding Regulations 2005*, take account of the following matters:

- the asset and liability structure of the scheme;
- its risk profile;
- its liquidity requirements; and
- the age profile of its members.

The trustees must send a copy of any recovery plan together with the associated schedule of contributions to the Pensions Regulator within five days of the date that schedule of contributions is certified.

The Pensions Regulator can fine trustees who have not taken reasonable steps to comply with these requirements.

Schedule of contributions

13.11A In relation to a defined benefit scheme subject to the new scheme funding rules a schedule of contributions is a statement setting out the contribution rates payable to a defined benefit scheme by or on behalf or the employer and the active members of the scheme, and the dates on or before which the contributions are to be paid.

A detailed description of the schedule of contributions that underpins the new scheme funding requirement introduced by the *Pensions Act 2004* (as well as has having underpinned the minimum funding requirement which had been introduced by the *Pensions Act 1995*) is described at **8.5** above.

The schedule of contributions must be certified by the actuary and the duty on the trustees to prepare or revise the schedule of contributions is not fulfilled, and the schedule of contributions cannot come into force until it has been so certified. The certificate must state that, in the opinion of the actuary, the schedule of contributions is consistent with the statement of funding principles and that, if so, the rates of contributions in the schedule are such that:

- where the valuation shows that the funding objective was not met, the statutory funding objective can be expected to be met by the end of the period in the recovery plan determined by the trustees or managers (but in the case of cross-border schemes where contributions from employers based in other EU member states are accepted this must be within 12 months after the effective date of the actuarial valuation); or

- where the valuation shows that the funding objective was met, the statutory funding objective can be expected to continue to be met for the period covered by the schedule. The schedule will not be in force until the actuary has so certified it.

If the actuary is not able to give the required certificate, the actuary must report the matter to the Pensions Regulator within five days after the end of the period within which the schedule of contributions had to be received by the trustees (i.e. within five days of the end of the 15-month period (12 months for EU cross-border schemes) following the valuation's effective date). This is the same requirement as also applies in the case where the actuary cannot certify the calculation of the scheme's technical provisions – see **13.10**.

Where the valuation had showed that the statutory funding objective was not met, the trustees must send a copy of their schedule of contributions together with an associated recovery plan to the Pensions Regulator within five days of the date that the schedule of contributions is certified.

The Pensions Regulator can fine trustees who have not taken reasonable steps to comply with these requirements and to fine an actuary who does not report a failure to be able to certify a calculation of the scheme's technical provisions within the permitted period.

The Pension Regulator is given the power under *s 231* of the *Pensions Act 2004* to impose a schedule of contributions – see **13.11C**.

The requirements on the trustees to report material non-compliance by the employer in making payments in accordance with the schedule of contributions, and the penalty that the Pensions Regulator may impose on the employer in such cases and on the trustees if they do not report the employer's non-compliance, are described at **8.5** above.

Reaching agreement with the employer

13.11B The trustees must strive to obtain the agreement of the employer:

(a) to any decision about the methods and assumptions which are to be used by the actuary in calculating the scheme's technical provisions;

(b)   to any matter which is to be included in the scheme's statement of funding principles;

(c)   to any recovery plan; and

(d)   to any matter to be included in the schedule of contributions.

Such agreement must be reached within the 15 months following the effective date of the actuarial valuation concerned (12 months for EU cross-border schemes).

If, however, *in extremis*, the trustees conclude that they will not be able to obtain the employer's agreement within this period to all or any of these matters, the trustees have the power to modify the future accrual of benefits under the scheme in order to obtain the employer's agreement. (The trustees have no power, however, to make any change in these circumstances that would adversely affect the subsisting rights of any scheme member or their survivor – see **6.4**).

If the trustees decide to make such changes to future pension rights they must record the scheme amendment in writing and notify the active scheme members within one month of the modification taking effect.

Where the trustees fail to reach agreement with the employer on any of the matters listed above, they must report this failure to the Pensions Regulator within five working days after the end of the 15 month deadline unless the scheme is a cross-border scheme with members in other European states in which case the deadline for reporting to the Pensions Regulator is within five working days after the end of the 12 months following the valuation's effective date.

Note, however, that under the trust documentation of some schemes a discretion is given to fix the rates of contributions payable to the scheme without the agreement of the employer. In these circumstances the trustees are not required to seek the agreement of the employer but they are required to consult with that employer.

The Pensions Regulator can fine trustees who have not taken reasonable steps to comply with these requirements.

Role of the Pensions Regulator

13.11C The Pensions Regulator is given powers to resolve difficulties arising in the operation of the new scheme funding provisions. These powers can be exercised where it appears to the Regulator (whether or not as a result of a report made to the Regulator) that:

• the trustees have failed to comply with the requirement to prepare or revise a statement of funding principles;

• the trustees have failed to obtain an actuarial valuation when required to do so;

- the actuary is unable to certify the calculation of the scheme's technical provisions or its schedule of contributions;

- the trustees have failed to comply with the requirement to prepare or revise a recovery plan;

- the trustees have failed to comply with the requirements to prepare or revise a schedule of contributions;

- the actuary is unable to certify a schedule of contributions;

- the employer has failed to make payments in accordance with the schedule of contributions and that failure is of material significance to the Pensions Regulator in the exercise of its functions;

- the trustees have been unable to reach agreement with the employer within the set timescale about one or more of the matters on which agreement is required.

The powers open to the Pensions Regulator in these circumstances are to make an order (a) to modify future benefit accruals under the scheme (but not any modification that would affect member's subsisting rights), (b) to give directions about the manner in which the scheme's technical provisions should be calculated, including the methods and assumptions which should be used in the calculation, (c) to give directions about how, and over what period, any failure to meet the statutory funding objective should be rectified, and (d) to impose a schedule of contributions on the scheme setting out the contributions to be paid and the dates by which they are to be paid.

Obtaining the advice of the actuary

13.11D The *Pensions Act 2004* stipulates that trustees must obtain the advice of their actuary before doing any of the following:

- making any decision about the actuarial methods and assumptions to be used in calculating the scheme's technical provisions;

- preparing or revising the scheme's statement of funding principles;

- preparing or revising a recovery plan;

- preparing or revising the schedule of contributions;

- modifying the scheme as regards the future accrual of benefits.

The Pensions Regulator can fine trustees who have not taken reasonable steps to comply with these requirements.

The *Pensions Act 2004* also imposes on actuaries the requirement to follow the relevant professional guidance in carrying out their duties in relation to the funding of defined benefit schemes. This will be contained in a guidance note issued by the Pensions Board of the Institute and Faculty of Actuaries.

Disclosure to members

13.11E The *Occupational Pension Schemes (Disclosure of Information) Regulations 1996 (SI 1996/1655)* are being amended to include new duties to disclose to members information relating to the funding of their defined benefit scheme. These requirements only apply once the new funding rules apply to the scheme. Trustees must make available copies of the following documents within two months following a request from scheme members and prospective scheme members, their spouses, any other scheme beneficiaries as well as relevant trade unions. Trustees may make a charge not exceeding the cost of copying, packaging and posting. They must also make the documents available for inspection free of charge at a reasonable place.

The documents concerned are:

- the statement of funding principles;
- the actuarial valuation, including the actuary's certificate relating to the calculation of the technical provisions;
- the actuarial report;
- the recovery plan;
- the actuary's certificate of adequacy of the contributions payable under the schedule of contributions.

The trustees must also inform the members of their right to request a copy of these documents and also the Pensions Regulator, and this is required to be mentioned in the *annual funding statement* which must be sent automatically every year to all members.

This annual funding statement must be issued by the trustees to all scheme members and beneficiaries annually. It applies to defined benefit schemes still operating under the MFR rules as well as those operating under the new funding rules.

The *Disclosure of Information) Regulations 1996* require trustees to include the following matters in the annual funding statement where the scheme is operating under the new funding rules:

- a summary, based on the most recent actuarial valuation and any subsequent actuarial reports of the extent to which the assets of the scheme were sufficient to cover its technical provisions;
- a summary of the estimate of the solvency position of the scheme as shown in the most recent actuarial valuation;
- a summary of any recovery plan; and
- a statement that the statement of funding principles, the actuarial valuation, the actuarial report, the recovery plan and the actuary's certificate of adequacy of the contributions are available on request.

Where the scheme is still operating under the MFR, the following information must be included in the annual funding statement:

- a summary of the funding position of the scheme as shown in the certificate required under *reg 14* of the *Occupational Pension Schemes (Minimum Funding Requirement and Actuarial Valuations) Regulations 1996 (SI 1996/1536)*, together with a statement showing the period over which any funding shortfall identified by such a certificate is to be corrected; and

- a statement on the availability of actuarial valuations, schedules of contribution, payment schedule, and statement of investment principles are available on request.

The draft *Occupational Pension Schemes (Disclosure of Information) (Amendment) Regulations 2005* also require the trustees of a scheme operating under the new funding rules to include with the scheme's annual report and accounts a copy of the following information: the statement of funding principles, the actuarial valuation or report, any recovery plan and the actuary's certificate on the adequacy of the schedule of contributions.

In its draft code of practice on funding defined benefit schemes issued in March 2005 the Pensions Regulator suggests that the annual funding statement will be member's primary source of information on funding matters. Therefore it argues that trustees need to make the document clear and understandable. The draft suggests the following information should also be included in the annual funding statement:

- an explanation of any changes in the funding position since the last statement in relation to the technical provisions or to the cost of securing with an insurance company accrued leaving service benefits, and of any difference between these two funding positions;

- a summary of the scheme's investment policy as it relates to achievement of the statutory funding objective; and

- a summary of the protection offered by the Pension Protection Fund (PPF) as it relates to the particular benefits promised by the scheme and who to contact if members need more information about the PPF.

Where an annual funding statement is due while the MFR continues to apply to the scheme, the Pension Regulator's draft code of practice suggests that trustees should include in the statement:

- if available, the funding position at the last full actuarial valuation in relation to the cost of securing with an insurance company accrued leaving service benefits;

- when the trustees expect to have in place the first schedule of contributions under the new regime; and

- a summary of the protection offered by the PPF as it relates to the particular benefits promised by the scheme and who to contact if members need more information about the PPF.

13.11E   *Trustees and the scheme actuary*

The draft code of practice suggests that in the case of active members, and in some cases deferred members trustees should issue the annual funding statement at the same time as annual benefit statements (where these are issued automatically). It also advises that trustees may if they wish combine the two statements in one document.

Other duties of scheme actuary

13.11F   Although both the *Pensions Act 1995* and the *Pensions Act 2004* have made important changes which affect the task undertaken by the scheme actuary, there are a number of duties that an actuary has long performed and in many cases continues to perform on behalf of the trustees of an occupational pension scheme.

- Until 6 April 2006, HMRC requires an actuarial valuation to be carried out on all large self-administered schemes using a common actuarial method and set of assumptions for the purposes of identifying and controlling pension fund surpluses – see **19.2**. Whenever the actuary carries out any valuation of the pension scheme, a formal report and actuarial certificate has had to be sent to HMRC within three months.

- In the case of a scheme that is or has been contracted out by either the Guaranteed Minimum Pension (GMP) test or the reference scheme test, the scheme actuary has been involved in various certification processes – see **13.18** below.

- The actuary must calculate what pension rights in the scheme are bought by an employee who brings a transfer value from a previous pension scheme. Similarly, the actuary calculates the transfer value due to an early leaver from the scheme – see **9.14**.

- The actuary is involved in calculations such as: the commutation rate for a pension to be exchanged for a cash lump sum, reduction rates in cases of early retirement and the cost of augmenting pensions for senior employees.

- In major reorganisations occasioned by takeovers or mergers involving the employing company, the actuary advises on bulk transfer arrangements – see **19.5**. Similarly, an actuary is involved if two or more existing pension schemes sponsored by the same employer are to be merged.

- When a scheme is wound-up the actuary will calculate how the assets are used to meet the current liabilities – see **19.9**.

- The actuary must provide figures for the auditors who prepare the company accounts so that a true and fair pension cost can be calculated – see **CHAPTER 15**.

Reference scheme test

13.12   From 6 April 1997 the reference scheme test replaced for future pensionable service the GMP test as the defined benefit basis for contracting out of the additional pension provided by the state. A scheme satisfies the reference scheme test if the scheme actuary certifies that it provides pensions for members that considered as a whole are broadly equivalent to, or better than, those provided by a reference scheme.

The reference scheme is based on producing a pension at age 65 based on 1/80th for each year of service of 90% of an employee's earnings between the National Insurance lower and upper earnings limits, averaged over the last three tax years, with a contingent spouse's pension set at 50% of the member's pension.

The scheme actuary must re-certify every three years that the scheme will provide a pension at least as good, or better than, that provided by the reference scheme for at least 90% of the scheme members. If the scheme fails the reference scheme test, it will cease to be able to contract out.

The actuary also has to confirm that any pre-6 April 1997 GMP rights that are retained in the scheme are adequately funded during the period up to 6 April 2007.

The method by which employees are contracted out, and whether they are contracted out at all, is chiefly a decision for the employer to take in consultation with employees and recognised trade unions.

The reference scheme test can be adopted if the actuary certifies that at least 90% of the employees to be contracted out will accrue benefits that are better than, or equivalent to, those of the reference scheme. If a considerable proportion of employees' earnings is non-pensionable, e.g. overtime, it might mean that the scheme could fail the reference scheme test. In other cases, if say, 5% of the employees fall below this threshold, the scheme can still contract them out. This might seem to be invidious, and some employers have decided that they will propose amendments to the scheme rules so that the benefits provided under the reference scheme are introduced as an 'underpin' to the main scheme benefits. That is to say, no member can ever accrue benefits at a rate less favourable than that provided by the reference scheme. There are other solutions – such as making overtime pensionable or contracting out on the money purchase protected rights test or contracting in to S2P.

Following proposals made by Alan Pickering in his simplification review which was published in July 2002, in December 2002 the Government consulted on legislative changes that would weaken the reference scheme test. The accrual rate would be reduced from 1/80th of average qualifying earnings in the last three years to 1/100th of career average earnings as revalued by Limited Price Indexation. Also, instead of qualifying earnings being 90% of earnings between the National Insurance lower and upper earnings limits, they could be based on all earnings. To date, these proposals have not been progressed.

The actuary of a scheme that is contracted out using the reference scheme test was formerly required to submit solvency certificates to the National Insurance Contributions Office once every three years. These were normally submitted with the renewed reference scheme certificate. This requirement to submit solvency certificates (Certificate T) has now been abolished.

Trustee relationship with scheme actuary

13.13   It is likely that both the trustees and the employer will on occasion need independent advice from an actuary. This is not a problem as the same actuary can advise both the employer and the trustees. Prior to 6 April 1997, in such situations, actuaries had to state clearly whom they were advising so that a conflict of interest could be avoided. If the actuary was advising the employer, the trustees may have judged it prudent in some circumstances to seek advice from another actuary.

As an example, suppose the employer wished to make use of a surplus to provide some benefit improvements. The employer may have asked for a fair estimate of their costs using the same basis as is used for identifying the pension cost in the company accounts, but may also have asked for a separate estimate of the cost using a more conservative funding basis which would be disclosed to members.

If the company wishes to buy or sell a part of the business, it will want the pension terms to work to its advantage; the trustees have to ensure the terms will not damage the interest of any members.

Since 6 April 1997 the problem has been resolved as the scheme actuary has been appointed by the trustees and it is to the trustees that the actuary is answerable. The trustees could face penalties if they were to rely on the advice of an actuary they had not appointed. If the scheme actuary, duly appointed by the trustees, is also to advise the sponsoring employer, the trustees must formally be informed that this will be the case and furthermore the actuary must alert all concerned to any potential conflict of interest. In such circumstances it should always be clear when advice is being given to the trustees and when it is being given to the employer. Actuaries appointed as the scheme actuary should usually communicate directly to the trustees.

The actuarial profession has developed a professional code of practice for scheme actuaries appointed under the *Pensions Act 1995* known as Guidance Note (GN) 29 *Occupational Pension Schemes – Advisers to Trustees or a Participating Employer*. It should be recommended reading for the trustees of all defined benefit schemes, and is available from the web site of the Faculty and Institute of Actuaries at http://www.actuaries.org.uk/files/pdf/map/GN29V5–0.pdf. Trustees should remember that if the actuary has reason to believe there is a material irregularity he or she must report the matter immediately to the Pensions Regulator – see **10.4** above.

Provision of information

13.14   Before 6 April 1997 it was the employer who had to provide the actuary with information which was relevant to a defined benefit scheme's funding position. From 6 April 1997, since the actuary must be appointed by the trustees, it has been the responsibility of the trustees to provide this information. As explained at **8.11** the employer now has an obligation to provide this information to the trustees who in turn are to pass it to their actuary.

Checklist 13

- Trustees of self-administered defined benefit schemes must appoint a suitably qualified scheme actuary. The actuary therefore must regard the trustees as the client to whom he or she owes a duty of confidence.

- The scheme actuary cannot be a trustee, nor connected with or associated with a trustee.

- The scheme actuary can also advise the sponsoring employer but must give notice if there is any conflict of interest. The trustees must be told if the scheme actuary also advises the employer.

- Scheme actuaries appointed under the *Pensions Act 1995* are bound to adhere to a professional code of conduct set out in Guidance Note 29.

- The actuary will carry out periodic actuarial valuations of the scheme to determine the scheme's liabilities, its assets and so the recommended contribution that needs to be made by the employer (net of any employee scheme contributions paid under the scheme rules).

- For valuations of defined benefit schemes where the effective date of the valuation is on or after 23 September 2005, the valuation must be carried out under the new scheme funding rules introduced by the *Pensions Act 2004*. These rules involve a scheme specific approach to finding and comply with the requirements of the European IORP Directive.

- The actuary must decide to use either a market value or a discounted value approach in calculating the value of the scheme's assets and liabilities.

- In relation to valuations with an effective date before 23 September 2005, the actuary must use a prescribed method and set of assumptions to apply the Minimum Funding Requirement (MFR).

- The actuary must certify that a scheme can contract out using the reference scheme test by providing benefits that meet an overall quality test.

- The actuary has a number of other important roles, such as calculating transfer values and transfer credits, commutation rates and the effect of proposed scheme reconstructions.

- The trustees of a defined benefit scheme have a statutory duty to ensure that the schedule of contributions is respected.

- The trustees must supply their scheme actuary with the information he or she reasonably requires.

- The actuary must use a prescribed method and set of assumptions to apply HMRC's surplus test but this disappears with effect from 6 April 2006.

- The scheme actuary must report to the Pensions Regulator any material non-compliance with the statutory requirements.

Chapter 14

Trustees and the pensions lawyer

Association of Pension Lawyers

14.1   Not all firms of solicitors are able to provide the specialised expertise needed for pensions work. Most of the larger firms will have a number of partners who specialise in acting for pension funds, and trustees of self-administered schemes tend to rely on their legal advice.

Individual solicitors and barristers may be members of the *Association of Pension Lawyers*, a grouping which is recognised by the Law Society.

> Susan Andrews
> Secretary to the Association of Pension Lawyers
> c/o Room 10
> PMI House
> 4–10 Artillery Lane
> London
> E1 7LS
> Web site: http://www.apl.org.uk.

The Association produces a quarterly journal *Pensions Lawyer* available on subscription (£60 pa at the time of writing) which contains good, detailed papers, written by pension lawyers but which are accessible to a wider audience. It is a very useful source of in-depth information on pensions legal issues. Those wishing to subscribe should contact the Secretary at the address above.

Services offered by pension lawyers

14.2   Pension lawyers are engaged to provide the following services:

- to prepare documentation for occupational pension schemes, including the trust deed and rules, and to advise on how they should be amended from time to time;

- to advise trustees on any aspect of law but in particular that relating to trust law and the statutory law applying to pension schemes;

- to advise trustees in difficult disputes brought by members or prospective members through the internal disputes resolution procedures or before the Pensions Ombudsman;

- to undertake litigation work through the courts;

- to provide legal advice, especially when changes to pension provision are being proposed, or when the trust deed and rules prove difficult to apply, perhaps because they are defective;

- to provide advice in merger and acquisitions work so that trustees of the scheme belonging to either the purchasing company or the vendor company may agree to the transfer of pension fund assets;

- to provide, in some cases, independent trusteeship services; and

- to advise on customer agreements between the trustees and investment managers.

Trustee relationship with pension lawyers

14.3   In the past pension lawyers have not been active in marketing their services but this is now changing with an increase in competition. Firms of solicitors now regularly compete for work in beauty parades before trustees. However, Law Society standards and codes may intervene and prevent a solicitor acting in a litigation matter because he or she has previously gained confidential knowledge that could be used unfairly to disadvantage the other side.

The trustees must appoint their own legal advisers. They would face penalties if they relied on the advice of a lawyer appointed by someone else, such as the sponsoring employer. This is not to say that the same lawyer cannot also act for the employer. In accordance with their own professional guidance, lawyers must not disguise any conflict of interest. The general remarks concerning an adviser's primary loyalty to either the employer or the trustees are particularly acute in the case of the pensions lawyer. Obviously, both the employer and the trustees will need independent legal advice in the case of a dispute between them. Even if there is no direct dispute, the trustees should ensure that they have taken independent legal advice. An example would be a payment out of a surplus to the employer: trustees would be foolish in the extreme to accept the legal advice of the lawyer who was acting for the employer. They must obtain advice from another source.

Whistle-blowing

14.4   Unlike other advisers, lawyers are to some degree excused from any 'whistle-blowing' duty (see **10.4** for a general discussion of the duty to report non-compliance to the Pensions Regulator). This special treatment of one particular grouping among the trustees' advisers derives from an important principle that lawyers should respect their clients' confidences. Of course, this would not protect a lawyer from prosecution if he or she colluded with any malpractice.

The *Pensions Act 2004* states that a person cannot be required under that Act to produce or permit the inspection of any 'protected item'. Here a 'protected item' is defined as:

- communications between a professional legal adviser and his/her client or any person representing that client if they are made in connection with the giving of legal advice to the client, or they are made in connection with, or in contemplation of, legal proceedings and for the purpose of those proceedings;

- communications between a professional legal adviser, his/her client or any person representing that client and any other person if they are made in connection with, or in contemplation of, legal proceedings and for the purpose of those proceedings;

- items which are enclosed with, or referred to in communications which are made in connection with the giving of legal advice to the client, or it is made in connection with, or in contemplation of, legal proceedings and for the purpose of those proceedings, and are in the possession of a person entitled to possession of them.

But any communication or item is not a protected item if it is held with the intention of furthering a criminal purpose.

Checklist 14

- Trustees should consult a pensions lawyer whenever they have any serious doubts about how they should carry out their duty under the legislation and in line with the trust deed and rules. This should ensure compliance with the law and that no breach of trust occurs.

- The trustees must not rely on legal advice from a lawyer who has been appointed by the employer or any other party. Any lawyer who is approached for advice must have been appointed by the trustees themselves.

- The services pension lawyers can provide are not limited to drafting scheme documentation and litigation. They can provide a wide variety of services including liaison with the supervisory authorities.

- Pensions law is a specialised area of legal expertise and so trustees will want to ensure that the lawyer they engage has relevant experience in dealing with pension schemes.

- Advice given to a client which is legally privileged on the ground that it is a protected item is not subject to the whistle-blowing requirements.

Chapter 15

Trustees and the fund accountant

Introduction

15.1   The trustees of almost all occupational pension schemes must appoint a scheme auditor and they may face penalties if they rely on the work of an auditor who has been appointed by the employer or some other third party. Certain kinds of occupational pension schemes, however, are exempt from the general requirement to have an appointed auditor in place. They include schemes with less than two members and death-benefit-only schemes. Also exempt are small self-administered schemes and executive pension schemes set up on a defined contribution basis, but only provided that certain conditions are met. These conditions include the requirement that all the members of the scheme should also be trustees of the scheme and that all decisions taken by the trustees must be unanimous (or would be unanimous if any trustees who are not members are disregarded).

Special rules apply to the appointment and removal of the scheme auditor and the exchange of information between auditor, employer and trustees – see CHAPTER 10.

Eligibility to be an auditor

15.2   The scheme auditor must be a person who is a member of a recognised supervisory body and is eligible for the appointment under the rules of that body. Furthermore, the auditor must:

- not be a member or trustee of the scheme concerned;

- not be a person employed by the trustees;

- not be the employer of any member of the scheme; and

- neither be an officer nor employee of a company, nor a partner or employee of a partnership, that is the employer of any member of the scheme.

The important principle is that the same individual must not act as both trustee and auditor to the same scheme, and by extension an auditor is ineligible to act for a pension scheme if anyone associated with that auditor is a trustee. This requirement goes further than those applying to the scheme actuary. If a partner or employee of an accountancy firm acts as a scheme trustee, that firm cannot supply the auditors to the pension scheme.

The trustees can appoint either an individual or a firm as the scheme auditor. Qualified auditors from elsewhere in the European Union may act as scheme auditors.

Pension scheme accounts

15.3   The *Occupational Pension Schemes (Requirement to obtain Audited Accounts and a Statement from the Auditor) Regulations 1996 (SI 1996/1975)* came into force on 6 April 1997 and require that:

- the trustees of an occupational pension scheme must obtain, as soon as is reasonably practicable and, in any event, not more than *seven months* after the end of the scheme year, accounts audited by the scheme auditor for that year. This provision has replaced the earlier requirement that the accounts had to be prepared within 12 months;

- the audited accounts must contain the information set out in the schedule to the *Requirement to obtain Audited Accounts Regulations 1996*; and

- the trustees should include a statement in the annual report that the accounts have been prepared and audited in accordance with the regulations. This replaces an earlier suggestion that at least two of the trustees should authorise the audited accounts since in this way the whole of the trustee board will be responsible for ensuring that the accounts have been prepared and audited in accordance with the statutory requirements.

In July 1996 the Accounting Standards Board (ASB) issued its Statement of Recommended Practice (SORP) entitled *Financial Reports of Pension Schemes*. A revised version of the SORP was published in November 2002. This sets out the recommendations, intended to represent current best practice, on the form and content of the financial statements issued by pension schemes. Although the SORP is, as its name suggests, not mandatory, the trustees who are responsible for producing an annual report and accounts for their schemes are encouraged to follow it. The *Requirement to obtain Audited Accounts Regulations 1996* in fact require the trustees to make a statement in the published accounts as to whether they have been prepared in accordance with the SORP. The statement must also indicate any material departures from the guidelines set out in section 2 of the SORP. Because of its importance, it is highly recommended that the trustees take a look at the SORP. It is a very helpful document. Copies are obtainable from:

> Pensions Research Accountants Group
> 145 London Road
> Kingston upon Thames
> KT2 6BR
> Tel: 020 8247 1264

Apart from the specified information covered by the SORP and the *1996 Regulations*, the audited accounts must show a true and fair view of the financial transactions of the scheme during the scheme year, the amount and disposition of the assets at the end of the scheme year and any liabilities of the scheme, other than to pay pensions and benefits after the end of the scheme year.

There must be a statement by the auditor as to whether or not contributions have been paid in accordance with the *schedule of contributions* (defined benefit schemes) or with the *payment schedule* (defined contribution schemes) as described at **8.3–8.7**.

After the failure to pay contributions by the statutory deadline, the most common reported act of non-compliance with the regulatory requirements (see **10.4**) has been the failure by trustees to produce their audited accounts within seven months of the end of the scheme year. Non-compliance with this requirement was formerly a criminal offence. The burden of proof needed, however, to mount a successful prosecution meant that enforcement of the requirement was difficult. On 3 April 2000, however, non-compliance was made subject to a civil penalty generally in the form of a fine and since then it has been easier to deal with such acts of non-compliance more quickly.

In April 2000, to mark the new regime, the former regulator, Opra, published a booklet *Getting Your Audited Accounts and the Auditor's Statement on Time – A Guide for Occupational Pension Scheme Trustees*. In the booklet Opra pointed out that:

> 'Preparing pension scheme accounts and making sure they are audited on time isn't just a question of keeping within the law and making us happy. As trustees, you will want to make sure the scheme is run in a businesslike way so that members can have confidence in it'.

In a separate booklet issued in June 2000, Opra issued further guidance on audited scheme accounts entitled *A Guide for People Involved with Insured Salary-Related Pension Schemes* because this was a type of scheme that was experiencing particular problems. The booklet contained a pro-forma time-table for scheme accounts preparation and audit running from twelve weeks before the scheme year end, when the trustees ought to have agreed with the auditor the provisional audit commencement date, until 26 weeks after the scheme year end when the trustees and auditor should both have signed off the accounts.

The Auditing Practices Board points out that the responsibility for obtaining the scheme's accounts is the responsibility of the trustees (who usually appoint an administrator to carry out this task). It adds, however, that auditors who are aware of a failure by trustees to obtain audited accounts within seven months of the end of the scheme year, but who fail to report this to the Pensions Regulator on a timely basis, risk being reported by the Pensions Regulator to their professional bodies and that this could result in fines and adverse publicity for the audit firm concerned. For further discussion of the scheme auditor's whistle-blowing duties, see **10.4**.

Scheme financial records and procedures

15.4   The *Occupational Pension Schemes (Scheme Administration) Regulations 1996 (SI 1996/1715)* specify receipts, payments and records that the pension scheme trustees must keep. As mentioned in CHAPTER 11, the trustees will inevitably have to rely on their pensions manager and the pensions administration department to carry out all the complex tasks involved in running the financial affairs of an occupational pension scheme. Nevertheless, it should be remembered as always that it is the trustees who are responsible for ensuring that the scheme is administered correctly and efficiently. For more details in this area, 'Part 6 – Financial Management' of *Tolley's Pensions Administration* is recommended reading.

Bank account

15.5   Under the *Pensions Act 1995* there are specific requirements on the trustees to keep any money they receive in a separate bank account held in their name. Similarly, if an employer is responsible for a pension payroll service and therefore makes payments to members, it must deposit any payments which it cannot pay over to members in a separate bank account.

Fraud prevention

15.6   Auditors are not present in the offices of the pension scheme administrators on a day-to-day basis supervising what is going on. They cannot themselves, therefore, prevent fraud. Rather it is up to the trustees themselves to be responsible for ensuring that the accounts are accurately prepared and that there are adequate controls, reporting systems and accounting records in place. Separate sections of the pension administration team should be used to: (a) calculate; (b) authorise; and (c) pay benefits, with different people involved at each of the three stages. Since the audit is carried out some time after the end of the accounting period, the main responsibility for the continuing prevention of fraud or any other malpractice rests with the trustees. However, a good auditor will inform the trustees of any administrative and accounting control weaknesses that are discovered during an audit.

The possibility of fraud should never be dismissed. It can take many forms including:

- the removal of monies from the pension scheme to defraud the beneficiaries;

- the removal of monies from the pension scheme to help a sponsoring employer in financial difficulties but which simply defrauds the scheme beneficiaries;

- employee or employer contributions not properly passed over to the scheme;

- the use of the scheme as a conduit for the removal of employer assets properly due to the employer's creditors;

- cheque frauds;

- unreported deaths;

- selling the scheme's assets at less than the true value;

- phantom pensioners (i.e. fictional beneficiaries of the scheme to whom benefits are fraudulently being paid from the scheme);

- simple theft;

- diversion or overpayment of transfer payments from the scheme and underpayment of transfer payments received by the scheme; and

- fraud connected with the scheme's investments including their use as unauthorised collateral.

This list is far from comprehensive. Again, detailed discussion of these topics is given in *Tolley's Pensions Administration*. It should be stressed, however, that failure to pay the correct level of benefits as a result of maladministration (see **11.4**) could jeopardise scheme resources to the same extent as fraud.

In November 2004 the Auditing Practices Board (APB) re-issued Practice Note No 15, *The Audit of Occupational Pension Schemes in the United Kingdom*. The Practice Note is available on the Internet at http://www.frc.org.uk/apb/publications/pub0357.html.

The general purpose of the Practice Notes issued by the APB is to assist auditors in applying the mandatory Statements of Auditing Standards in particular circumstances and industries. Practice Note 15 therefore gives guidance to auditors on how to apply the general Auditing Standards when they are auditing an occupational pension scheme. The Practice Note is very clearly written and pension fund trustees might find it very useful as a standard reference work. In particular, the section of the Practice Note dealing with the treatment of Standard Auditing Statement 300 (accounting and internal control systems and audit risk assessments) makes valuable reading for pension fund trustees. The Practice Note states:

' ... the responsibilities of trustees for ensuring that the scheme is properly administered and its assets properly safeguarded apply irrespective of a scheme's size or administrative arrangements, and the attitude, role and involvement of each scheme's trustees are likely to be fundamental in determining the effectiveness of its control environment'.

The Practice Note advises auditors to take the following factors into account when they are to consider the attitude, role and involvement of a scheme's trustees for the purpose of carrying out their duties under SAS 300:

- the amount of time committed by individual trustees;

- the skills and qualifications of individual trustees;

- the regularity and effectiveness of trustee meetings;

- arrangements to monitor adherence to the scheme's Statement of Investment Principles;

- training undertaken by trustees;

- compliance with industry guidelines (for example the Myners principles)

- the independence of trustees from each other and from the employer;

- the dominance of an individual trustee (or employer) over the investment and administration policies;

- adequacy of minutes of trustee meetings;

- the division of duties between trustees;

- the involvement of trustees in supervision and control procedures, including matters such as cheque-signing arrangements;

- the adequacy of the accounting records and access of the trustees thereto;

- trustees' attitude towards third parties to whom they delegate the conduct of scheme activities; and

- arrangements for the trustees to monitor scheme income and expenditure.

The APB issued *Audit Risk and Fraud – Supplementary Guidance for Auditors of Occupational Pension Schemes* in May 2005 to take account of the introduction of a series of international standards on Auditing (ISAs) which have replaced the earlier Statements of Auditing Standards (SAS) for accounting periods beginning on or after 15 December 2004. This Bulletin updates Practice Note 15 in the light of these ISAs as well as updating that guidance to reflect the establishment of the Pensions Regulator and the reforms made by the Pensions Act 2004.

Trustee relationship with accountant

Which accountancy firm?

15.7   Trustees and employers may wish to employ different accountancy firms for the pension fund accounts and the company accounts so that there is no possibility of a conflict of interest. This was a firm recommendation of the House of Commons Social Security Committee investigating the Maxwell affair. One example of a possible conflict of interest is whether the accountants auditing the employer accounts should immediately report the matter to the trustees if they spotted that employer contributions were not being regularly paid to the pension fund. (This was before the requirement on the trustees to enforce a schedule of contributions/payment schedule – see **8.5–8.6**.)

However, the Pension Law Review Committee disagreed with the House of Commons Social Security Committee stating that trustees should be free to appoint an auditor acting for the employer provided that the terms of engagement are clearly set out, the roles and responsibilities of employer, trustees and auditor are clearly defined and that the areas of conflict are known.

Guidelines from the Chartered Accountants' Joint Ethics Committee ban accountancy firms from being appointed as independent trustees to the pension scheme of any company for which they are also acting as an insolvency practitioner.

Trustee responsibilities to auditors

15.8 The trustees' responsibilities are set out in the *engagement letter* sent by the auditor to the trustees, which is normally repeated every three years. The trustees will acknowledge their understanding of these responsibilities in a letter of representation on the accounts which they send to the auditors each year prior to the auditors signing their opinion. The Practice Note 15 (see **15.6** above) gives detailed guidance, with examples of appointment and engagement letters.

Whistle blowing

15.9 As discussed at **10.4** the auditor must blow the whistle to the Pensions Regulator if he or she finds any material irregularity.

Company accounts: FRS 17 and IAS 19

15.10 Accountants engaged by the company will need to account for pension costs in the company's profit and loss account. It used to be normal practice for pension costs to be based solely on the contributions actually paid by the company into the pension fund. So a company taking a contribution holiday would receive an immediate fillip in its figures. Such a system fails to match revenue and costs as they are earned and incurred, which can be seriously misleading.

As a result, the Statement of Standard Accounting Practice No 24 (SSAP 24) was developed. It was first applied in July 1988. The overall aim of SSAP 24 was to give a *true and fair* figure for the cost to the company of providing pension benefits, and works by trying to spread any variations from the regular cost over longer periods.

From the point of view of the trustees of the occupational pension scheme, SSAP 24 had few direct implications. How pension costs are accounted for in the company's accounts, however, may influence the employer's willingness to sponsor variable-cost defined benefit schemes over fixed-cost money purchase schemes. It should be noted that the disclosure requirements associated with SSAP 24 meant that company accounts were obliged to begin to give more detail of the associated pension scheme.

In 1999, the Accounting Standards Board (ASB) issued Financial Reporting Exposure Draft 20 (known as FRED 20) which set out the proposals for a new accounting standard on the treatment of pensions and other retirement benefits in the company accounts. FRED 20 immediately began to cause considerable consternation because the proposed methodology to be applied to accounting for the costs of defined benefit schemes was bound to generate greater volatility in company accounts.

Despite the consternation caused, the ASB proceeded with the development of the new standard and, in November 2000, it published *Financial Reporting Standard 17 'Retirement Benefits'* or FRS 17 as it is universally now known. Upon its publication, Sir David Tweedie, the then Chairman of the ASB commented:

> 'Pension cost accounting has for a long time been an impenetrable black box to users of accounts. This new standard will help all interested parties to understand the implications for a company of running a defined benefit pension scheme. It may not be popular with some who would like the present obscurity to remain but transparency of information must be preferable. It should mean that decisions about pension provision are made on a better informed basis. In my view, the UK now has the best standard in the world for accounting for pensions and I would expect it to trigger similar reviews in other countries.'

The key feature of FRS 17 is that the market value of a defined benefit pension scheme's surplus or deficiency will appear as an entry in the balance sheet of the sponsoring employer's company accounts. Under the existing standard SSAP 24, the company's balance sheet showed the accrual of the difference between the contributions paid and the amount charged to profit.

Under FRS 17, the company's profit and loss account shows the relatively stable ongoing service cost, interest cost and expected return of assets measured on a basis consistent with international standards. The effects of fluctuations in market values of the pension fund's assets and liabilities are not seen as being part of the operating results of the business and are treated in the same way as revaluations of fixed assets, i.e. they are recognised immediately in the second performance statement, known as the Statement of Recognised Gains and Losses (STRGL). The ASB argues that this use of the STRGL copes with problems of volatility.

However, in practice, many finance directors were not convinced and feared that the volatility caused by market changes in the pension fund's assets and liabilities would damage the financial credibility of the sponsoring company. In particular, large negative numbers in the STRGL stemming from a defined benefit scheme deficiency tend to be seen by financial analysts and, importantly, the company credit-rating agencies as a debt to the employer. If a company's credit rating is lowered as a result, it will make it much more expensive for the company to borrow money.

Part of the difficulty is that, unless further qualifications are made in the company's accounts, a pension fund surplus is assumed to be akin to an asset of the company and a deficiency is, as mentioned above, seen as a debt. Yet a surplus cannot simply be paid over to the employer – see **19.3**. Similarly, an employer normally has the right at any stage to end any further accrual of pensions, which will change the FRS 17 numbers. The employer also has the option to wind up the scheme. Any deficiency arising in the scheme's fund on winding up becomes a debt on the employer to the extent defined in the legislation. Where the wind-up began before 10 May 2004, the cost of wind-up might not prove too daunting to an employer since the debt to the employer in respect of the accrued rights of non-pensioner members was capped at the cost of cash equivalent transfer values at the minimum MFR level. Since 11 June 2003, however, a decision by an employer to put a defined benefit scheme into wind up has become a very expensive option since the legislation now requires all the scheme's liabilities to be secured on 'full buy-out' terms, meaning the liabilities have to be secured by the purchase of non-profit immediate or deferred annuities from an insurance company, as explained at **19.10–19.11**. The overall point is that the company sponsoring the defined benefit scheme and the defined benefit scheme itself are two separate legal entities but a surplus or deficit in the pension scheme will affect the accounts of the sponsoring employer.

While all these difficulties exist, it should be borne in mind that FRS 17 or any other accounting standard has not materially increased or decreased the cost of running a defined benefit scheme. It merely changes the way that the cost of providing a defined benefit scheme is accounted for in the company accounts of the sponsoring employer.

FRS 17 did not have to come into force in relation to company accounts immediately, although companies had been able voluntarily to operate it for accounting periods ending on or after 22 June 2001. On 2 July 2002, however, the ASB proposed to extend the transitional arrangements for the adoption of FRS 17 and so defer the mandatory requirement for its full adoption. In the meantime, UK financial statements would continue to have to include disclosure of information prepared in accordance with FRS 17 either in the footnotes or, where the standard is voluntarily adopted early, in the main financial statements. This proposal to defer full implementation of FRS 17 was put into effect on 25 November 2002.

The ASB's decision to defer full implementation was a direct result of the announcement by the International Accounting Standards Board (IASB) that it had added to its agenda a project to reconsider the provisions of the corresponding international standard IAS 19 *Employee Benefits*. Under European requirements, IASB accounting standards are to become mandatory throughout the Union for companies listed on recognised stock exchanges.

Because it was going to take the IASB some time before it issued proposals, the ASB decided it should act immediately. Without the proposed amendment, companies with accounting periods ending after 22 June 2002 would have been required to adopt FRS 17 in full for their interim statements at December 2002, and would then face the risk of having to change their accounting a second time when they were required to use IASB standards for their group accounts from 1 January 2005.

Since 1 January 2005 European companies listed on a recognised exchange must use IAS 19. UK companies which are not listed on a stock exchange may continue to use FRS 17 or may opt to use IAS 19. But the old SSAP 24 can no longer be used to account for any company's pension costs.

IAS 19 itself was amended in late 2004 and allows companies to choose between two different ways of accounting for pension costs:

- either gains and losses have to be recognised in the profit and loss account of the company only to the extent that they represent more than 10% of the greater of the assets or liabilities of the pension scheme and, if they do have to be recognised, they can be spread over a period equal to the expected future working lifetime of the scheme's active members; or

- the gains and losses are recognised outside the profit and loss account in a second performance statement known as the Statement of Recognised Income and Expense (SORIE) which is very similar to the STRGL used by FRS 17.

Checklist 15

- Trustees must appoint a suitably qualified scheme auditor.

- The scheme auditor cannot be a trustee nor connected with or associated with a trustee.

- The same auditors can provide audit services to the scheme trustees and the sponsoring employer subject to rules governing professional conduct.

- Trustees must supply their scheme auditor with the information he or she reasonably requires.

- Scheme accounts are governed by a Statement of Recommended Practice (SORP) and the *Occupational Pension Schemes (Requirement to obtain Audited Accounts and a Statement from the Auditor) Regulations 1996*, and must be received by the trustees not more than seven months from the end of the scheme year.

- Auditors can advise the trustees on ways to improve internal controls to ensure risks of maladministration and fraud are minimised,

---

but the responsibility for the proper financial management of the scheme rests with the trustees, while the day-to-day financial management is carried out by the scheme administrators.

- How employers which sponsor defined benefit schemes account for the cost of doing so in their company accounts has become an important issue.

Chapter 16

Investing pension fund assets

Introduction

Insured schemes

16.1   Around one quarter of all employees who are active members of occupational pension schemes belong to schemes in which all the benefits are guaranteed by one insurance company. The employer has simply entered into an *insurance contract*, not specifically an investment management contract. Employer- or employee-nominated trustees of insured schemes have no direct input in determining their scheme's investment policy.

If the number of employees working in a company, or the size of the pension fund, ever reaches a critical threshold, economies of scale would suggest that the scheme stops being a wholly insured scheme and instead becomes a *self-administered scheme*, i.e. a scheme where the trustees take control of their scheme's overall investment strategy.

Self-administered schemes

Managed funds

16.2   The term *managed fund* describes an arrangement where the trustees of a self-administered scheme have entered into an investment management contract with an insurance company, and the scheme's funds are invested in a pooled arrangement along with the funds from many other schemes. The trustees do not have a direct input into the investment policy but they can decide to switch to another managed fund or decide that the pension fund is large enough to become a segregated fund. Pooled funds are also operated by unit trust groups.

Segregated funds

16.3   The term 'segregated fund' describes the situation where the trustees of an occupational pension fund have entered into a contract with one or more investment managers who manage the assets of that pension fund independently of any other pension funds. The trustees are responsible for formulating the overall investment policy to be followed by their investment manager or managers.

The largest UK occupational funds are self-administered schemes run as segregated funds, although the trustees will in many cases have decided to keep part of the scheme's assets in managed or pooled funds run by an investment manager, a unit trust or an insurance company.

Trustee investment powers

16.4   The trust deed and rules governing the occupational pension scheme should give the trustees very wide powers of investment. In the past, if they had not done so, the trustees would have been bound by quite severe limitations on the permitted range of investments, which were imposed by default by the *Trustee Investments Act 1961*. The coming into force of the *Trustee Act 2000* gives trustees in general much more modern investment powers, but in practice the investment powers of pension fund trustees are in any case governed by the terms of their trust deed and rules which for the most part have long given the trustees the power to invest in a wide range of investment assets.

There are a number of general principles that trustees must observe in exercising their investment powers.

The most important principle is that trustees must take the same amount of care in exercising any investment power as ordinary prudent men or women would take 'if they were making an investment for the benefit of other people for whom they felt morally bound to provide'.

The general duty to take advice is especially relevant. Trustees who have not taken investment advice cannot be said to have acted in a prudent and reasonable way; even if they acted sincerely and in good faith. Trustees should ensure that the investment advice they receive is objective and of high quality.

Trustees can, of course, reject the advice, since responsibility for the pension fund lies ultimately with them. However, it is clear that they should not reject advice arbitrarily simply because they disagree with it. They would need to be convinced that to follow the advice was imprudent and unreasonable. In practice, they would have taken further advice from another reputable source.

Under the *Trustee Act 2000* trustees have had a general duty to consider the need for diversification of the investments and the suitability of the kind of investments made. Also the *Pensions Act 1995* and the *Pensions Act 2004* have added considerably to the statutory duties placed on occupational scheme trustees in matters concerning investment.

Financial services legislation

16.5   The *Financial Services Act 1986* made it a criminal offence to carry on an investment business without proper authorisation. The *Financial Services and Markets Act 2000* maintains this position. Since, in general, the trustees of an occupational pension scheme are not authorised, it follows that all the activities that define the carrying on of regulated activities under the 2000 Act must be undertaken by another, authorised, party.

In cases of doubt, trustees should check the *bona fides* of an investment manager directly with the FSA.

> Financial Services Authority
> 25 The North Colonnade
> Canary Wharf
> London
> E14 5HS
> Tel: 020 7676 1000
> Fax: 020 7676 1099
> Web site: http://www.fsa.gov.uk.

Trustees do not need to be authorised themselves if all day-to-day decisions relating to the scheme's management are taken by an authorised investment manager. This does not mean that effective control over investment policy is no longer in the hands of the trustees: but it does mean that it is very dubious that unauthorised trustees can be involved in individual decisions to buy or sell particular assets.

Amendments made to the *Financial Services and Markets Act 2000 (Carrying on Regulated Activities by Way of Business) Order 2001 (SI 2001/1177)* on 6 April 2005 effected a number of decisions on which HM Treasury had consulted as part of its review of the operation of the *Financial Services and Markets Act 2000*. The changes made are intended to give pension fund trustees more freedom in making investments.

- The expression 'routine or day to day decisions' should be replaced with 'day to day decisions' in the *Business Order* to provide greater scope of decisions which pension fund trustees are permitted to take.

- Pension fund trustees should be permitted to invest in pooled investment vehicles and contracts of insurance in addition to the products in which they are already permitted to invest.

- Unauthorised trustees should only have to obtain and consider independent advice rather than to act in accordance with it.

- Unauthorised trustees should be able to take advice from professional firms which operate under Part XX of the 2000 Act (Part XX firms are professionally qualified and subject to the discipline of designated professional bodies, e.g. actuaries).

The Treasury also agreed that the possibility of allowing in-house experts (who are not authorised by the FSA and who do not operate under Part XX of the 2000 Act) to provide advice to unauthorised trustees should be kept under review.

Pensions Act 1995

16.6   The *Pensions Act 1995* makes it clear that from 6 April 1997, subject to the trust deed and rules, the trustees have the same power to make an investment of any kind as if they were absolutely entitled to the assets of the scheme. The Act probably therefore has rendered void any requirement that the sponsoring employer must approve how the trustees exercise their powers. Any restriction imposed by the trust deed and rules probably will relate to the types of investment in which the trustees are permitted to invest. For example, the trust deed and rules may ban the trustees completely from making any investments in the business of the sponsoring employer.

If the trustees delegate their powers of investment to a fund manager who is authorised under the *Financial Services and Markets Act 2000*, the trustees cannot be held responsible for that fund manager's acts or defaults provided that they have taken all steps to satisfy themselves that the fund manager has the '*appropriate knowledge and experience*' for managing the investments of the scheme, that it is carrying out its work competently, and is complying with all the requirements made under the *Pensions Act 1995* relating to pension fund investments.

The trustees can also delegate their powers of investment under the same conditions, and without liability to a fund manger who is not authorised under the *Financial Services and Markets Act 2000*, if it concerns investment business not covered by the scope of that Act, e.g. cash or property.

Pensions Act 2004

16.6A   The impetus for the changes made in the 2004 Act has come from two sources: the need for the UK to comply with the European IORP Directive which introduces minimum prudential standards for any institution for occupational retirement provision in order to promote cross-border schemes and the full implementation of the recommendations made by Paul Myners (see **CHAPTER 17**).

The *Pensions Act 2004* makes the following changes in relation to trustees' investment duties:

- It alters the requirements made by the *Pensions Act 1995* in relation to the statement of investment principles that trustees must prepare and maintain (see **16.9**).

- It adds to the requirements in the *Pensions Act 1995* generally requiring trustees to exercise their powers of investment in accordance with regulations.

- It provides that where the trustees have delegated responsibility for investment to a fund manager then that fund manager generally has to exercise its responsibility in accordance with regulations.

- It requires that trustees, before making investment decisions, must obtain and consider 'proper advice' on whether the investment is satisfactory.

What these requirements mean in detail is set out in the *Occupational Pension Schemes (Investment) Regulations 2005* which have been issued in draft at the time of writing.

(a) The trustees of defined benefit scheme, or the delegated fund manager, must consider scheme funding requirements (including the statement of funding principles (see **13.9**) when making investment decisions.

(b) The powers of investment, or the discretion, must be exercised in a manner calculated to ensure 'the security, quality, liquidity and profitability of the portfolio as a whole' – but this means that the aim is to reflect the 'prudent person' principle and does not mean that that scheme's investments should show profitability at all times.

(c) The scheme's investments should be predominately invested in 'regulated markets' and any assets not invested in a regulated market should be kept at a prudent level. Note that any investment that the trustees have made into a collective investment scheme is treated as an investment on a regulated market if the actual investments held in the collective investment scheme are themselves invested in a regulated market. A 'regulated market' essentially is any securities market which is 'regulated, operates regularly, is recognised by the local competent authorities, is open to the public, is adequately liquid and has adequate arrangements for unimpeded transmission for income and capital to the order of investors, and in respect of which adequate custody arrangements can be provided for the investment when it is dealt in on that market'.

(d) The scheme's assets must be properly diversified in such a way as to avoid excessive reliance on any particular asset, insurer or group of undertakings to avoid accumulations of risk in the portfolio as a whole. Investments in assets issued by the same issuer or by issuers belonging to the same group must not expose the scheme to excessive concentration of risk.

(e) Investment in derivative instruments (see **16.11**) may be made only in so far as they contribute to a reduction of investment risks, or facilitate efficient portfolio management, and any such investment must be made so as to avoid excessive risk exposure to a single counterparty and to other derivative operations.

The requirements made by the *Occupational Pension Schemes (Investment) Regulations 2005*, however, do not apply to schemes with fewer than 100 active and deferred members, although the trustees of such schemes (and any fund manager to whom the trustees have delegated their investment powers) must in exercising their powers of investment have regard to the need for diversification of investments, 'in so far as appropriate to the circumstances of the scheme'. Nor do these requirements apply to wholly insured schemes.

The *Pensions Act 2004* also introduces the new requirements relating to *trustees' knowledge and understanding* which are discussed at **5.1A**. These include the requirement that the trustees must be 'conversant' with their statement of investment principles (that is to say, they must be familiar with, and understand, its contents and purpose) and also that they have knowledge and understanding of the principles relating to the funding of occupational pension schemes and the investment of the scheme's assets and other matters that may be set out in regulations.

Investment committees

16.7   Subject to any restriction imposed by the trust deed and rules, the trustees can delegate their investment powers to a sub-committee of two or more trustees, but if they do they will still all remain responsible for the acts and default of this investment committee. Note in this context also that, if member-nominated trustees have been appointed under the trustees' *appropriate rules*, they must not be allocated functions that differ from other employer-nominated trustees, but that this may not be the case with member-nominated trustee directors in the case of a corporate trustee – see **4.12**. This anomaly disappears with the introduction under the *Pensions Act 2004* of the new requirements for member-nominated trustees and trustee directors. In the case of a board or trustees or of a corporate trustee, the legislation explicitly excludes the making of any rule that excludes an individual nominated by the members from 'the exercise of functions exercisable by other trustees or trustee directors by reason of the fact that he or she has been nominated by the members' – see **4.32**. However, more generally, pension fund trustees as a whole will continue to retain the ultimate responsibility and legal liability for the decisions of the investment sub-committee unless the sub-committee in turn has properly delegated those decisions to a properly appointed person.

Paul Myners held as a key investment principle that it was 'good practice for trustee boards to have an investment sub-committee to provide appropriate focus'.

As explained at **5.1F**, the code of practice issued by the Pensions Regulator to implement the trustee knowledge and understanding requirements introduced by the *Pensions Act 2004* states where the trustee takes on a specialist role such as the chair of an investment sub-committee, there is an expectation that the investment knowledge and understanding for that role is deeper, broader and more technical than that of the trustee which invests exclusively in insurance policies.

Statement of Investment Principles

16.8   The trustees must prepare and maintain from time to time a written statement setting out the principles governing decisions about scheme investments. The *Pensions Act 2004* and the *Occupational Pension Schemes (Investment) Regulations 2005* in redrafting the legislation governing statements of investment principles have made only two major changes of substance. First, the statement must now be revised at least every three years rather than 'from time to time' as previously required by the *Pensions Act 1995*. Secondly, trustees are now required explicitly to disclose their 'risk management methodology', rather that simply their policy on 'risk'.

In order to prepare or revise such a statement, the trustees must obtain and consider written advice from a professionally qualified adviser. The trustees must also consult with the employer who sponsors the pension scheme but are not required by the legislation to secure the employer's agreement to the statement of investment principles in contrast to the requirement to do so in relation to a statement of funding principles (see **13.9**).

The statement of investment principles must cover policy on the following matters:

- the kinds of investments to be held;

- the balance between different kinds of investments;

- the investment risk measurement methods and risk management processes to be used;

- the expected return on investments;

- the realisation of investments; and

- the trustees' policy on using the voting rights attached to the shares held by the fund in companies and on socially responsible investment issues (see **16.26** below).

Trustees who do not comply with the requirements of the *Pensions Act 1995* regarding their investment duties risk being fined, by the Pensions Regulator.

The requirement to prepare and maintain a statement of investment principles does not apply to wholly insured schemes, nor to small schemes with less than 12 members and where all the members are trustees of the scheme and decisions must be made unanimously.

The trustees' Statement of Investment Principles should be a key document governing the scheme, changing as the scheme changes. For example, the investment principles governing a small scheme with no pensioner members and a young workforce will be very different from those governing a large scheme with a higher proportion of pensioners and deferred pensioners than active members. The importance of the requirement for a Statement of Investment Principles lies in the fact that the trustees must set out their own investment standards in the document and then are bound to comply with those self-same standards.

Asset management

16.9   The fund that financially underpins an occupational pension scheme is not static. It is a dynamic system with money constantly moving. Except when there is a complete, but temporary, *contribution holiday* for employers and employees (or perhaps it is a non-contributory scheme as far as employees are concerned), there is a regular flow of contributions into the scheme. New members may also bring transfer credits into the scheme from other pension schemes.

Similarly, the investments or assets already in the fund will also generate income. For example, shares in companies will give rise to income from dividends, property let to businesses will bring in rental income and interest will accrue from cash deposits.

Some or all of this income can be used to meet the cost of paying benefits and the scheme's expenses such as paying the scheme's advisers their fees, and meeting any day-to-day administrative costs for which the scheme rather than the employer is responsible.

However, any excess income can be used to make fresh investments. Likewise, existing financial assets can be sold and the money re-invested to buy other assets.

It may be that in a very mature scheme, the inflow of money from contributions and investments is no longer enough to meet the scheme's expenses and the cost of paying benefits. In this event, a carefully controlled sale of assets will need to be managed to release the required money.

If assets are bought and sold at random it is likely that the fund will perform very badly. If a fund is to meet its desired objectives, all financial advisers are agreed that it must be properly managed according to a thought-out plan: the process of asset management. Asset management, however, does not mean that the plan that is adopted need be inflexible and that investment opportunities should be ignored if they do not immediately fit in with that plan.

Conventionally, asset management is thought of as taking place at three levels; each of which requires a differing level of involvement from the trustees.

Level	*Trustee involvement*
Strategic asset management	High involvement
Tactical asset management	Medium involvement
Stock and individual asset selection	Low involvement

Strategic asset management

16.10   This is the level of the overall and long-term investment policy. It involves primarily the process known as *asset allocation* (i.e. how the fund's investments are divided between the various asset classes). When trustees, following the advice of their actuary or other financial advisers, decide how the pension fund's assets should be divided up into the various asset classes, they are said to be following a *top-down approach*.

The major asset classes are:

- *UK equities* – Ordinary shares in companies traded on the UK stock exchange.

- *Overseas equities* – Ordinary shares traded on foreign stock exchanges.

- *Junior market equities* – Ordinary shares in companies that do not fulfil the requirements for a listing on the main stock market.

- *Private equity (including venture capital)* – Investment in private companies not listed on a stock market.

- *Property* – Either direct ownership of buildings that are let commercially or for residential accommodation or pooled investments in a property fund.

- *Commodities* – Investments in any raw material or agricultural product such as oil, platinum, coffee, cattle.

- *Fixed-interest bonds* – Investments in securities issued by companies, local authorities and governments which give a fixed rate of interest for a predetermined length of time. The fixed-interest securities issued by the UK Government are called gilts.

- *Index-linked bonds* – Securities, usually issued by the Government, where the interest and capital repayments are linked to the movements in the Retail Prices Index.

- *Cash/short-term deposits* – Cash that is invested at high short-term rates.

- *Other assets* – Can include works of art, yachts, rare coins etc.

Each of these asset classes has particular characteristics. For example, looking at long periods of time during the 20th century, equities have outperformed fixed-interest securities. However, they seem to be inherently more risky. In bad trading conditions, companies reduce the dividend paid to their shareholders or even pay no dividend at all. Similarly, share prices rise and fall, and, of course, if a company fails, the shares may become worthless.

In the case of a defined benefit scheme, after taking advice from the scheme's actuary, trustees will know the future pattern of liabilities that the scheme must meet. This can guide them in deciding how the fund should be divided up between the various asset classes.

For example, a defined benefit scheme which is long-established in an industry that is contracting in size may have many more pensioners and deferred pensioners than active members. Employee contributions will tend to fall and its trustees will need to realise its assets in the near future in order to pay pensions. Such a scheme may hold a high proportion of fixed-interest stock which will mature in the near future.

Another defined benefit scheme may be recently established in a growth industry with a very young workforce. The scheme will need to build up its fund but will have a comparatively low level of liabilities in the near future. Such a fund could invest in assets which are more difficult to turn into liquid cash at short notice. Examples are property and equities which are asset classes thought to be more likely to register high growth over long periods.

It was the view of Paul Myners, and one that is embodied in his investment principles (see **17.4** and **17.5**), that the mandate given by the trustees to the investment manager or managers, and the scheme's trust deed and rules 'should not exclude the use of any set of financial instruments, without clear justification in the light of the specific circumstances of the fund'.

A new strand of thinking, however, has developed in recent years in relation to the kind of investments that should be held by a defined benefit scheme. The key ideas were set out by Jon Exley, Shyam Mehta and Andrew Smith in 1997 in a paper published by the Institute of Actuaries entitled *The Financial Theory of Defined Benefit Pension Schemes*. The position taken is that fixed-interest and index-linked bonds provide a better match than equities for defined benefit liabilities. Nevertheless, although bonds provide a better match for their liabilities, the majority of pension schemes continue to hold a significant proportion of their assets in equities. This is because it is commonly held that equities are expected to give rise to higher long-term investment returns than bonds. The downside of this extra expected return is that it comes with risks attached. After adjusting for the risks, it is argued that equities do not reduce the cost of providing defined benefit pensions. Furthermore, there is no guarantee that equities will always outperform bonds.

In 2001, the trustee of the Boots Pension Scheme announced that, over the 15 months ending in July that year, it had authorised the selling of all the scheme's equities and short-term bonds and had moved all its assets into high-credit-rated long-term bonds. John Ralfe, then a member of the Trustee Investment Committee of the Boots Pension Scheme, saw three main arguments in favour of this move, which had caused a sensation in the pensions world:

(a) it increased members' security by matching assets to liabilities with the result that the value of the assets should always be enough to pay all pensions;

(b) it reduced investment management charges and dealing costs in the case of the Boots Pension Scheme from £10m pa down to £250,000 pa; and

(c) it reduced the company's risk by removing the possibility that, by holding equities, a deficit could be created that would have increased employer contributions.

The views put forward by Exley, Mehta and Smith are grounded in corporate finance theory. They are, however, not accepted by many actuaries who believe that equities are an appropriate investment for pension funds to hold when matched against the liability to pay a pension that will not fall until several years into the future. Opinions are sharply divided and exchanges of view have on occasion been heated.

Financial instruments

16.11   These include the following:

- *Financial futures* – contracts binding two parties in a sale or purchase at a specified date at a price which is fixed at the time the contract is made.

- *Traded options* – a contract under which the payment of a sum of money gives a right, but not an obligation, to buy or sell something at an agreed price on or before a specified date.

- *Convertibles* – fixed-interest securities that can be converted into equities on predetermined terms.

- *Warrants* – a stock market security with its own market price which can be converted into a specific share at a predetermined price.

- *Swaps* – an instrument that allows investors to exchange payment streams such as those from interest rates, holding currencies and equity returns

Such financial instruments are in one sense just as much assets and a government bond or an ordinary share in a listed company. They can be bought and sold on regulated markets at an open, market price. Yet, in considering any of them as an asset, it should be remembered that they are ultimately derived from the existence of the fundamental assets classes listed in **16.11** above.

Financial mechanisms

16.11A   There are a number of mechanisms that investment managers can used to try and enhance their investment returns. Some are listed below and the definitions are those supplied by Mercer Investment Consulting:

- *Arbitrage* – profiting from differences in price when the same or equivalent investment is traded on two or more markets in more than one form. By taking advantages of monetary disparities in prices between markets, arbitrageurs perform the economic function of making these markets trade more efficiently.

- *Leverage* – using borrowed money to increase returns.

- *Program trading* – computerised trading used primarily by institutional investors, typically for large volume trades, where orders from the trader's computer are entered directly into the market's computer system and executed automatically.

- *Short position* – whereby an investor sells a stock that he does not currently own. The investor is expecting the stock value to fall, thereby making a profit when the position is closed at the lower price. (Note that the opposite term, *long position*, in fact simply means that an investor currently owns a security, contract or commodity.)Tactical asset management

16.12   The overall strategic decisions are not implemented in an inflexible way. For example, the trustees may have put down a *benchmark* stipulating that the fund is to retain 40% of its total value in overseas equities. That is a long-term average. It could be that during a world-wide recession with generally falling stock markets, the trustees may be advised that it is temporarily better to hold a smaller percentage in the form of equities generally and a higher percentage in cash on short-term deposit. Such decisions will involve the trustees but will be recommended by financial advisers such as the pension consultant as well as the investment managers themselves.

In practice, one might find that the scheme's Statement of Investment Principles will set out the trustees' benchmarked asset allocation policy as in the following table.

Asset class	Benchmark	Allowable range
UK equities	40%	30% to 50%
Overseas equities	20%	10% to 30%
UK fixed-interest bonds	12.5%	7.5% to 17.5%
UK corporate bonds	10%	5% to 15%
Index-linked bonds	7.5%	5% to 10%
All overseas bonds	5%	0% to 10%
Property	2.5%	0% to 5%
Cash	2.5%	0% to 5%

In other words, although the benchmark, for example, for UK equities is that they should represent 40% of the pension fund, the investment manager is free to decrease or increase that weighting anywhere in the range from 30% to 50% of the fund.

In any case, market movements in asset prices will mean that the weighting will change without the investment manager being involved in buying one asset class and selling another. For example, suppose during a year UK equities fell in market value and UK fixed-interest bonds (gilts) rose in market value. In this instance, therefore, assuming at the start of that year the scheme held each of the assets at its exact benchmark proportion, the scheme's UK equities portfolio would drop below its 40% benchmark and the UK gilts portfolio would rise above its 12.5% benchmark simply because of the overall market movements.

If the overall market movements were sufficiently large, the UK equities portfolio would drop through the 30% bottom end of its permitted range, and the UK gilts portfolio would break through its 17.5% ceiling. At this point, the fund managers would seek to rebalance the fund and would begin buying UK equities to bring the scheme's UK equities portfolio back up over 30% of the fund, and begin selling UK gilts to bring the UK gilts portfolio back down below 17.5% of the fund.

Of course, the result of the trustees' policy is that the investment manager buys assets which are currently falling in value and sells assets which are currently rising in value. This may seem to some to be a strange thing to want to do at that time.

On the other hand, trustees who decide to adopt an asset allocation policy are not seeking to maximise the scheme's investment performance over the short term but rather to pursue a long-term investment strategy which usually involves a degree of matching different kinds of assets against different kinds of liabilities.

Hedge funds and absolute return mandates

16.12A There is also a trend, for example, towards the use of 'hedge funds' which may be seen as investment arrangements where the fundamental asset classes and other financial instruments are actively managed within flexible guidelines. Often hedge funds do not have well-defined benchmarks, but rather an 'absolute return' objective or target relative to cash whereby the trustees mandate the investment manager to achieve a specified rate of return rather than, say, mandating them to achieve a return that beats by a specified margin a relevant return achieved by an index which tracks a particular asset class.

In setting such mandates trustees must ensure that they can properly manage the associated risks. Such mandates may in a sense suggest a move away from current benchmarked asset allocation policies to the old mandate given in the 1970s and 1980s which was 'to maximise the investment return and minimise the investment risk'.

Mercer Investment Consulting defines a hedge fund as' a fund that seeks to generate investment returns by using non-traditional investment strategies, utilising mechanisms such as short selling, leverage, programme trading, arbitrage and tools such as options, futures, swaps and forwards (derivatives in general)'.

In many ways it is useful for trustees when considering their strategic asset allocation policy to distinguish between 'assets' and 'mandates'. The asset is the fundamental entity which is owned by the scheme – such as a share in Tesco, or an office block – and the mandate (or 'strategy') is the guidelines set by the trustees to their investment manager on how the assets are to be managed and what objectives are set in terms of the various factors such as investment return, fees, liquidity and volatility.

Stock and individual asset selection

16.13   An investment policy that concentrates on individual stock selection is called a *bottom-up approach*. But even if, as in most cases, a *top-down approach* has been adopted, the decision to buy, say, Glaxo in December 1987 but not to buy, say, Polly Peck is obviously of vital importance since Glaxo soared and Polly Peck went bust.

The trustees will not usually be involved in decisions about which particular shares to buy and sell. As explained above, the *Financial Services and Markets Act 2000* prohibits trustees who are not authorised from being involved in day-to-day decisions – and individual stock selection is perilously close to a day-to-day decision. In the main, these decisions will be left to the investment managers.

There are certain exceptions. Trustees might want to be involved in the discussions of whether to invest in, say, a privatisation issue. Particularly large purchases and sales in a directly-managed property portfolio might also mean closer discussion with the trustees.

Trustees will want to ensure that stock selection is properly diversified and that shares in any particular company do not represent too large a percentage of the overall fund. Shares in a large, blue-chip, UK company will rarely form more than 6% or 7% of the total value of any fund.

Similarly, trustees may lay down certain guidelines that set specific restrictions on stock selection. For example, the trustees of a pension fund in a particular industry may prefer to see the pension fund invest in that industry and it is rare that trustees will object to shares being held in a competitor company. Trustees may also wish to invest in a Venture Capital Fund which invests in small businesses in the specific geographical area of the country where most of the pension fund members are located. Such restrictions should not be allowed to jeopardise the overall financial return of the pension fund. See also the discussion of socially responsible investment at **16.26** below.

The law now restricts pension fund investment in the sponsoring employer – see **16.22**.

Appointing investment managers

16.14   The trustees must appoint the investment manager or managers. They must not rely on the advice of an investment manager who has been appointed by a third party unless that appointment was made on behalf of the trustees.

In-house investment managers

16.15   Where the employer is a bank, insurance company or another financial institution, the associated occupational pension scheme is usually provided by the employer's in-house investment managers. However, some of the UK's larger occupational pension schemes outside the financial sector also employ their own in-house investment management teams. In some cases these in-house investment management teams also compete to take on business from other, unconnected, occupational pension schemes.

Very large schemes can achieve cost savings by using in-house investment teams and there is an obvious advantage in having the expertise at hand, uniquely dedicated to the needs of just one pension fund. Internal communication between trustees and investment managers should ensure a very intimate involvement in the investment process for the scheme's trustees. One possible disadvantage lies in the great difficulty trustees would have in changing in-house managers if they were to lose confidence in them. Some schemes use a combination of in-house and external investment managers.

In the case of the pension funds in the Maxwell Group of companies, the investments were managed by a financial institution that also formed part of the same group of companies. Nevertheless, there have been few calls to ban in-house investment management, but there are implications for custodial services – see **16.23** below.

External investment managers

16.16   Most occupational pension schemes use external investment managers since the benefits of scale of employing an in-house team only begin to emerge when the total assets managed are very large, perhaps well in excess of £1bn.

Trustees may engage just one investment management firm to look after all the fund's assets, or two or more may be appointed either with the same or differing investment briefs.

Trustees have a completely different relationship with external investment managers compared to any of the other professional advisers they may hire. The trustees are likely to build up a long-term and intimate relationship with their actuary or pension consultant. The relationship with the investment manager will usually depend on the investment manager attaining performance targets over relatively short periods of three to five years. Research conducted by Russell/Mellon CAPS, the investment information services provider, shows that on average trustees stay with an investment manager for just over seven years.

16.16   *Investing pension fund assets*

The trustees do not usually have a completely direct relationship with the investment managers although trustees and investment manager will usually meet together at least quarterly to review progress. The relationship is often mediated by the pension consultant or actuary.

Trustees
↓↑
Actuary/Pension Consultant
↓↑
Investment Manager

Appointment of investment managers

16.17   The appointment of the investment manager will be governed by the trust deed and rules: it may be the responsibility of the trustees as a whole, or a sub-group of trustees who form an investment committee.

Generally, the overall investment policy will have been developed by the trustees and the scheme's pension consultant. Once developed, the policy may indicate what kind of investment managers are needed.

The pension consultant is then usually asked to draw up a shortlist of potential investment managers for the scheme. Some trustees responsible for the appointment make visits to the premises of the investment management and spend time discussing the requirements.

The short-listed investment managers will come to meet the trustees and make presentations. Those who are responsible for the appointment will usually put some emphasis on the investment manager's past performance. Eventually a decision will be made and the investment manager or managers are appointed.

Some criticism is now being made of the role of the pension consultant in drawing up the shortlist. It has been alleged that the consultants need to play safe and only tend to nominate the larger well-known firms of investment managers. If the consultants recommended a smaller player who turned out to perform badly, the consultant could be blamed by the trustees and employer for having gone out on a limb. If they recommend the large firms and they perform badly, it is less likely that the consultant will be blamed for having taken the consensus view.

In the recent past, however, the largest investment managers have not dominated the market to the same extent as previously. In part this has been because some of the investment managers have lost clients through lower investment performance. In part it has been as a result of greater use of smaller specialist investment managers. In June 2005 the *Financial Times* published research showing that in 2004 the 20 largest investment managers collectively managed £286.4 bn of assets belonging to segregated funds. Some 40%of this amount was managed by the four largest investment managers. There is still a high concentration of assets in the biggest four investment funds, but it represents a considerably smaller proportion than in the recent past. The comparable percentage among the top 20 investment managers in 1997 was 62%.

Types of investment managers

Balanced/specialist managers

16.18   A balanced fund manager will manage assets across a range of asset classes. The breakdown between the classes will reflect any asset allocation policy worked out by the trustees unless the trustees have given the fund manager discretion to determine the asset allocation policy itself.

A specialist fund manager will manage assets only in one asset class. This is usually, and has long been, the case with property because of the specialised nature of the market. However, specialist managers may now offer expertise in other niche markets, such as Far East equity markets or Government bonds.

Many occupational pension schemes hire a mix of balanced and specialist investment managers.

Active/passive managers

16.19   An active investment manager will try to achieve an overall return from the investments which is superior to an agreed performance benchmark.

A passive manager will try to achieve through stock selection the same weighting in the investment portfolio as makes up some standard index of investments. For example, if managing a portfolio of UK shares, that portfolio of UK shares could be made up of shares in the same weighted proportions as in the FTSE 100 index. The aim is to achieve the same performance as the chosen index.

Again, a mix of active and passive fund managers may be hired by the trustees of an occupational pension scheme.

Customer agreements

16.20   Since the coming into force of the *Financial Services Act 1986*, investment managers and the pension fund trustees have had to enter into a signed customer agreement. This is a lengthy document and should establish all the contractual terms governing the relationship.

It is highly recommended that the trustee's legal adviser should check the contract to ensure that it is satisfactory. The customer agreement should settle the question of fees. In the UK, investment managers usually levy their charges for the provision of investment services to pension fund trustees by means of what is known as an *ad valorem fee*. This is a fee that varies as an annual percentage of the funds being managed according to the absolute amount of these managed funds. The following is a purely hypothetical example of such a scale adopted by the balanced, active investment manager of a £50m pension fund.

Slice of fund	Fee as a percentage	Amount
On the first £12m	0.6% p a	£72,000
On next £30m	0.3% p a	£90,000
On £8m balance	0.15% p a	£12,000
Total £50m	0.348% p a	£174,000

The table is given simply to explain how the *ad valorem* fee system works, but since it is hypothetical it should not used a benchmark. (Note that the fees are expressed in this table as a *percentage* of the value of the fund because that is how most of us tend to express one number as a proportion of another. But investment managers tend to express fees not as percentages but as *basis points*. A basis point is 1/100th of a percentage point, i.e. rather than say that the fee was 0.4% of the fund managed, the investment manager would say that it was set at 40 basis points.)

Such direct fees will also vary according to the portfolio of assets being managed. An investment manager looking after only equities is likely to charge double the rate of an investment manager looking after only bonds. Similarly, an active manager will probably charge more than double the rate of a passive manager. In both cases, the differences in the rates of charges can be justified by the differences in the complexity of the task that the investment manager is being asked to perform. Such a charging structure, although it can be criticised on some grounds, has at least the virtue of being clear and easily visible.

Bundled brokerage and soft commissions

16.20A The customer agreement should also deal with one issue that has long been a concern in the industry. This is the visibility of certain transaction charges that might be met by the pension fund. In particular, the concern relates to soft commission, or *softing* and *bundling*.

Softing refers to the practice whereby services or products (such as computers and information services) are provided by the broker to the investment manager, in part exchange for a predetermined minimum level of the commission-bearing business of carrying out the transactions relating to the investment manager's clients, such as pension funds.

Bundling refers to the practice whereby the investment manager's payment to the broker includes not only a payment to meet the cost of the broker's intermediation services but also the cost of the 'soft' products or services provided by the broker to the investment manager.

The concern is that, under such practices, trust funds can be used in deals whose prime purpose is to gain commission for the investment manager. This expenditure is in practice incurred on the trustees' behalf by the investment manager. This is because the commissions are added to the cost of the purchase, or deducted from the proceeds of the sale, of the asset involved in the transaction and settled against the pension fund's account with the custodian. As Paul Myners said in his March 2001 review of institutional investment: 'In other words, they are paid directly by the pension fund.'

Soft commission is not illegal and the current practice and regulatory framework make it difficult for trustees to opt out of such arrangements, but one of the leading pension consultancies described soft commission back in the early 1990s as a 'murky practice' and called for it to be made unlawful.

Paul Myners in his review of institutional investment proposed that investment mandates should always incorporate a management fee inclusive of the cost of any external research, information or transaction services acquired or used by the investment manager, rather than having these costs passed on to the pension fund.

On 27 July 2001, the Treasury announced how it proposed to carry forward this aspect of Paul Myners' recommendations, an aspect to which the Treasury obviously accorded a high degree of importance, since it commented that responses to the consultation exercise it had carried out after the publication of Paul Myners' review had to led it to believe that the problem was 'if anything, greater than Mr Myners originally suggested'. The Treasury's chief concerns was that the issue suggested that:

- there were insufficient competitive pressures in investment broking and market-making activities; and

- the present obligation under the financial services legislation for 'best execution' (i.e. getting the best deal possible for your client) was not working properly to protect pension funds.

The Government acted to amend the two sets of investment principles devised by Paul Myners (see **17.3**). The relevant principles now state that:

'Trustees, or those to whom they have delegated the task, should have a full understanding of the transaction-related costs they incur, including commissions. They should understand all the options open to them in respect of these costs, and should have an active strategy – whether through direct financial incentives or otherwise – for ensuring that these costs are properly controlled without jeopardising the fund's other objectives. Trustees should not without good reason permit soft commissions to be paid in respect of their fund's transactions.'

The Treasury also asked Paul Myners to develop a set of indicative questions that would help pension fund trustees require better disclosure of the investment costs their fund incurs, and obtain clearer incentives for their managers and brokers. In response, in October 2001, Paul Myners suggested the following ten questions that should be addressed by the trustees to their investment managers:

'1. What is your best view of the level of transaction costs – including not only commission but also market impact and opportunity cost – borne by our fund during the reporting period?

2. What action have you taken to minimise transaction costs while still dealing effectively?

3. Please explain any major differences between the level of costs incurred by you on our behalf and those incurred by other managers as reported in reputable surveys.

4. Were commission rates uniform across all transactions, and if not, what determines the commission rate on a transaction? Explain trend rates on these.

5. Which dealing venues and methods did you choose for our portfolio, why, and how did your choices affect our dealing costs?

6. Which brokers did you deal through and how did you select them?

7. Where you are not using an execution-only broking service, please list other services that you buy or benefits that you receive from the broker concerned – such as research and access to Initial Public Offers (IPOs). Please explain how you evaluate the benefit these generate for us relative to the cost.

8. If you make use of both external research and in-house research, explain what distinguishes the former, for which we pay an additional charge, from the latter, which is covered by your management fee, and how you decide which to use.

9. Explain your rules on entertainment of your staff by brokers and those with whom you transact on our behalf where we bear the cost. Make available the records you keep, your policy guidelines and the approximate number, type and overall value of the events attended.

10. If you wish to make a case for soft commission arrangements, explain how our interests are better served by the broker providing you with services rather than securing lower commission costs for us.'

The Treasury advised trustees to compare the answers given by different investment managers with a view to understanding the extent to which:

•   the fund is incurring a higher or lower level of transaction costs through the trustees' investment manager than would be normal for similar mandates with this or other managers;

•   the investment manager satisfactorily addresses any conflicts of interest between its own commercial interests, those of its associated and other clients and of the trustees' pension fund; and

•   the investment manager is proactively seeking to increase the efficiency of execution of transactions to buy and sell assets though innovation, including the use of new dealing venues, new technologies, the terms of customer agreements and financial instruments.

The Treasury also stated:

'Trustees should be clear that their responsibility is not simply limited to asking the initial question. Where appropriate they must challenge the resulting answers if they are incomplete or unsatisfactory. In line with the principles of investment, they should ensure that they have the appropriate skills and information to address these issues. In particular, they should ensure that those providing advice on these issues have expertise in transaction issues. Trustees should consider the full range of transaction costs, including custody, foreign exchange and deposit arrangements.'

One problem, of course, is that investment managers prepared stock answers to the questions which Paul Myners has devised.

Although the Treasury stated that its preference is for these issues to be tackled through market mechanisms and commercial negotiations, it recognised that this represents a 'significant challenge, especially for pension fund trustees'.

The Treasury had already asked the Financial Services Authority (FSA) to explore how investment managers comply with the 'best execution' rule and this has now been widened to take in the issues presented by the use of soft commissions and the bundling of services. The FSA published *CP 176: Bundled Brokerage and Soft Commissions* in April 2003 and proposed that investment managers would no longer be able to incur costs for services additional to dealing without the customer's express agreement. It reported that up to 40% of total commission spend was used to acquire services additional to dealing. In its *Policy Statement 04/13* in May 2004 and *Policy Statement 04/23* in November 2004, the FSA confirmed that it was limiting the scope for softing and bundling to execution services and investment research and would work with bodies representing investment managers to develop a solution to secure improved management of conflicts of interest through increased transparency and accountability to clients and better payment and pricing mechanisms for both execution and research services.

In March 2005 the FSA published *CP 05/5 Bundled brokerage and soft commission arrangements: proposed rules*. These proposed rules confirm the FSA's position that investment managers' use of commission should be limited to the purchase of 'execution' and 'research' services. This paper also includes details of the work done by the investment management and broker sectors, with the involvement of pension fund trustees, in developing measures to enhance transparency and accountability in soft commission and bundled brokerage arrangements.

The paper sets out the services the FSA considers as legitimately falling within the definition of execution and research, which can therefore be paid for from commission under the new regime, and what it views as being non-permitted services. The FSA is proposing that non-permitted services include, amongst other things, computer hardware, seminar fees and travel or entertainment costs.

The FSA does not propose to state whether particular market pricing and information services are permitted or not but has set guidelines against which all services should be evaluated. The FSA has stated that it expects investment managers to apply these principles to determine whether particular goods and services they propose to acquire with commission are permitted services. They must be able to justify this decision to their clients and the FSA if asked. The FSA, however, has also stated that it is satisfied that the proposals out forward by the investment management representative bodies are a credible way of addressing the lack of transparency and accountability that had been identified. These proposals include:

- descriptions of investment managers' policies, processes and procedures in the management of trading commissions paid on behalf of clients;

- client specific information on how commissions paid have been generated and how they have been used, including a split between amounts of commission spent on execution on the one hand and research on the other;

- reports will be issued by investment managers to UK pension funds from the first quarter of 2006; and

- the encouragement of forward-looking discussions between brokers and fund managers on how commission should be split between research and execution.

Performance measurement

16.21 Trustees of occupational pension funds are urged by the National Association of Pension Funds (NAPF) to subscribe to one of the professional performance measurement services. Performance measurement will allow trustees to judge in an objective manner how their investment managers are performing by obtaining the figure for their fund's quarterly and annual investment return and allow them to compare that performance either with other pension funds over the same period or with the relevant benchmark.

Calculating investment performance is not a totally straightforward exercise. Looking at the market value at the beginning and end of the scheme year will take no account of the flow of money into the scheme from contributions and transfer credits and the flow of money out of the scheme to pay for benefits, transfer payments and administration costs. The performance measurer will need to use *money-weighted* or *time-weighted* techniques to establish the investment performance, allowing for this flow of money into and out of the fund. In brief, a money-weighted technique measures the actual investment return of a particular fund while a time-weighted technique measures what the performance would have been assuming new money had been invested evenly during the period under consideration.

In making comparisons, trustees will also have to consider the degree of *discretion* that they have given the investment manager. If UK equities have performed badly over the period, but the trustees' *asset allocation* policy limits the percentage of the fund that should be held in UK equities, the effect may have been to raise the investment return in comparison to other funds where the investment managers have had complete discretion to decide the scheme's asset allocation policy.

Trustees will want to use performance figures achieved by their investment managers in deciding whether they should be retained or replaced. However, they should give any investment manager a reasonable period over which to gauge performance: a three-year minimum is often recommended. Indeed it forms part of Paul Myners' investment principles (see **17.3–17.5**) that clear timescale(s) of measurement and evaluation should be agreed before the appointment of an investment manager, such that the trustees agree not to terminate that appointment before the expiry of the evaluation timescale by reason of underperformance alone.

It should also be remembered that changing investment managers always involves some cost and investment risks. Trustees are now being advised to appoint a specialist *transition manager* when a change of investment managers is proposed. The aim is to ensure that the transition is effected in the most efficient way so that risks are controlled and costs minimised. The NAPF issued a guide *Transition Management Made Simple – What a Trustee Needs to Know* in November 2001 which gives useful advice in this area.

Because an investment manager knows that the investment performance of the funds it manages will be measured (and also that its mandate will be retained, increased, reduced or removed altogether as a result of that eventual measurement), just *how* the investment performance is measured is bound to influence the investment manager's behaviour.

For example, if a balanced, discretionary fund manager is going to be judged against the median performance of other balanced, discretionary fund managers, then it is very likely that this investment manager will seek to maintain an asset allocation policy that does not differ substantially from the typical asset allocation policy adopted by most balanced, discretionary managers (the so-called 'herd instinct'). To do otherwise is to risk producing an investment performance that differs substantially from the median result.

One problem in such a strategy is that the asset allocation assumed by such a manager trying to achieve the default median performance may be unsuitable for the needs of the pension fund in question, because the assets are not likely to match its liabilities (e.g. a mature fund with a high proportion of pensioners might be thought to require a high proportion of its fund in bonds, but setting a performance target of beating the median fund's performance might be thought to entail having a much higher proportion of the fund in equities).

In fact, many trustees have moved away from the practice of comparing their fund's performance against the median achieved by other pension funds. Instead, with the advice of their investment consultant, often associated with the firm of the scheme's actuary, trustees often set customised performance benchmarks for their investment manager or managers. Russell Mellon, the investment information services company, reports that the proportion of pension funds in its universe that had adopted a scheme-specific benchmark rose from just 4% in 1990 to over 85% by the end of 2003.

These benchmarks rely on the trustees having made an asset allocation policy decision, again with the help of an investment consultant, such that it is decided, for example, that 20% of the fund should be invested in European equities. That fund's investment manager charged with looking after the fund's European equities might then be given the annual performance target of beating by a certain specified margin the year-on-year change in one of the relevant indices measuring the investment return on European equities.

But just as one can criticise the shortcomings of measuring the investment performance of a pension fund against the median achieved by a large number of other, often dissimilar funds, the customised benchmark approach is also not without its difficulties.

One particular difficulty is the choice of the relevant index for the asset class chosen (for example, the portfolio of shares in European companies held by the investment manager may differ from the shares making up the Index). The choice of an index, and how closely the investment manager is expected to track that index, will affect whether the investment manager feels able to buy or sell any particular share. This could be a 'sub-optimal investment strategy'.

As Paul Myners notes in his review of institutional investment:

> 'The customised benchmark approach relies on asset allocation being carried out in a system with limited resources and suboptimal systems of performance measurement. As many of the ultimate customers (that is, trustees) lack expertise to interpret critically the issues and difficulties inherent in the advice they are given, they have little choice but to follow it. Yet they – and not those providing the advice – retain full legal responsibility for their decisions.'

When going through the process of selecting an investment manager, the trustees are usually also interested in that manager's previous track record. In May 1999 a new UK Investment Performance Standard (UKIPS) was introduced via the former Pension Fund Investment Performance Code Monitoring Group, now known as the UK Investment Performance Committee. The code sets out how investment managers must present their own investment performance figures. Although the code is voluntary, in practice it is unlikely that pension fund trustees would want to continue to employ investment managers who did not comply with the UKIPS requirements. The code is internationally recognised and the UK version requires the investment manager to have its performance figures independently verified.

Self-investment

16.22   Self-investment (known more correctly as *employer-related invest-ment*) can take the form of the pension fund owning shares held in the sponsoring company, making loans made to the sponsoring company or the occupational pension scheme owning and leasing back the employer's business premises.

In fact, the trust deed and rules of many schemes have always specifically prohibited any level of self-investment.

During the 1990s there were many instances of the sponsoring company running into financial difficulties. The trustees, who were often senior executives of the company, had borrowed money from the pension fund to help with company cash-flow problems. The company, none the less, went into liquidation and the beneficiaries were left not only jobless but with pension promises that were underfunded or completely worthless.

It was always commonly held that the assets of the occupational pension scheme were at arm's length from those of the company. Where, however, there was self-investment, this could not be true.

As a result of these problems, the *Occupational Pension Schemes (Investment of Scheme's Resources) Regulations 1992 (SI 1992/246)* came into force on 9 March 1992. They restricted to 5% the proportion of the resources which most kinds of occupational pension schemes may invest in the sponsoring company, or any other company associated or connected with it. The legislation was later contained in the *Occupational Pension Schemes (Investment) Regulations 1996 (SI 1996/3127)* and is now found in the *Occupational Pension Schemes (Investment) Regulations 2005* (issued in draft at the time of writing).

The regulations include transitional provisions that give schemes time to reduce any existing self-investment to within the permitted limit.

These regulations have prohibited most kinds of pension scheme from making any loan to the sponsoring employer (regardless of whether or not the loan exceeds the 5% limit).

Any breach by trustees of the self-investment rules is a serious offence which would result in severe fines and in serious cases the Pensions Regulator could instigate criminal proceedings where the breach of the self-investment rules is deliberate or fraudulent.

The employer-related investment restrictions do not, however, apply to small schemes such as small self-administered schemes and executive pension schemes, provided certain conditions are met, including having all the members as trustees and requiring all decisions to be taken unanimously.

Custodial and administrative arrangements

16.23   Custody and administration refers to:

- the safekeeping of all investment securities;

- the process of settlement ensuring that money is paid out for securities that are purchased and that money is received for securities that are sold;

- the transfer of all documentation resulting from the purchase and sale of the securities;

- the collection of dividends resulting from shareholdings;

- carrying out other corporate actions, in particular exercising the voting rights attaching to shares owned by the pension fund;

- the reclaiming of tax;

- the necessary action where discretionary decisions arise in cases of corporate actions or capital changes, such as a new rights issue of shares etc; and

- the full accounting of all transactions and the production of regular financial reports.

The custodian's role in essence is to make the investment decision an actual reality; it comprises all the backroom activities necessary in the investment process.

Given that it is a very different kind of activity from the actual investment decision itself, many investment managers contract out this role to a custodian, often a bank, while other investment managers will work with an associated company acting as the custodian.

The term *global custodian* has emerged to describe the services offered by a custodian skilled in working with several separate investment managers. In such cases, the trustees appoint the global custodian completely independently of whom they choose as their investment managers.

Trustees should pay particular attention to the custodial and administrative arrangements set out in the customer agreement that they sign with their investment managers. It is important, especially in the light of the Maxwell scandal in the early 1990s, that trustees take reasonable steps to ensure that money cannot be removed fraudulently from the pension fund assets held by the custodian.

The investment manager and custodian should make up any fraudulent loss that they were in a position to prevent.

Procedures which may help include:

- reviewing the authorisation procedures for the transfer of any assets out of the pension fund account;

- specifying the accounts to which money can be transferred; and

- ensuring advance notification for any transfer of money above a stated amount.

The major hazards associated with custody are as follows:

- misappropriation through fraud (including computer/electronic systems fraud), and the use of, or failure to detect, forged documents of title or transfer documents, wilful or accidental destruction of records or documents, theft and other loss of documents, including while in transit;

- delivery otherwise than in accordance with authorised instructions;

- the improper use of one customer's investments to settle or secure another's obligations;

- failure to:

  - maintain adequate records identifying an individual customer's entitlement to, and status of, investments;

  - account for entitlements to benefits and tax recoveries; and

  - respond to corporate events (such as preferential share issues to existing shareholders);

- unauthorised use of customers' investments for the custodian's own purposes or commingling of customers' investments with the custodian's own investments in such a way as to place customer's investments at risk in the event of the custodian's insolvency;

- custodians defaulting, in particular when customers' investments are held in an overseas jurisdiction where laws and market practice restrict the recovery and separate identification of investments; and

- deficiencies in documentation such that the division of responsibilities in the event of loss as between customer, an authorised firm and any third parties is unclear.

The 1995 collapse of Barings Bank heightened concerns about the soundness of the custody function. Since 6 April 1997 the *Occupational Pension Schemes (Disclosure of Information) Regulations 1996 (SI 1996/1655)* have required trustees to give the name of their custodian in their annual report to members.

In the wake of the recommendations made in March 2001 by Paul Myners, the Government issued in February 2002 a consultation paper discussing his proposal that there should be a statutory requirement for pension fund trustees to appoint a custodian who is completely independent of the employers who sponsor the pension scheme (see **17.6**). The Government's view was that there was no clear-cut evidence that the existence of an independent custodian within the chain of pension scheme management would do much to prevent fraud. Indeed the Government expressed the view that such a legislative requirement could merely succeed in giving scheme members a sense of security that would not be matched in practice.

The February 2002 paper asked for opinions on whether the appointment of independent custodians should be governed by legislation or by a code of good practice, but also went on to explore other ways of improving pension fund security against fraud. Most of these alternative avenues for promoting security involved tightening up on the customer agreement between the trustees and the investment manager (see **16.21** above).

Stock lending

16.24   The customer agreement should, in particular, be clear about whether and under what conditions *stock lending* is permitted.

Stock is lent by the custodian to institutions involved in the trading of shares for short periods of time in return for a fee. The fee may be passed on to the pension fund, or simply used to reduce the level of fees charged by the custodian.

In normal circumstances, there is no particular risk to the pension fund but the trustees need to ensure that the trust deed and rules of the scheme actually permit stock lending. Trustees would also need to ensure that their fund was reasonably indemnified in case of any default.

Corporate governance issues for trustees

16.25   As at 31 December 2003, the ownership of UK shares was broken down as shown in the table below.

Ownership of total UK equity, 31 December 2003

	£ billion	% of total
Rest of world	441.7	32.3%
Insurance companies	236.9	17.3%
Pension funds	219.8	16.1%
Individuals	203.9	14.9%
Unit trusts	27.2	2.0%
Investment trusts	31.2	2.3%
Other financial institutions	151.3	11.1%
Charities	15.9	1.2%
Private non-financial companies	9.9	0.7%
Public sector	0.3	0.0%
Banks	30.1	2.2%
TOTAL	1,368.0	

Source: Office of National Statistics

The table indicates that the proportion of UK shares owned by UK self-administered pension funds was just over 16% as at the end of 2003. In other words, the trustees of these pension funds owned around one-sixth of British Industry. This represents, however, a much smaller proportion than was the case in 1989 when UK self-administered pension funds ownership of UK equities peaked at over 30%, nearly twice the proportion held today.

Corporate governance is the term used to describe the relationship between the owners of the shares, those who control those shares and the directors of the companies in which the shares are invested. In the case of occupational pension schemes, therefore, it refers to the relationship between trustees, the investment managers of pension funds and the management boards of companies in which the pension funds have invested.

Until the late 1980s institutional investors were not overtly involved in the management decisions of the companies in which they invested. If performance was poor, the investors would pull out and invest elsewhere. Such a policy is not tenable indefinitely, and institutional investors as shareholders have begun to be more involved in pressing for change.

The key issue for the trustees of occupational pension schemes is how the voting rights that go along with share ownership are exercised. The National Association of Pension Funds (NAPF) urges all its members to exercise their shareholder votes whenever possible. Trustees wishing to ensure that this happens must first check that the customer agreement they sign with their investment managers and custodian services makes the relevant provisions, and secondly see that these provisions are observed in practice. Trustees should also consider if they should engage the services of one of the voting services agencies who prepare profiles of companies and alert investors to upcoming issues to be discussed at annual general meetings. There has also in the past been concern that voting instructions issued by pension funds have not always been executed.

The development of corporate governance should strengthen the links between companies and those who invest in them. The *Institutional Shareholders Committee* issued way back in December 1991 a Statement of Best Practice on Corporate Governance whose main points include the following:

(a)   Institutional investors should encourage regular, systematic contact at senior executive level to exchange views and information on strategy, performance, board membership and quality of information.

(b)   Institutional investors will not wish to receive price-sensitive information as a result of such dialogue but may agree to accept it on an exceptional basis as the price of a long-term relationship, although this would require that they suspend their ability to deal in the shares.

(c)   Institutional investors are opposed to the creation of equity shares that do not carry full voting rights.

(d)   Institutional investors should support boards by a positive use of voting rights, unless they have good reasons for doing otherwise. Reasons for voting against a motion should be made known to the board beforehand.

(e)   Institutional investors should take positive interest in the composition of boards of directors, with particular reference to:

    (i)   concentrations of decision-making power not formally constrained by checks and balances appropriate to the particular company; and

    (ii)   the appointment of a core of non-executives of appropriate calibre, experience and independence.

(f)   Institutional investors support the appointment of compensation and audit committees.

(g)   Institutional investors encourage disclosure of the principles upon which directors' emoluments are determined.

(h)   In takeover situations institutional investors will consider all offers on their merits and will not commit themselves to a particular course of action until they have reviewed the best and most up-to-date information available.

(i)   In all investment decision-making institutional investors have a fiduciary responsibility to those on whose behalf they are investing, which must override other considerations.

The last point is crucial. Consider an institutional investor which has 30% of the share capital of Company A. This 30% represents the funds of ten occupational pension schemes, each of whom own 3% of Company A's shares. In each pension fund, shares in Company A represent 5% of the total pension fund. Company A makes a hostile takeover bid for Company B. Company B has an occupational pension scheme which is one of the ten schemes with a 3% holding in Company A. The institutional investor will owe a fiduciary duty to the trustees of the pension fund of Company B who might be expected to oppose the takeover.

The hostile bid fails, then Company B makes a counter hostile bid for Company A. As a result, the shares of Company A rapidly rise in the market. The institutional investor will consider the offer on its merits and the trustees of the ten occupational pension funds may urge the institutional investor to accept the bid. If the takeover were to fail, the share price of Company A would fall again and an opportunity for the beneficiaries of the pension funds to have profited from the high bid price would have been lost. The institutional investor would not have acted in the interest of the pension fund beneficiaries.

The issue that trustees should consider is that although they own the pension fund assets on behalf of the scheme's beneficiaries, effective control of the fund lies with the institutional investor, the investment manager, who is none the less bound by the customer agreement with the trustees.

During the 1990s recommendations by a number of committees were made concerning the proper relationship between institutional investors and the boards of directors of the companies in which those institutions invested. The recommendations of the Cadbury Committee, the Greenbury Committee and the Hampel Committee have had a crucial impact on the development of corporate governance in the UK, especially on sensitive issues such as levels of company directors' pay and contract conditions. Furthermore, pension funds, as one of the largest institutional shareholders of UK companies, have a key role to play in the current major review of company law.

In July 1999 the report of the committee of inquiry into UK Vote Execution, known as the Newbold Committee, was published. It examined the problems that pension funds were actually having in executing the voting rights that attached to their shareholdings. The report recommended that regular, considered voting should be regarded as a fiduciary responsibility by pension fund trustees to the membership. It also encouraged trustees to develop written voting policies which included setting down procedures to ensure that, where voting was delegated to the custodian or investment manager, the votes had indeed actually been lodged. In fact, the *Occupational Pension Schemes (Investment) Regulations 1996 (SI 1996/3127)* were amended with effect from 3 July 2000 so that trustees are required to publish in their statement of investment policy (see **16.9**): 'their policy (if any) in relation to the exercise of the rights (including voting rights) attaching to investments'.

The review of institutional investment in the UK conducted by Paul Myners and published in March 2001 (see **CHAPTER 17**) considered the corporate governance issue in depth. The review found that there was a lack of active intervention by institutional investors (i.e. mainly self-administered pension funds and insurance companies) in the companies in which they invest. This was so even where there was a reasonable expectation that this would enhance the value of investments.

As a result, Paul Myners recommended that UK law should incorporate a duty on those responsible for the investment of pension scheme assets actively to monitor and communicate with the management of the companies in which they invest, and that they exercise their right to vote as shareholders, where, after taking into account the costs of any action, there was a reasonable expectation that such activities were likely to enhance the value of the investment.

In particular, Paul Myners suggested that UK law should adopt a similar requirement to that already in place in theUSA. This recommendation was generally supported by the Confederation of British Industry and the Trades Union Congress.

In its official response to Paul Myners' review, the Government indicated that it would propose legislation in this area (see **17.6**), and in February 2002 it published a consultation paper setting out its proposals. Subject to views expressed in response to the consultation paper, the Government proposes to frame a general requirement to the effect that:

'[those who are] responsible for the investment of the assets of a retirement benefits scheme must, in respect of any company or undertaking (wheresoever resident or incorporated) in which they invest such assets, use such rights and powers as arise by virtue of such investment in the best interests of the members and beneficiaries of such scheme'.

The important point was that this proposed *activism duty* would apply to the pension fund trustees as well as the investment managers. The duty would be applied to the trustees and investment managers of both defined benefit and defined contribution occupational pension schemes, regardless in the latter case of whether or not the members had any discretion as to how monies are invested.

The duty would also generally apply irrespective of the size of the occupational pension scheme, although the costs of actively engaging with companies and exercising shareholder votes for small schemes might well mean that in practice no action was normally taken. This was because to do so would simply not be in the members' best financial interests because the cost would be disproportionate. (The requirement would not be applied to a small self-administered scheme (SSAS) where all the members are trustees of the scheme and those trustees invest the scheme's assets directly.)

The proposed new duty would override any contrary provision in a scheme's trust deed and rules but the trustees could vary the wording of the requirement in the customer agreement with their investment manager in so far as the investment manager is instructed to comply with a specific trustee voting policy.

It is likely that the trustees would have had to disclose to their members their approach to the activism duty, including details of how they would ensure that this statutory duty would be met, possibly through the existing statement of investment principles (see **16.9**) or through the scheme's annual report and accounts (see **9.32**).

In the event, however, in response to the Government's February 2002 consultation on proposed legislation on shareholder activism, the Institutional Shareholders Committee (see above) issued a guidance note on the role of institutional shareholders in shareholder activism on 21 October 2002. The proposals set out in the new statement of principles include strengthened responsibilities for institutional shareholders and their agents, as well as the proposal that the new principles should be included in industry fund management contracts.

Socially responsible investment

16.26   In the famous case between the National Coal Board Trustees of the Mineworkers' Pension Scheme and the National Union of Mineworkers heard before the then Vice Chancellor Sir Robert Megarry in 1984 (*Cowan v Scargill*), the Vice Chancellor said:

'In considering what investments to make the trustees must put on one side their own personal interests and views. Trustees may have strongly held social or political views. They may be firmly opposed to any investment in South Africa or other countries, or they may object to any form of investment in companies concerned with alcohol, tobacco, armaments or many other things. In the conduct of their own affairs of course they are free to abstain from making such investments. Yet if under a trust investments of this type would be more beneficial to the beneficiaries than other investments, the trustees must not refrain from making the investments by reason of the views that they hold.'

Nevertheless, since that judgment the whole issue of socially responsible investment has gained ground. SRI covers a range of areas including the following:

- *Economic issues*, for example whether to invest in local venture capital funds to support the local economy where members and beneficiaries live.

- *Political issues*, for example whether to invest in countries with considerable human rights abuses or even to exercise corporate-governance-type pressures on companies who make donations to political parties.

- *Environmental issues*, such as the adoption of a policy of favouring green investments and pressurising companies who are perceived to damage the environment.

- *Ethical issues*, for example whether to invest in companies making armaments.

Since 1984, some evidence has begun to accrue to suggest that purely on financial grounds it may be imprudent to invest in, say, polluting industries since they will become less profitable on a *polluter pays* principle while heightened public awareness will make companies producing environmentally acceptable products more competitive. The result is that socially responsible investment policies are held to be permissible, even desirable, *provided all other things are equal*. The December 1998 Consultation Paper issued by the then DSS reports that the Government believes that pension scheme trustees should consider in a positive way how their funds are invested. It states: 'We believe that trustees should be free to consider moral and social issues in relation to their investments, provided trustees adhere to the obligations placed on them by trust law and always put the beneficiaries' interests first'.

From 3 July 2000, the trustees have been required to state in their policy 'the extent (if at all) to which social, environmental or ethical considerations are taken into account in the selection, retention and realisation of investments'. This policy statement must be included in their overall Statement of Investment Principles as explained at **16.9** above.

Additional voluntary contributions

16.27 All occupational pension schemes have had to offer their active members an opportunity to make additional voluntary contributions (AVCs). In a money purchase scheme, this may often be an opportunity simply to pay more than the minimum employee contribution required under the scheme rules. In some defined benefit schemes, there will be an opportunity to purchase 'added years' pensionable service via an AVC arrangement. In most defined benefit schemes, however, AVC vehicles are money purchase vehicles offered by an external third party provider.

In many cases a choice of providers is offered. For example, a scheme may offer a deposit-based investment provided by a building society and a with-profits type investment provided by an insurance company.

What is often forgotten is that the trustees of the occupational pension scheme have a duty to ensure that the AVC investments being offered to active members are well managed and represent good value. Trustees should be as concerned with the investment performance of the AVC vehicles as they are with the performance of the pension fund itself. The reality of this duty became apparent at the time of the recent difficulties of Equitable Life, which was the UK's largest provider of AVC policies, although in practice it is not reasonable to have expected trustees to have foreseen the particular difficulties that Equitable Life was to experience.

Trustees should consider what the effect of any charges that are borne by the members will mean for those members who are able only to contribute comparatively modest amounts – any fixed charges will disproportionately penalise this group. Similarly, many active members who pay AVCs have an eye on early retirement possibilities. In certain insured AVC arrangements there are quite severe early surrender penalties for those who do not continue to pay contributions for the full-term of the policy. This may not be made clear to the members by the AVC provider at the time they start out on the policy, and in certain instances the capital sum they have accumulated when they want to draw their pension turns out to be less than the total AVCs that they have paid in. This is unacceptable and trustees should act to protect the interests of their members who entrust their savings to an AVC arrangement provided by the scheme. As an aside, this is one reason that Equitable Life had such a good reputation prior to its troubles: its charges were among the lowest in the market and its administration procedures were very efficient.

The decision by the Treasury to allow from April 2001 certain employees to contribute from the same earnings to both an occupational pension scheme and a personal or stakeholder pension scheme (an easement known as *partial concurrency*) was in itself likely over time to have a huge impact on the AVC and FSAVC markets. This is in part because personal and stakeholder pensions can be taken in part as a tax-free lump sum as this is not open to members of FSAVC schemes or any AVC contract entered into since 8 April 1987. Yet the arrival of *full concurrency* as an intrinsic feature of the new pensions tax regime on 6 April 2006reduces the need for occupational pension schemes to offer AVCs still further. As a result the government has legislated in the *Pensions Act 2004* so that the requirement on trustees to provide AVCs is removed. In practice it is expected that most schemes will continue to keep their existing AVC arrangements open at least to those members who currently contribute to them.

The valuation of bonds and equities

16.28   UK pension funds hold most of their assets in bonds (chiefly those bonds issued by governments and in particular those issued by the UK government) and in the ordinary shares (equities) issued by companies listed on the world's major stock markets. Both bonds and equities normally give rise to an income stream. Both kinds of assets also normally give rise to a capital gain or loss if and when the pension fund comes to sell them in the market.

If you divide the income generated by a bond or an equity by the price of that bond or equity, you find out the 'yield' of that investment. It follows therefore that when the price of a bond or share rises, the yield will fall and when its price falls, the yield will rise.

But how are bonds and equities valued? There are a number of traditional measures.

Equities

16.29   The *dividend yield* is the value of the dividends paid out per share during a year by a company, divided by that company's current share price and the result is expressed as a percentage. As explained above, the higher the company's share price, the lower the dividend yield and vice versa. Dividend yields either reflect actual past dividends (*historic yields*) or best-guess forthcoming dividends (*prospective yields*). The amount of dividends paid out by a company essentially reflects its level of profits. However, companies can distribute profits by buying back shares instead of distributing dividends. Also, some companies that have made no profits and so have paid out no dividends can still have high share prices because investors guess that they will be profitable in future.

For example, last year the ABC Company paid out a total net dividend of 50 pence per share. Its current share price is 339.5 pence. The historic dividend yield is 14.7%.

The *earnings per share* figure is the company's earnings after corporation tax divided by the number of shares in issue. It tells you the total amount earned for each share during the year. It should be noted that not all of these earnings are distributed to the shareholders. Some will be kept to reinvest in the company.

16.29 *Investing pension fund assets*

For example, last year the ABC Company had post-tax profits of £1.276bn and had issued to date 1,446,155,227 shares. The earnings per share figure is therefore 88.2 pence.

The price/earnings ratio (p/e ratio) is the ratio of the share price divided by the earnings per share. One way of looking at this is to say that it tells you how many years of profits are needed to equal the current market value of the company. The higher the price/earnings ratio, the greater is the expectation among investors that the company's profits will grow. Price/earnings can also be based on past data (*historic ratios*) or the estimated profits over the coming year (*prospective ratios*). The price/earnings ratio always moves in the opposite way to the dividend yield.

For example, the ABC Company's share price was 339.5 pence. Its earnings per share was 88.2 pence. Its historic price/earnings ratio was therefore 3.8.

Bonds

16.30   UK pension funds mostly buy long-dated gilts, that is to say bonds issued by the UK Government which will pay a fixed amount of interest each year until their redemption date, which is more than 15 years from the date they were first issued. After the 15-year period the Government will buy them back at their issue price.

The *coupon* is the fixed amount of interest payable each year by the gilt. It is expressed as a percentage of the issue price. So a *Treasury 8pc '21* is a gilt which will pay each year a coupon of 8% of its issue price until the last payment made in 2021, when the original amount borrowed by the Government will be repaid. This amount is known as the *redemption price*.

UK bonds are actively traded and their market price will normally be different from their *redemption price*.

The *current yield* (also known as the *running yield* or the *interest yield*) of the bond is calculated by dividing the bond's coupon by the bond's current market price and expressing the result as a percentage. Therefore as the price of a bond rises, its current yield will fall, and vice versa.

For example, on 3 May 2005 , the Treasury 8pc '21 had a market price of £139.61. The current yield was therefore 5.73%.

The *redemption yield* takes account of the fact that the Government will pay the investor holding the bond the bond's redemption price when it matures. This gives rise to a capital gain or loss depending on whether the current market price is higher or lower than the redemption price. (Note that immediately before the bond's redemption date, the market price of the bond will equal its redemption price.) This capital gain or loss is in addition to the guaranteed future stream of income from the bond. Professional investors will therefore take into account the current value of the capital gain or loss implied by the current market price as well as the future flow of coupons. The formula for calculating the redemption yield is a little complicated but the redemption yield is printed in each day's *Financial Times*. For example, on 3 May 2005, the Tr 8pc '21 had a redemption yield of 4.51%.

Checklist 16

- Trustees of self-administered schemes have a duty to invest under the 'prudent men and women' principle and have a duty to take advice. They also have a higher standard of care expected of them – of having 'knowledge and understanding' of relevant matters.

- The *Financial Services and Markets Act 2000* precludes trustees who are not authorised from taking the day-to-day investment decisions – these must be delegated to an authorised investment manager.

- Trustees have the power to make investments as if they were absolutely entitled to them.

- The trustees' use of their investment powers cannot be made subject to the employer's consent.

- The trustees must prepare, maintain and then comply with a *Statement of Investment Principles* which should be a key scheme document.

- The trustees must, with advice, decide on the relative allocation of scheme's resources among the various asset classes and in many ways this will be affected by the nature of the scheme's emerging liabilities and, where applicable, also by the minimum funding requirement or from 23 September 2005 by the new scheme funding rules under which the trustees of defined benefit schemes must also prepare and from time to time review and if necessary revise a written statement of funding principles.

- The trustees of a self-administered scheme must appoint the scheme's investment manager or managers and must not rely on the investment advice of a manager appointed by a third party unless that appointment was made on behalf of the trustees.

- Trustees should be happy about the content of the customer agreement between themselves and the investment manager and ensure that it has been checked by their lawyer. The agreement should be completely transparent regarding the investment manager's fees.

- Trustees ought to subscribe to one of the performance measurement services. Trustees should also agree with their investment managers at the time of their appointment over what period of time their

---

performance will be assessed, and not dismiss them before the end of that period on the ground of poor investment performance.

- Self-investment (employer-related investment) is subject to strict statutory limits and may be banned altogether by the trust deed and rules.

- Trustees should be vigilant about custody arrangements to ensure that they are efficient and contain safeguards to prevent fraud.

- Trustees should not seek to avoid their corporate governance responsibilities and should employ the voting power of shares that are held by the fund. Trustees ought to consider becoming active shareholders of the companies in which they invest, where this is in the best interests of their members, in the light of the voluntary approach to strengthening the role of institutional investors in the governance of the companies of which they are part owners.

- Trustees are not prevented from taking ethical and other socially responsible investment issues into consideration but this must not displace their duty to invest the funds for the financial benefit of their members.

- Trustees also have a duty to ensure that in-house AVC arrangements represent good value and offer satisfactory investment performance.

Chapter 17

Investment issues after Myners

Introduction

17.1   In his budget speech of 21 March 2000, the Chancellor of the Exchequer announced that he had asked Paul Myners, then Chairman of Gartmore Investment Management, to look at whether there were factors discouraging institutional investors from investing in smaller firms' and to report back with recommendations by the next Budget. Paul Myners subsequently issued in May 2000 a wide-ranging consultation paper in which he stated:

'Pension fund trustees do not in general seem to be drawn from the ranks of those experienced in investment. Anecdotal evidence suggests that while some pension funds do have high quality training programmes for trustees, many trustees receive little training. Moreover, most are employed, and in practice appear to have limited time to devote to their duties, which of course extend beyond simply investment decision making.

Given this, and given also pension funds' objectives as set out above, it seems reasonable that trustees' major concern is likely to be to avoid what they perceive as underperformance. With limited time and expertise available to meet this goal, one would expect them to rely heavily on professional advice and to feel most comfortable replicating the practices and decisions of others.'

He then asked those considering the consultation paper whether this was a valid description of the approach of a significant number of pension fund trustees and whether trust law provided an appropriate basis for pension scheme governance, particularly investment decisions.

Paul Myners made a interim report to the Chancellor of the Exchequer and also to the Secretary of State for Social Security (now Secretary of State for Work and Pensions) in November 2000. This was so that he could himself respond to the separate Government consultation exercise on the minimum funding requirement (MFR) by recommending that it should be abolished because, among other things, he saw it as seriously distorting pension fund investment decisions.

His overall response was made in his final report *Institutional Investment in the UK: A Review* which was published on 6 March 2001, the day before the Chancellor's Budget speech. This is an important document and should be required reading for all pension fund trustees. It is available on the Treasury web site at http://www.hm-treasury.gov.uk/media//843F0/31.pdf.

The recommendations made in that report, which were accepted in principle by the Chancellor the day following its publication, form the substance of this chapter.

Following the publication of Paul Myners' review, the Government launched a two-month further consultation period ending on 15 May 2001. On 27 July 2001, the Treasury announced how it proposed to carry forward one particular recommendation that Paul Myners had made. This concerned how a pension fund's investment transaction costs, such as brokers' services, should be met (see **16.19**). Later, on 2 October 2001, the Treasury published its overall, detailed response to *Institutional Investment in the UK: A Review*.

Voluntary code for pension fund investment

17.2   A key component of Paul Myners' review was the drawing up of two sets of investment principles for pension funds, one for defined benefit schemes and one for defined contribution schemes. The Treasury made some minor revisions to these sets of principles and issued the revised sets of principles as part of its detailed response to Paul Myners' review.

The Government's policy is that pension fund trustees should adopt these principles as best practice, and expects them to disclose publicly their compliance with them on a voluntary basis. However, as recommended by Paul Myners himself, there was to be a public assessment carried out by the Government of the effectiveness of the principles in bringing about the desired changes two years after the publication of the review. The Government assessment began in March 2003 and published its conclusions in December 2004.

The Government proposed at the onset of the assessment that the principles, as revised, should not apply to insured occupational pension schemes, where in effect the trustees have delegated responsibility for all investment decisions except for the choice of the fund manager. It should also be noted that insured occupational pension schemes are subject to the separate review that was undertaken by Ron Sandler, as commissioned by the Treasury following a recommendation by Paul Myners for such a review. The Sandler review embraced all retail savings products, not only insured pension schemes, and was published in July 2002.

The Government did not exempted other small schemes from the new requirements set out by Paul Myners but stated that it recognised that it was more difficult for small schemes to implement certain elements of the revised principles. The Government's view is that the appropriate course of action is for the trustees of a scheme in this position to explain why they have not implemented the element in question.

Revised text of principles

17.3 We reproduce below the text of the principles devised by Paul Myners in *Institutional Investment in the UK: A Review* as revised by the Government and released on 2 October 2001. The Government's proposed changes outlined in December 2004 are reported at **17.6** below.

As explained above, there are two sets of principles: the first relates to defined benefit schemes and the second to defined contribution schemes.

Defined benefit pension schemes

DB Principle 1. Effective decision-making

17.4 Decisions should be taken only by persons or organisations with the skills, information and resources necessary to take them effectively. Where trustees elect to take investment decisions, they must have sufficient expertise and appropriate training to be able to evaluate critically any advice they take.

Trustees should ensure that they have sufficient in-house staff to support them in their investment responsibilities. Trustees should also be paid, unless there are specific reasons to the contrary.

It is good practice for trustee boards to have an investment sub-committee to provide the appropriate focus.

Trustees should assess whether they have the right set of skills, both individually and collectively, and the right structures and processes to carry out their role effectively. They should draw up a forward-looking business plan.

DB Principle 2. Clear objectives

Trustees should set out an overall investment objective for the fund that:

● represents their best judgement of what is necessary to meet the fund's liabilities given their understanding of the contributions likely to be received from employer(s) and employees; and

● takes account of their attitude to risk, specifically their willingness to accept underperformance due to market conditions.

Objectives for the overall fund should not be expressed in terms which have no relationship to the fund's liabilities, such as performance relative to other pension funds, or to a market index.

DB Principle 3. Focus on asset allocation

Strategic asset allocation decisions should receive a level of attention (and, where relevant, advisory or management fees) that fully reflect the contribution they can make towards achieving the fund's investment objective. Decision-makers should consider a full range of investment opportunities, not excluding from consideration any major asset class, including private equity. Asset allocation should reflect the fund's own characteristics, not the average allocation of other funds.

DB Principle 4. Expert advice

Contracts for actuarial services and investment advice should be opened to separate competition. The fund should be prepared to pay sufficient fees for each service to attract a broad range of kinds of potential providers.

DB Principle 5. Explicit mandates

Trustees should agree with both internal and external investment managers an explicit written mandate covering agreement between trustees and managers on:

- an objective, benchmark(s) and risk parameters that, together with all the other mandates, are coherent with the fund's aggregate objective and risk tolerances;

- the manager's approach in attempting to achieve the objective; and

- clear timescale(s) of measurement and evaluation, such that the mandate will not be terminated before the expiry of the evaluation timescale for underperformance alone.

The mandate and trust deed and rules should not exclude the use of any set of financial instruments, without clear justification in the light of the specific circumstances of the fund. Trustees, or those to whom they have delegated the task, should have a full understanding of the transaction-related costs they incur, including commissions. They should understand all the options open to them in respect of these costs, and should have an active strategy – whether through direct financial incentives or otherwise – for ensuring that these costs are properly controlled without jeopardising the fund's other objectives. Trustees should not without good reason permit soft commissions to be paid in respect of their fund's transactions.

DB Principle 6. Activism

The mandate and trust deed should incorporate the principle of the US Department of Labor Interpretative Bulletin on activism. Trustees should also ensure that managers have an explicit strategy, elucidating the circumstances in which they will intervene in a company; the approach they will use in doing so; and how they measure the effectiveness of this strategy.

DB Principle 7. Appropriate benchmarks

Trustees should:

- explicitly consider, in consultation with their investment manager(s), whether the index benchmarks they have selected are appropriate; in particular, whether the construction of the index creates incentives to follow sub-optimal investment strategies;

- if setting limits on divergence from an index, ensure that they reflect the approximations involved in index construction and selection;

- consider explicitly for each asset class invested, whether active or passive management would be more appropriate given the efficiency, liquidity and level of transaction costs in the market concerned; and

- where they believe active management has the potential to achieve higher returns, set both targets and risk controls that reflect this, giving the managers the freedom to pursue genuinely active strategies.

DB Principle 8. Performance measurement

Trustees should arrange for measurement of the performance of the fund and make formal assessment of their own procedures and decisions as trustees. They should also arrange for a formal assessment of performance and decision-making delegated to advisers and managers.

DB Principle 9. Transparency

A strengthened Statement of Investment Principles should set out:

- who is taking which decisions and why this structure has been selected;

- the fund's investment objective;

- the fund's planned asset allocation strategy, including projected investment returns on each asset class, and how the strategy has been arrived at;

- the mandates given to all advisers and managers; and

- the nature of the fee structures in place for all advisers and managers, and why this set of structures has been selected.

DB Principle 10. Regular reporting

Trustees should publish their Statement of Investment Principles and the results of their monitoring of advisers and managers. They should send key information from these annually to members of these funds, including an explanation of why the fund has chosen to depart from any of these principles.

Defined contribution pension schemes

DC Principle 1. Effective decision-making

17.5   Decisions should only be taken by persons or organisations with the skills, information and resources necessary to take them effectively. Where trustees elect to take investment decisions, they must have sufficient expertise and appropriate training to be able to evaluate critically any advice they take.

Where scheme members are given a choice regarding investment issues, sufficient information should be given to them to allow an appropriate choice to be made.

Trustees should ensure that they have sufficient in-house staff to support them in their investment responsibilities. Trustees should also be paid, unless there are specific reasons to the contrary.

It is good practice for trustee boards to have an investment sub-committee to provide appropriate focus.

Trustees should assess whether they have the right set of skills, both individually and collectively, and the right structures and processes to carry out their role effectively. They should draw up a forward-looking business plan.

DC Principle 2. Clear objectives

In selecting funds to offer as options to scheme members, trustees should:

- consider the investment objectives, expected returns, risks and other relevant characteristics of each fund, so that they can publish their assessments of these characteristics for each selected fund; and

- satisfy themselves that they have taken their members' circumstances into account, and that they are offering a wide enough range of options to satisfy the reasonable return and risk combinations appropriate for most members.

DC Principle 3. Focus on asset allocation

Strategic asset allocation (for example for default and lifestyle options) should receive a level of attention (and, where relevant, advisory or management fees) that fully reflects the contribution they can make to achieving investment objectives. Decision-makers should consider a full range of investment opportunities, not excluding from consideration any major asset class, including private equity.

DC Principle 4. Choice of default fund

Where a fund is offering a default option to members through a customised combination of funds, trustees should make sure that an investment objective is set for the option, including expected returns and risks.

DC Principle 5. Expert advice

Contracts for investment advice should be open to competition, and fee rather than commission based. The scheme should be prepared to pay sufficient fees to attract a broad range of kinds of potential providers.

DC Principle 6. Explicit mandates

Trustees should communicate to members, for each fund offered by the scheme:

- the investment objective for the fund, its benchmark(s) and risk parameters; and

- the manager's approach in attempting to achieve the objective.

These should also be discussed with the fund manager concerned, as should a clear timescale(s) of measurement and evaluation, with the understanding that the fund mandate will not be terminated before the expiry of the evaluation timescale for underperformance alone.

Trustees, or those to whom they have delegated the task, should have a full understanding of the transaction-related costs they incur, including commissions. They should understand all the options open to them in respect of these costs, and should have an active strategy – whether through direct financial incentives or otherwise – for ensuring that these costs are properly controlled without jeopardising the fund's other objectives. Trustees should not without good reason permit soft commissions to be paid in respect of their fund's transactions.

DC Principle 7. Activism

The mandate and trust deed should incorporate the principle of the US Department of Labor Interpretative Bulletin on activism. Managers should have an explicit strategy, elucidating the circumstances in which they will intervene in a company; the approach they will use in doing so; and how they measure the effectiveness of this strategy.

DC Principle 8. Appropriate benchmarks

Trustees should:

- explicitly consider, in consultation with their investment manager(s), whether the index benchmarks they have selected are appropriate; in particular, whether the construction of the index creates incentives to follow sub-optimal investment strategies;

- if setting limits on divergence from an index; ensure that they reflect the approximations involved in index construction and selection;

- consider explicitly for each asset class invested, whether active or passive management would be more appropriate given the efficiency, liquidity and level of transaction costs in the market concerned; and

- where they believe active management has the potential to achieve higher returns, set both targets and risk controls that reflect this, giving managers the freedom to pursue genuinely active strategies.

DC Principle 9. Performance measurement

Trustees should arrange for measurement of the performance of the funds and make formal assessment of their own procedures and decisions as trustees. They should also arrange for a formal assessment of performance and decision-making delegated to advisers and managers.

DC Principle 10. Transparency

A strengthened Statement of Investment Principles should set out:

- who is taking which decisions and why this structure has been selected;

- each fund option's investment characteristics;

- the default option's investment characteristics, and why it has been selected;

- the agreements with all advisers and managers; and

- the nature of the fee structures in place for all advisers and managers, and why this set of structures has been selected.

DC Principle 11. Regular reporting

Trustees should publish their Statement of Investment Principles and the results of their monitoring of advisers and managers. They should send key information from these annually to members of these funds, including an explanation of why the fund has chosen to depart from any of these principles.

Result of the assessment

17.5A   In December 2004 the Treasury published '*Myners principles for institutional investment decision- making: review of progress*'. The document is available at
http://www.hm-treasury.gov.uk/media/DCB/53/myners_principles_web.pdf.

The report also acted as a consultation document both setting out the results of the Government's review of the extent to which the Myners principles have been effective in bringing about behavioural change, as well as seeking views on its findings and proposals for change.

The review itself was based on evidence which had been collected during the period of assessment, some of which had already been made public. This evidence included a structured qualitative study of 14 pension schemes, which had been published in November 2003, and a quantitative survey of trustees representing 1,580 occupational schemes, which had been published in July 2004.

The December 2004 *review of progress* reported that action was certainly being taken on a voluntary basis by many schemes. Over half of all trustees surveyed agreed that the Myners principles provided guidelines for best practice, and 'had encouraged formalisation of previously ad hoc behaviour, leading to trustees being better informed and addressing issues they would not otherwise have considered'.

The review found that schemes representing a majority of occupational scheme members had taken formal decisions to act – in some way and to some extent, not necessarily resulting in full implementation – on six of the ten key issues covered by the principles. Larger schemes (those with more than 1,000 members) which represented more than 90% of total scheme membership were significantly more likely than smaller schemes to have taken action on the issues arising from the principles.

Around 70% of schemes reported that they were fully, or mostly, compliant with the principles in aggregate. Yet the Treasury's review remarked that this self-assessment of overall progress might be in itself a matter of concern, as it did not appear to be borne out by the progress which the survey indicated had been made against each principle individually. Also the review found that 18% of all schemes had taken no action on the principles during the two years following their publication.

The review identified the following areas where the Treasury had found progress was lagging, and 'where pension funds are therefore not yet likely to be serving their members' and sponsors' interests as well as they might':

- many trustee boards have not yet attained the levels of skill, expertise and resourcing necessary to achieve the improvements in investment decision making envisaged by Myners. This overarching deficit is a contributor to the other areas of poor progress;

- a continuing lack of clarity of the respective roles of trustees and their advisers;

- insufficient resources being devoted to the asset allocation process, relative to its impact on total fund returns;

- a continuing mismatch in perception between trustees and fund managers over the investment time horizons managers to which are working;

- insufficient promotion of shareholder engagement;

- poor quality of commentary on, and disclosure of, progress in implementing the principles.

Proposed changes

17.5B　In the December 2004 review of progress, the Treasury proposed to strengthen and amplify the Myners principles in respect of the areas where it judged progress had lagged. These proposed revisions are as follows:

- the chair of the trustee board should be responsible for ensuring that trustees taking investment decisions are familiar with investment issues and that the board has sufficient trustees for that purpose;

- for funds with more than 5,000 members, the chair of the board and at least one-third of trustees should be familiar with investment issues (even where investment decisions have been delegated to an investment subcommittee);

- funds with more than 5,000 members should have access to in-house investment expertise equivalent at least to one full-time staff member familiar with investment issues;

- as well as contracting separately for investment and actuarial advice (as the principles currently require), in relation to investment advice, funds should also contract separately for strategic asset allocation and fund manager selection advice;

- trustees should provide the results of monitoring of their own performance to members, and ensure that key information provided to members is also available on a dedicated pension fund web site.

The Government also stated that it would explore the practicalities of a voluntary, independently compiled report on compliance with the Myners principles by trustees. These might be similar to the reports issued by the Audit Faculty – formerly known as the Financial Reporting and Auditing Group (FRAG) of the Institute of Chartered Accountants in England and Wales – which have been commissioned by custodians to demonstrate to clients their compliance with various internal control procedures. The Treasury sees such a development as helping to provide an informed commentary on how the principles are being implemented, and helping trustees to validate and benchmark their decision-making procedures more effectively.

The *review of progress* document contains drafts of how the Myners principles would be reworded to incorporate the proposed changes outline above.

Legislative proposals

17.6   Although the Government's formal response to Paul Myners' review issued on 2 October 2001 stressed that it wanted pension fund trustees to adopt the investment principles voluntarily as best practice, with the caveat the they should disclose publicly their compliance with them, the response also listed two areas where the Government was considering whether to introduce legislation in the near future. These two areas of proposed legislation were as follows:

- where pension fund trustees are taking an investment decision, they should be able to take it with the skill and care of someone familiar with the issues concerned;

- UK law should incorporate an activist duty (similar to the one imposed under US legislation) on those responsible for the investment of pension scheme assets so that pension fund trustees or their investment managers intervene when necessary in the governance of the companies in which the pension fund holds shares.

The first of these two areas has now been incorporated into the legislation but is now generally known as the trustee 'conversance' and 'knowledge and understanding requirements' and are explained at **5.1A**.

On 4 February 2002 the Government issued further consultation papers outlining its proposals for legislation in these two areas, plus a further paper asking whether legislation would be necessary in a third area, custody, where Paul Myners had suggested that legislation was needed. The issues regarding custody and corporate governance are discussed in **CHAPTER 16** (see **16.23** and **16.25** respectively), but in both cases the Government later confirmed that the results of the consultation have led, at least in the immediate term, to a decision not to go down the legislative route but instead to rely on the existing requirements and voluntary codes.

Checklist 17

- Trustees of an occupational pension scheme are strongly advised to read *Institutional Investment in the UK – A Review* and the Treasury's December 2004 assessment of compliance with the principles and its proposed changes.

- Trustees should be familiar with the set of investment principles applying to their scheme and should adopt these principles as best practice.

- Trustees should disclose publicly their compliance with these investment principles, explaining why in any particular case they have departed from any of those principles.

- The Government began to assess the level of voluntary compliance with the investment principles in March 2003 and reported in December 2004 setting out some proposed changes to principles.

- A key investment principle set by Paul Myners is that where trustees elect to take investment decisions, they must have sufficient expertise and appropriate training to be able to evaluate critically any advice they take and this requirement has now been introduced by the Pensions Act 2004 as a legislative requirement.

- Pension scheme trustees are not required to become investment experts but they should have sufficient expertise to be able to evaluate whether the advice they receive is complete, up to date and based on appropriate assumptions, and should exercise their own judgement when considering and acting upon advice.

Chapter 18

Conduct of trustee meetings

Introduction

18.1   The following description of how Robert Maxwell chaired a trustee meeting was given by a former trustee of Mirror Group Pension Fund to the House of Commons Social Security Committee:

> 'The style of the meetings was that you would be kept waiting around for hours, including senior Directors and Editors of newspapers, and suddenly he would whirl in his shirt sleeves and conduct two hours of business in five or six minutes. You just could not raise matters, they were steamrollered through. The helicopter would arrive, and out he would go in a puff of smoke, and you were left asking, "what was that?"

> At one stage we asked for verbatim minutes to be taken, because we were so unhappy that minutes as recorded did not agree with all our understandings of what happened at the meeting. Often minority viewpoints frequently expressed by myself and other trustees were just simply not recorded and there was no comeback. We could protest, but still we were not able to get meetings scheduled, we could not raise agenda items and we could not get the minutes published. There was also quite a lot of manipulation in the way the meetings were held. They could be held at two days' notice, with no access to the previous minutes, no agenda, and the reports and valuations were placed before you at the meetings. It is very difficult to wade through all that detailed information at one minute's notice.'

Clearly, in such a meeting, trustees are unable to carry out their duty of care towards the scheme's beneficiaries and a breach of trust is almost certain.

The trust deed and rules may specify how trustee meetings are to be conducted or it may give the trustees power to make their own regulations on how they should operate. What is important is that there should be formal rules of conduct which are observed. That is not to say that the meeting itself should be unduly formal in tone.

Who chairs the trustee meeting?

18.2   The trust deed and rules may specify who should chair the trustee meetings or alternatively simply state that the trustees should make their own rules on how a chairman is appointed. In practice, the appointment is usually in the gift of the employer.

Setting the agenda

18.3   An occupational pension scheme has its own regular annual calendar marked by the need to issue trustee reports, consider auditor's reports, listen to reports from the investment manager, decide on the level of discretionary increase to pensions and the like. Other items, such as the need to exercise a discretionary power as to who is to receive a death-in-service lump sum, can arise at any time in the year. Actuarial reports may be on a three-yearly cycle. Important items such as a merger with another scheme, or a major change in benefit design will require detailed discussion. Trustees will also want to consider wider issues that may arise from time to time. For example, the trustees may need to discuss the effect on the scheme of any new legislation.

Much of the agenda will necessarily be set by the needs of the scheme. It will be usual, therefore, for the scheme's pensions manager, who ordinarily acts as the secretary at the trustees' meeting, to prepare an agenda to include all the matters of business that must be considered. This will then be agreed with the chairman.

However, matters raised by trustees at the last meeting and which it was agreed would appear on the next meeting's agenda must not be forgotten.

It may be best practice for the secretary to the meeting to send to each trustee a reminder notice of the approaching trustee meeting and ask if he or she has items that should be placed on the agenda.

Reaching decisions

18.4   Probably most trustee meetings reach most of their decisions purely by resolution. A piece of paper is circulated, discussed and nodded through. No formal vote is taken.

Yet to be valid any decision must be passed by a quorum at a meeting and to this end the trust deed and rules or the trustees' own formal regulations should specify how many trustees have to be present to form that quorum. In the case of a corporate trustee, the quorum may be specified in the Articles of Association. In practice either two-thirds or a majority of the trustees is usually specified as the quorum. In cases where 'member trustees' and 'management trustees' are separately distinguished, the rules may specify that a minimum number from each trustee category must be present for the meeting to be quorate.

The trust deed and rules or the trustees' own regulations should also specify whether the trustees are to act by unanimous or majority decision. (If they do not, then under the *Pensions Act 1995* decisions must be by majority, whereas the previous default under trust law required unanimity. This provision technically only applies to meetings of trustees rather than the trustee directors in the case of a corporate trustee.) If a vote is evenly split, it should similarly be specified if the chairman is to have the casting vote.

The *Occupational Pension Schemes (Scheme Administration) Regulations 1996 (SI 1996/1715)* also set out rules governing the proper notice that must be given to each trustee of trustee meetings. Normally, notice should be sent not less than ten working days before the meeting. Meetings can be held at shorter notice where this is necessary as a matter of urgency to make a decision. The notice must specify the time, date and place of the meeting. If an individual trustee finds that he or she has not been invited to a meeting, or meetings at short notice were held without his or her consent, the trustee can complain to the Pensions Regulator. The trustee responsible for convening meetings, i.e. the chairman of the trustees, could be fined or removed by the Pensions Regulator if he or she fails to take reasonable steps to ensure the proper conduct of meetings. Again, technically these regulations only apply to meetings of trustees, not of trustee directors in the case of a corporate trustee.

It is important to remember that each individual trustee bears a collective responsibility for any action or inaction of the trustee body. If a trustee knows that a decision will constitute a breach of trust, he or she is not absolved simply by voting against it.

Recording decisions

18.5 The *Pensions Act 1995* requires trustees to ensure that there are written records of all their meetings, including meetings of any trustee sub-groups.

The *Occupational Pension Schemes (Scheme Administration) Regulations 1996* require that these records should at least contain the following details:

- the date, time and place of the meeting;
- the names of all the trustees invited to the meeting;
- the names of the trustees who attended the meetings and those who did not attend;
- the names of any professional advisers or any other person who attended the meeting;
- any decision made at the meeting; and
- whether, since the previous meeting, there has been any occasion where a decision has been made by the trustees and if so, the time, place and date of such a decision; and the names of the trustees who participated in that occasion at which a decision was made.

Although the wording of the Act does not apply to meetings of trustee directors, it would seem to be a good idea that trustee directors should adopt a comparable standard of record keeping.

It is not intended under the Act that records of trustee meetings should necessarily be disclosed to scheme members. Rather, the intention is that all trustees, including any who may not have been involved when any decision was taken, should have access to these records. The minutes of trustees' meetings may be automatically copied to the scheme's auditors and also made available where relevant to the scheme's other advisers, in particular the scheme actuary and scheme lawyer.

In a court case known as *Re Londonderry's Settlement*, the Court of Appeal held that minutes of trustee meetings containing the reasons the trustees had exercised their discretionary powers in a particular way do not have to be disclosed to the beneficiaries of the trust. This principle stands even though the minutes are considered to be the property of the trust. The confidentiality of the minutes is a long-standing principle and based on the view that individuals could not be called upon to serve as trustees and to exercise the discretionary powers given to them by the trust deed if, in the absence of bad faith, they were to have their reasons called into question either by the beneficiaries or by the court. It should be noted, however, that if the trustees do give their reasons, those reasons are then open to question.

The Scheme Administration Regulations require a record to be kept of trustees' decisions taken at a meeting but do not specify the amount of detail that needs to be recorded on how the trustees came to make that decision in that particular way. It might be thought that the trustees should not record the reasons they arrived at a particular decision, but in view of the *Wednesbury Principles* (see **5.4**) it might be useful if the minutes could demonstrate that the trustees did consider all the relevant facts, and just as importantly, did not take into consideration any irrelevant facts, in arriving at their decision. If the trustees can be shown to have:

- asked themselves the correct questions;

- directed themselves correctly in law; in particular they must adopt a correct construction of the trust deed and rules; and

- not arrived at a perverse decision, i e a decision to which no reasonable body of trustees could arrive;

then neither the Pensions Ombudsman nor the courts are likely to overturn a decision made by trustees properly using their discretionary powers. It should be noted that in the case of *Wilson v The Law Debenture Trust Corporation* the judge held that, in the absence of evidence to the contrary, the presumption is that the trustees have exercised their discretion properly.

Furthermore, in the *Wilson* case the judge held that, in the absence of any evidence of impropriety, the court will not compel the trustees of a pension scheme to disclose the reasons they exercised their discretion in any particular way. However, this needs to be set against the statutory powers given to the Pensions Ombudsman to force discovery of scheme documents. These statutory powers are set out at *ss 149* and *150* of the *Pension Schemes Act 1993*. The Pensions Ombudsman in investigating a complaint may require any person responsible for the management of the scheme to which the complaint relates to furnish information or produce documents relevant to the investigation.

On 25 April 2002 the Pensions Ombudsman issued a determination involving a complaint brought by Mr Allen against the corporate trustee of the TKM Group Pension Scheme. The determination is reported as *C Allen Determination by the Pensions Ombudsman*. The main issue was that the trustee had refused to disclose minutes of a meeting during which Mr Allen's application for an unreduced early retirement pension had been refused. The determination is of interest because of the remarks made by the Pensions Ombudsman to the effect that an absence of a breach of law does not mean there is no act of maladministration – see **11.4**, where this part of the Pensions Ombudsman's determination is quoted.

In other words, just because there is no legal duty on trustees to make a copy of their minutes available to a complainant, this does not imply that in actually refusing to do so, the trustee could not be committing an act of maladministration. The Pensions Ombudsman went on to state:

'As a matter of good administrative practice trustees should provide reasons for their decision to those with a legitimate interest in the matter and, subject to the need to preserve rights to privacy of individual members, should also make the minutes of their meeting available to scheme members. I can see no good reason for the trustee not to have done so in this case and the failure of the trustee to do this for Mr Allen was also maladministration. Not knowing the basis on which an adverse decision is taken is itself an injustice.'

The Editor of the Pensions Law Reports series commented that this determination sat uncomfortably with the *Wilson* case cited above, but that comments made in the case of *Edge v Pensions Ombudsman* when it was before the High Court (see **9.1**) tended to support the idea that reasons must sometimes be given. He hoped that a suitable case would come before the courts so that the matter might be clarified.

Although not specifically relating to a pension scheme, the Privy Council concluded in the case of *Schmidt v Rosewood Trusts Ltd* heard in 2003 that a beneficiary's right to seek disclosure of trust documents is best approached as one aspect of a court's inherent jurisdiction to supervise, and where appropriate to intervene in, the administration of trusts. This judgment also stressed, however, that where a court becomes involved in a case where there are issues as to personal or commercial confidentiality, the court may have to balance the competing interests of different beneficiaries, the trustees themselves and third parties with the result that any disclosure may have to be limited and safeguards may have to be put in place. There is therefore no automatic rule that means the trustees must disclose a trust document that may damage the interests of third parties.

Frequency of meetings

18.6   How many trustee meetings are needed in a year will depend on the kind of scheme. Trustees of a small insured scheme may meet only once a year. Most large occupational pension schemes will meet at least quarterly. The trust deed and rules or the trustees' own formal regulations will usually specify that a special meeting may be called by any one of the trustees. Sometimes a special resolution can be passed without physically calling a meeting if all the trustees are willing to sign a copy of the resolution. There is no particular reason why video-conferencing technology could not be used if this would facilitate full attendance of all the trustees. However, it is more practicable to schedule the next four or so meetings on a rolling basis well in advance. Trustees should ensure that attendance at a trustee meeting takes priority over other work commitments and that they prepare adequately for the meeting by reading thoroughly any relevant papers sent in advance of the meeting, as well as considering seriously whether there might be any unintended implications of the decisions that are to be taken at the meeting. For example, if one particular clause of the trust deed and rules is to be amended, it is sometimes the case that there is a cross-reference to that clause elsewhere in the trust documentation and that by making the intended change, the cross-reference means that an unintended change is also made.

Checklist 18

- In practice, the decision on who chairs the trustees is usually made by the employer.

- In practice, the agenda of the trustees' meeting will be set by the chairman working with the pensions manager (secretary of the trustees), but any trustee can table an agenda item.

- The trust deed and rules or the articles of association of a corporate trustee should specify the quorum necessary for any decision to be valid and whether decisions are to be unanimous or by majority.

- Proper notice of at least ten working days should normally be given to each trustee and the notice should also specify the time, date and place of the meeting, although the requirement can be overridden when as a matter of urgency it is necessary to make a decision.

- Proper minutes of each meeting must be kept.

- Although the law does not require the trustees to let a complainant see minutes of the meeting at which his or her complaint was considered, it may amount to maladministration if the trustees decide not to do so.

- Trustees should not meet too infrequently.

- Trustees should prepare themselves adequately for the meeting.

Chapter 19

Special situations

Pension fund surpluses

19.1   During the 1980s and the 1990s, a number of factors, including in particular the high investment returns achieved from equities, combined to give rise to substantial surpluses in very many defined benefit schemes. From the employer's perspective, once a substantial surplus began to accumulate, the most desirable outcome is for the employer's contributions to be discontinued until the surplus can be run off. In some cases, employers sought not only an extended employer contribution holiday, but also a payment, subject to a free-standing tax, from the surplus.

In many cases, however, the scheme's members felt that the benefits of superior investment returns should also be used to benefit them and they sought to have employee contributions reduced and benefits improvements made.

From the point of view of the trustees, provided the scheme actuary's approval was granted to the surplus being used in these ways, their major duty was to ensure that they took into consideration the interests of all the different classes of potential beneficiaries and that requirements of the trust documentation were always observed.

The view of one other major player, HM Treasury, was also important. It also wished to see pension fund surpluses reduced. It argued that full tax relief was being given unnecessarily since more assets were being held than were needed to provide the benefits and were being used to depress the employer's taxable profits.

Yet, as employer contribution holidays were renewed and further rounds of benefit improvements were granted, two factors were surreptitiously beginning to increase schemes' liabilities. First, pensioner longevity was increasing but the actuaries' mortality tables had failed to keep up with this improvement. Second, the world's developed economies were settling into a period of prospective low price inflation. If future price inflation is low, the real value of bonds will be eroded more slowly than in times of higher inflation, and so bond prices will be higher than they would otherwise have been. If bond prices are higher, the yield on bonds will be lower. The overall cost therefore of matching pensioner liabilities buy buying bonds will rise.

The benefit improvements that had been made, including those which had arisen from statutory requirements such as limited price indexation on pension rights built up from 6 April 1997, had also, of course, increased the value of schemes' liabilities.

19.1   *Special situations*

The dawning of the new century coincided with a three-year global bear stock market, and pension fund asset values plummeted. Surpluses were converted into deficits, and low inflation meant that employers found that they could not easily increase the prices of the goods and services they sold to offset the higher contributions they once again needed to pay.

The Finance Act 1986

19.2   The *Finance Act 1986* introduced new requirements on pension fund surpluses and clarified the existing law.

On using the projected accrued benefit method and assuming that the margin of investment returns over earnings growth is 1.5%, as well as making various other assumptions, if a self-administered defined benefit scheme runs a surplus of over 5%, action must be taken to reduce it to not more than 5% within, in most cases, the following five years.

If no action is taken, the scheme will lose part of its tax exemption.

The trustees can decide to reduce the surplus using any combination of the following:

- suspension or reduction of employer contributions for up to five years;

- suspension or reduction of employee contributions for up to five years;

- improvement of scheme benefits (in particular past service benefits) up to HMRC limits; and/or

- payment of some or all of the surplus to the employer, taxed at 35%.

If a payment from the fund is given to the employer, the actuarial value of the surplus cannot be reduced to less than 5%.

Valuations must be sent to HMRC at intervals of, currently, not more than three and a half years.

These rules will, however, disappear on 6 April 2006 with the introduction of the new pensions tax regime, although any payment made by a registered scheme from a fund surplus to the employer will still be subject to the free-standing 35% tax.

Payment of surplus to the employer

19.3   One legislative provision is that no payment out of the fund can be made to the employer until at least Limited Price Indexation (LPI) (that is, annual increases in line with the retail prices index limited to 5% in any one year) has been guaranteed on all pensions in payment and all future pensions when they come into payment.

The *Pensions Act 1995* has provided since 6 April 1997 that where the trust deed and rules permit a payment out of surplus to be made to the employer, that power can only be exercised by the trustees. Furthermore, the trustees can only exercise that power if:

- it results from a statutory surplus as defined in the *Finance Act 1986*;
- the trustees are satisfied that it is in the members' interests;
- limited price indexation is in place for all pension rights; and
- notice has been given to the members (including pensioners).

Members have two months from this first notice to respond to the trustees. The trustees must then send a second notice informing members of the trustees' decision and the members will have a further three months from the second notice to take any complaint to Opra. No payment to the employer can be made if a complaint is still outstanding.

The *Pensions Act 2004* will substitute new provisions governing how any payment can be made from a pension fund surplus to the employer and prevents trustees from making a payment to the employer unless:

- they have a certificate from a prescribed person that the assets and liabilities of the scheme have been calculated and verified in accordance with new regulations to be issued, and stating the maximum amount of the payment that may be made;
- the payment does not exceed the maximum amount given on the certificate;
- the trustees are satisfied that it is in the interests of the members for the payment to be made;
- where appropriate, the employer has requested, or consented to, the payment;
- the Pensions Regulator has not issued a freezing order against the scheme under *s 23* of the Pensions Act; and
- scheme members have been notified in accordance with the requirements to be set out in regulations.

Because of the introduction of a higher threshold before a payment to the employer may be made, the new rules do not include the requirement that, before a payment may be made to the employer, 5% limited price indexation (LPI) protection must be extended to all scheme pensions (over and above the protection in respect of rights accrued after 1997 provided by the main statutory LPI provisions). Guaranteed pension increases, as required by the LPI legislation or by scheme rules, will, however, be included in the assessment of liabilities for the purpose of the full buy out calculation, and this will be set out in the new regulations.

The *Pensions Act 2004* also introduces transitional powers for trustees to amend scheme rules to take account of the repeal of the former provisions first introduced by the *Finance Act 1986*. In any pension scheme where the current rules allow payments to the employer other than in order to comply with HMRC requirements, but which may have been constrained by the requirements in the *Pensions Act 1995*, trustees may choose to revive their original powers, limit them or leave them unchanged. In schemes where rules are framed so as only to allow payments in circumstances specified under the *Finance Act 1986* requirements, trustees may choose whether and how they wish to take a power to make payments of surplus to the employer. The pre 6 April 2006 HMRC requirements for tax approval have generally required scheme rules to prohibit payments of surplus except with HMRC approval and in accordance with the requirements introduced by the *Finance Act 1986*. In both cases, any new rules will be subject to the overriding provisions of the *Pensions Act 2004*, and trustees:

- must be satisfied that such a rule change is in the interests of scheme members;

- can only make one such decision;

- must make it within five years of the commencement of these provisions; and

- must give written notice to the employer and scheme members that they plan to change the scheme rules on payments to the employer.

Practice on surpluses

19.4   Among the larger schemes, pension fund surpluses have typically been reduced by a combination of benefit improvements and employer contribution holidays. Figures released by HMRC show that cumulatively since the measures set out in the *Finance Act 1986* came into effect, statutory surpluses have been reduced as in the following table:

Method of reduction	Number of schemes	Amount of reduction (£ million)
Contributions holiday (employer)	2,997	13,394
Contributions holiday (employee)	190	262
Contributions reduction (employer)	1,613	4,762
Contributions reduction (employee)	258	851
Payment to employer*	293	1,217
Increase in benefits	1,867	9,079
New benefits	220	175
TOTAL		29,740

Figures relate to the period 1987/88–2002/03 and represent the total amount to be eliminated by each of the methods indicated. Some of the reductions would be made in years after 2002/03. (Note that the total number of schemes cannot be deduced as some scheme surpluses are reduced using more than method.)

* The figure for payments to employers excludes the amount paid over by schemes reported to be wound up in each year.

Source: HMRC

In the three tax years 1995/1996 to 1997/98 the total amount of surpluses reduced by any combination of the methods of reduction listed in the table totalled £4,586 million. In contrast in the three tax years 2000/01 to 2002/03 the total amount of surpluses reduced in these ways totalled a mere £124 million, less than 3% of the earlier total. The mid-1990s was the high point of surplus reductions, given the high investment returns then. The following table shows the number of schemes reporting a surplus of over 5% and of under 5%, on the Finance Act 1986 basis in running three-year totals

Period	Number of schemes with surplus over 5%	Aggregate value of surplus (£ million)	Number of all schemes reporting	% of schemes with surplus over 5% of all schemes
94/95 to 96/97	750	4,444	5,593	13.4%
95/96 to 97/98	1,029	4,795	8,063	12.8%
96/97 to 98/99	877	4,127	8,092	10.8%
97/99 to 99/00	448	1,233	7,220	6.2%
98/99 to 00/01	186	220	7,101	2.6%
99/00 to 01/02	116	147	7,078	1.6%
00/01 to 02/03	71	125	5,995	1.2%

Source: HMRC

In an on-going scheme, it seems that surpluses can be dealt with, if not always amicably, at least practically in the context of the normal industrial relations life of the company. Nevertheless, several major court cases during recent years have centred on the question of *who owns a surplus?*

The Court of Appeal, giving its judgment in the case of *National Grid Co plc v Mayes & others* set out some basic principles which have become fairly well established. These are as follows:

- A court will always try to ensure that the rules of the pension scheme, as set out in the trust deed and rules, are followed (provided they are not overridden by legislation) and the court's approach should be 'practical and purposive, rather than detached and literal', ie to try to follow what was actually intended and to construe the wording in a reasonable and practical way – this principle was famously set out in the case of *Mettoy Pension Trustees v Evans*.

- When an employer exercises a power given to it by the trust deed and rules, the employer will not necessarily be treated as a fiduciary (i.e. the employer can look to its own interests) but nevertheless the employer must not, without reasonable and proper cause, take action which is 'calculated or likely to destroy or seriously damage the relationship of confidence and trust between employer and employee'. This is the 'implied duty of good faith' set out in the case of *Imperial Group Pension Trust v Imperial Tobacco Ltd* (see **8.2** above).

- Employees have no automatic right to a surplus revealed by an actuarial valuation but they have 'a reasonable expectation that any dealings with that surplus, whether by the employers or the trustees of the scheme acting within the powers of the scheme, will pay a fair regard to their interests, since the express purpose of the scheme is to provide benefits for their retirement'. This principle was set out in the case of *Re Courage Group's Pension Schemes* (see **7.1**).

- To the extent that an employer is under an obligation to make contributions, it is fair for some purposes to regard those as part of the employees' overall remuneration package, just as much as contributions made by the employees from their salaries and wages, a comment made by the judge in the case of *Thrells Ltd (1974) Pension Scheme in Liquidation v Lomas*.

- It is not the case that members of a contributory pension scheme have interests in the application of a surplus equivalent to rights of property – a point affirmed by the Court of Appeal in *National Grid Co plc v Mayes & others*.

However thought-provoking these general principles may be, members, employers and trustees should not be misled into thinking that they are the starting point in deciding whether or not any particular course of action is permitted when it comes to considering how an actuarial surplus will be used in any particular case. When it came to setting out its judgment in the *National Grid* case, the Court of Appeal said that: 'The solution to the present problem lies within the terms of the scheme itself, and not within a world populated by competing philosophies as to the true nature and ownership of an actuarial surplus'.

In the event, the Court of Appeal's own judgment in the *National Grid* case was overturned by the Law Lords. This latter judgment centred on the specific interpretation of the scheme's trust documentation and so does not invalidate any of the general principles set out above. The House of Lords' eventual decision in the case, however, has been seen as evidence that the courts should also take a practical and commercial view of the way in which pension schemes operate.

In the decision of the Court of Appeal in July 1999 in the case of *Edge v Pensions Ombudsman*, Lord Justice Chadwick dealt with the duty of trustees to consider the interests of all the classes of beneficiaries who could benefit from a pension fund surplus. The trustees would want to consider the circumstances in which the surplus had arisen but he added that, having done so, the trustees would not be bound to take any particular course as a result of that consideration, provided it was a matter of the use of trustee discretion. He said: 'The essential requirement is that the trustees address themselves to the question of what is fair and equitable in all the circumstances. The weight to be given to one factor as against another is for them'. See **9.1** above for further discussion on this point about the use of the trustees' discretionary power in agreeing to how a surplus should be used.

Mergers and takeovers

19.5   If one company (the vendor company) runs an occupational pension scheme, and sells a business or subsidiary company to another company (the purchasing company) which also runs an occupational pension scheme, then part of the vendor's pension scheme is likely to be transferred to the purchaser's pension scheme.

The two companies will negotiate a deal in the normal way. The normal way means that the vendor will want to sell at the highest price possible and the purchaser will want to buy at the lowest price possible. The sale will be clinched by a purchase and sale agreement.

The Occupational Pensions Board gave trustees the following advice in *Pension Trust Principles*:

'You will need to be particularly clear about your duty to act in accordance with the trust deed and rules if the employer is engaged in the sale and purchase of an undertaking which involves a bulk transfer of members and assets out of or into the scheme. The two employers involved will have entered into a sale agreement which will cover the pension terms of the transferring employees and the associated financial arrangements. You and your fellow trustees will not normally be parties to the agreement, and indeed the trustees of the two schemes may not have been consulted fully, if at all. You must ensure that you act strictly in accordance with the trust deed and rules, even if the terms of the sale agreement differ from these. The employers will have to solve any difficulties that arise.'

The trustees of the vendor company's scheme must not transfer too great a proportion of their fund to the new fund as this would not be in the interests of beneficiaries who remain.

The trustees of the purchasing company must not accept an influx of new members without ensuring that adequate new funding is also transferred into the fund as this will not be in the interests of either the existing or the transferring beneficiaries.

The members who are being asked to transfer will want to ensure that their existing expectations will be realised in the new scheme.

Under the *Occupational Pension Schemes (Preservation of Benefit) Regulations 1991 (SI 1991/167)*, bulk transfers of members from one scheme to another scheme may be permitted without the consent of the members involved. However, the actuary to the transferring scheme must certify that the past service rights and expectations to be provided to the transferring members in the new scheme are equivalent on an overall basis to their past service rights and expectations in the original scheme. Even if the actuary gives such a certificate, it does not absolve the trustees of the transferring scheme from their fiduciary duty to the members involved. Actuaries will also inform the trustees of any matters that they did not taken into account in issuing their certificate but which they think the trustees ought to consider in coming to their decision.

If an entire company is taken over by another, the latter will become the principal employer of the former company's pension scheme. If then the scheme of the company that has been taken over is to be merged with another scheme sponsored by the company that has now become the principal employer, the situation from the point of view of the two sets of trustees is the same as just described, i.e. they must act in the interests of their own members – see also the discussion of issues concerning bulk transfers at **9.8**.

In cases of a group of companies, the principal employer may want to have admitted into membership of a pension scheme employees who work for other employers in the group. Those employees may be members of another pension scheme which is to be wound up or they may not currently be members of any pension scheme. The usual approach would be to adhere those other employers in the group as participating employers to the scheme's trust deed. In such cases, the trustees of the pension scheme concerned must ensure that adequate bulk transfer payments are made to cover any past service rights that are in future to be provided by their scheme. The future contribution rates made by these employers must also be in line with actuarial recommendations. If the existing scheme is running a surplus it might not be acceptable for the new employers to benefit immediately from a contribution holiday. Rather they would be expected to contribute at the recommended rate for a minimum period of time. This issue was the subject of court action in the case of *Hillsdown Holdings v Pensions Ombudsman* (see **7.1**) where the judge distinguished between an employer who takes a contribution holiday in respect of a category of existing members and an employer who introduces a large class of new members and takes a contribution holiday in relation to them so as to accelerate the effect of the contributions holiday in relation to the existing members.

Sometimes in the past when a well-funded scheme was merged with a less well-funded scheme, the trustees agreed to ring-fence some of the assets for the members of one of the schemes, so that these members were protected if the scheme was subsequently wound up. However, changes made by the *Pensions Act 1995* in the priority order for paying liabilities on winding up mean that such ring-fencing agreements made on or after 6 April 1997 may not be effective in this event.

All of the above discussion is based on the premise that the employer with a pension scheme is selling a business to another employer who also runs a pension scheme. Of course, that is not always the case. Before 6 April 2005, the *Transfer of Undertakings (Protection of Employment) Regulations 1981 (SI 1981/1794)* (TUPE) specifically singled out future rights under an occupational pension scheme as an employee benefit that did not automatically transfer from one employer to another when a business changes hands. The regulations embodied in domestic legislation the requirements of the European Acquired Rights Directive, and these also originally excluded future occupational pension scheme rights from the scope of the protection afforded to employees on transfers of businesses. Yet the Directive was amended in 1998 so that each member state could decide whether this exclusion should continue.

Sections 257–258 of the *Pensions Act 2004* and the *Transfer of Employment (Pension Protection) Regulations 2005 (SI 2005/649)* now require the transferee employer to provide a minimum level of pension provision for the transferred employees in cases where their previous employer provided some form of occupational pension scheme to those employees.

Sections 257–258 of the 2004 Act differ from the requirements of the main *TUPE Regulations* because the provisions in the Act do not require the new employer to provide the same pension provision as is the case with all the other terms and conditions of employment.

Instead, the *Pensions Act 2004* requires that where the transferee employer wishes to offer a defined benefit occupational scheme to the transferring employees, this scheme must either meet the Reference Scheme Test (see **13.12**) or meet the alternative requirements set out in the *Transfer of Employment (Pension Protection) Regulations 2005*. These regulations stipulate that these alternative requirements are that the scheme must provide benefits worth at least the equivalent in present value of 6% of a member's pensionable pay, excluding the member's own contributions, for each member. The employee cannot be required to contribute more than of 6% of pensionable pay.

Where the transferee employer wishes to offer the transferring employees a defined contribution occupational scheme or a stakeholder pension scheme, the employee must be able to decide on the amount of contributions on his or her own contributions which the employer is then required to match pound of pound up to a 6% of basic pay (the employer is free to contribute more than this, but is not required to do so).

These new requirements to provide minimum pension benefits to the transferring employees must, nevertheless, be qualified by the effect of the European Court of Justice in the cases of *Beckmann v Dynamco Whicheloe Macfarlane Ltd* and *Martin & ors v South Bank University*. In those cases, the ECJ held that the exception granted under the Acquired Rights Directive that allows occupational pension schemes to be excluded from the overall protection offered by the TUPE Regulations, must be applied narrowly and strictly interpreted. As a result, the ECJ held that the exception granted applied, as in the wording of the Directive, only to 'old-age, invalidity and survivors' benefits', and so would not be applied to a benefit where it is paid not on the ground that the employee had reached the relevant retirement age, but on the ground that he or she had become entitled to early payment of a pension and a retirement lump sum by reason of either dismissal for redundancy or on early retirement. The ECJ stated in the *Martin* judgment:

'Early retirement benefits and benefits intended to enhance the conditions of such retirement, paid in the event of early retirement arising by agreement between the employer and the employee to employees who have reached a certain age...are not old-age, invalidity or survivor's benefits under supplementary company or inter-company pension schemes within the meaning of Article 3(3) of Directive 77/187.'

Scheme reconstructions

19.6　In some circumstances, following reorganisations such as a merger or a change in the benefit design policy by the employer, employees who joined a scheme before a certain date may continue to be active members building up rights to further benefits but no new members are admitted into membership. Instead, new employees are possibly offered membership of another occupational pension scheme, a group personal pension arrangement or a designated stakeholder pension scheme. In such cases, the responsibility of the trustees of the scheme that is closed to new members remains solely the members of that scheme. They must ensure that those members receive their due benefits when they fall due in the normal way. The funds held by the closed scheme can only be used in accordance with the trust deed and rules and the trustees cannot transfer those assets gratuitously to the other pension scheme for the benefit of the new employees.

In other cases, new members are admitted into the existing scheme but into a new section where differing rules apply, while those who remain in the original section of the scheme enjoy *grandfathered* rights. An example might be a defined benefit section which is closed to new members but where existing members are given grandfathered rights. New employees are offered membership of a newly created money purchase section within the same scheme. In this case the scheme trustees owe a fiduciary duty to the members of both sections.

In such a situation as just described where, say, there is a significant surplus in the pension scheme, there might be no particular reason in principle why the trustees could not agree to some of that surplus being run off to provide the employer contributions to the money purchase pensions of the new members, provided always that this did not disadvantage the reasonable pension expectations of the members of the final salary section. If effect, it would be equivalent to a continuing contribution holiday for the employer. However, for this to happen it is very important for the pension scheme's trust deed and rules to make it clear that the surplus accrued in the final salary section of the scheme can be applied for the benefit of the new members in the money purchase section of the scheme, even if it is already clear that the two sections form part of one overall pension scheme.

This problem arose in the High Court case *Kemble v Hicks* where the scheme's governing documentation failed to make this point explicit. Subject to the particular facts of that case, Justice Rimer observed:

'But it does appear to me that the establishment of the money purchase scheme involved what was, within that overall scheme, a scheme quite separate from the final salary scheme and to which different considerations applied ... It seems to me to follow that, to the extent that the surplus in [the final salary scheme] was thereafter used to fund the employer contributions to the money purchase scheme, the money purchase scheme members were thereby improperly and unfairly subsidised by the final salary scheme members, because the surplus remained held on the trusts of the final salary scheme.'

The facts of *Kemble v Hicks* are very specific to that case, but in March 2000 the Pensions Ombudsman upheld a complaint against Barclays Bank which has closed its final salary scheme to new members and opened instead a new money purchase scheme, but again within one overall pension scheme with a common set of trustees. The Pensions Ombudsman agreed that the new money purchase scheme was part of one overall scheme incorporating the final salary scheme, but he did not consider that the new money purchase scheme was part of the pre-existing final salary scheme. If there was no provision in the documentation for a cross-subsidy, there could be no legal basis for the employer's contributions to the money purchase scheme to be paid out of the surplus in the final salary scheme. The Pensions Ombudsman directed the employer to repay contributions with interest to the pension fund.

This determination by the Ombudsman was, however, rejected on appeal to the High Court by Justice Neuberger in the case of *Barclays Bank plc v Holmes*. He decided that the correct interpretation of the scheme's trust documentation was that it constituted a single trust fund subject to two separate schemes, with the result that the bank was not obliged to pay contributions into the fund while the fund was in surplus. Justice Neuberger also made it clear that *s 67* of the *Pensions Act 1995*, which acted at the time to prevent any scheme amendment being made which would worsen the 'accrued rights' of members without their consent (see **6.3**), did not mean that having a pension fund surplus preserved for the benefit of the members could count as an 'accrued right' that had to be protected under that section of the Act. He said that: '[I]t cannot sensibly be contended that a member of a pension scheme has any 'right', let alone an 'accrued right' to or in relation to a surplus.'

It must be said that life becomes more difficult for trustees where a common pension fund guarantees the benefits of several different classes of active members, with different scales of benefit rights, as well as those of deferred pensioners and pensioners. Trustees must act equitably towards all classes of the membership.

Prompted by the emergence of funding deficits (see **19.10**) especially since 2001, the sponsoring employers of a high proportion of the UK's final salary schemes have taken action to cut future pension costs by making changes to these schemes. In many cases, the employer has invoked its power under the trustee deed and rules and begun to wind up the scheme (see **19.9–19.13** below). In other cases, alternative action has been taken including:

- closing the final salary scheme to new entrants but allowing existing members to continue to build up further rights as described above;

- requiring employees to pay higher contributions or offering them a choice of paying higher contributions in order to maintain the same accrual rate (e.g. 1/60th) or continuing at the same employee contribution rate while moving to a lower rate of accrual (e.g. 1/80th) for future service;

- redesigning certain aspects of the pension scheme (e.g. removing or reducing enhanced terms for early retirement); and

- closing the final salary scheme not only to new entrants but also to further accrual of benefits for the existing members: this can be done in two ways:

  - existing members accrue no further pensionable service (e.g. a member with 15 years' pensionable service will build up no more years of service even if he or she remains an employee for another 15 years) but their benefits will still be calculated on their final pensionable earnings as at the time the benefits become due (e.g. on the date they retire); or

  - existing members accrue no further pensionable service and are treated in the same way as a deferred pensioner with their benefits being calculated using their final pensionable earnings as at the date further pensionable service ended, subject to statutory revaluation thereafter (see **9.22**).

None of the options listed above falls foul of the legal principle that amendments to schemes must not reduce the pension rights that have already been accrued (see **6.3**) since they all relate only to pension rights built up, or the lack of them, from the date of the change.

There are potential legal problems for the employer in taking up any of these options if the employees can show that there are either express or implied terms in their contracts of employment that indicate that they have a contractual right to continue to build up final salary benefits. Closing a final salary scheme to further accrual is highly likely to give rise to difficult industrial relations for the employer. See also the discussion at **7.5**.

Speaking at the spring 2003 conference of the Pensions Management Institute, Chris Mullen, National Head of Pensions at law firm Pinsent Curtis Biddle, described the issues that the trustees needed to consider during such changes, especially the option of closing the scheme for future accrual.

First, it is highly probable that the trustee body will contain members of senior staff of the sponsoring employer who have received advice from external sources and who are implementing the change. The trustee body itself must also take independent legal advice as to how to proceed. This legal advice must be kept confidential to the trustees who are bound to carry out their duties under the trust deed and rules and to act in the interests of all members (not just the active members). There is therefore a conflict since it would not be proper for senior employees of the employer who are charged with putting this new policy into effect to be privy to the details of the legal advice received by the trustees. It is true that the trustees can also take into account any duty they may have to have a care for the employer's interests, but in such circumstances where the change is being proposed by the employer, usually with external legal advice that is confidential to the employer, the trustees would seem also to have duty to seek their own confidential and independent legal advice. It is suggested that those trustees who are also senior staff of the employer might absent themselves from the meeting between the other trustees and their legal advisor. Alternatively, the trustees may appoint an independent trustee to take legal advice and act in their name on this issue.

Second, as already noted at **7.1**, the High Court in the case of *Hillsdown Holdings v Pensions Ombudsman* has made it clear that in certain circumstances it is correct for the trustees to negotiate with the sponsoring employer. It is perfectly proper, therefore, to bargain with the employer in the circumstances where the employer has proposed to close the scheme to future accrual. For genuine bargaining to take place, it is therefore all the more important that the legal advice that the trustees receive is kept confidential from the employer. The main options open to the trustees are:

- to agree to the proposal or to suggest alternatives (e.g. a lower accrual rate going forward; moving to a career average design; asking the employees to agree to pay higher contributions);

- to bargain for better protection for member's accrued rights (e.g. retaining a link to final pensionable earnings at the date the member ceases to be an employee; buying out members' rights using deferred or immediate non-profit annuities); and

- to refuse agreement to the closure of the further accrual. Although this may prompt the employer to wind up the scheme immediately, it is also possible that the employer may not wish to do this since it would also immediately crystallise any debt to the employer under the *Occupational Pension Schemes (Deficiency on Winding Up etc.) Regulations 1996 (SI 1996/3128)* or the *Occupational Pension Schemes (Employer Debt) Regulations 2005 (SI 2005/678)* which replace the 1996 Regulations if the scheme winds up or the debt on the employer arises on or after 6 April 2005– see **19.10** and **19.11** below.

If, having taken independent legal advice, the trustees of the scheme are of the opinion that the employer is asking them to agree to a proposal that is in conflict with their duties under the trust deed and rules of the scheme or of statutory provisions, the trustees should consider going to the court for directions.

Employer ceases to trade

Independent trustee

19.7 Under new requirements introduced by the *Pensions Act 2004*, the insolvency practitioner (or the Official Receiver) who has been appointed because the employer has become insolvent must, where that employer sponsors a pension scheme set up under a trust, inform the Pensions Regulator, the Board of the Pensions Protection Fund (see **23.1B**) and the current trustees that the insolvency event has occurred. It is then the responsibility of the Pensions Regulator to take whatever steps are needed to ensure that, if required, an independent trustee, registered with the Pensions Regulator, is put in place.

The Pensions Regulator also has the power in these circumstances to appoint a trustee, who could be a member or other lay-trustee, rather than an independent trustee. It also can determine whether the employer, the scheme, or both, should meet the costs of any trustee (whether independent or not) that the Pensions Regulator appoints.

The *Occupational Pension Schemes (Independent Trustees) Regulations 2005 (SI 2005/703)* provide for the Pension Regulator to compile and maintain a register of persons who satisfy the conditions for registration as an independent trustee. Any independent trustee that the Pensions Regulator appoints upon the insolvency of an employer sponsoring a trust based occupational pension scheme must be from the register.

Prior the changes made by the *Pensions Act 2004*, it was the responsibility of the insolvency practitioner or Official Receiver to ensure that at all times there was an independent trustee in place, and if not, it fell to the insolvency practitioner or Official Receiver to appoint one. The Department for Work and Pensions reported, however, that in practice either this duty was often not observed or it was observed but that the net effect was to create unnecessary expenditure that had to be met from the scheme which in practice delivered no real benefit to the members. Indeed, there were also many instances of very high fees being charged by independent trustees which were paid at the cost of reducing the benefits that could otherwise have been paid to the members.

If an independent trustee was not appointed, the only recourse for members of the scheme who felt that such an appointment would be in their interests was to apply to the Court to force the insolvency practitioner or Official Receiver to do so but such a course would involve costs which might well be prohibitively high for the members.

In summary, therefore, the new system means that independent trustees will not be appointed by the Pensions Regulator unless it judges this to be necessary. The existing trustees can be supplemented by lay member trustees appointed by the Regulator. The Regulator will also determine whether the costs are met by the scheme or the employer or both. Where independent profession trustees are appointed by the Pensions Regulator they must be listed on the Regulator's register, and this should also ensure that the fees charged will not be unreasonable.

Winding up a pension scheme

19.8   An occupational pension scheme may be wound up due to a number of reasons, not all of them detrimental for the members concerned. A large employer with several schemes may wish to harmonise them into one scheme with superior benefits. A larger employer may have bought out a smaller employer and wish to move its members into its own scheme. However, in other cases, it may be that the employer may no longer choose to include an occupational pension scheme among the benefits offered to its employees or the employer may have become insolvent.

Which legislative requirements apply when an occupational pension scheme is wound up depend on the date the scheme went into wind-up. In relation to wind-ups which begin on or after 6 April 2005, the date the Pension Protection Fund (PPF) – see **23.1 B** – came into being, the following legislation applies:

* *Section 71A* of the *Pensions Act 1995* which allows the Pensions Regulator to modify the trust deed and rules of a scheme to secure its winding up. This section is amended by the *Pensions Act 2004.*

* *Section 72A* of the *Pensions Act 1995* which requires the trustees to keep the Pensions Regulator informed about the progress being made to complete the winding up of their scheme. This section is also amended by the *Pensions Act 2004.*

* *Sections 72B* and *72C* of the *Pensions Act 1995* which give the Pensions Regulator power to issue directions to facilitate the winding up of a scheme including when it concludes that the trustees are failing to make due progress and requires the trustees to comply with those directions. These sections are also amended by the *Pensions Act 2004.*

* *Section 73* of the *Pensions Act 1995* which has been substituted in its entirety by the *Pensions Act 2004.* This key piece of the legislation sets out the preferential liabilities on winding up that apply when a defined benefit occupational pension scheme commences winding up on or after 6 April 2005 – see **19.9** below.

* *Section 73A* of the *Pensions Act 1995* which has been introduced by the *Pensions Act 2004* deals with the operation of the scheme during the winding up period – see **19.10** below.

- *Section 73B* of the *Pensions Act 1995* which has also been introduced by the *Pensions Act 2004* makes supplementary provisions relevant to *ss 73* and *73A*.

- *Section 74* of the *Pensions Act 1995* which deals with the discharge of liabilities by insurance etc. This section is amended by the *Pensions Act 2004*.

- *Sections 75* and *75A* of the *Pensions Act 1995* deal with the situation of a debt becoming due from the employer when the scheme's assets are insufficient to secure the liabilities. *Section 75* is amended by the *Pensions Act 2004* while *s 75A* is a new section inserted by the *2004 Act*.

- *Sections 76* and *77* of the *Pensions Act 1995* deal with the situation where there are excess assets on winding up. These two sections are amended by the *Pensions Act 2004*.

The main regulations made under the *1995 Act* relevant to schemes winding up on or after 5 April 2005 are the *Occupational Pension Schemes (Winding Up) Regulations 1996 (SI 1996/3126)*. These regulations have been amended by subsequent legislation, notably:

- the *Occupational Pension Schemes (Winding Up and Deficiency on Winding Up etc) (Amendment) Regulations 2004 (SI 2004/403)*

- the *Occupational Pension Schemes (Winding Up, Deficiency on Winding Up and Transfer Values) (Amendment) Regulations 2005 (SI 2005/72)*, and

- the *Occupational Pension Schemes (Winding Up etc) Regulations 2005 (SI 2005/706)*.

In addition, the *Occupational Pension Schemes (Employer Debt) Regulations 2005 (SI 2005/678)* are important in that they set out the level of debt due from an employer on insolvency, scheme wind up or withdrawal by an employer from a multi-employer scheme. They also state when there is a debt due to a defined contribution occupational pension scheme. These regulations completely replace the *Occupational Pension Schemes (Deficiency on Winding Up etc) Regulations 1996 (SI 1996/3128)* with effect from 6 April 2005.

These recent amendments to the various earlier regulations have effected a fundamental change which has had retrospective effect from 11 June 2003. This was the date when the government announced that if a scheme began to wind up on or after that date, at a time when the employer was not insolvent, then the debt on the employer would be calculated on the basis that both pensioner members and non-pensioner members of the scheme would receive the full value of their benefits by reference to the cost of buying immediate and deferred annuities from insurance companies. Securing the benefits in this way is known as a 'full buy-out'.

Previously the debt on the employer in relation to the non-pensioner members was much less demanding since it was based on the cost of providing the cash equivalent transfer values based on the minimum funding requirement

(MFR). The announcement meant that since 11 June 2003 it has been very unattractive for a solvent employer to 'walk away' from a defined benefit scheme and leave its non-pensioner members with benefits worth far less than they had previously been led to expect.

From 15 February 2005 the requirement for the debt on the employer to be calculated on full buy-out terms was also applied to wind-ups commenced on or after that date in cases where the employer was insolvent.

Preferential liabilities on winding up

19.9   *Section 73* of the *Pensions Act 1995*, inserted by *s 270* of the *Pensions Act 2004*, puts in place a new priority order which applies to occupational pension schemes which begin winding up on or after 6 April 2005 and so coincides with the coming into operation of the Pensions Protection Fund (PPF) – see **23.1B**.

Essentially, if the assets of a defined benefit which is covered by the PPF has assets which immediately before the employer's insolvency are not sufficient to meet the scheme's 'protected liabilities' and no scheme rescue is possible, the Board of the PPF will assume responsibility for the scheme and the responsibility of the trustees for the scheme comes to an end. If the scheme, however, has sufficient assets to meet the scheme's 'protected liabilities', the Board of the PPF will not assume responsibility for the scheme and the trustees retain responsibility for winding up the scheme. In this case, the trustees must secure the scheme's liabilities in compliance with the requirements of the new priority order. Here 'protected liabilities' refer to:

- the cost of securing benefits for or in respect of scheme members that correspond to the compensation which would be payable in accordance with s 162 of the *Pensions Act 2004* if the PPF's Board assumed responsibility for the scheme – see **23.1B;**

- the liabilities of the scheme other than liabilities to or in respect of members;

- the estimated cost of winding up the scheme.

A rule setting out a priority order on a wind-up defines the relative importance of the benefits and the order in which the assets are to be used to purchase these benefits. No benefits given a lower priority may be secured from the assets of the scheme until all the benefits awarded a higher priority have been secured.

The new statutory priority order which applies for when a defined benefit occupational pension scheme begins winding up on or after 6 April 2005 is as follows:

(a)   certain pensions or benefits paid by insurance contracts purchased before April 1997 that cannot be surrendered or where the surrender value does not exceed the liability secured by the contract;

(b)   any liability for pensions or other benefits to the extent that the amount of the liability does not exceed the corresponding PPF liability, other than a liability within paragraph (a);

(c)   remaining voluntary contributions not covered in (b);

(d)   any other scheme benefits not covered in (a), (b) and (c).

The priority order and other measures in the new *ss 73, 73A, 73B* inserted into the *Pensions Act 1995* and the amended *s 74* of that Act are aimed at ensuring that broadly speaking individual scheme members will be no worse off if their scheme winds up than they would be if the PPF were instead to assume responsibility for the scheme and pay compensation to members.

Operation of scheme during wind-up

19.10   *Section 73A(2)* of the *Pensions Act 1995* provides that the trustees must ensure that, during a winding up period, any pensions or benefits paid to or in respect of a scheme member are reduced, so far as necessary, to reflect the liabilities that will be satisfied under the priority order in *s 73(4)*. It also provides that trustees may take such steps as necessary to recover any overpayment or pay any shortfall arising from the requirement to reduce pensions and benefits.

Section 73A(3) stipulates that during a winding up period no benefits may accrue under the scheme rules and no new members can be admitted to the scheme, yet these restrictions are qualified by *ss 73A(4)* to *73A(6)* so that pension increases and any accrual derived from the investment of payments made in respect of a defined contribution section can continue.

Section 73A(7) and *(8)* allow regulations to require the trustees or managers of a scheme to adjust the entitlements of a person to a discretionary award (such as an enhanced ill-health pension) or to a survivor's benefit in certain circumstances. The aim is to prevent a discretionary award during the winding-up period increasing the cost to the scheme of discharging the liabilities in respect of a member.

Section 73A(9) stipulates that if any person other than the trustees has powers under the scheme's trust deed and rules to distribute the assets of a scheme during a winding up, then those powers are overridden so that, subject to *ss 73, 73A* and *73B*, they may instead be exercised by the trustees.

Running as a closed scheme

19.11   *Section 38* of the *Pensions Act 1995* (as amended by the *Pensions Act 2004*) allows the trustees of defined benefit schemes in some cases to defer winding up their scheme even if the rules of the scheme would require in the circumstances the prevailing for the scheme to be wound up. In such cases, usually following the insolvency of the sponsoring employer, no new members will normally be admitted to the scheme and no member will normally build up any future pensionable service. Such a course would only be taken if the scheme were sufficiently well funded for it to be likely to be able to meet its liabilities as they fall due.

Section 153 of the *Pensions Act 2004* deals with the situation where a scheme rescue is not possible and, although the scheme has sufficient assets to meet the protected liabilities under the PPF, the high level of the scheme's liabilities mean that the scheme's trustees cannot secure a buy-out quote for the scheme's pension liabilities from one or more insurance companies. Under these circumstances, the trustees must apply to the Board of the PPF for authority to continue to run their scheme as a closed scheme. They must clearly demonstrate that a full buy-out has not been possible.

Checklist 19

- Surpluses only ordinarily arise in defined benefit schemes and, in an on-going scheme, are simply any positive balance of the actuarial value of the scheme's assets less the actuarial value of the scheme's liabilities.

- A modest surplus provides a cushion against adverse market conditions but a large surplus is not desirable from the employer's viewpoint since the assets might be better used to invest in the employer's business.

- Until 6 April 2006, the tax legislation requires surpluses to be reduced once they have reached a specified size.

- In the past surpluses have been reduced by payments from the fund to the employer, subject to a tax deduction, but this is becoming more difficult to achieve.

- Surpluses have usually been reduced by a combination of benefit improvements and discretionary pension increases combined with an employer contribution holiday.

- Trustees must be vigilant in ensuring that, as a result of any bulk transfer of members into the scheme, the scheme receives a payment that meets the extra pension liabilities taken on and that, on a bulk transfer out of the scheme, the departing members will have their reasonable expectations met but that the payment is not excessive.

- When new classes of active members are created in the same scheme following a scheme reconstruction, the scheme trustees must act equitably to all the classes of members, including the existing deferred pensioners and pensioners.

- Many final salary schemes are now closed to new members and sponsoring employers are seeking other ways to contain future costs including closing schemes to further accrual for existing members. Trustees should ensure that in such circumstances they obtain independent and confidential legal advice and should consider negotiating with the employer.

- If the employer ceases to trade because of insolvency, the Pensions Regulator may appoint, in the case of a defined benefit scheme, an independent trustee.

- Following the insolvency of the employer, defined benefit schemes which begin to wind up on or after 6 April 2005 will become the responsibility of the Board of the Pension Protection Fund (PPF) if the degree of underfunding means that the scheme's 'protected liabilities' cannot be met by the scheme and there is no prospect of a corporate rescue. Otherwise it will normally remain the responsibility of the trustees to wind up the scheme and secure its liabilities in line with the revised priority order for securing benefits.

Chapter 20

Resolution of individual disputes

Introduction

20.1   It is possible that from time to time the industrial relations life of a company will witness a collective dispute concerning a pensions issue which has arisen simply because the occupational pension scheme is inevitably considered as an element of the employees' terms and conditions of employment. In such a case, the trustees should not normally be involved directly because the matter is part of the industrial relations life of the company as a whole. Resolution of any dispute may be the responsibility of a special pensions negotiating forum or other negotiating committee as discussed in **CHAPTER 7**.

In contrast, when a dispute arises not as part of the industrial relations of the employer, the trustees may well become involved. In an occupational pension scheme of any size, individual disputes are bound to occur – sadly in some cases as a result of maladministration. In too many cases, the dispute arises over inaccurate data, a subject discussed at **11.4**. Yet many disputes arise because of poor communications. Poor communications frequently result in a mismatch between the realities of a member's pension entitlement and what he or she may have held as a genuine expectation. The communications issues addressed in **CHAPTER 9** are, therefore, directly relevant in a considera-tion of disputes.

Ultimately, any dispute involving a member will usually involve the trustees because they are the party with overall responsibility, but more particularly because the legislation now gives them a specific role in resolving such disputes.

Internal dispute mechanisms

20.2   *Section 50* of the *Pensions Act 1995* requires the trustees of an occupational pension scheme to establish a disputes resolution scheme that will deal with complaints from members. The requirements of that section and those of the *Occupational Pension Schemes (Internal Dispute Resolution Procedures) Regulations 1996 (SI 1996/1270)* are currently in force but they are prospectively to be replaced by the new measures contained in the *Pensions Act 2004*. We first explain the current arrangements, then outline the new measures.

Currently s 50 of the *Pensions Act 1995* requires the trustees of an occupational pension scheme to establish a disputes resolution scheme that will deal with complaints from:

- the active, deferred and pensioner members of the scheme;

- a widow, widower or surviving dependant of a deceased member of the scheme;

- a prospective member of the scheme – that is anyone who under his or her contract of employment or the scheme rules:

    - is able voluntarily to become a member of the scheme; or

    - will become able voluntarily to join after the end of a waiting period; or

    - will be admitted automatically to the scheme unless he or she chooses not to do so; or

    - may be admitted to the scheme at the employer's invitation with the employer's consent;

- anyone who has been one of the above within the previous six months of making the complaint; and

- any person who claims to be in one of the above four categories, even if the scheme's administrators dispute that this is the case.

A complainant can ask a representative to pursue a complaint on his or her behalf.

First stage

20.3   Currently, dispute resolution involves a two-stage process. The individual makes a complaint that is considered by, say, a pension administrator who must make a reply which should include an explanation for the decision, referring to any part of the scheme rules, trust deed, or legislation that has formed the basis for the decision. The reply should also refer to the complainant's right, if dissatisfied, to ask the trustees or managers of the scheme to consider the dispute. The reply should contain a reminder that the services of the Pensions Advisory Service (TPAS) (see **20.7**) are available to assist members and beneficiaries of the scheme in connection with any difficulty which remains unresolved. TPAS's address must be given.

The reply from the scheme should be sent within two months of the date of the application for a decision, except in exceptional circumstances. If a scheme is unable to reply within that time because, for example, they are seeking information that may take longer, they should send an interim reply explaining the reason for the delay and an expected date for a substantive reply.

Once the reply has been sent, the complainant has a right of appeal to the trustees. The complainant has a maximum of six months in which to exercise this right of appeal.

Second stage

20.4   Under the second-stage arrangements the trustees' response to the appeal should, again, contain an explanation for their own decision, referring to any part of the scheme rules, trust deed, or legislation that has formed the basis for the decision. If the trustees have exercised discretion in arriving at the decision under dispute it is not a requirement that they make the reasons for their decision public, although they may do so if they wish (see **18.5**). Trust law does not require trustees to give reasons since to do so could fetter their decisions in future. However, the decision of the trustees should refer to the relevant part of the scheme rules or trust deed that gives them the right to exercise their discretion in a given case.

The second-stage reply from the trustees should also contain information about the services of TPAS (see **20.7**) and the Pensions Ombudsman (see **20.8**), so that should the complainant remain dissatisfied with the explanations given, he or she may refer his complaint, ideally first to TPAS and then, if still unresolved, to the Pensions Ombudsman for consideration and possible investigation.

The reply from the trustees should be sent within two months from the receipt of the application from the complainant. If this is not possible, an interim reply must be sent within this time saying when the matter will be considered by the trustees. It will be open to a complainant to refer his or her complaint to TPAS or the Pensions Ombudsman if the handling of the complaint is unduly protracted.

Disputes which can be excluded

20.5   Certain disputes are excluded from the scope of an internal dispute procedure. These are disputes that have been accepted for investigation by an outside agency such as TPAS, the Pensions Ombudsman, an employment tribunal or the courts.

New requirements

20.6   *Section 273* of the *Pensions Act 2004* replaces the current *s 50* of the *Pensions Act 1995* with a new *s 50* and *ss 50A and 50B*, and sets out revised requirements relating to the dispute resolution arrangements for occupational pension schemes. It will allow the trustees to decide if their internal disputes resolution procedure should have a single stage or two or more stages. The new requirements will apply to existing schemes in relation to new disputes made on or after 23 September 2005. Any disagreement that was on-going before that date must continue under the old rules until that internal dispute procedure comes to an end.

The trustees will remain responsible for ensuring that dispute resolution arrangements are made and implemented. A pension dispute is to be defined as being a dispute about matters relating to the scheme between the trustees of the scheme and anyone 'with an interest in the scheme'. The trustees' dispute resolution arrangements must provide a procedure for any person with an interest in the scheme to be able to apply to the trustees of the scheme to make a decision on the matters of the dispute.

The new *s 50A* sets out the meaning of 'person with an interest in the scheme' and this reflects the definitions currently set out in the *Internal Dispute Resolution Procedures Regulations 1996*. A person with an interest in the scheme is:

(a) a member of the scheme;

(b) a widow, widower, or surviving dependant of a deceased member of the scheme;

(c) a surviving non-dependant beneficiary of a deceased member of the scheme (i.e. in relation to a deceased member of an occupational pension scheme, a person who, on the death of that member, is entitled to the payment of benefits under the scheme);

(d) a prospective member of the scheme (i.e. a person (i) who is able, at his or her own option, to become a member of the scheme, or (ii) will become so able if he or she continues in the same employment for a sufficiently long period, or (iii) will be admitted to the scheme automatically unless he or she makes an election not to become a member, or (iv) may be admitted to the scheme subject to the consent of this or her employer);

(e) a person who has ceased to be within categories (a) to (d); or

(f) a person who claims to be such a person who is mentioned in categories (a) to (e) and the dispute relates to whether he or she is such a person.

Where a dispute is referred to the trustees for a decision, the trustees must make a decision *within a reasonable period* of receiving the application and notify the applicant of the decision again *within a reasonable period*. Under *s 90* of the *Pensions Act 2004* the Pensions Regulator is required to issue a code of practice on what constitutes a *reasonable period*. The Pensions Regulator issued its draft of this code for consultation in April 2005 and this suggested that reasonable periods within which the trustees must make a decision on the dispute and notify the applicant of that decision are, in the case of a one-stage procedure, four months; and anything other than one stage procedures, 10 months. Nevertheless, the Pensions Regulator would not expect trustees or managers to delay where they are able to respond to the application sooner. Under the code, as drafted, the person who brought the dispute should be informed of the decision as soon as practicable after the decision has been made, usually within seven days. The Pensions Regulator states that it expects there to be a sufficient period of time built into the 10-month period to allow the applicant to consider the first stage decision and seek advice on it if necessary.

The *Occupational Pension Schemes (Internal Dispute Resolution Procedures) Regulations 2005* (in draft at the time of writing) stipulate that when the trustees notify the person bringing the dispute of their decision, they must also give that person:

- a statement that The Pensions Advisory Service (TPAS) is available to assist members and beneficiaries of the scheme in connection with any difficulty with the scheme which remains unresolved and the address at which TPAS may be contacted;

- a statement that the Pensions Ombudsman may investigate and determine any complaint or dispute of fact or law in relation to a scheme made or referred to in accordance with the Pension Schemes Act 1993 and the address at which he may be contacted.

Schemes which are to be exempt from the requirement to have an internal disputes resolution procedure are those where every member of the scheme is a trustee and those with no more than one member.

Certain disputes will be exempted from these procedures. These are those where proceedings have already been begun in respect of this dispute in any court or tribunal, or if the Pensions Ombudsman has begun an investigation of the matter. Again, further exemptions may be set out in future regulations.

The *new s 50B* sets out the matters which are to be included in the dispute resolution procedure. The procedure:

- must provide for the representation of a person in order for an application for the resolution of a dispute to be made or continued where (i) that person dies, (ii) that person is a minor or a person otherwise incapable of acting, or (iii) in any other case, that person nominates a representative.

- may include provision about the time limits for making an application for the resolution of a dispute but further provides that the procedure must (in the case of a person with an interest in a scheme as mentioned in categories (e) or (f) above) require a six-month time limit for making the application.

- must set out details about how the application is to be made; what information should be included in the application; and the way in which decisions are to be reached and given.

- must provide for the dispute resolution procedure to cease if, after the application is made, the dispute becomes one in respect of which proceedings have been commenced in any court or tribunal or the Pensions Ombudsman has commenced an investigation as a result of a complaint made or a dispute referred to him.

The Pensions Advisory Service

20.7   If the internal dispute resolution mechanism fails to satisfy the individual who has made the complaint or if the individual has difficulties in making his complaint via the internal dispute mechanism, he or she can approach the Pensions Advisory Service (TPAS). The Service maintains a network of volunteers, who are experts in the field of occupational pensions, who can take up most problems directly with the scheme administrators or trustees on behalf of any beneficiary of that scheme. TPAS has traditionally worked in close liaison with the Citizen's Advice Bureaux. Formerly supported by voluntary donations, the Service now receives a government grant.

In general, TPAS works by a process of negotiation and conciliation, relying very much on good will. It cannot undertake formal arbitration services nor can it initiate legal action.

TPAS offers its services free of charge.

Local TPAS volunteers can be approached via the local Citizens' Advice Bureaux or the London headquarters:

> The Pensions Advisory Service (TPAS)
> 11 Belgrave Road
> London
> SW1V 1RB
> Pensions helpline: 0845 6012923
> General office tel: 020 7630 2250
> Fax: 020 7233 8016
> email: enquiries@pensionsadvisoryservice.org.uk
> Web site: http://www.opas.org.uk.

Under the *Occupational Pension Schemes (Disclosure of Information) Regulations 1996 (SI 1996/1655)*, trustees must notify members of the role and the address of TPAS. This may usually be included in the Pension Handbook.

In its latest report, TPAS reported that the problems brought to it by members of occupational pension schemes were broken down as follows:

Type of enquiry	2003/04 percentage
Poor administration	30%
Clarification of entitlement	19%
Poor advice t	13%
Transfers	11%
Early retirement/ill-health	8%
Scheme closure	5%
Other	14%

In recent years an area which began to cause concern was that of incorrect early retirement quotations. TPAS commented that all too often serious mistakes occur in the calculation of benefits on which members are expected to base fundamental, financial decisions. Yet trustees and administrators sometimes seek to avoid the consequences of this mis-information by hiding behind the fact that when the quotation was given it was described as being an estimate. TPAS takes the view that the word 'estimate' cannot be used to excuse a mistake that results in figures significantly lower than those first given.

Pensions Ombudsman

20.8 If TPAS is unable to resolve a difficult dispute to its own satisfaction and feels that the complainant has a good case, it may, with the individual complainant's consent, pass the case to the Pensions Ombudsman. Similarly, if the individual is dissatisfied with the action taken by TPAS, he or she can direct the complaint to the Pensions Ombudsman. (A complainant has a right to approach the Pensions Ombudsman directly, bypassing TPAS, once he or she had tried the internal disputes resolution procedure. The Pensions Ombudsman and TPAS, however, both prefer the complainant to try TPAS first.) The Pensions Ombudsman may be contacted as follows:

> The Pensions Ombudsman
> 11 Belgrave Road
> London
> SW1V 1RB
> Tel: 020 7834 9144
> Fax: 020 7821 0065
> email: enquiries@pensions-ombudsman.org.uk
> Web site: http://www.pensions-ombudsman.org.uk.

Jurisdiction

20.9 The Pensions Ombudsman can investigate:

- complaints made by, or on behalf of, actual or potential beneficiaries of an occupational or personal pension scheme who allege that they have 'sustained injustice in consequence of maladministration in connection with any act or omission of a person responsible for the management of the scheme';

- complaints made by, or on behalf of, a person responsible for the management of an occupational pension scheme who 'in connection with any act or omission of another person responsible for the management of the scheme' alleges maladministration of the scheme;

- complaints made by, or on behalf of, the trustees or managers of an occupational pension scheme who 'in connection with any act or omission of any trustee or manager of another such scheme' allege mal-administration of the other scheme;

- disputes of fact or law that arise in relation to an occupational or personal pension scheme between a person responsible for the management of the scheme and an actual or potential beneficiary who is a party to the dispute and which has been referred to the Pensions Ombudsman by, or on behalf of, that actual or potential beneficiary; and

- disputes of fact or law that arise between the trustees or managers of an occupational pension scheme and another person responsible for the management of the scheme or any trustee or manager of another occupational pension scheme and which has been referred to the Pensions Ombudsman by any of the parties to the dispute.

In the above, the term 'managers of the scheme' is defined as the trustees or managers themselves and the employer. Under separate regulations (the *Personal and Occupational Pension Schemes (Pensions Ombudsman) Regulations 1996 (SI 1996/2475)*) the Pensions Ombudsman is also given jurisdiction to investigate and determine complaints made against the scheme 'administrator'. Here 'administrator' means generally any person concerned with the administration of the scheme other than a manager of the scheme and so can cover the scheme actuaries and other advisors.

In the case of *R (on the application of Britannic Asset Management Ltd) v Pensions Ombudsman*, the Court of Appeal held that, although *s 146(4)* of the *Pension Schemes Act 1993* gave power to Parliament to pass regulations that would give the Ombudsman jurisdiction to issue determinations affecting those 'concerned with the financing or administration of, or the provision of benefits under, the scheme', in the event the regulations mentioned above did so only in relation to 'those concerned with the administration of the scheme' and that, as a consequence, the Pensions Ombudsman does not have jurisdiction over 'those concerned with the financing of a scheme' nor with 'the provision of benefits under the scheme' unless they are also concerned with the administration of the scheme. In coming to this decision, the Court of Appeal drew a distinction between a person who undertook 'an act of administration concerned with the scheme' and a person 'concerned with the administration of the scheme'.

Following the Court of Appeal's judgment, the Pensions Ombudsman stated that:

> 'The people who need the law's protection are not those in charge of the funds but those from whom money has allegedly been filched. A legal system which concentrates on preventing alleged maladministration from being called to account is failing the people.'

In the event the government responded by including a measure in the *Pensions Act 2004* to widen the Pensions Ombudsman's jurisdiction so that he can investigate complaints involving 'one-off'' acts of administration. This has been done by inserting a new subsection into *s 146* of the *Pension Schemes Act 1993* which stipulates that:

> 'a person or body of persons is concerned with the administration of an occupational or personal pension scheme where the person or body is responsible for carrying out an act of administration with the scheme'.

Yet this new measure will not have retrospective effect and will only apply to disputes and complaints heard by the Pensions Ombudsman in relation to a matter which arises on or after 6 April 2005.

The term 'actual or potential' beneficiaries refers to:

–   a member of the scheme, i.e. someone who is or has been an active member of the scheme;

–   the widow, widower, or any surviving dependant of a deceased member of the scheme;

–   from 1 December 2000, a person entitled to a pension credit as against the trustees under the pension sharing on divorce provisions;

–   a person claiming to be a member or the widow, widower or surviving dependant of the member; and

–   a person who is or has been entitled to the payment of benefits under the scheme.

Following the enactment of the *Child Support, Pensions and Social Security Act 2000*, the Pensions Ombudsman may now also deal with:

●   complaints made by, or on behalf of, an independent trustee who alleges maladministration of the scheme in connection with an act or omission committed by the other trustees or former trustees of the scheme (but not by another independent trustee);

●   any dispute between different trustees of the same occupational pension scheme provided that the dispute has been referred to the Pensions Ombudsman by at least half of the trustees to the scheme. (This includes any dispute in schemes where an independent trustee is to be appointed because of the insolvency of the employer and which arises between an independent trustee of the scheme and the other trustees or former trustees, but not with another independent trustee, and which has been referred to the Pensions Ombudsman by, or on behalf of, the independent trustee who is party to the dispute);

●   any question relating, in the case of an occupational pension scheme with a sole trustee, to the carrying out of the functions of that trustee and which has been referred to the Pensions Ombudsman by, or on behalf of, the sole trustee.

The second point listed immediately above is important because it allows the trustees to ask the Pensions Ombudsman to clarify for their benefit any scheme rule that is unclear. This may be attractive as a cheaper option for the pension fund than taking the matter to the courts.

Other extensions of the Pensions Ombudsman's jurisdiction include being able to accept complaints made against the employer in connection with personal pension schemes (including therefore stakeholder pension schemes legally established as personal pensions).

Since the regulations governing internal dispute resolution came into force, the Pensions Ombudsman regulations have been amended to exclude from his jurisdiction cases that have not been subject to the internal dispute resolution procedures, although the Ombudsman has the discretion to take on such cases where it seems reasonable to him that he should do so – for example when it seems there is no real prospect of the trustees issuing a response to the claimant. The Pensions Ombudsman has discretion to accept a case if he is satisfied that a complaint has been made to the scheme and the trustees have replied even if the internal dispute resolution procedure was not correctly followed.

The Pensions Ombudsman cannot act in a case where court proceedings have already started or when a court has already given a final decision. However, an amendment made by the *Child Support, Pensions and Social Security Act 2000* allows the Pensions Ombudsman to accept a case if it has been previously referred to a court or employment tribunal but has subsequently been discontinued other than on the basis of a binding settlement. On the other hand if, after the Pensions Ombudsman has already taken up a case, one of the parties to the dispute starts legal action in a court, then any party to the legal proceedings can apply to the court to have those legal proceedings halted. The court will usually agree to halt the proceedings if the matter is seen to fall within the scope of the Pensions Ombudsman.

In normal circumstances, there is a three-year time limit for making a complaint or referring the dispute. The period runs from the date of the act, or failure to act, that gave rise to the dispute or from the date the complainant first learned of the problem.

Procedure

20.10   Legislation prevents unnecessary overlap between the remits of the Pensions Regulator and the Pensions Ombudsman. Broadly, the role of the Pensions Regulator is one of *enforcement* and that of the Pensions Ombudsman is *adjudication*.

If the Pensions Ombudsman feels there is prima facie evidence of maladministration (see also **11.4**), the Pensions Ombudsman will write to the trustees, managers, scheme administrators (such as an insurance company) or employers and ask for their observations. This in itself may prompt a settlement of the dispute, or the Ombudsman may decide that the complainant does not have a case. Further correspondence may follow and the Pensions Ombudsman has extensive powers to insist on the production of relevant documents or relevant information. An oral hearing may be set up. At the end of the process the Pensions Ombudsman gives a determination, with reasons and in writing, to the complainant and to the trustees/managers/administrators/employers.

Directions

20.11 Where the Pensions Ombudsman finds that a party has been guilty of maladministration, he can issue a direction to remedy the effect of that maladministration. The remedy will be to put the complainant in the position he or she would have been in if the maladministration had not occurred. So, if a benefit was promised that was too high, there may be maladministration, but the Pensions Ombudsman will not uphold the incorrect benefits promise. Restitution can be made, however, if there was injustice resulting in financial loss, for example, if the complainant can show that he or she relied on an incorrect benefit promise of too high a benefit to enter into financial commitments. Similarly, the maladministration may have given rise to an overpayment which the trustees are bound to try and recover. Since the overpayment resulted from a mistake, there is no general provision in law that allows the beneficiary to retain the overpayment. However, if the beneficiary can show that the overpayment has been spent as a result of a financial transaction that he or she would not otherwise have entered into then the Pensions Ombudsman may issue directions to prevent any injustice resulting from the original maladministration. The Pensions Ombudsman can also direct that sums of up to £1,000 can be paid to a complainant as compensation for distress and disappointment suffered in consequence of maladministration.

Under the *Occupational Pension Schemes (Disclosure of Information) Regulations 1996 (SI 1996/1655)*, trustees must notify members of the function and the address of the Pensions Ombudsman.

Maladministration and breaches of the law

20.11A We discussed the concept of 'maladministration' at **11.4** and in particular the Pensions Ombudsman's argument that maladministration can occur irrespective of whether or not there is a breach of the law is explored in the relation to the non-disclosure by trustees of scheme documentation as discussed at **18.5**. In the case of *Henderson v Stephen Harwood & ors* heard in January 2005, Mr Justice Park had cause to discuss this distinction.

He pointed out that, so far as relevant to this case, the Pensions Ombudsman has jurisdiction:

- to determine *complaints* about maladministration which is alleged to have caused injustice (under *s 146(1)(a)* of the *Pension Schemes Act 1993*); and

- to determine *disputes* of fact or law (under *s 146(1)(c)* of the *Pension Schemes Act 1993*).

He acknowledged that *complaints* about maladministration are not within the ordinary jurisdiction of the courts, but *disputes* of fact or law about pension schemes are. As a result in relation to cases involving disputes of fact or law the Pensions Ombudsman and the courts share jurisdiction.

He also explained that appeals from decisions of the Pensions Ombudsman had established that in such cases the Ombudsman could not disregard established legal principles. Mr Justice Park gave as an example a case in which, if a beneficiary of a pension scheme begins proceedings in court against the employer over some grievance connected with the scheme, but the court decides that, although it can see why the beneficiary feels that he has a grievance, nevertheless as a matter of law the employer has no liability to him.

Yet, if that beneficiary has not begun proceedings in court, but instead makes a *complaint* to the Pensions Ombudsman, the Ombudsman cannot give a decision that the employer or the trustees are liable. Mr Justice Park cited the cases of *Westminster City Council v Haywood* and *Wakelin v Read* in support of this limitation of the Pensions Ombudsman's powers.

Wakelin v Read is cited in fact because it illustrates the same principle but from the converse effect. If beneficiaries bring before the Pensions Ombudsman a *dispute* which they might have brought by way of a civil action in the ordinary courts, and in the event the court would have awarded some form of relief to them, the Pensions Ombudsman must also award relief. Mr Justice Park stated that the Pensions Ombudsman cannot deny relief on the ground that, as he sees the matter, the beneficiary is an undeserving complainant. Mr Justice Park cites the judge, Mummery LJ in the *Wakelin v Read* case:

' ... it was not right that there should be a different answer as to the substance of the dispute according to whether the dispute was decided by a court or by the Ombudsman'.

Yet, in setting down the courts' view of what the Pensions Ombudsman may or may not do, Mr Justice Park pointed out that there was one qualification to the above. He said:

'What I have said is entirely correct if the matter which the beneficiary brings before the Pensions Ombudsman rather than before a court is a *"dispute"* within s 146(l)(c) of the [*Pension Schemes Act 1993*]. It may be different, however, if the subject matter is a complaint of maladministration and consequential injustice within s 146(l)(a). Maladministration in itself is not a matter which is actionable in the ordinary courts, but allegations of maladministration are matters which a complainant can raise before the Ombudsman, and which the Ombudsman can investigate and determine. If he finds that there has been a case of maladministration which has caused injustice, but that there has been no breach of contract or other form of civil wrong for which relief could have been obtained in a conventional civil action, the Ombudsman may be able to grant a measure of relief in a situation where a court could not have done so. The matter is not entirely clear on the authorities. The main relevant case is *Westminster City Council v Haywood* ... I will not examine the case here, but I believe that the effect can accurately be summarised as follows. There is as yet no authoritative decision that the Pensions Ombudsman can award monetary compensation for distress and inconvenience caused by maladministration, but if he can the amount of it can only be modest.'

Appeals

20.12   The Pensions Ombudsman can make a direction which is enforceable by a court. The decision is final and binding. The only recourse from a determination of the Pensions Ombudsman is an appeal to the High Court, or in Scotland to the Court of Session, purely on a point of law.

Despite this restriction, many trustees and employers have appealed to the courts against a determination issued by the Pensions Ombudsman after he has upheld a complaint or dispute brought by a scheme member. In many cases the court has accepted that the appeal is truly on a point of law rather than a finding of fact and has gone on to reverse the Ombudsman's determination.

The appeal procedure, however, raises a difficult problem. The Pensions Ombudsman is a law tribunal available at no cost to the complainant. Yet in the case of an appeal from a determination of the Pensions Ombudsman, the losing party at the High Court, if represented, has to meet the costs of the winning party. In practice, therefore, if a complainant succeeds with the Pensions Ombudsman but the trustees/employer appeal to the High Court, the complainant faces a serious financial risk of having to meet the costs if he or she is represented in the Court to oppose the appeal. The net result is that the individual complainant is likely to choose not be represented in the appeal.

In the early 1990s, the practice developed with the first Pensions Ombudsman of offering to appear in an appeal if the court felt that this would be of assistance. The second Pensions Ombudsman originally found this approach odd since elsewhere in the judicial system it does not happen that a lower tribunal appears to assist a court to make a judgment on appeal. Instead, the practice developed of the Pensions Ombudsman writing a letter to the judge setting out the arguments. However, criticism from judges in the High Court led the second Ombudsman to revert to the earlier practice of being represented in the appeal. If the appeal reversed the earlier determination, the Ombudsman at first had to bear the cost of both parties. This was later held not to be correct because if the Ombudsman had not been represented, no costs would have been recoverable from him and the appellant would still have been faced with the costs of the action. It was therefore decided that if the appeal was successful in the High Court, the Pensions Ombudsman would have to bear the cost only of the additional expenditure incurred by the successful appellant resulting from the Pensions Ombudsman's being represented. Later, however, this practice was again reversed and the full cost once again fell on the Ombudsman's office. The third Pensions Ombudsman has now decided that he will not be represented on appeals unless they raise a question of the legal jurisdiction of the Pensions Ombudsman.

The overall result is that if the trustees/employer appeal against a determination issued by the Pensions Ombudsman, it is quite probable that they will be the only party heard by the judge in the High Court. Such a situation is rather unsatisfactory.

The idea has been suggested that a note should be added to any determination issued by the Pensions Ombudsman concerning the right of individual scheme members to seek costs orders from the court to protect them in the event of an appeal proceeding. To what extent individual complainants would be willing to go through this procedure, and if they did so, to what extent High Court judges would regard such applications sympathetically is far from clear.

The Edge case

20.13 In July 1999, in the case of *Edge v Pensions Ombudsman*, the Court of Appeal ruled that the Pensions Ombudsman could not carry out any investigation where no effective remedy could be given, because any directions issued by the Pensions Ombudsman would be unenforceable because they would also necessarily affect the interests of those who had not been represented during the investigation. In short, it seemed that the Court of Appeal had seriously curtailed the role of the Pensions Ombudsman. Suppose, for example, a death benefit had been paid to one person by the trustees and not to another. Would the Court of Appeal's judgment mean that the Pensions Ombudsman could not accept a complaint from the legal spouse as it would affect the interests of the person who had instead been granted the death benefit, since that person under the current rules could not be a party in the carrying out of the Pensions Ombudsman's determination? It would also seem to make any form of 'class action' impossible.

In what was a clear statement of support for the Office of the Pensions Ombudsman, and indeed for the Pensions Ombudsman himself, the then Government Minister of State with responsibility for pensions explained that measures would be introduced into the Child Support, Pensions and Social Security Bill, then before Parliament, to ensure that the Pensions Ombudsman could continue to carry out his role.

Essentially the new measures would have allowed the Pensions Ombudsman to join to a case under investigation those whose interests may be affected by the outcome of the case. The Pensions Ombudsman would therefore have been permitted to appoint a person to represent a group of members or potential members who had the same interest in the complaint or dispute. He would also have had the power to order that the costs of legal expenses in a particular case should be met from the pension fund. This new extension would not have applied to any cases that have not been referred to the Pensions Ombudsman before the date the measure brought in by *s 54* of the *Child Support, Pensions and Social Security Act 2000* had actually been brought into force. In December 2001 the Department for Work and Pensions circulated draft amending regulations which had to be made before the new measures could come into force.

In the event, however, after a long period, on 18 March 2003, the Government announced that it would not be introducing the new regulations, and that *s 54* of the Act would not be brought into force. The Minister of State stated:

'We have considered very carefully the comments received as a result of consultation on the draft amendment rules. We are concerned that the changes made by section 54 would not be as beneficial as originally envisaged and that they would also add a further layer of complexity to an area of legislation which needs to be simplified and not complicated further. This would not be in line with Government policy which is to simplify the rules governing disputes and complaints about personal and occupational pensions whenever possible. The principles underlying the changes are sound but we want to explore how they can be made to work as effectively as possible. We do not want to bring into effect legislation which is complex and moreover does not fully achieve what is needed. We will consider how best to resolve this in the light of the Pensions Green Paper and its key messages of simplification and protection.'

No further developments have since occurred in relating to the *Edge* case. Inevitably, the Government's turn around will be seen by some as a victory for the judges in a long-running turf war they have waged against the office of the Pensions Ombudsman; for the lawyers, many of whom did not favour *class actions* being determined by the Pensions Ombudsman; and possibly also for trustees and employers on the ground that any weakening of the office of the Pensions Ombudsman strengthens their hand against members bringing a complaint.

The combination of the Pensions Ombudsman not generally being able to appear in the High Court, Court of Appeal, or House or Lords to defend his determination and the effect of the decision in *Edge* are seen by many as a process of gradually eroding the powers of the Pensions Ombudsman.

In many ways this is likely in practice to make life easier for trustees who may well wish to appeal against a determination of the Pensions Ombudsman which is adverse to them. The cost of access to the courts is generally seen to be prohibitively expensive to individual scheme members unless they are very wealthy, or are entitled to legal aid, or are granted in advance an order by the court so that the pension fund will meet their costs if they lose on appeal. Nevertheless, the current arrangements for dealing with breaches of the law and maladministration in relation to pension provision leave much to be desired, in terms of a rational approach.

The courts and tribunals

20.14   As just discussed, a civil court case is usually a prohibitively expensive route for an individual member or beneficiary to follow in trying to resolve a dispute. However, in an extreme case the court has jurisdiction to grant an order that representative beneficiaries of a pension fund are entitled to pursue claims with their costs being met from the pension fund itself. This is only likely to occur in a group action. However, it is common to find pensions issues appearing as an employment law case in an employment tribunal, often in unfair dismissal cases where, for example, loss of future pension rights might need to be quantified.

Checklist 20

- Trustees must ensure that there is in place an internal disputes resolution procedure.

- If the complainant is unhappy with the trustees' decision, he or she can call on the Pensions Advisory Service (TPAS) to mediate in the dispute.

- If the complainant is dissatisfied with the result of mediation by TPAS, he or she can take the matter to the Pensions Ombudsman, or TPAS may refer the case to the Pensions Ombudsman if it feels the trustees are being unreasonable. Trustees must comply with the determinations of the Pensions Ombudsman, with an appeal to the High Court being permissible only on a point of law.

- The issue of how costs are met in an appeal from a determination of the Pensions Ombudsman to the High Court may be thought to be rather unsatisfactory.

- Members can bring legal action through the courts or, in employment-related matters, an employment tribunal.

Chapter 21

Breaches of trust

Introduction

21.1 The trustees are collectively responsible for any breach of trust that might be committed. If a trustee believes that a breach of trust is being committed but fails to convince the majority of the trustees to take preventative action, he or she should seek professional advice.

Trustees owe a duty of care to each and every beneficiary of the occupational pension scheme. Any trustee who fails to carry out his or her *fiduciary* duty as set out under the trust deed and rules could be found by the courts or the Pensions Ombudsman to have committed a breach of trust. All the trustees are likely to be held individually and collectively liable for this breach. Even if a trustee was not directly responsible for a breach of trust, he or she could be sued. If it is found that the trustees have committed a breach of trust which results in a loss of scheme assets, they could be personally liable to restore the loss.

A breach of trust is also likely to be of material significance to the Pensions Regulator. Under the *Pensions Act 2004* the Pensions Regulator has power to seek an injunction from the courts in order to prevent any misuse or misappropriation of the assets of an occupational pension scheme.

Trustees, therefore, bear an important level of responsibility. In practice, it is recognised that trustees who carry out their duties honestly and prudently should not be exposed to unlimited liability. In **CHAPTER 22** various forms of protection for trustees are examined. However, the protection will depend on the severity of the breach of trust committed.

One pragmatic form of protection for trustees against being taken to court for an alleged breach of trust is the sheer expense of mounting such an action. The cost is too prohibitive for all but the richest individuals. However, the Pensions Ombudsman could also rectify a breach of trust by issuing a determination that might also order that restitution should be made personally by the trustees themselves. The services of the Pensions Ombudsman are provided at no cost to the complainant. As an alternative, a trade union or other group using representative beneficiaries could help to bring an action for breach of trust through the courts and in some exceptional cases the court might agree that the cost of bringing the action could be met from the pension fund itself.

Breaches of trust can be categorised in various ways.

Unintentional and innocent

21.2   It is likely that many unintentional and innocent technical breaches of trust occur every day. A member may have taken voluntary retirement and the pension should have been reduced because it was going to be paid early. An administrative error occurred and the member received an unreduced pension, part of which was taken as a lump sum. The error comes to light a few years later. The trustees may feel it inappropriate to reduce the pensioner's income at that point and the lump sum is probably long spent. The error occurred in the pensions administration department but the trustees are responsible. The pension fund has suffered loss as a benefit was paid out but not in accordance with the trust deed and rules.

Negligent and culpable

21.3   In a negligent and culpable breach of trust the trustees will have acted carelessly but still in good faith. They may have used fund assets to buy a new computer system from a persuasive salesman from a small software house without commissioning a proper study and without taking independent advice. Once bought, the software package proves totally inadequate, and when the trustees seek compensation they find that the software house has gone into liquidation.

Culpable and fraudulent

21.4   In a culpable and fraudulent breach of trust one or more of the trustees will have attempted to misappropriate, or succeeded in misappropriating, the scheme's assets. This could include a case of a director who is also a trustee taking an unauthorised loan from the pension fund to stem a disastrous cash-flow problem in the company. There is *wilful misconduct*.

Breaches of statutory law

21.5   Trustees might also act in breach of some statutory requirement. Examples could include the *Equal Pay Act 1970*, the *Race Relations Act 1975*, the *Sex Discrimination Act 1975*, the *Pension Schemes Act 1993*, the *Pensions Act 1995*, the *Disability Discrimination Act 1995*, the *Data Protection Act 1998*, the *Welfare Reform and Pensions Act 1999*, the *Financial Services and Markets Act 2000*, and the *Pensions Act 2004*.

Checklist 21

- Trustees who commit a breach of trust that results in a loss of scheme assets can be personally liable to restore that loss.

- All the trustees could be found to be individually and collectively liable for a breach of trust committed by just one trustee.

- It is important that those undertaking the responsibility of acting as trustees should take their duties seriously and be satisfied that there are in place adequate measures to give them protection from the results of unintentional or negligent breaches of trust.

- Trustees may also face penalties if they are found to have acted in breach of a statutory requirement.

Chapter 22

Protection for trustees

Introduction

22.1   Any trustee who commits a *culpable and fraudulent* breach of trust may have to face prosecution for a criminal offence. The only protection, as such, is that the individual may qualify for legal aid.

Trustee Act 1925

22.2   In certain circumstances, trustees may be excused breaches of trust through *s 61* of the *Trustee Act 1925*. Three conditions set out in the Act have to be satisfied.

The trustees:

* must have acted honestly;
* must have acted reasonably; and
* 'ought fairly to be excused'.

It is probable therefore that trustees are protected in cases of *unintentional and innocent* breaches of trust. But if the trustees were *negligent and culpable* it is more difficult to see how they can be excused under this measure.

It is likely that the court would consider it important whether the trustees sought legal or other professional advice in relation to the action which led to the breach of trust. If the trustees were following legal advice, the court is likely to hold that they were acting reasonably.

Statutory protection

22.3   The *Employment Rights Act 1996* offers comfort to trustees (including directors of a corporate trustee) in as much as it:

* offers protection to employee trustees against unfair dismissal by the employer if the dismissal was related to the carrying out of their trustee duties (see **8.9**); and

* offers protection to employee trustees who are subjected to any detriment by their employer because of decisions they have taken as trustees – an example might be that an employee is deliberately passed over for promotion by the employer because he or she argued against a rule change favoured by the employer (see **8.9**).

The *Pensions Act 1995*, which introduced the above two measures before they were re-enacted in the *Employment Rights Act 1996*, also makes clear that trustees are not normally responsible for any act or default of any properly appointed and authorised fund manager (see **16.6**) while the *Pensions Act 2004* offers protection to trustees who carry out their duty to report breaches of the law to the Pensions Regulator preventing them from being sued for breach of confidence (see **10.4**).

Indemnity and exoneration clauses

22.4   The trust deed and rules should contain an indemnity clause which excuses trustees from liability arising from a breach of trust except in cases of *wilful negligence* or *wilful misconduct*. The trust deed and rules may specify that the indemnity is given by the pension fund or by the employer.

In short, the trustees' acknowledged liability for the loss brought about by the breach of trust is financially covered in such circumstances by the fund or the employer.

Instead of, or in addition to, an indemnity clause, the trust deed and rules may contain an exoneration clause. The trustees are simply exonerated from responsibility for any action or lack of action on their part which led to a financial loss for the pension fund – always provided that there was no *wilful negligence* or *wilful misconduct*.

The trustees would bear no personal liability to meet the amount of the shortfall.

If the fund simply meets the cost of the trustee's indemnity, no beneficiary is financially more secure as a result of the court's or Pensions Ombudsman's decision that a breach of trust has taken place. Provision that any shortfall in the fund will be met by the employer is either of very limited or no value at all if the employer has gone into liquidation.

The position is not so clear if some trustees were kept unaware of the wilful misconduct being carried out by others. All action or inaction by trustees is legally held to result from a unanimous decision. The innocent trustees might then have to bring a legal action against the guilty trustees: a course with particular difficulties if the other trustees have disappeared or are already bankrupt. A partial solution may be found with special types of indemnity insurance.

It must be said that the possible scope of the various forms of exoneration clause found in trust deeds is not always very clear. In some cases, the courts have held that a widely drawn clause could exonerate even deliberate breaches of trust. There is actually little legal authority for the idea that it is contrary to public policy to exclude liability for gross negligence by an appropriate exoneration clause clearly worded to have that effect. Lord Justice Millet of the Court of Appeal has acknowledged that there is now a widespread view that these clauses 'have gone too far'. In his opinion, if such clauses are to exclude exemption for wilful misconduct or gross negligence, this should be done by Parliament enacting new legislation. Certainly there is a strong feeling that such clauses should not be available to excuse a professional independent trustee in such cases.

The lead case in this area is that of *Armitage v Nurse* where the Court of Appeal held that an exemption clause could exclude the trustee from liability for loss to the trust fund: 'no matter how indolent, imprudent, lacking in diligence, negligent or wilful he may have been, so long as he has not acted dishonestly'. As may be seen, the Court of Appeal held that even 'wilful' action by the trustee could be exempted by such a clause as long as the trustee was not actually fraudulent.

In December 2002, the Law Commission published a consultation paper, *Trustee Exemption Clauses (Consultation Paper 171)*. The paper examines the current law and practice relating to trustee exemption clauses, considers the economic implications of regulation of such clauses, sets out the options for reform and makes provisional proposals for change on which views were invited.

The tenor of the dilemma the Law Commission experienced in dealing with this issue is best summed up in the following two paragraphs taken from its consultation paper.

'The Law Commission does not believe that an absolute prohibition on all trustee exemption clauses is justifiable at present. One of the advantages of the trust is its flexibility and its adaptability to different factual circumstances and to different kinds of relationship. To deny settlors all power to modify or to restrict the extent of the obligations and liabilities of the trustee would have a very significant impact on the nature of the trust relationship. The trust would inevitably become more inflexible. We are particularly concerned that excessive regulation of trustee exemption clauses may deter lay trustees from assuming the responsibility of trusteeship in the first place.

At the same time, the Law Commission does believe that there is a very strong case for some regulation of trustee exemption clauses. Their increased use in recent years has without doubt reduced the protection afforded to beneficiaries in the event of breach of trust. While there is a need to maintain a balance between the respective interests of settlor, trustee and beneficiary, we believe that the current law is too deferential to trustees, in particular professional trustees who hold themselves out as having special knowledge skills and experience, charge for the services they provide and insure themselves against the risk of liability for breach of trust.'

In an interesting determination (J00273) issued in April 2000, the Pensions Ombudsman formulated a set of principles for guidance derived from a number of key court cases to determine whether the trustees' legal costs, where not met by the other party, can be met from the pension fund. He held that if there is an express indemnity clause allowing costs to be recovered from the fund even if there has been misconduct then those costs can be taken from the fund, provided that the trustees have not been guilty of wilful default. However, if there is an exoneration clause but no indemnity clause, any liability for legal costs is undertaken personally by the trustees and the exoneration clause cannot defeat that liability.

Liability and negligence insurance

22.5   Insurance companies have made negligence insurance available, which may be most important if any indemnity provision cannot be made because the employer has gone into liquidation. If negligence insurance is provided, it should be in the name of the trustees (even if the employer meets the cost of the premiums).

It is to be expected that any negligence insurance will exclude claims arising out of *wilful negligence* or *wilful misconduct*. Because the non-fraudulent trustee can suffer claims as a result of breaches of trust carried out by his or her fraudulent colleagues, some negligence insurance will now cover cases of fraud where trustees other than those who acted fraudulently have claims made on them. The insurance company will require extensive and precise details on the trustees and their advisers. The cost of such insurance is high, and generally relates to the size of the pension fund's assets.

Limitations on indemnity and exoneration clauses and liability and negligence insurance

22.6   *Section 33* of the *Pensions Act 1995* specifically provides that, with certain exceptions, liability for any breach of an obligation placed on trustees by law to take reasonable care, or exercise skill in the carrying out of their investment duties, cannot be excluded or restricted by any prior agreement such as an exoneration clause in a trust deed. *Section 33*, however, does not mean, according to the Department for Work and Pensions, that trustees need to be held personally liable. If there is an indemnity clause, the trustees can still have recourse to its protection, although under the terms of that clause cases of *wilful negligence* or *wilful misconduct* are likely to be excluded as explained above.

More specifically, however, the trustees cannot be indemnified out of the scheme assets for any fines or penalties for offences for which they have been convicted or which have been imposed by the Pensions Regulator for breach of the requirements of the Act. Furthermore, the scheme assets cannot be used to pay insurance premiums for any liability insurance that would cover such fines or penalties. If trustees accept reimbursement out of the assets of the scheme to cover any fine or penalty, they are guilty of an offence and are liable on summary conviction to a fine and on conviction on indictment to imprisonment or a fine or both.

Employer reimbursement policies

22.7 Reimbursement policies are sometimes provided by insurance companies to cover the employer against costs arising out of a breach of trust committed by the trustees. They do not therefore offer protection to the trustees themselves but are a means for the employer to insure against additional costs stemming from the need to honour an indemnity clause or from simply having to pay higher contributions into the pension scheme.

Legal costs

22.8 Trustees might need to initiate court action in some circumstances, perhaps to clarify the nature of their powers to deal with a situation not envisaged in the trust deed and rules (although in some circumstances the Pensions Ombudsman may also be able to determine the issue – see **20.7** above). In other cases, the trustees may need to go to court to pursue litigation against another party, or indeed to defend the fund against hostile litigation. It is important that the trustees are not personally liable to meet the legal costs involved. Trustees are therefore able to approach the court for a preliminary ruling that their costs can be met from the pension fund before embarking on the litigation itself. Some lawyers now advise trustees to ensure that they are insured for any costs incurred in defending themselves in a criminal action. They argue that a trustee could be prosecuted for a criminal offence such as some kind of illegal share-dealing or tax evasion.

Liability of a corporate trustee

22.9 At **3.3** above, we discussed how it was very common for there to be a corporate trustee responsible for a pension scheme rather than a group of individual trustees. The corporate trustee will normally be set up as a limited company. If the members of a pension scheme run by a corporate trustee needed to sue their trustee for breach of trust they would be suing a limited company rather than individuals. In practice this is not likely to result in much recompense since the corporate trustee will usually have very few assets. The corporate trustee could then become insolvent. (Independent corporate trustees, if set up as a trust corporation, must in contrast have more significant assets.)

The directors of the corporate trustee (known generally as 'trustee directors') owe fiduciary duties to that company. However, in the case of *HR v JAPT*, which was heard in the High Court in 1997, it was held that there is no direct fiduciary relationship between the directors of a corporate trustee and the beneficiaries of the pension scheme. The only fiduciary relationship to which the beneficiaries of the pension scheme could be a party would be with the corporate trustee company itself.

Generally speaking, the directors of a corporate trustee are not automatically liable for breaches of trust committed by the corporate trustee, even if the director or directors concerned were involved in the breach.

A court can impose liability upon a director of a company in cases where, on the evidence, the wrongdoer was the company, but only where the actions of that director involve an assumption of personal liability. Therefore, a director of a corporate trustee could be personally liable to the beneficiaries of the pension scheme if that director had taken a risk that was 'commercially unacceptable' because it might jeopardise the position of others.

Otherwise, in such cases involving a corporate trustee it may be possible for redress to be obtained by indirect means. For example, some members might sue the corporate trustee and on the basis of the judgment in that case succeed in having that corporate trustee wound up. The members could then require the liquidator of that company to sue the former directors so that anything that was recovered could then be distributed to them.

Also through the principle of third party accessory liability the directors of a corporate trustee can be liable for a breach of trust committed by the corporate trustee if it can be shown that they knowingly assisted in a dishonest and fraudulent act carried out by the corporate trustee itself.

Protection after winding up

22.10   If the trustees complete a winding up of a pension scheme, it is sensible for them to obtain insurance cover to protect them from the possibility of future claims from scheme beneficiaries of whom they were unaware at the time of the winding-up. Of course, there may have been a indemnity clause in the scheme's trust deed and rules, and in theory this may continue. However, if the indemnity was backed by the employer and the reason for the winding up was the employer's insolvency, this indemnity will now be of little value.

It is also possible that *s 61* of the *Trustee Act 1925* could be of help (see **22.2** above) but the trustees may not wish to rely on a court finding in their favour, especially if it can be shown that the failure to pay the correct benefits was due to maladministration or an act of negligence.

There are also statutory discharge provisions contained in *s 19* of the *Pension Schemes Act 1993* and *s 74* of the *Pensions Act 1995*. For defined benefit schemes starting to wind up on or after 6 April 1997, *s 74* of the *Pensions Act 1995* is the more important of these provisions, but it does not protect trustees if scheme members or beneficiaries have in fact not received their correct benefit during the winding-up.

All these considerations make continuing cover after the completion of the winding-up by means of a suitable insurance contract an important issue for the trustees.

Checklist 22

- A court might excuse trustees who have committed a breach of trust if they have actually acted honestly and reasonably.

- The *Employment Rights Act 1996* offers protection to trustees against unfair dismissal or from being subjected to any detriment by the employer.

- The *Pensions Act 1995* offers trustees protection from being pursued for breach of trust because of losses caused by a properly appointed and authorised fund manager.

- The *Pensions Act 2004* offers protection to trustees who report breaches of the law to the Pensions Regulator from being sued for breach of confidence.

- The trust deed should contain adequate indemnity and/or exoneration clauses protecting the trustees except in cases of wilful misconduct.

- In certain circumstances the *Pensions Act 1995* removes the power of a trust deed to exclude or restrict the liability of trustees if they fail to take care or exercise skill in the carrying out of their investment duties.

- The trustees cannot be indemnified out of the pension fund for any fines or penalties that they have been ordered to pay by the Pensions Regulator, nor can the fund be used to meet insurance premiums that would cover such fines or penalties.

- Liability and negligence insurance are available, except where wilful misconduct has been demonstrated, to protect trustees who have been ordered to make restitution – such insurance may be operative where the employer is insolvent and not able to indemnify the trustees.

- Trustees who need to approach the court to decide a question or otherwise make a ruling may be granted by a preliminary ruling made by that court the right to have the legal costs met from the pension fund.

- The Pensions Ombudsman may also be able to help where there is dispute among the trustees.

- Trustees who complete a winding up of their schemes are advised to ensure that they remain protected against future claims from members or beneficiaries who failed to receive their due benefits.

Chapter 23

Compensation schemes

Introduction

23.1   In the past, if an occupational pension scheme defaulted, and its beneficiaries did not receive the pension entitlement which had already accrued to them (without considering the loss of any future expectations of pension benefits), some mechanisms existed to mitigate their loss. Yet for members of many schemes the compensation available might be absolutely minimal or completely non-existent. Following the Maxwell debacle, there were calls for a comprehensive compensation scheme where members' loss derived from dishonesty. The Government responded via the *Pensions Act 1995* which established a Pensions Compensation Board (PCB) and Pensions Compensation Scheme.

The developments, however, could not deal with the results of funding problems that have arisen in defined benefit, and more specifically, in final salary occupational pension schemes caused principally by the three-year bear market in the world equity markets during the period from 2000 to 2002, the prospect of low inflation which caused bond yields to fall and the significant increase in scheme liabilities arising from the increasing longevity of pensioners.

These funding problems in an on-going scheme backed by a sufficiently strong sponsoring employer are not necessarily catastrophic, although they are often uncomfortable. The employer can increase its contributions, employees can agree to increase their contributions, or to accept a lower rate of benefit for future service. The employer may close the final salary scheme to new entrants or even to future accrual and early retirement terms can be made less generous. In some schemes, members have given their consent to a worsening of their already accrued benefits. Yet the expected benefits continue to be met from the fund as they fall due.

Where, however, the employer is insufficiently strong or the employer's covenant to the scheme and its members is weak, then it is likely that the employer either:

- becomes insolvent, leaving the trustees' to wind up an under-funded scheme and the members facing the prospect of future pension income that is much lower than they had expected and in some cases of no pension income from the scheme at all;

- or remains in business but stops contributing to the scheme with the result that the scheme goes into wind-up – if this occurred before

11 June 2003, the debt to the employer was calculated on a weak basis so that, given the priority order for securing benefits then in place,only a small proportion of the level of non-pensioners' expected benefits could be secured.

In view of the deteriorating situation, and the large distress being caused, the government decided to introduce in the *Pensions Act 2004* two new compensation schemes. These are:

- the Financial Assistance Scheme to help members of under-funded defined benefit schemes where the employer became insolvent and the scheme entered into wind up during the period 1 January 1997 to 5 April 2005 inclusive;

- the Pension Protection Fund to help members of under-funded defined benefit schemes where the employer has become insolvent and where the scheme enters in wind up on or after 6 April 2005.

Financial Assistance Scheme

23.1A   *Part 6* of the *Pensions Act 2004* establishes the Financial Assistance Scheme (FAS) which is to be financed using government resources. The FAS is to deliver financial help to members of under-funded, defined benefit schemes which have entered winding-up during the period 1 January 1997 to 5 April 1997.

In February 2005, the government reported that it had identified at least 380 schemes in which around 65,000 members might be potentially eligible for financial assistance. Final confirmation that any of these schemes will definitely qualify for the FAS cannot be made until the *Financial Assistance Scheme Regulations 2005*, which were issued in draft for consultation in April 2005 and then laid before Parliament in June 2005 until schemes have been formally assessed under those criteria.

The FAS will provide assistance to members of defined benefit pension schemes only if the sponsoring employer is insolvent. Although the scheme must have entered into wind-up during the period 1 January 1997 to 5 April 2005, a scheme will not be excluded from the FAS just because the employer becomes insolvent after 5 April 2005 but the scheme will be excluded if the insolvency of the employer occurs after the end of the period by which schemes must have notified the FAS of their potential eligibility. This date will be set in the definitive version of the regulations. Trustees of schemes which may be potentially eligible, even if the winding-up of that scheme has now been completed, should ensure that they notify the FAS before this cut-off date.

The FAS, at least initially, will provide financial assistance to those within three years of their scheme's normal pension age as at 14 May 2004. The assistance will top up individuals' pensions to a level broadly equivalent to 80% of the core pension rights accrued in their scheme. The core benefits are specified in the *Financial Assistance Scheme Regulations 2005* but do not include annual pension increases. Payments will begin when the member reaches 65 and assistance will only be provided to those whose core benefits equal or exceed the equivalent of £10 a week. A cap is applied on the total amount of assistance and pension payable so that payments from the FAS may not top up members' pensions to more than £12,000 per year.

Payments will be backdated to the date to the later of 14 May 2004 or when the member reaches 65. Such backdated payments are likely to be in lump sum form.

A surviving spouse of a deceased scheme member who was, or would have been, within three years of their scheme pension age on 14 May 2004 will be eligible to receive payments from the date of the death of the member, regardless of the survivor's age. The widow's/widower's pension will be set at 50% of the member's level of assistance.

Further details of the FAS are available at http://www.dwp.gov.uk/lifeevent/penret/penreform/3_fas.asp.

The FAS will not be able to assist the members of under-funded schemes which have gone into wind-up during the period 1 January 1997 to 5 April 2005 but where the employer has not become insolvent before the notification date mentioned above. This will in particular affect schemes whose trustees negotiated with their sponsoring employer during the winding-up process to compromise the debt to the scheme that had arisen on the employer under the former *Occupational Pension Schemes (Deficiency on Winding Up etc.) Regulations 1996 (SI 1996/3128)*. Before 11 June 2003, such scheme wind-ups with a still solvent employer would give rise to a debt on the employer based on the minimum funding requirement cash-equivalent basis which would generally not be sufficient to ensure non-pensioners' pension expecta-tions would be met. Wind-ups beginning on or after that date, however, give rise to a debt on the employer calculated on the full buy-out cost of securing these expected benefits – see **19.8** for more details.

Although the legislation generally provides for a statutory debt on the employer when a defined benefit winds up, there is no requirement in the legislation itself to enforce the debt on the employer. In the case of *Bradstock Group Pension Scheme Trustees Ltd v Bradstock Group plc* the High Court established the principle that trustees could agree with the employer to compromise the debt. In reaching their decision, the trustees would be able to take into account factors relating to the scheme and wider factors such as the survival of the sponsoring employer and the active member's job security. It is also possible that over time, the trustees could obtain more money from the sponsoring employer than they would achieve by seeking to enforce the whole statutory debt and this might be especially the case if enforcing the debt would drive the employer into insolvency.

Yet many were concerned that the licence given by the courts to the trustees had caused many trustees too readily to agree compromise deals with the sponsoring employers that would put them in breach of their fiduciary duty of care for all the members of the scheme – continuing employment for active members is not a benefit for deferred pensioners in the scheme, for example. In retrospect, compromising the debt and keeping the employer in business has overruled the member of an under-funded defined benefit scheme from receiving any help from the FAS.

Section 38 of the *Pensions Act 2004* gives the Pensions Regulator the ability to issue a contribution notice where there has been avoidance of employer debt to a scheme in relation to any such act provided that the act first occurred on or after 27 April 2004 and the Regulator issues the notice within six years of that act.

Since 6 April 2005 the trustees role in any such compromise negotiations should be in accordance with the guidance issued by the Pensions Regulator and which is described at **7.5**.

An unhappy example of a compromise scheme was the subject of a Westminster Hall Parliamentary debate on 22 February 2005 initiated by Mr. David Chidgey MP concerning the APW Pension Scheme. He said:

'Prior to June 2003, employers could wind up their schemes and pay only the minimum funding requirement—the MFR debt—which was usually between a fifth and a seventh of the cost of the annuities. It was understood by most Members [of Parliament] that after those regulations came into force, no solvent employer would be able to close an underfunded pension scheme.

However, unscrupulous employers began to realise that the common law that enabled trustees to compromise a debt could still be used if they could show that the new buyout debt would force the employer into bankruptcy. In fact, because the new buyout debt was so much larger than the MFR debt, the new regulations gave employers more scope to compromise.

In the case of APW, the MFR deficit was about £7.8 million, compared with a buyout debt of £55 million. Therefore, while it could be argued that the MFR level of debt could be met over 10 to 20 years—so the trustees would refuse to compromise it—it was obvious from the accounts that the APW group could not afford £55 million all in one go to buy the annuities. Furthermore, APW knew that if it allowed its pension scheme to keep going beyond April 2005, the trustees would not be open to any compromise. They would simply allow the firm to go into liquidation, knowing that the scheme members would receive 90 per cent. of their pensions from the new Pension Protection Fund. APW would also have known that, although the new financial assistance scheme would be a further incentive to trustees not to compromise, at that time the trustees had no concrete information to go on. The Pensions Bill merely stated that all the detail would be provided by subsequent regulations. Therefore, the trustees had no way of knowing whether the APW scheme would be eligible and, if it were, how much it would receive and whether a limit would be placed on members' pensions.

The choice was between forcing the firm into liquidation over the pension debt and leaving members hostage to fortune on the vagaries of the FAS, and the best possible compromise, which would still only secure 20 to 30 per cent. of members' deferred benefits. Should anybody think that the threat by APW directors to put the firm into liquidation was a bluff, I am assured that the trustees received a written ultimatum that unless they agreed to the compromise drawn up in November, the directors would file for bankruptcy the next day. To add insult to injury, the trustees were also told that APW's American parent would then buy the firm back out of bankruptcy, free of the £55 million pension debt, at a knockdown price. So the compromise was made and the bombshell fell on hundreds of scheme beneficiaries, many of whom found their expectations of a secure retirement in ruins. Members were left distraught, having to rethink their lives.'

Pensions Protection Fund

23.1B   The Pension Protection Fund (PPF), made under *Part 2* of the *Pensions Act 2004*, came into being on 6 April 2005. Its main function is to provide compensation to members of eligible defined benefit pension schemes, when the employer has become insolvent and there are insufficient assets in the pension scheme to cover the scheme's *protected liabilities*. The PPF is funded through various compulsory annual levies which are charged on those defined benefit occupational pension schemes which are covered by the PPF known as *eligible schemes*, and also by the assets that are taken over by the Board of the PFF when it assumes responsibility for a scheme, and the investment return achieved by investing those assets.

The PPF provides two levels of compensation. For those members who have reached their scheme's normal pension age or those who are either already in receipt of survivors' pension or a pension on the grounds of ill health, the PPF will pay compensation so that the initial level of compensation payable generally is equal to 100% of the pension in payment immediately before the assessment date. The part of this compensation that is derived from pensionable service on or after 6 April 1997 will be increased each year in line with the Retail Prices Index capped at 2.5% in any one year.

For the active members and deferred pensioners who have not yet reached their scheme's normal pension age the PPF will generally pay 90% of the pension an individual had accrued immediately before the assessment date as revalued in line with the Retail Prices Index capped at 5% for each year between the assessment date and the commencement of the compensation payments. This compensation is subject to an overall cap set at £27,777.78 in 2005/06 and will be raised annually in line with the increase in national average earnings. This equates to a maximum benefit of £25,000 in 2006/07 at age 65 (since 90% of £27,777.78 is £25,000). The cap is adjusted according to the age at which compensation comes into payment. Once compensation is in payment, the part that derives from pensionable service on or after 6 April 1997 will be increased each year in line with the Retail Prices Index capped at 2.5%. Compensation will also be paid to certain survivors.

The PPF Board can alter the levies to meet its liabilities. If necessary, however, the amount of compensation could be reduced and the revaluation and indexation rates can also be adjusted if circumstances so dictate.

Special levy arrangements apply in 2005/06, the first year of the operation of the PPF. From 2006/07, apart from the *general levy* which is payable by all occupational and personal pension schemes, and the *fraud compensation levy* which will be raised from all occupational pension schemes that are eligible for the Fraud Compensation Fund (see **23.2**), eligible schemes will be required to pay the following levies:

- The *pension protection levies* will be set by the Board of the PPF which, as currently envisaged, will need to raise approximately £300 million a year to meet the PPF's ongoing liabilities. They will comprise:

    - the *scheme-based pension protection levy* which is based on the level of a scheme's liabilities relating to members and also, if the Board of the PPF considers it appropriate, the number of members within a scheme, the total amount of pensionable earnings of active members within a scheme and/or any other scheme factor as set out in regulations;

    - the *risk-based pension protection levy* which is based on the funding level of a scheme and, in some cases, the risk of the sponsoring employer becoming insolvent. If the Board of the PPF considers it appropriate, it may also take account of a scheme's asset allocation and/or any other risk factor as set out in regulations.

In the longer term, the *Pensions Act 2004* requires that at least 80% of the pension protection levies must be raised through the risk-based pension protection levy. During the early years, however, this will be phased in.

- The *administration levy* will be used to pay for the initial start up costs and ongoing administrative costs of the PPF. The initial start up costs will be collected over a three-year period.

- The *PPF Ombudsman levy* which goes to fund the work of this new Ombudsman.

The process whereby an eligible scheme will come under the PPF is fully explained in detail by the PPF's booklet *Guidance for Trustees,* which is available from the PPF at http://www.pensionprotectionfund.org.uk/trustee_guidance_-_bookmarked_pdf_version.pdf.

Board of the Pensions Protection Fund (PPF)
Knollys House
17 Addiscombe Road
Croydon
Surrey
CR0 6SR
Tel: 0845 600 2541
Text phone: 0845 600 2542

Fax: 020 8633 4903
Email: information@ppf.gsi.gov.uk
Web site: http://www.pensionprotectionfund.org.uk/.

Events to be notified by the trustees

23.1C The trustees of eligible pension schemes covered by the PPF are required by *s 69* of the *Pensions Act 2004* to notify the Pensions Regulator when certain events occur in relation to the scheme but only if specified conditions are met. This notification regime stems from one of the main statutory aims of the new Pensions Regulator which is to reduce the risk of situations arising which may lead to compensation being payable from the PPF. Apart from *s 69* itself these requirements are set out by the *Pensions Regulator (Notifiable Events) Regulations 2005 (SI 2005/900)* as modified by the general directions issued by the Pensions Regulator under *s 69(1)* of the *2004 Act* and the code of practice issued by the Pensions Regulator on the overall notifiable events framework.

The notifiable events requirements set out four conditions as listed below.

- Condition A: The value of the scheme's assets is equal to, or greater than, the value of the scheme's liabilities calculated either under the last MFR valuation or under the last risk-based PPF buy-out level. Here 'risk-based PPF buy-out level' means the level of funding needed to provide members with the amount of compensation to the level that can be offered by the PPF in accordance with the actuarial valuation specified by *s 179* of the *Pensions Act 2004* to determine scheme underfunding for the purposes of the risk-based PPF levies.

- Condition B: The trustees have not incurred a duty to make a report to the Pensions Regulator (or its predecessor, Opra) in the previous 12 months because they had reasonable cause to believe that failure by the employer to make a payment to the scheme in accordance with the most recently agreed schedule of contributions was likely to be of material significance.

- Condition C: The decision by the trustees to compromise a debt owed to the scheme by the employer relates to a debt such that the full amount owed is less than 0.5% of the scheme's assets calculated at present under either the last MFR valuation or the last risk-based PPF valuation.

- Condition D: The change in the employer's credit rating is other than a change from investment grade to sub-investment grade where that credit rating is supplied by a recognised credit rating agency.

The trustees are required to report to the Pensions Regulator if any of the following scheme events occur unless the conditions specified are also met:

- Any decision by the trustees to take action which will, or is intended to, result in any debt which is or may become due to the scheme not being paid in full must be notified unless conditions A, B and C are all satisfied.

- Two or more changes in the posts of the scheme auditor and the scheme actuary within the previous 12 months must be notified to the Pensions Regulator, unless both conditions A and B are satisfied.

- A decision by the trustees to make a transfer payment to, or accept a transfer payment from, another scheme where the value of that transfer is more than the lower of 5% of the value of the scheme's assets and £1.5 million must be notified unless both conditions A and B are satisfied.

- A decision by the trustees to grant benefits, or a right to benefits, on more favourable terms than those provided for by the scheme rules, without either seeking advice from the actuary or securing additional funding where such funding was advised by the actuary must always be notified.

- A decision by the trustees to grant benefits, or a right to benefits, to a member where the cost of this benefit is more than the lower of 5% of the value of the scheme's assets and £1.5 million must be notified unless both conditions A and B are satisfied.

The requirement on the trustees is to report such notifiable events, when the conditions are met, in writing and as soon as is reasonably practicable.

Note that other notifiable events must also be reported to the Pensions Regulator by the sponsoring employer, again depending on which of Conditions A to D apply. In practice the employer may ask that the responsibility for reporting these events is carried out either by the trustees or the pensions administrator.

Fraud Compensation Fund

23.2   A Compensation Scheme came into effect on 6 April 1997 administered by the Pensions Compensation Board (PCB) and which was designed to protect the members of occupational pension schemes that are set up as trusts if:

- the sponsoring employer is insolvent;

- the value of the assets of the scheme has been reduced and there are reasonable grounds for believing that the reduction was caused by mis-appropriation, fraud or some other prescribed offence;

- the amount of the shortfall means that for defined benefit schemes the value of a scheme's assets is less than the specified protection level; and

- it is reasonable in all the circumstances for the PCB to assist the scheme members.

The Fraud Compensation Fund applies to both defined benefit and defined contribution occupational pension schemes.

The Pensions Compensation Board remains responsible for considering applications for fraud compensation until 31 August 2005 when the Board of the Pensions Protection Fund takes over that responsibility.

If a fraud compensation application is made by a eligible defined benefit scheme within the PPF's assessment period, this will not significantly change the process of assessment. The PPF guidance, however, stresses that it is important to be aware that any fraud compensation payments may count towards the value of the pension scheme's assets and will therefore need to be settled before a valuation is obtained. The result is that the PPF's assessment period for a pension scheme cannot end until the application has been finally settled because the amount of fraud compensation must be taken into account in the actuarial valuation to ascertain whether there are sufficient assets to enable the pension scheme to wind-up outside of the PPF.

Compensation will be paid if the value of the assets has been reduced since the relevant date and the Board considers that there are reasonable grounds for believing the reduction was attributable to an act or omission constituting an offence as set out in regulations. The relevant date in the case of schemes established under trust remains 6 April 1997.

The maximum payment that may be made from the Fraud Compensation Fund is an amount equal to the value of the loss less any recovered funds. The Fraud Compensation Fund is financed by the fraud compensation levy.

Financial Services Compensation Scheme

23.3   Following the collapse of a UK insurance company, the Government of the day brought in the *Policyholders Protection Act 1975*. This guaranteed that all members and beneficiaries of an occupational pension scheme that was fully insured would receive at least 90% of their accrued pension benefit in the event of the insurance company becoming insolvent. There was no cash ceiling on the amount of compensation stipulated in the Act and the fund to cover such claims was financed by a levy on insurance companies. The security of the members and beneficiaries depended on the employer having paid over all the due contributions to the insurer, on the scheme trustees not undertaking any assignment or pledge on the insurance contract, and on the trustees ensuring that all payments out of the scheme were to genuine beneficiaries of that scheme.

This provision has now been revoked and replaced by the Financial Services Compensation Scheme.

In the case of the collapse of a financial services company regulated under the requirements of the *Financial Services Act 1986*, or its successor legislation, the *Financial Services and Markets Act 2000*, there has been only very limited compensation to mitigate any loss suffered by an occupational pension scheme which had invested scheme assets with the failed company.

Under the rules of the former Investors Compensation Scheme (ICS), pension funds were classed as multiple investors and received the same compensation as a single individual investor. The scheme paid out 100% of the first £30,000 invested, and 90% of the next £20,000 invested. This gave a maximum £48,000 compensation. In the case of the failure of a bank (such as BCCI) or a building society, compensation offered by the Deposit Protection Board was limited to 90% of the first £20,000, i.e. £18,000.

The recent reforms taking place in the world of financial services provided an opportunity to review the former compensation and default protection schemes covering those activities which now all fall under the scope of the Financial Services Authority (FSA).

As a result there is now a single compensation scheme – the Financial Services Compensation Scheme (FSCS). The FSCS is a company, independent of the FSA, whose function it is to administer arrangements for assessing and making compensation payments in accordance with rules made by the FSA. These arrangements apply where regulated firms are in liquidation or are otherwise unable to meet their obligations to consumers.

However, as a matter of policy, it was concluded that the FSCS should focus on those consumers who are least able to sustain financial loss. The new compensation limits follow closely those existing under the former schemes. They are as follows:

Asset type	Compensation calculation	Maximum
Deposits	100% of first £2,000 and 90% of up to £33,000 of any remaining loss	£31,700
Investments	100% of first £30,000 and 90% of up to £20,000 of any remaining loss	£48,000
Long-term insurance	At least 90% of the value of the policyholder's guaranteed fund at the date of default	No maximum

The situation for pension fund trustees is set out in the FSA's Compensation Sourcebook rules and can be summarised as follows:

(a)   If the claim is in respect of lost deposits, pension fund trustees are unable to claim compensation from the FSCS unless the claimant is a trustee of a small self-administered scheme, or the trustee of an occupational pension scheme of an employer that is neither a 'large company', nor a 'large partnership', nor a 'large mutual association'.

(b)   If the claim is in respect of designated investment business, pension fund trustees *are unable* to claim compensation from the FSCS *unless* the claimant is a trustee of a small self-administered scheme or the trustee of an occupational pension scheme of an employer that is neither a 'large company', nor a 'large partnership', nor a 'large mutual association'.

(c)   If the claim is in respect of a contract of long-term insurance arising from the failure of an insurance company or friendly society, pension scheme trustees *are able* to claim compensation from the FSCS.

Under the FSA's Compensation Sourcebook the following definitions are applied:

- A 'large company' is a *body corporate* that does *not* qualify as a 'small company' under *s 247* of the *Companies Act 1985*. Under *s 247* a company is regarded as a 'small company' essentially if it is a company that satisfies at least two of the following criteria:

  - it does not have more than 50 employees;

  - its turnover is not more than £5.6m;

  - its balance sheet total is not more than £2.8m.

- A 'large partnership' is a partnership or unincorporated association with net assets of more than £1.4m.

- A 'large mutual association' or unincorporated association is one with net assets of more than £1.4m.

Unpaid contributions

23.4   *Section 124* of the *Pension Schemes Act 1993* allows certain unpaid pension contributions to be paid into the occupational pension scheme by the Government in circumstances where the employer has become insolvent. The unpaid contributions can be employer contributions or employee contributions. The employee contributions must have actually been deducted from employees' pay. However, provided the contributions had actually been deducted from the employee's pay but not paid to the scheme, the Government could pay an equivalent amount to the scheme. As regards unpaid employer contributions, compensation paid by the Government is limited to the lower of the following:

- employer contributions due in respect of the 12 months before the employer became insolvent;

- an amount equal to 10% of the total paybill over the 12 months before the employer became insolvent;

- in the case of a defined benefit scheme, the amount certified by an actuary as necessary to meet the scheme's liability.

The schedules of contributions (defined benefit schemes) and payment schedules (defined contribution schemes) required by the *Pensions Act 1995* (see **8.3**) should ensure that non-payment of contributions is restricted to relatively short periods before an employer insolvency occurs.

Contracted-out schemes

23.5   Prior to 6 April 1997 members of contracted-out schemes also built up rights, albeit reduced rights, in SERPS. In the event that a scheme, that retains liability for either pre-6 April 1997 contracted-out GMPs, or protected rights, is wound up and the scheme's resources have been so depleted that they are unable to secure the GMPs or protected rights perhaps by using insured, non-profit annuities, the DWP will treat the state scheme premiums as having been paid.

The relevant legislation is contained in *sub-paras (3A)* to *(3E)* of *para 5* of *Sch 2* to the *Pension Schemes Act 1993* and *regs 49* and *50* of the *Occupational Pension Schemes (Contracting-out) Regulations 1996 (SI 1996/1172).*

In effect this means that any deduction from the individual's entitlement to SERPS which would have been made because that individual had been contracted out while a member of the scheme will not in the event actually be made. The SERPS pension payable is the same as if the individual had never been contracted out. With the abolition of future rights to GMPs on 6 April 1997, the compensation has only affected contracted-out rights built up from 1978 to 1997.

In relation to contracted-out rights built up since 6 April 1997 in an occupational pension scheme contracted out by the reference scheme test, the state will meet the cost of restoring lost rights using what are known as the *deemed buyback* provisions inserted into *Sch 2* to the *Pension Schemes Act 1993*. For rights to additional pension from SERPS and S2P to be restored, the following conditions must be satisfied:

- The contracted-out scheme must have entered into wind-up after 5 April 1997.

- The sponsoring employer must be unable to make up the shortfall in funding.

- The remaining funds must be less than the amount needed to restore the additional pension rights.

- The scheme must be less than 100% funded under the minimum funding requirement provisions (see **13.7**).

- The amount available in the scheme in relation to a particular individual member must be less than the amount that would have been available if the scheme had been 100% funded on winding up.

For each affected member, the amount available to restore rights to additional pension from the state is the lower of:

- the *technical amount* which is equal to the amount required to restore the member's additional pension to the level it would have been if the member had not been contracted out under the scheme; and

- the *MFR transfer value* which is equal to what would have been the value of the member's accrued pension rights if the scheme had wound up funded at 100% of the MFR. But where the *MFR transfer value* is less than the *technical amount*, the amount that is to be restored is reduced by the same proportion.

Deemed buyback provisions also operate in relation to occupational pension schemes contracted out on the protected rights test but only in relation to losses which have arisen out of the unlawful removal of fund assets.

When S2P replaced SERPS for the future accrual of additional pension on 6 April 2002, the then existing regulations setting out the factors to be used in the deemed buyback calculations ceased to be valid and so deemed buyback could not operate. It was not until the *Occupational Pension Schemes (Contracting-out) (Amount Required for Restoring State Scheme Rights) Amendment Regulations 2005 (SI 2005/891)* were laid before Parliament on 31 March 2005 and subsequently came into force on 21 April 2005 that deemed buyback once again became available in practice,

In relation to the Financial Assistance Scheme and schemes where the employer has not become insolvent (**23.2**), the Minister for Pensions in a statement to the House of Commons on 4 April 2005 explained:

'As solvent employers have a duty to support their schemes and provide the benefits members were expecting, it is right that the FAS focuses on insolvent employers. We have however taken action to facilitate operation of the arrangements for deemed buy back which enables some members of severely under-funded contracted-out pension schemes in wind-up, who meet the qualifying conditions, to choose to be reinstated into the state system. On 31 March we laid new regulations to speed up the process and ensure schemes get their calculations quickly. These regulations clarify that as well as being available to members of some insolvent schemes (helping ensure that the funding allocated to the FAS can help as many people as possible), this option is also available to some members in schemes with solvent employers.'

EU Insolvency Directive and the Francovich case

23.6 On 20 October 1980, the European Community adopted Council Directive (EEC) 80/987 which deals with the approximation of the laws of the European Community member states relating to the protection of employees in the event of the insolvency of their employer.

The preamble of the Directive states that it has been adopted because: '... it is necessary to provide for the protection of employees in the event of the insolvency of their employer, in particular to guarantee payment of outstanding claims ...'

Article 8 of the Directive says:

'Member states shall ensure that the necessary measures are taken to protect the interests of employees and of persons having already left the employer's undertaking or business at the date of the onset of the employer's insolvency in respect of rights conferring on them immediate or prospective entitlement to old-age benefits, including survivors' benefits, under supplementary company or inter-company pension schemes outside the national statutory social security schemes.'

The Directive is binding on all member states who were required to bring in national legislation to enforce the Directive within 36 months of its notification (i.e. by October 1983).

In 1992, the European Court of Justice decided the case of *Francovich v Italy*. Italy was judged to have failed to implement the Employer's Insolvency Directive and, as a result, the plaintiff, Signor Francovich, could claim damages from the Italian Government to compensate him for the loss he had suffered.

The UK Government's view is that it has complied with the requirements of Directive by implementing the requirements of *s 124* of the *Pension Schemes Act 1993* which deal with unpaid contributions (see **23.7** above). However, there is a body of legal opinion that believes that the Directive acts more broadly to protect employees' pension rights upon the insolvency of their employer.

As discussed at **19.10**, there is a requirement for the trustees of defined benefit schemes that are found to be underfunded on a winding up to pursue the employer for the required deficiency payment. However, because the deficiency payment is currently calculated on the MFR basis, it may not actually be sufficient to secure each member's accrued rights in full in the situation where the scheme is winding up. Furthermore, if the employer is insolvent, the unsecured status of the employer's debt to the trustees means that in practice the debt may not be recoverable. It is argued, therefore, that these legislative measures, made under *s 75* of the *Pensions Act 1995*, cannot be said to implement the Directive either. Employees whose pension rights held in a defined benefit scheme are not fully bought out during the winding up of a scheme, in a case where the employer has become insolvent, may therefore be advised to pursue a claim against the UK Government for failure to implement the Directive, along the lines of the *Francovich* case.

It is of note that in January 2003 the Iron and Steel Trades Confederation trade union announced that it was considering taking legal action against the Government on these grounds. The announcement was made after 800 workers had lost their jobs when Allied Steel and Wire went into receivership in July 2002. The company had sponsored two final salary pension schemes that are being wound up but which are unlikely to have sufficient assets to secure more than two-thirds, and possibly less, of the non-pensioners' accrued pension rights. Although noting the planned introduction of the Financial Assistance Scheme and the Pension Protection Fund, the trade union decided that it was in the best interests of their members to press ahead with this challenge. In November 2004, Mr Justice Evans-Lomb in the High Court, stated that the case should be referred to the European Court of Justice.

Checklist 23

- The *Pensions Act 2004* has established the Financial Assistance Scheme and the Pension Protection Fund to provide financial assistance to members of under-funded defined benefit schemes.

- The *Pensions Act 1995* set up a new compensation scheme for members of trust-based occupational pension schemes – compensation is only payable if the employer is insolvent and the loss occurred through misappropriation. The scheme will in future be administered by the Board of the Pension Protection Fund.

- The operation of the Financial Services Compensation Scheme provides little comfort to the trustees of an occupational pension scheme except in relation to a contract of long-term insurance arising from the failure of an insurance company or friendly society.

- If an employer becomes insolvent not having paid contributions due to a pension scheme, the state can make up for the missing contributions up to a specified limit.

- GMPs and notional GMPs from protected rights built up until 6 April 1997 are guaranteed by the state and the deemed buyback provisions operate in relation to periods of contracted-out employment after that date..

- The EU Insolvency Directive instructs member states to protect employees' pension entitlement on the insolvency of the employer.

Chapter 24

Training opportunities for trustees

Introduction

24.1   Greater emphasis was placed on the proper training of trustees following the 1991 revelations of the Maxwell scandal. Stress must be placed on the quality of training offered, always bearing in mind that trustees drawn from company management or the employees generally are not expected to become professional pension experts. Indeed, as has so often been mentioned in this book, one of the duties of all trustees is to take professional advice. Training courses offered to trustees should therefore not be geared so much towards improving their technical understanding of pensions but rather emphasising the need for trustees to understand that:

• they, the trustees, are in control;

• they, the trustees, bear the responsibility for the safekeeping of the trust funds;

• they, the trustees, must question keenly their advisers, including the pensions manager, who are all answerable to them; and

• they must never become complacent.

It was notable that there was no requirement in the *Pensions Act 1995* for trustees to receive any training at all, although as noted at **8.8** the *1995 Act* stipulated that trustees are entitled to paid time off work to perform trustee duties and undergo training. However, the first of Paul Myners' principles developed in 2000 for the trustees of both defined benefit and defined contribution schemes (see **17.4** and **17.5**) is that:

'Decisions should be taken only by persons or organisations with the skills, information and resources necessary to take them effectively. Where trustees elect to take investment decisions, they must have sufficient expertise and appropriate training to be able to evaluate critically any advice they take.'

The subsequent developments leading to the new obligations on trustees of occupational pension schemes to be conversant with their trust documentation and other key documents and to have relevant knowledge and understanding as set out in *ss 247–249* of the *Pensions Act 2004* are explained at **5.2**. These legislative requirements clearly require the trustees of occupational pension schemes to receive training.

The '*Scope Documents*' described at **5.3** and reproduced in **APPENDIX 1** are intended to serve as the basis for a draft syllabus and qualification for trustee training to be developed by the Financial Services Skills Council and the Qualifications and Curriculum Authority, although it will not be mandatory for trustees to take the qualification.

April Alexander, director of education and communications at the Pensions Regulator, said:

> 'Access to good quality and affordable learning is vital for trustees. We are already working with training providers to ensure that trustees will be able to comply with the legal requirements on knowledge and understanding, which are due to come into force in April 2006.
>
> Trustees' learning needs vary according to the size and type of the pension schemes they run, and we have just completed research into free online learning which would benefit trustees of small schemes with few resources. Among a large random sample of trustees there was almost universal recognition that levels of expertise are not high enough and there is a very marked appetite for access to e-learning.

These knowledge and understanding requirements should give trustees the confidence they need to run their schemes and to challenge their advisers before they make decisions. It is important that advisers are also well-versed in the trustee knowledge and understanding requirements.' The Pensions Management Institute (PMI) (see **11.1**) launched in 1993 the *Trustee Certificate of Basic Pensions Knowledge* which gives formal recognition of an individual trustee's basic knowledge of what is involved in undertaking pension trustee work.

The certificate is awarded to those who successfully complete a short examination. The examination is available, on a totally voluntary basis, to all pension fund trustees as well as to any other interested individual.

The examination lasts about one hour and takes the form of answering multiple-choice questions designed to test basic knowledge across the syllabus. Each item either poses a question or makes a statement which requires completion. This is followed by four possible responses, one of which is the correct response. Candidates' answers to each item will therefore be (a), (b), (c) or (d). The examination does not involve writing essays.

The 26 topics listed below form the basis of the syllabus:

- pension arrangements and membership;
- regulatory framework;
- HMRC requirements before April 2006;
- HMRC requirements from April 2006;
- basic concepts of a trust;
- fundamentals of trusteeship;
- different forms of trusteeship;

- main duties of trustees;
- powers of trustees;
- discretions of trustees;
- trustees' liabilities and protections;
- winding up and/or merging schemes;
- trustee meetings;
- powers of delegation and responsibilities of trustees;
- collection and investment of contributions;
- keeping of records and calculations of benefits;
- disclosure of information;
- annual report;
- individual and bulk transfers;
- typical investment objectives of trustees;
- different classes of investments;
- characteristics of the different classes of investments;
- different investment management structures;
- investment performance and monitoring and investment manager meetings;
- custody of scheme assets;
- role of the actuary; and
- valuations and scheme funding.

The examination should be taken after a short period of experience of being a trustee, and some background reading and attendance at a trustee training course run by a consultancy, training provider, trade union or other body. The PMI itself does not run trustee training courses nor does it recommend or endorse any particular training courses. It has assembled a list of providers of trustee training courses which is available on request from the address below or from the PMI's web site.

Further information can be obtained from:

Education Secretary
The Pensions Management Institute
PMI House
4–10 Artillery Lane
London
E1 7LS
Tel: 020 72471452
Fax: 020 73750603
Web site: http://www.pensions-pmi.org.uk.

Checklist 24

- Trustees do not have to be pension experts – they have professional advisers for that purpose.

- Trustees should, however, understand that they are responsible for the safe keeping of the pension fund and that it is vital that they take their duties seriously – training should be directed to this end.

  Trustees must comply with the requirements set by the *Pensions Act 2004* so that they are conversant with their trust documentation and other key documents and have knowledge and understanding of relevant matters.

- Trustees must be given paid time off work to undertake their trustee duties and to undergo training. The principles put forward by Paul Myners state that trustees should receive training in relation to investment matters.

- The scope documents will serve as the basis draft syllabus and qualification for trustee training to be developed by the Financial Services Skills Council and the Qualifications and Curriculum Authority.

- Trustees should consider taking the PMI's *Trustee Certificate of Basic Pensions Knowledge* which is not biased towards those who are good at writing essays.

- There are many training providers in the marketplace – regularly updated lists are available from the PMI.

The combined DB/DC scope document

Trustees are required to have knowledge and understanding about the law relating to trusts and to pension schemes generally.

Unit 1 The law relating to trusts

This includes an understanding of the special nature of a pension trust and the duties, obligations and powers of trustees to operate pension schemes in accordance with the law and with the trust deed and documents.

1a   The definition and nature of a pension trust

Including the separation between the scheme and the employer.

1b   Fiduciary duties

Including the obligation to act prudently, taking into account the needs of all beneficiaries.

1c   Conflicts of interest

Especially the range of situations which may give rise to conflicts and how those conflicts may be managed.

1d   Professional advice and decision making

Especially the need for obtaining professional advice (where appropriate) in reaching decisions.

1e   The role of advisers and suppliers to the scheme

Including (as appropriate) actuaries, benefits consultants, financial advisers, fund managers, lawyers and statutory independent trustees.

1f   The particular role and use of advisers where a scheme or employer is under threat or a scheme is in wind-up.

1g   Fitness and properness to act as trustees

Including the need for regular attendance at meetings.

1h   Taking office

Especially personal duties and responsibilities.

1i   Ceasing to hold office

Especially continuing personal liability for past decisions.

1j   Investing funds

Especially trustees' responsibility to act prudently.

1k   Operating the scheme in accordance with the trust deed, rules and subsequent amendments

Including the power to delegate functions while retaining responsibility.

1l   The role of the auditors

Including internal and external auditors.

1m   Protections offered to trustees

1n   The importance of sound administration arrangements

Including risks, controls and contingency planning.

Unit 2 The law relating to pensions

This includes occupational pensions legislation (in outline) and the key provisions of related legislation that affects pension schemes and impacts on the role and activities of trustees.

2a   Occupational pensions legislation, including:

- key provisions of the *Pensions Act 2004;*
- key remaining provisions of the *Pensions Act 1995;*
- the Pensions Regulator, Codes of Practice and guidance.

2b   Disputes resolution, including:

- Internal Disputes Resolution Procedure;
- the role of the Pensions Advisory Service;
- the role of the Pensions Ombudsman.

2c   Pensions related legislation

Including the impact of other key provisions on the running of pension schemes.

2d   The tax privileges and requirements for occupational pension schemes.

2e   The interface between occupational schemes and state pensions provision.

2f   The particular powers of the regulator in the event of disagreement between the trustees and the employer.

Trustees are required to have knowledge and understanding about the principles relating to the funding of occupational pension schemes and the investment of the scheme's assets.

Unit 3 Investment: defined benefit (DB) and defined contribution (DC) occupational arrangements (including AVCs)

This includes the different types of assets available for investment and their characteristics.

3a   Capital markets

> *Including, in broad terms, the effect of economic cycles.*

3b   The major asset classes and their characteristics.

3c   The implications of overseas investment

> *Including foreign exchange risk.*

3d   The existence of specialised asset classes, instruments and techniques.

3e   Risk v reward, especially:

- the nature of risk;
- the risk/reward profile of each asset class.

3f   Valuation of assets (DB schemes only), for example:

- actuarial valuations;
- company balance sheets.

3g   With profits arrangements and how they work (as appropriate).

Unit 4 Funding: defined benefit (DB) occupational arrangements

This includes the principles relating to the funding of occupational DB schemes and the way in which funding is dependent upon the financial circumstances of the sponsoring employer and the value of the liabilities of the scheme.

4a   How the funding for occupational DB pension arrangements works.

4b   The nature of the employer/trustee relationship and the effect of pension liabilities on the sponsoring employers.

4c   The nature and strength of the employer covenant and its ability and willingness to meet the costs of members' benefits

> *Especially an awareness of the employer's business and its risk exposure.*

4d   How liabilities are valued.

4e   Funding targets

> *Including how funding targets are set in relation to the underlying value of the liabilities.*

4f   Potential risks to the scheme

> *Including those arising from financial instability of the sponsoring employer or corporate restructuring.*

4g   The impact of trustee powers

> *Including the financial and reputational impact of exercising discretions.*

4h   Transfers and bulk transfers in and out of schemes.

4i   Additional pension funding by employees, including (where appropriate):

- additional voluntary contributions (AVCs) and added years arrangements;

- free standing additional voluntary contributions (FSAVCs);

- stakeholder pensions;

- salary/bonus sacrifice;

- personal pension arrangements.

Unit 5 Contributions: defined benefit (DB) occupational arrangements

This includes the principles relating to the funding of occupational DB schemes and the way in which contribution levels are dependent upon the funding of the scheme.

5a   The assumptions underlying the contribution calculations, including:

- the process of setting contributions and the relationship between these contributions and the scheme's liabilities;

- the effect of the assumptions on valuations of the fund.

5b   The nature and status of professional advice.

5c   Funding deficits

> *Including the requirements placed on trustees where there is an actual or potential funding deficit and disagreement between them and the employer(s) on the rate of contributions required to correct it.*

Unit 6 Strategic asset allocation: Defined-benefit (DB) occupational arrangements

This includes the principles relating to the suitability of different asset classes to meet the liabilities of the scheme.

6a   How to fund particular future benefits

> *Especially through selecting an appropriate mix of asset classes.*

6b   The process of strategic asset allocation.

6c   Reviewing asset allocation decisions

> *Especially where there is a change in status or maturity of the scheme.*

Unit 7 Funding: defined contribution (DC) occupational arrangements (including AVCs)

This includes the principles relating to the funding of occupational DC arrangements and the risks borne by scheme members.

7a   How the funding for occupational DC pension arrangements works

> *Including expenses of the scheme especially in the event of a wind-up.*

7b   The risks borne by members.

7c   The implications of contracting out.

Unit 8 Investment choices: defined-contribution (DC) occupational arrangements (including AVCs)

This includes the principles relating to the choice of investments.

8a   Investment strategy and member investment choices.

8b   Administration procedures specific to DC arrangements, including:

- the responsibilities of trustees in relation to effective administration;
- the risks to member benefits.

Unit 9 Fund management: defined-benefit (DB) and defined-contribution (DC) scheme arrangements (including AVCs)

This includes the principles of fund management and how performance can be measured.

9a   The Statement of Investment Principles (SIP)

> *Especially the investment considerations necessary to meet the provisions of the SIP.*

9b   Measuring performance including the use of indices.

9c   The ownership of assets

> *Especially the implications for trustees in relation to corporate governance.*

9d   The structure of investment portfolios.

9e   The selection of fund managers

> *Including how the process is managed.*

9f   Continuing review of investment arrangements.

Trustees need to be conversant (i.e. familiar) with the documents that are particular to their own scheme so that they are able to make use of those documents in carrying out their functions.

Unit 10 The scheme's trust deed and scheme rules

This includes any subsequent amending documents.

10a The duties, powers and discretions of trustees

> *Under their own trust deed, rules and amendments.*

10b The balance of power between employer and trustees

> *Including when it is appropriate to exercise various trustee powers especially where a scheme or employer is under threat or a scheme is in wind-up.*

10c Classes of members in the scheme

> *Including eligibility for membership.*

10d Benefits offered

> *Including the circumstances under which they are payable and how the payments are made.*

Unit 11 The scheme's Statement of Investment Principles (SIP)

11a Responsibilities for investment decisions

> *Including why this structure has been selected and, if appropriate, the terms of reference of the investment sub-committee.*

11b The investment objectives

> *Including the reasons for them (DB schemes) and/or the reasons for the range of funds offered (DC arrangements).*

11c The asset allocation strategy (DB schemes only)

> *Including how the strategy has been arrived at.*

11d Investment mandates

> *Including an understanding of the nature of the contract between the trustees and their advisers.*

11e Fee structures (DB schemes only)

> *Including why these structures have been selected.*

11f Charges (DC arrangements only).

11g The type of investments undertaken (DB schemes only).

11h Socially responsible investment and corporate governance.

Unit 12 The scheme's Statement of Funding Principles (SFP) (defined benefit schemes only)

12a Responsibilities for preparing the SFP.

12b The scheme's statutory funding objective.

12c Contents of the SFP.

12d Review of the SFP

Including changes to the status of the scheme.

Unit 13 Other relevant scheme documents

This includes the scheme booklet, announcements and member communications, minutes of meetings that record current policy and the annual report.

13a Scheme booklet, announcements and other member communications.

13b Actuarial valuation and advice

Especially the key elements of the most recent actuarial valuation and subsequent advice.

13c Minutes of meetings, including:

- their importance;
- policy decisions recorded in them.

13d Annual report and accounts.

13e Any significant insurance policy

13f Any significant agreement or contract.

Including those with delegated authorities or professional advisers.

13g Any trustee approved procedures, including:

- the internal disputes resolution (IDR) procedure;
- appointment of all classes of trustees;
- appointment of chairperson.

13h Statement of compliance with the Myners' Principles (where appropriate).

13i Terms of reference of any sub-committee (where relevant).

13j Memorandum and Articles of corporate trustee (where applicable).

13k The scheme business plan

Including a skills audit (where applicable) and/or training plan.

13l Trustees should be aware of where all original documents are kept and of the arrangements for their custody, safekeeping and access.

Index

A

Absolute returns 16.11A
ACA: *see* Association of Consulting Actuaries
accountants 9.1, Chapter 15
Accounting Standards Board, 9.4, 15.3, 15.10
active investment manager 16.19
active members 9.15–9.19
actuarial methods and assumptions 13.4–13.6, 13.10
actuary 9.4, 9.6, 10.1, 10.2, 12.1, Chapter 13, 16.10, 16.16–16.17
additional pension 1.7, 1.8
additional voluntary contributions (AVCs) 1.9, 8.4, 16.27
administrative agreement 11.2
administrator of pension scheme 8.12, Chapter 11, 12.4, 15.4, 20.3
adoption leave 9.4
advice, financial 9.37
advisers Chapter 10
age discrimination 9.8
aggregate funding method 13.6
alternative arrangements (trustee selection) 4.5, 4.14, 4.16, 4.17, 4.20
amendment power 6.3, 7.1A–7.1B, 8.2
annual funding statement 13.11E
annual report 9.38
annuity rates 9.3
APL: *see* Association of Pension Lawyers
appointment of trustees 4.1, 4.23, 8.2
appropriate rules (trustee selection) 4.5, 4.6, 4.15–4.16, 4.18–4.20
approved schemes 1.3
arbitrage 16.11A
Article 119: *see* Article 141EC
Article 141EC 9.2
asset management 16.9–16.12A
see also investment
Association of Consulting Actuaries 12.1

Association of Corporate Trustees (TACT) 3.4
Association of Pension Lawyers (APL) 14.1
Association of Pensioneer Trustees (APT) 3.7
attained age method 13.6
auditor Chapter 15, 8.4, 10.2, 10.4
augmentation 9.13, 13.7
automatic membership 9.8
AVCs: *see* additional voluntary contributions
average salary schemes 1.5

B

balanced investment manager 16.18
ballots (selection of trustees) 4.15, 4.21
ballots (statutory consultation procedure) 4.20
beauty parades 10.5
Beddoes judgment 22.8
beneficiary 1.15, 8.1, 21.1
benefit design 9.10, 12.5, 13.7
see also scheme reconstructions, takeovers
benefit statements 9.36–9.37
bonds 16.10
bottom-up approach 16.13
breach of confidentiality 8.10, 10.4, 22.3
breach of statutory law 5.10, 21.5
breach of trust 1.15, Chapter 21
bridging pensions 9.3
bulk transfers 9.14, 13.3, 19.5
bundled brokerage 16.20A

C

cash balance schemes 1.5
cash deposits 16.10, 23.3
chairman (of trustees) 18.2
Chartered Accountants' Joint Ethics Committee 15.7
Child Support, Pensions and Social Security Act 2000 1.8, 1.13, 4.5, 4.29

children's pensions: *see* survivors'
  pensions
Citizens Advice Bureaux 20.7
closed schemes 19.11
Civil Partnership Act 2004 1.13, 5.7
committee of management: *see*
  management committee
communications 9.33, 12.6, 20.1
  see also information, duty to
  disclose
commutation rates 9.3, 13.7
Companies Acts 3.3, 4.12
compensation schemes Chapter 23
compromising debts 7.5, 23.1A,
  23.1C
conflicts of interest for adviser 10.2
consultants Chapter 12, 16.16–16.17
consultation by employer
  7.1A–7.1B
contract-based pensions Preface, 2.1
contracted-in schemes 1.7
contracted-out deduction (COD)
  1.7, 1.8
contracted-out schemes 1.7, 13.7,
  23.5
contributions 8.3–8.7, 9.3, 9.10,
  23.4
contribution holiday 16.9, 19.2
contribution notices 7.5
contributory schemes 1.9
controlled investments 2.2
conversance requirement 5.1A,
  5.1K–5.1L, 6.2A
convertibles 16.11
corporate governance 16.25
corporate trustee 3.3
cost 1.11
coupon 16.30
court costs 20.12, 21.1, 22.8
current unit method 13.6
current yield 16.30
custodians 3.8, 10.2, 16.23
customer agreements 16.20

D

data controller 11.6
data processor 11.6
Data Protection Act 1998 1.13, 11.6
death-in-service lump sum 5.5

debt on the employer 8.5, 8.6, 19.8
deed poll 2.5
deferred pensioners 1.5, 9.13, 9.14
deficit on winding up 19.9, 23.1A,
  23.1B
defined benefit schemes 1.5
defined contribution schemes 1.5
delegation of trustees' powers 11.3
Department for Work and Pensions
  (DWP) 1.13
dependant, definition of 5.7
dependants' pensions: *see* survivors'
  pensions
derivatives: *see* financial instruments
detrimental modifications 6.4
direct payment arrangement 1.16,
  2.7
Disability Discrimination Act 1995
  1.13, 9.1, 9.7
disclosure: *see* information, duty to
  provide
discretionary powers 3.6, 5.4, 8.2,
  9.1, 9.21
disputes Chapter 20
  see also industrial relations
dispute resolution scheme
  20.2–20.6
disqualification as trustee 4.2
dividend yield 16.29
divorce 5.7, 6.2, 9.30
duties of trustees 5.1–5.2, 10.1,
  16.4, 21.1
DVDs 9.41
DWP: *see* Department for Work and
  Pensions

E

early leavers 1.5, 9.20–9.24
  see also transfer values
early retirement 9.12, 13.7, 19.5,
  19.6
earnings per share 16.29
ECJ: *see* European Court of Justice
embedded independent trustee 3.5
employer, role of Chapter 8
Employer-financed retirement
  benefit schemes 1.4, 4.13
employer-nominated trustees 4.23,
  4.26

employer-related investment (ERI)
16.13, 16.22, 21.5
employment protection 8.9, 22.3
Employment Rights Act 1996 1.13,
8.8, 8.9
Employment tribunals 8.8, 8.9
Employment Tribunals Act 1996
1.13
entry age method 13.6
equal treatment 1.14, 9.2–9.3
Equal Pay Act 1970 1.13
equity 1.15
see also trust law
equities 16.10, 16.29
ERI: *see* employer-related
investment
European law 1.14, 9.2
European Court of Justice (ECJ)
1.14, 9.2, 9.3
executive pension schemes 1.6,
15.1
exempt-approved schemes 1.3
exoneration clause 22.4, 22.6

F

Faculty of Actuaries: *see* Institute of
Actuaries
fees 3.4, 3.5, 3.7, 4.4, 10.5, 12.1,
16.20
final salary underpin 1.5
final salary schemes 1.5
Finance Act 1986 8.3, 19.2, 19.4
Finance Act 2004 2.10, 5.7, 6.1
Financial Assistance Scheme (FAS)
1.5, 23.1A
financial futures 16.11
financial instruments 16.11
financial mechanisms 16.11A
Financial Services and Markets Act
2000 1.13, 2.2, 2.16, 9.37,
16.5, 16.6, 16.13, 16.20
Financial Services Authority (FSA)
5.9, 16.5, 16.20A, 23.3
Financial Services Compensation
Scheme 23.3
Financial support directions 7.5
fixed interest bonds 16.10, 16.30
fixed-term workers 9.9
fraud 15.6, 16.23, 21.4, 23.2

Fraud Compensation Scheme 23.2
fraud on a power 8.2
fund manager: *see* investment
manager
funded unapproved retirement
benefit schemes (FURBS) 1.4,
1.10
funded schemes 1.10
FURBS: *see* funded unapproved
retirement benefit schemes

G

gilts 13.9, 16.10
GMP: *see* guaranteed minimum
pension
good faith, implied duty of 8.2
Goode Committee: *see* Pension Law
Review Committee
grandfathering 19.6
group personal pensions 1.1,
2.6–2.9
guaranteed minimum pension (GMP)
1.8, 9.13, 9.15, 13.7, 23.5
guaranteed transfer value 9.16

H

handbook 9.35
hedge funds 16.12A
HMRC 1.3, 1.13, 5.5, 5.7, 6.1, 8.1,
12.10, 13.7, 19.2, 19.4
holding trustee 3.8
House of Commons Social Security
Committee 1.15, 10.4, 15.7,
18.1

I

IAS 19: *see* International Accounting
Standard 19
ICS: *see* Investors Compensation
Scheme
ill-health pensions 5.8
increases 1.8, 9.26–9.27, 19.3
indemnity clauses 22.4–22.5
indemnity insurance 9.1
individual trustees 3.2
independent trustee 3.5, 4.3, 19.7
Independent Pension Trustees Group
(IPTG) 3.5
index-linked bonds 16.10

industrial relations 1.11, 3.6,
Chapter 7, 19.1, 19.4
industry-wide schemes, trustee
requirements 4.13
Industrial Tribunals Act 1996 1.13
information, duty to provide 8.11,
9.31–9.43,10.7, 13.7,13.11E,
13.15, 15.3
Insolvency directive 23.6
insolvent employer 13.9,
19.7–19.11, 23.4–23.6
insured schemes and benefits 1.6,
12.11, 16.1, 23.3
Institute of Actuaries, Faculty of
Actuaries 9.4, 13.2, 13.9
IORP Directive 1.14, 1.15, 6.1,
13.8, 16.6A
Institutional Shareholders
Committee 16.25
interim deed 6.1
International Accounting Standard
19 (IAS 19) 15.10
international benefits 12.7
internet and intranet sites 9.42
investment 12.8, Chapter 16
investment committees 4.12, 16.7
investment manager 9.2,
16.14–16.19, 23.3
investment powers 16.4,
16.6–16.6A
Investors in People 11.4
IR12: *see* Practice Notes
irrevocable trusts 1.15

K

Knowledge and Understanding: *see*
Trustees' Knowledge and
Understanding

L

late joiners 5.9, 9.11
Law Society 14.1, 14.3
leaflets 9.40
legal adviser Chapter 14, 12.9
leverage 16.11A
liability insurance 22.5–22.6
limited price indexation (LPI): *see*
increases
long position 16.11A

long-service benefit 9.14
LPI: *see* limited price indexation

M

maladministration 11.4, 15.6, 20.1,
20.9, 20.11A
managed funds 16.2
management committee 3.6, 4.28,
5.5
maternity leave 9.4
meetings Chapter 18
member-nominated trustees
4.4–4.22, 4.29–4.34
mergers: *see* takeovers
MFR: *see* minimum funding
requirement
minimum age requirements 9.8
minimum funding requirement
(MFR) 8.5, 9.23, 13.1, 13.7
minutes (of trustee meeting) 18.5
mis-selling of personal pensions
2.4
money purchase schemes 1.5
money purchase underpin 1.5, 9.17
money-weighted returns 16.21
Myners Report 1.15, 10.1, Chapter
17

N

national insurance contributions 1.7
National Insurance Contributions
Office 3.2
negligence insurance 22.5–22.6
negotiations with the employer 7.2,
7.5
new employees 9.15
newsletters 9.39
nomination (as trustee) 4.7, 4.30
non-contributory schemes 1.9
normal pension age 9.15
not-contracted-out schemes 1.7
notifiable events 7.5, 23.1C

O

Occupational Pensions Board 5.1,
7.1, 8.1, 19.5
Occupational Pensions Regulatory
Authority (Opra): *see* Pensions
Regulator

Ombudsman: *see* Pensions
Ombudsman
OPB: *see* Occupational Pensions
Board
Opra: *see* Pensions Regulator
opting out 5.9, 9.18
overriding legislation 6.2

P

participating schemes 1.7
part-time employees 9.3
passive investment manager 16.19
paternity leave 9.4
pay-as-you-go schemes 1.10
payment schedule 8.6, 15.3
payments to employer 19.2–19.4,
21.5
p/e ratio: *see* price/earnings ratio
Pension Protection Fund (PPF) 1.5,
13.6, 19.7–19.9, 19.11, 23.1B
Pension Schemes Act 1993 1.13,
9.23, 23.5
pensionable earnings cap 1.4, 9.16
pensioneer trustees 3.7
pensioner action groups 9.25
pensioners 9.25–9.28
see also statutory consultation
procedure
Pensions Advisory Service (The)
(TPAS) 20.4–20.7
pensioner trustees 4.28
Pensions Act 1995 1.13, passim
Pensions Act 2004 1.13, passim
pensions consultative committees
3.6, 4.28, 9.26
Pensions Law Review Committee
1.15, 6.2, 10.4, 11.1, 15.7
Pensions Management Institute
(PMI) 11.1, 24.1
pensions manager Chapter 11
Pensions Ombudsman 9.16, 9.26,
20.8–20.13, 21.1
Pensions Regulator 1.16, passim
performance measurement 16.21
period of office (as trustee) 4.10,
4.18–4.20, 4.24–4.26
personal data 10.6
personal pensions 1.1, 2.2 – 2.9, 8.7,
9.19

PMI: *see* Pensions Management
Institute
PMI Trustee Group 11.1
Policyholders Protection Act 1975
23.3
pooled funds: *see* managed funds
power of amendment: *see*
amendment power
powers of the employer 8.2
powers of trustees 5.1, 5.3
prescribed rules (trustee selection)
4.5, 4.21
preservation requirements 9.13
price/earnings ratio 16.29
priority rule 19.9–19.10
programme trading 16.11A
projected accrued benefit method
13.6, 19.2
projected unit method 13.6
promotion of personal and
stakeholder pension schemes
2.2, 9.44
property 1.15, 16.10, 16.12
protected liabilities 19.9
protected modifications 6.4
protected rights 1.8
prudence 16.4

Q

quality certification 11.4
quorum (for trustee meeting) 18.4

R

Race Relations Act 1975 1.13, 9.1
Recovery plans 13.11
redemption price 16.30
redemption yield 16.30
reductions in yields 2.17
reference scheme test 1.8,
13.11–13.12
register of prohibited persons 4.3
register of occupational pension
schemes 1.1, 3.2
registered pension schemes 1.3, 5.5
reimbursement policies 22.7
relevant events 4.16
relevant filing system 11.6
religion or belief, discrimination on
the grounds of 9.11

removal of trustees 3.3, 4.1, 4.8, 4.24–4.26
reporting non-compliance 8.10, 10.4, 14.4, 15.9, 22.3
reselection (as member-nominated trustee) 4.25
retirement annuity contracts 2.2
retirement counselling 12.12
retirement of trustee 4.24
revaluation requirements 9.22
running yield 16.30

S

salary-related schemes 1.5
schedule of contributions 8.5, 13.11A, 15.3
scheme reconstructions 19.6
  see also benefit redesign
Scope documents 5.1B, Appendix 1
segregated funds 16.3
selection (as trustee) 4.14, 4.15
self-administered schemes 1.6, 16.2–16.3
self-investment: *see* employer-related investment
SERPS: *see* state earnings related pension scheme
settlement (of investment transactions) 16.23
settlor 1.15, 8.1
Sex Discrimination Act 1976 1.13
Sexual orientation 5.7, 9.10, 9.21
short position 16.11A
short service benefit 9.15
small self-administered schemes (SSAS) 1.6, 4.13, 15.1
socially responsible investment (SRI) 16.8, 16.13, 16.26
Society of Pension Consultants (SPC) 12.1
soft commission 16.20A
solicitor: *see* legal adviser
SORP1: *see* Statement of Recommended Practice No.1
SPC: *see* Society of Pension Consultants
specialist investment manager 16.18
SRI: *see* socially responsible investment

SSAP24: *see* Statement of Standard Accounting Practice No 24
Stakeholder pensions 1.1, 1.15, 2.1, 2.10–2.13, 4.2, 8.3, 8.7, 9.37, 16.27
State Earnings Related Pension Scheme (SERPS) 1.7, 1.8, 9.23, 23.5
statement of funding principles 13.9
state pension age 9.3
State Second Pension (S2P) 1.7, 1.8, 9.23, 23.5
statement of investment principles 16.8
Statement of recommended practice No. 1 (SORP1) 15.3
Statement of standard accounting practice No 24 (SSAP24) 15.10
statutory consultation procedure (trustee selection) 4.5, 4.7, 4.14–4.15, 4.17–4.20, 4.22–4.23, 4.27
statutory funding objective 13.5, 13.8
statutory law 1.13
statutory modifications 6.5
stock lending 16.24
stock selection 16.9, 16.13
strategic asset management 16.9–16.10
subsisting rights 6.4
surpluses 7.1–7.2, 7.4, 9.5, 9.7, 9.20, 14.3, 19.1–19.4
survivors' pensions 5.7, 9.24, 9.29
swaps 16.11

T

TACT: *see* Association of Corporate Trustees
tactical asset management 16.9, 16.12
takeovers 9.7, 16.25, 19.5
technical provisions 13.5–13.6, 13.8–13.11E
time off, paid 8.8
time-weighted returns 16.21
top-down approach 16.10
top-up schemes 1.4, 1.10

trade unions 3.6, 4.7, 4.14, 4.28,
    Chapter 7, 21.1
    see also industrial relations
traded options 16.11
training 8.8, 11.4, 12.13, 24.1
transfer payment: *see* transfer value
transfer values 9.23, 13.7
transfers: *see* bulk transfers
trust corporation 3.4
trust deed and rules Chapter 6, 14.2,
    passim
trust law 1.15, 4.22, 5.1, 8.1, 8.2,
    9.1,10.1, 10.3
Trustee Act 1925 3.3, 4.1, 22.2
Trustee Act 2000 16.4
Trustee Certificate of Basic Pensions
    Knowledge 24.1
Trustee Investment Act 1961 16.4
trustee body Chapter 3, 4.26–4.27
trustee directors 3.3, 4.1, 4.12, 4.24
Trustees' Knowledge and
    Understanding (TKU)
    5.1A–5.1M, 10.1
Trustee Panel 11.1A
TUPE requirements 9.5
type A events 7.5

U
unapproved schemes 1.3, 1.4, 4.13
unbundled GPP arrangement 2.9
unfair dismissal: *see* employment
    protection

unfunded unapproved retirement
    benefit schemes (UURBS)
    1.4
unfunded schemes 1.4, 1.10
UURBS: *see* unfunded unapproved
    retirement benefit schemes

V
vacancies (for position as trustee)
    4.9, 4.15, 4.19, 4.20, 4.21,
    4.27–4.28, 4.31
VAT 3.3
venture capital 16.10, 16.13,
    16.26
videos 9.41
voluntary membership 9.26

W
waiting periods 9.8
warrants 16.11
Wednesbury principles 5.4, 9.1,
    18.5
welfare activities 9.21
Welfare Reform and Pensions Act
    1999 4.5, 8.3, 8.7, 9.23
whistle blowing: *see* reporting
    non-compliance
widowers' pensions: *see* survivors'
    pensions
wilful negligence or misconduct
    21.4, 21.5
winding-up 19.8–19.11, 22.10